Psychological Theory and Educational Reform
How School Remakes Mind and Society

For more than a century educational reformers have looked for a breakthrough in the sciences of psychology and pedagogy that would dramatically improve the effectiveness of schooling. This book shows why such an ambition is an illusion. Schools are institutions that attempt to balance the needs of a bureaucratic society that funds them with the personal goals, interests, hopes, and ambitions of the students who enroll in them. Reform efforts attempt to realign that balance without any clear conception of how the two are related. This book offers a theoretical account of the relation between the minds of learners and the institutional structure of the school that would account both for the ways that schooling remakes minds and societies and for the reasons such institutions are resistant to change.

Professor David R. Olson is Professor of Human Development and Education at the Ontario Institute for Studies in Education of the University of Toronto. He was educated at the University of Saskatchewan and University of Alberta and was a Post-Doctoral Fellow at the Harvard Center for Cognitive Studies, where he worked with Jerome Bruner. He has been a Fellow at the Stanford Center for the Behavioral Sciences, the Netherlands Institute for Advanced Studies, and most recently the Wissenschaftskolleg zu Berlin. He is author of some 300 articles and book chapters and author or editor of 14 books, including *The World on Paper* (Cambridge University Press, 1994), and editor with Nancy Torrance of *The Handbook of Education and Human Development* (1996). He is a Fellow of the Royal Society of Canada and holds honorary degrees from Gothenberg University (Sweden) and the University of Saskatchewan. He was named University Professor in 1998.

Psychological Theory and Educational Reform

How School Remakes Mind and Society

DAVID R. OLSON
University of Toronto

CAMBRIDGE
UNIVERSITY PRESS

KH

PUBLISHED BY THE PRESS SYNDICATE OF THE UNIVERSITY OF CAMBRIDGE
The Pitt Building, Trumpington Street, Cambridge, United Kingdom

CAMBRIDGE UNIVERSITY PRESS
The Edinburgh Building, Cambridge CB2 2RU, UK
40 West 20th Street, New York, NY 10011-4211, USA
477 Williamstown Road, Port Melbourne, VIC 3207, Australia
Ruiz de Alarcón 13, 28014 Madrid, Spain
Dock House, The Waterfront, Cape Town 8001, South Africa

http: // www.cambridge.org

First published 2003

Printed in the United States of America

Typeface Palatino 10/13 pt.   *System* LaTeX 2$_\varepsilon$ [TB]

A catalog record for this book is available from the British Library.

Library of Congress Cataloging in Publication Data
Olson, David R., 1935–
Psychological theory and educational reform : how school remakes mind and society /
David R. Olson.
   p. cm.
Includes bibliographical references (p.) and index.
ISBN 0-521-82510-5 (hardback) – ISBN 0-521-53211-6 (paperback)
1. School management and organization.   2. Educational psychology.
3. Educational change.   I. Title.
LB2806 .O47   2003
370.15 – dc21   2002034982

ISBN 0 521 82510 5 hardback
ISBN 0 521 53211 6 paperback

11/22/04

For Jerry Bruner

Contents

Preface

For some time I have been struck by the fact that whereas the psychological understanding of children's learning and development has made great strides, conspicuously through the pioneering work of Jean Piaget, Lev Vygotsky, and the Cognitive Revolution beginning in the 1960s, the impact on schooling as an institutional practice has been modest if not negligible. With most of my colleagues, I had assumed that if only we knew more about how the mind works, how the brain develops, how interests form, how people differ, and, most centrally, how people learn, educational practice would take a great leap forward. But while this knowledge has grown, schools have remained remarkably unaffected.

Thus, whereas the research assures us that what people learn depends upon what they already know, in school what they learn depends upon what the school mandates. Whereas the research suggests that people learn because they are intrinsically interested or because they love learning, in school they pursue knowledge because, as they say, they "need the credit." Whereas researchers insist that learning is inspired by the search for meaning and the growth in understanding, what, in fact, they learn depends upon what books, chapters, or pages they believe they are responsible for.[1] For the theorist, the growth of mind is spontaneous and continuous; for the school, it is a matter of obligation and duty.

---

[1] When the distinguished McGill psychologist John Macnamara was asked by his students prior to the final examination what they were responsible for, he replied, "You are responsible for the welfare of your immortal soul!" I am indebted to Michael Corballis for this anecdote.

This disparity between our knowledge of the mind and the practices of the school underlies many of the traditional criticisms of the school – its bookishness, its penchant for parceling knowledge into arbitrary packages called subjects, its remoteness from "felt needs" and direct experience of the learner, its impersonal forms of discourse, its objective standards, its extrinsic goals – and motivates many urgent calls for reform of the school to fit the advances in the learning sciences.

In fact, attempts to make schools more "child-centered" were common for much of the 20th century. But Ravitch's (2000) review of the effects of these attempted "progressivist" reforms argued that not only did they fail to raise academic standards, if anything they lowered them, especially for the less gifted students. And now many accuse schools of presiding over falling standards, thereby placing "the nation at risk," and call for more desperate measures ranging from radical changes in administration and ownership, such as charter schools, to increased surveillance of teachers and students through new regimens of testing. The provisional reports on the impact of these most recent reforms are at best mixed. Yet all the while conspicuous and soluble problems are ignored: School libraries wane, classroom resources are depleted, after-school programs are phased out, and discouraged and underpaid teachers leave the profession in droves, some 40% in the first 3 years, thereby limiting the opportunities for school improvement (*Guardian Weekly,* Aug. 30–Sept. 5, 2001, p. 8).[2]

The checkered history of deep reforms and urged reforms – what the economist A. Hirschman (2001) has called "reform mongering" – requires us to think again about schooling. The problem, I believe, is that the theories that gave us insight into children's understanding, motivation, learning, and thinking have never come to terms with schooling as an institutional practice with its duties and responsibilities for basic skills, disciplinary knowledges, grades, standards, and credentials. As long as schools are seen only as environments for personal growth, the nature and effects of schooling as an institution will be overlooked. Conversely, as long as schools are seen as institutions for achieving social goals and standards, the nature of personal growth and understanding will be overlooked. Around such axes the rhetoric of educational reform revolves.

---

[2] In some urban districts teachers are said to leave their systems on average after 3 years (Goertz, 2001, p. 54). They leave primarily because of job dissatisfaction and desire to pursue other careers (Ingersoll, 2001).

What is required, then, is an advance in our understanding of schools as bureaucratic institutions that corresponds to the advances in our understanding of the development of the mind. What is required is a better understanding of the relation between psychological theory and educational reform. When achieved, many of the so-called failures of schooling may come to be seen rather as optimal solutions to deep-seated social problems and practices. The reliance on rules, the bookishness, the responsibilities assigned to students, the earning of credentials, and the traditional pedagogical methods may all emerge as solutions adopted for good reasons rather than as miseducative rituals. Seeking credits will be seen as just as valid a basis for study as is pursuing one's interests. Indeed, "If you have an interest, pursue it in your own time" or "Keep it to yourself" as Gradgrind or the masters at Leamy's National School might say (McCourt, 1996); we have more serious matters to attend to – such as earning a credential in maths. Duty and responsibility must find their place along with interest and understanding if we are to understand schooling.

If we are to understand schooling and its relation to mind and society, we must begin by formulating and then addressing a thorny theoretical puzzle: On the one hand are the child's growing understanding, subjectivity, intentionality, and responsibility. On the other is the school's responsibility for shaping persons to fill certain prespecified social roles in an increasingly bureaucratic society. A too sharp distinction between persons and institutions makes much good science irrelevant to the understanding of schooling, whereas conflating the two hides the effects of the schooling from our view, reducing it to just one more factor in personal and social development. As long as schools are charged with the responsibility for awarding the credentials that indicate one's competencies to perform the society's work – their historical and valued function – one can tune the system to make it more inclusive and effective but not markedly alter its structure. Only in the final two chapters of the book do I address how one may at least begin to do this tuning.

Only distinguishing persons as intentional beings from institutions as bureaucratic agents allows the universal institutional features of schooling to come into view. The most fundamental of these universal features is the reallocation of responsibility from a person to a public institution; the institution of the school assigns a new identity and determines who one will become. This realignment is achieved through other universal features of schooling, including classification, grading, curriculum, surveillance, and credentialing. These institutional features, as I shall explain, are responsible for two truths that have remained largely unexplained, the facts that even radical school reforms tend to have limited if not negligible effects and, second, schooling as an institutional process itself has dramatic and irreversible cognitive and social effects. These effects are sufficiently important that schooling is widely viewed as essential to full participation in a modern society as well as a requisite ingredient of modernization. Once the institutional autonomy of the school is recognized, we will be able to see in a new way an array of traditional issues in the study of education, including the nature of abilities, of learning, of thinking, and, most important, of intentionality, responsibility, and accountability. I conclude by sketching a new framework for thinking about schooling that honors equally the subjectivity of the learner and the normative structures of a modern bureaucratic society.

In part my account is a product of a somewhat recent history of the field of educational studies. In response to the loss of faith in the educational establishment, and partly because of its isolation from the more basic disciplines, educational studies opened their arms to the specialist disciplines of history, anthropology, sociology, philosophy, and psychology. These disciplines provided a new seriousness to educational studies and led to an exhilarating burst of basic research of relevance to education "broadly conceived," in the phrase of the Spencer Foundation, a major supporter of educational research including much of my own. My own career coincides with this transformation. Educational research had been largely an actuarial science of predicting achievement on the basis of a variety of factors such as intelligence quotient (IQ) and socioeconomic status (SES). In the 1960s the study of education began to be much more integrated into the basic disciplines of history, anthropology, sociology, psychology, and the like. However, this infusion of more specialized disciplinary knowledge created an unanticipated problem, namely, that schooling as a largely autonomous institutional process was almost completely lost sight of. Rediscovering the fundamental nature of schooling in the midst of these specialist studies is one of the goals of this book.

This book, in one sense, is an extension of my work on literacy in that it is premised on the, to me, inescapable and overwhelming impact of writing on the formation of modern bureaucratic societies. Schooling in large part is an initiation into a written "documentary" tradition. Whereas in *The World on Paper* (1994) I focused on the evolution of writing systems and their impact on the thinking and consciousness of individual readers and writers as they learn to read, write, and interpret texts, in this book I examine the school as embedded in a bureaucratic social system in which writing and the documentary tradition are central organizing features. This requires a much clearer distinction between a literate person and a literate society. When I came to terms with societal literacy (with thanks to Georg Elwert, 2001, and to Dorothy Smith, 1990a), I realized that I was in a position finally to address the question of why the now abundant studies of individual learning and human development had made so little impact on the institutional practices of schooling. Further, I realized that I was not alone in having neglected the fact that school is not simply an environment for human development but an institution with its own entitlements and obligations. Few writers acknowledge that the school is an institution that imposes its own boundaries and forms on human development by specifying the criteria or norms against which development and achievement are to be judged.

I dedicate this book to Jerome Bruner, who not only has been a longtime mentor and friend but set the stage for the argument of this book both by showing the essential role that education plays in human development and by demonstrating how development could be addressed in an intentionalist, sociocultural frame of reference. My book could be read as an elaboration of chapter 3 of Bruner's *The Culture of Education* (1996), in which he poses the antinomy between education as human development versus education as social reproduction. Whereas Bruner addressed this antinomy by urging schools to be more participatory, collaborative, and given over to constructing rather than receiving meanings, I address it by exploring the impact of the institutional dimensions of a bureaucratic society with its norms, rules, procedures, and laws on the organization of schooling and the formation of mind. Bruner was also the first reader of this book, and my indebtedness is transparent throughout these pages.

I must also express my gratitude to the Ontario Institute for Studies in Education of the University of Toronto and its Dean for the encouragement and support provided over many years. More specific gratitude is owed to the incomparable Wissenschaftskolleg zu Berlin and its directors, Wolf Lepenies, Jurgen Kocka, Joachim Nettelbeck, and Rinehart Meyer-Kalkus, for the year-long fellowship that made the drafting of this book possible. I would also like to express my thanks to the readers, informants, and critics who helped me shape my argument and my text, especially Keith Oatley, Janet Astington, Clifford Christensen, Ray Jackendoff, Lynd Forguson, Frank Smith, Jack Goody, Joan Peskin, Michel Ferrari, Jerry Lazare, Wolfgang Edelstein, Rick Volpe, Renata Valtin, Helen Moore, Jens Brockmeier, Keith Sawyer, Ian Winchester, Carol Feldman, Dieter Sadowski, Fritz van Holthoon, and Yehuda Elkana. Nancy Torrance, with the help of Nancy Mayes, did an enormous amount of work in getting the volume ready for publication, and I am grateful for their efforts.

Toronto, November 2002

PART I

THE DISCOURSE OF EDUCATION

1

The Discourse of Educational Reform

> Philosophizing should focus about education as the supreme human
> interest in which ... other problems, cosmological, moral, logical, come
> to a head.
>
> (J. Dewey, 1984, p. 156)

Few regard educational theory as the queen of the sciences. Educational
theory tends to be regarded as an applied science if a science at all. Yet
education, like government, economics, and law, defines a special space
that requires one to cross traditional disciplinary borders as well as frontiers between theory and practice. Because educational theory requires
a framework that embraces a rich diversity of knowledge, it is an ideal
candidate for the position as, if not the queen, at least the handmaiden
of the sciences. Educational theory has rarely risen to that challenge.
Most of the discourse on education is either a defense of the traditional
or an urgent call for reform. The discipline has been slow to articulate
the space in which such debate takes place.

Setting out that frame is one of the major intellectual tasks of this new
century. The end of the 20th century, marked by remarkable progress
in the specialized sciences, gives way to the 21st, in which the larger
problem stands out in bold relief – What is the relation between these
bits of specialized knowledge that have been carefully constructed so as
to honor their autonomy? As Yehuda Elkana (2000) has pointed out, the
Enlightenment, of which the specialized sciences are the fullest flower,
succeeded only by marginalizing the question of the relation between its
specializations. The problem is visible everywhere. Psychology has as its
domain the mental life of individuals, but most psychologists recognize

that the contents of consciousness are defined interpersonally and socially. Sociology, law, and economics have as their domains the action
of groups and institutions, but most sociologists, legal theorists, and
economists recognize that social practices are lodged in the consciousness of individual minds. Economists develop impersonal laws of the
market but recognize that such laws – essentially those for maximiz-
ing personal gain – are routinely violated by personal whim, allegiance,
charisma, habit, or conformity. One is not being melodramatic to say
that these specialized scientific disciplines face a crisis.

The basis of the crisis, I believe, is what appears to be an unbridgeable
gap between the institutional and the personal: between the formal as
embodied in large-scale institutions and the informal as embodied in
individual minds and local culture; between the fixed, public rules and
subjective, private intuitions; between the objectively given and the
subjectively taken; between social norms and intentional actions; between custom and law; between written record and local interpretation.
The gap is also manifest in disciplinary contexts. In linguistics, it is the
gap between the formal rules of the grammar, insisted upon by parents
and pedagogues, and the implicit pragmatic knowledge of speakers; in
law, it is that between the formal law as stated and its contextual interpretations assigned by the courts; in literature, it is between what a text
specifies and what a reader can bring to it; in psychology, it is between
algorithmic cognitive processes detailed by the cognitive scientists and
the contextualized, subjective judgments of rational and responsible
human agents; in sociology, between social norms and local practice.

In educational discourse, the problem is clearest of all. John Dewey
formulated it in terms of the "child" and the "curriculum." It is the chasm
between what the society through its institutions defines, mandates, and
assesses in its curriculum of study and what teachers and children make
of it in their subjective and intersubjective mental lives. In its most local
form, it is the gap between the child as a person and the child as a
member of a defined school population, a class. In its most political it
is the widening gap between proposals for school reform, one group
seeing the achievements of the collective as primary, the other seeing
the experience, beliefs, and goals of individual learners as primary. It is
only a slight overstatement to say that if we could solve the educational
theory problem, the rest would be easy. "Solve" may be a bit ambitious,
"address" more realistic.

Admittedly, the so-called mature disciplines are unlikely to rush to
take up a lead offered by educational theory. Dewey, one of the leading

philosophers of the 20th century, despaired of ever being taken seriously by other philosophers because he based his analysis on the study of education. Although he rarely referred to his own work, he once wrote:

Although a book called *Democracy and Education* was for many years that in which my philosophy, such as it is, was most fully expounded, I do not know that philosophic critics, as distinct from teachers, have ever had recourse to it. I have wondered whether such facts signified that philosophers in general, although they are themselves usually teachers, have not taken education with sufficient seriousness for it to occur to them that any rational person could actually think it possible that philosophizing should focus about education as the supreme human interest in which, moreover, other problems, cosmological, moral, logical, come to a head. (Dewey, 1984, p. 156)

Dewey's "bottom-up" pragmatism is now recognized as standing on all fours with any other philosophical tradition at the same time its value as educational theory is seen by many as at an all-time low; for many modern critics Dewey is seen as the problem rather than as the solution (Ravitch, 2000). Yet Dewey's theory was the last theory broad enough to justify characterization as a "theory of education" (he preferred the expression "science of education"), because he viewed education in a social context, integrating considerations of a democratic society on one hand and the nature of children's lived experience on the other. In that sense Dewey stands as the paradigm for all such theory.[1] I share both Dewey's optimism and his pessimism. Education provides an ideal context for grappling with the large problem of the relation between persons and institutions. But even if progress can be made there, one cannot be optimistic that educational theory will be seen as sufficiently "queenly" to be read carefully beyond its own borders. Whether or not it is adopted beyond its own borders, addressing the dilemma in the study of education is of importance in its own right and it defines the purpose of this book.

Not that educational researchers have slumbered in Dewey's shadow. Despite considerable scholarship and important local advances, it is widely conceded that educational thought and research lack an organizing theory and consequently cannot be regarded as science (Elkind, 1999). Pedagogy is a central concern of educational research, but pedagogy refers primarily to practices of teaching, not to the broader question

---

[1] Two superb, comprehensive accounts of the life and work of John Dewey have recently appeared: Westbrook (1991) and Ryan (1995). A readable introduction to the intellectual ferment of Dewey's time is provided by Menand (2001).

of why teaching is required in the first place. A sufficient number of theories have been applied to education – Thorndike's laws of learning, Skinner's theory of behavior modification, Erikson's theory of personality, Thurstone's theory of primary mental abilities, Berlyne's theory of motivation, Piaget's theory of mental development, Vygotsky's theory of cultural appropriation, Bruner's theory of knowledge construction – to have kept researchers and writers occupied for almost a century. For reasons that are not hard to grasp, such research has been motivated by the goal of improving education whether through upgrading either teachers, programs, or materials, including books and computers, or through improving the quality and equity of the pedagogical interaction through an improved understanding of learners and improved teaching techniques.

Why have these efforts not turned into an educational theory? I can suggest at least three reasons. The first is the problem of deciding just what is meant by a "theory." A theory is a conceptual system, that is, a system of concepts with four properties. First, the concepts refer to entities that can be identified or pointed out and referred to. Second, the concepts are linked logically to one another to form a network allowing for inference and for some concepts to be defined in terms of others. And third, a theory is composed of causal laws linking concepts to each other. The theory thereby allows prediction and explanation of the events specified in it. All conceptual understanding has these properties so we must add a fourth, namely, that the theory is amenable to documented elaboration and refinement. With these four in place we would have what Thomas Kuhn referred to as a paradigmatic "normal science." It has been argued, following Kuhn's (1962) analysis of scientific revolutions, that education is in a preparadigmatic state, that is, lacking an organizing framework, indeed, awaiting such a framework.

Currently, the study of education is essentially an applied field, a domain of practice rather than theory, and unified not by theory but by a practical concern, namely, educating our children and training teachers to do so effectively: hence, the inchoate programs of study in most schools of education. But even practical activities may, with increased understanding, mature into theories. Theories, however, abstract from the complexity of everyday events and practices. After all, Galileo succeeded in formulating a theory of motion only by delimiting his attention to a prescribed area, simple objects in rectilinear motion in frictionless space, while deliberately ignoring the "causes" of motion. Morrison (1974) and Pacey (1974) have described the long and complex history of how practical knowledge of engineering survived and grew before it came to be dominated by theory. Perhaps education is like engineering, accumulating local knowledge while waiting for the development of a theoretical framework sufficiently broad to incorporate and explain that more local and contextualized knowledge and practice.

Second, once we acknowledge the value of theory, we must decide what kind of a theory it is to be. Is it to be a cause–effect model as one encounters in the physical sciences or a more rational–intentional theory that one meets both in Dewey and in the more advanced biological and cognitive sciences? As Cziko (2000) has noted, if you put a glass of warm water into a refrigerator, the temperature of the water drops to match that of the refrigerator. But if you put a bird into a cool room, the bird's temperature remains unchanged. Part of the bird's biology is directed to maintaining constant body temperature. Analogously, successful students know that if the teacher's explanation is inadequate, they may fill in the missing bits from the textbook, a peer, or a parent, thereby maintaining a certain standard even in an impoverished environment. Cause and effect models are largely inappropriate.

Behaviorism was the attempt to explain action in simple causal terms. These days it is difficult to find a defender of behaviorism, yet the dominant tradition of educational research continues to rely on analysis of variance (ANOVA) models that attempt to isolate the causal factors such as dispositions and traits in the individual and various factors in the environment that may account for behavior. A population of persons or a classroom of children continues to be treated as a field of grain, the yield of which could be attributed to such causal factors as the quality of the seed, the days of sunlight, the quantity of rain, and the amount of fertilizer. Researchers continue to search for independent variables that account for some, however small, percentage of the variance of some dependent variable such as school achievement.[2] Thus putative causal factors such as intelligence quotient (IQ), social class (SES), school type, teaching method, and classroom organization continue to be examined to determine their effects on learning with little regard for the fact that children are more like the bird mentioned earlier than like the glass of water. What has yet to be recognized is that individual children making up the population, unlike individual plants, may have their own

---

[2] Researchers in Nordic countries may perhaps be forgiven for seeing a room full of bobbing tow-headed children as analogous to a field of ripened grain; for the rest of us there is no excuse.

goals, interests, beliefs, and intentions to which explanations must ultimately appeal. It is individuals who are ultimately responsible for their learning and their actions. Questions of intentionality and responsibility, plans and goals of the persons so affected, are nowhere to be seen in such educational theorizing.

The kind of theory chosen also determines what is to be taken as real, the individual learner or the groups individuals participate in, namely, school classes. Different causal laws are applicable in the two cases. The laws that apply to the learning of an individual have everything to do with intentionality, including understanding, consciousness, and responsibility. The laws that apply to the group of children, the class, on the other hand, average out intention and responsibility in order to assess the effects of independently determined variables such as class size, type of student, form of the curriculum, and form of assessment on the mean and standard deviation of some criterion variable such as mathematical achievement. The former appeals to such intentional states as beliefs and goals; the latter, to more direct cause–effect relations. Thus both the entities taken as real – individuals or classes – and the types of explanatory relations appealed to – intentional or causal – must be carefully distinguished.

Intentional versus social causes are not distinguished in educational theory. This results, as we shall see, from the tendency in Anglo-American tradition to treat social institutions as if they were merely aggregations of individuals. Consequently, the personal and the social are routinely conflated, both when research designed to assess the impact of some variable such as social class or quality of teaching is used as explanation of the personal, intentional learning of individuals, and vice versa, when psychological theory whether learning theory, ability theory, or, for that matter, Piagetian theory, is used to mandate programs of study and norms or standards of achievement. Intentional causation, the "first-person" beliefs and intentions of teachers and learners, does not map onto the social causation, the "third-person" variables found to be predictive of average class achievement. In my view, failure to distinguish persons from institutions is responsible in large part for the hodgepodge of contradictory claims manifest in current proposals for educational reform.

A third problem in constructing a framework theory for education is inherent in the changing nature of the entities under discussion. A rigorous science assumes that the entities postulated retain their properties through time, an assumption that is clearly violated in any developmental theory, including education, in which neither the characteristics of individuals, the attitudes about child rearing, nor the goals of education remain invariant through time. These changing attitudes and goals of education mirror major historical changes, as we shall see. Social institutions such as the family have always turned sons and daughters into husbands, wives, farmers, cooks, or whatever, on the basis of a kind of evolved, collective wisdom. What is new in the age of bureaucracy is a new faith in the exteriority of knowledge, that is, the belief that knowledge can be made explicit, that it is a public commodity that has a value, that can be bought and sold, that can be stored and transmitted, and for which both learners and schools may be held accountable. It is therefore inappropriate to describe historical changes in education in terms of a single criterion such as rising or falling standards.

What is less obvious is the role that institutions have come to play in this bureaucratic age. Explicit knowledge can be used, it is believed, to design institutions rationally to achieve specific goals, and schools are one such institution. Institutions are now called upon to do what formerly was taken to be the product of private virtue and wisdom. It was the Second World War that discredited the Enlightenment view of the perfectibility of humankind, the view that had been used to justify and to reform education for the preceding two centuries. What became clear in the aftermath of that war was that those who committed the greatest atrocities were often the most cultured and best educated. Contrary to the dream of the Enlightenment, education does not civilize human beings. So much for the perfectibility of humankind.

What has replaced the hopefulness of the Enlightenment, I suggest, is the view that it is institutions, not persons, that are perfectible.[3] Whereas individuals may prefer personal gain to social justice, institutions can be created that, it is believed, ensure that justice triumphs over greed. What we are called upon to do is to establish appropriate institutional forms; institutions, unlike persons, we now believe, are perfectible. In a sense this is the old Marxist view but with an important difference. The Marxists hoped to kill two birds with one stone, namely, perfect the institutions and in that way perfect the individual as well. That is, for the Marxists, the Enlightenment goal of the perfection of the individual was to be achieved through social, institutional means: Collectivize the

---

3 Although I thought this to be an original discovery, I later discovered that Hirschman (1970, p. 114) referred to the belief in the perfectibility of human institutions as a "typical American conviction."

farms, share the modes of production, and everyone will not only share the benefits but learn the essential human virtues.

The new view abandons the Enlightenment hopes altogether. People are just fine as they are; they do not need to be changed in any basic way. What they need to learn is to participate in the institutions, not just to achieve personal goals, but also to contribute to the perfection of those institutions, to make them more effective in achieving their specialized goals. Ideally, they need to learn not only to participate effectively in those institutions but also to criticize them, to make them more accessible, more just, and more humane. In such an institutional context it is no more realistic to address questions of personal beliefs independently of the society's knowledge and its institutions than it is to address questions of personal virtue independently of the courts and respect for law. The personal is completely embedded in the institutional. I examine this issue in detail in Chapter 14.

Like all single-minded goals, the goal of perfecting our institutions is perhaps doomed to failure because institutions, like persons, are prone to creating and then preserving narrow interests that others experience as oppressive. We could, presumably, create institutions in which everyone learned the "appropriate" cultural knowledge, but the methods needed to do so would be oppressive indeed. Individuals, too, have rights, in Canada guaranteed by the Charter of Rights, including the right to remain silent and the right to hold wildly quixotic beliefs.

Whether or not the belief in the perfectibility of institutions is warranted, modern societies are defined by their institutions, including their schools. But here is the catch: We must learn to think about our institutions with their rights and responsibilities while thinking about persons as individuals with theirs. We must avoid the temptation to reduce one to the other. Whereas persons may be thought of as a kind of institution and institutions may be thought of as a kind of person, it is a mistake, I believe, to see schooling either as just socialization or as just human development. By clearly distinguishing persons from institutions and by recognizing schools as the conflictual space[4] in which persons and institutions negotiate their goals and achievements, we may take some steps toward advancing the study of education.

---

[4] Bruner (1996) described such a conflictual space in terms of three antinomies: individuals versus cultures, local versus universal, and talent-centered versus tool-centered. Antinomies require trade-offs rather than reconciliation.

My purpose, then, is to advance an account, not of all education, but of its institutional form, namely, schooling, an account that views learners, teachers, and schools themselves in intentionalistic terms, adopting a vocabulary of agency, intentionality, responsibility, and accountability. Such an account will allow us to see the quite different and sometimes incommensurable responsibilities of students, teachers, and schools and will provide a framework for relating individuals to their public institutions, beginning with the school.

2

Educational Theory and Educational Reform

By now, it is clear to many that the liberal school-reform balloon has burst.

(S. Bowles & H. I. Gintis, 1976, p. 5)

Rarely have . . . reformers really understood the character of schools as social institutions.

(D. Tyack, 1995, p. 209)

It is too early to know whether, in the aggregate, charter schools improve school achievement compared to appropriate . . . controls.

(H. Gardner, 2000, p. 46)

For reasons that are not difficult to grasp, educational discourse focuses largely on issues of reform rather than issues of theory. Although there have been a small number of major educational reforms, such as the shift from ecclesiastical to secular schools and that from elite to mass education, the current calls for reform are directed more to standards and efficiency than to a radical change in purpose or goal. In these debates, if theory is mentioned at all, it is only to find someplace to lay the blame for alleged failures. The purpose of this chapter is to trace the often contradictory demands for educational reform to the deeper theoretical problem of the relations between persons and institutions.

Although all public institutions are subject to critical scrutiny, education is perhaps more so. Indeed, public education is under attack on a number of fronts. It is accused of perpetuating the inequalities between races, religions, and genders as well as those between the rich and the poor. It is accused of being bloated and inefficient, allocating only about one-half of educational resources to teaching and learning. And most serious of all, it is accused of presiding over falling academic standards that are said to yield an ill-trained workforce, untapped talent needed for the global economy, and failing grades in international comparisons of student performance in reading, writing, and mathematics.

Although there are dissenters like Franz Kafka (1999/1910, p. 17), who claimed "Education has done me great harm," a sentiment he repeated nine times in a matter of a few pages, adding, "Education tried to make another person out of me than the one I became," it is almost universally accepted that education is one of the primary vehicles of modernization (Triebel, 2001). Current criticism assumes the universal benevolence of education, and focuses on what are taken to be systemwide failures that result in unacceptable levels of student performance. A typical, if somewhat dated, indictment was *A Nation at Risk* (National Commission on Excellence in Education, 1983), sponsored by then President Reagan's secretary for education, which claimed that educational failure was sufficiently acute to jeopardize the standing of the United States in the world and required urgent reforms in school programs, assessment practices, and research to produce "excellence in education." A more balanced analysis of American education from the 1960s (Meyer, 1961) also called for reforms, focused on improving the programs of study, materials, teaching, accountability, and access to information technology. Since the 1980s reform has focused almost exclusively on issues of accountability, whether in the form of increased surveillance of students, teachers, and schools or of institutional reforms that highlight accountability to taxpayers. These include measures to specify learning outcomes, to outlaw "social promotion," and to apply the principles of the market to schooling as an institution. Although it is difficult to object to any program that aspires to higher standards, it is equally difficult to be optimistic about the measures proposed to achieve them.[1]

Indeed, many find it difficult to take broad criticisms seriously. Only a decade ago Japanese schooling and Japanese economic and managerial

---

[1] I have made no attempt to distinguish the rhetoric of reform in Canada, the United States, Britain, Australia, and New Zealand. On my admittedly sketchy reading criticisms are similar, focusing largely on issues of standards and accountability and to a lesser extent on issues of equity (wealthy countries are willing to share everything except their money). Similarities between systems by and large swamp differences because of the almost universal characteristics of schooling as an institutional practice with its shared goods, shared curricula, common textbooks, group pedagogies, testing, and credentials.

policies were equally valorized because of Japan's rapid economic growth and low unemployment, whereas by the beginning of the 21st century as the U.S. economy showed rapid growth, Japan's "opaque financing structure and rigid hierarchical management culture" came to be seen as liabilities (*London Review of Books*, September 2, 1999, p. 14). Schooling in the United States may not have been as maladaptive as *A Nation at Risk* had insisted (Levin, 1998, p. 5; Berliner & Biddle, 1995). Even the author of that original report acknowledged that schools were inappropriately blamed for poor academic achievement (Bell, 1993; see Rothstein, 2002).

Nonetheless, in some contexts setting higher standards and pursuing them relentlessly have proved useful. Exemplary schools (Lightfoot, 1983; Mortimore et al., 1988), exemplary programs (Greeno et al., 1998; Schauble, Klopfer, & Raghavan, 1991; Clay, 1998), exemplary systems (Comer, 1988; Resnick & Hall, 1998), exemplary instructional approaches (Brown, 1997; Egan, 1997), exemplary curricula (Gardner, 1999), and exemplary teachers (Holt, 1968) have all been described. Almost no one with any experience in the public schools has failed to encounter one or more teachers who were remarkable in both maintaining a comfortable atmosphere in their classrooms and at the same time straightforwardly pursuing high academic goals. I had two such teachers; surely you did too. There are two well-known problems. The first is that the effects of even model programs often cannot be sustained (Cook et al., 1999; Linn, 2000).[2] The second, widely acknowledged (Sarason, 1998; Jackson, 1990, p. 7), is that such practices cannot be generated by a formula: That is, they are not generalizable. Each exemplary program or practice is exemplary in its own way. Tolstoy, in *Anna Karenina*, noted a similar if reversed pattern in regard to unhappy families – each unhappy family is unhappy in its own way.

What is remarkable about the often-vehement criticism of the school is that no one seriously suggests that schooling is a failed social experiment and should be abolished. The talk is of upgrading schools, never closing them. This anomaly should strike us as remarkable. It is understandable that professionals associated with schooling would seek to preserve the school; few organizations vote themselves out of existence.

---

[2] No more so in education than in business. Tom Peters, who created a whole mystique about excellence in business in *In Search of Excellence* (Peters & Waterman, 1982), heralded exactly those types of firms that are now before the courts. So too the book *Best Practices* (Hiebeler, Kelly, & Ketterman, 1998) celebrated Enron, the company now notorious for defrauding investors.

But the demand for schooling arises not only from the professionals but also from the whole society. Typical is the view expressed in *The Guardian Weekly*: "The link between education and the chance of ending poverty, increasing child life expectancy, cutting population growth and improving farm production is beyond question" (Dec. 9–15, 1999, p. 13). Not only do nations take pride in the percentage of the children of particular ages attending school and even greater pride in the percentage of students graduating, child welfare generally is judged by such international agencies as the United Nations Children's Fund (UNICEF) and the United Nations Educational, Scientific, and Cultural Organization (UNESCO) on the basis of the availability of schooling. Parents, too, seek education for their children even if practices are hopelessly primitive (E. Goody & Bennett, 2001) and even if such schooling provides little or no economic advantage (Jencks, 1972; Lancey, 1996; Bloch, 1998). Schools are valued and vilified, often in the same breath, but rarely dissolved.

In fact, far from being a failure, schools are one of the modern world's more successful social experiments. Like politics, law, and economics, education, it seems, is here to stay. Although education in a very general sense is characteristic of all societies, perhaps even nonhuman primate societies, education as an institutional practice is tied to a particular level of social organization (J. Goody, 1986; Lancey, 1996, p. 199). In ancient Mesopotamia formal schools were created for training scribes and for training priests. In feudal China (10th century B.C.) schools were established to teach the "six arts" to children of the privileged classes. In the T'ang dynasty, seventh century A.D., a complex examination system was developed for the selection of individuals for administrative roles in government. In the West, specialist education for the clergy, for the military, for governors, and for the sons of wealthy landowners goes back to classical Greek and Roman times (Harris, 1989). But public education, that is, education mandated by and supported by the state, began only with the formation of nation states, those "imagined communities" (Anderson, 1983) with frontiers, a national language, laws, economies, citizens, and taxpayers. Just as a clerical education was essential for preserving the church in the Middle Ages, so public schools are seen as essential for creating and preserving the modern state. Nation-states see education as essential to their continuity; it is also seen as above the provincial concerns of a particular nation, as a "universal human right" (UNESCO, 1995). Education is now widely perceived as essential to becoming a full human being and therefore as worthy of being institutionalized universally in the form of schooling.

Recognizing the importance of schooling and creating institutions that achieve their goals are two quite different things. Viewed over a period of roughly 500 years, the striking impression is of how little schools have changed. Meyer, Boli, and Thomas (1994, p. 15) claim that the "extraordinary uniformity of their fundamental character [results from the] institutional environment common to organizations in national societies throughout the world system." Schools have always had classes, levels, teachers, and, perhaps most importantly, books. As Grendler (1989) pointed out, schooling exploded in 13th-century Italy; in 1333 it was decreed that public officials and judges must be able to read and write to hold their jobs. Murray (1978), too, noted that "the golden age for careerism via the schools . . . began with the twelfth century" (p. 220). And Davis (1975) reports the salutary effects of reading and schooling after the invention of printing. Teaching children to read in 15th-century Germany was much as it is today (see Figure 1). Classrooms in North America are now much as they were in 1900 (see Figure 2).

The few irreversible reforms in schooling that did occur historically did little to alter its basic form. The principle shifts were in matters of increasing inclusiveness, from the elite to the entire population, increasing systematicity and length, from two or three years to some twenty in modern times, and increasing content, from basic literacy to a general, comprehensive education. While these and other changes are important and warrant extensive discussion (see Chapter 11), schools as institutions are sufficiently similar across time that one would have no difficulty in recognizing a school in 3rd-century b.c. Athens or a bush school in 20th-century Ghana.

It is more difficult to assess the success of calls for reform or, for that matter, attempted reforms. Tyack and Cuban's (1995) history of U.S. educational reform concluded that most attempts at reform failed because they ignored the nature and history of public schools. They describe successful reform as a kind of "tinkering," trying out various proposals and selecting the institutional arrangements that produce an acceptable compromise between local conditions and diverse social interests such as access and equity and the match to the perceived needs of a market economy. The transformation of the school that began in the first half of the 20th century in which the educational philosophy of John Dewey figured prominently is now seen as part of a general social change rather than as the direct result of particular attempts at educational reform

Liber Faceti docens mozes ho

minū: p̄cípue Iuuenū/ ín fupplementū íllo&/quí a Cathone
erāt omíffí:p Sebaftíanū Brant: ín vulgare nouíter trāflatus

FIGURE 1. Pictorial representation of 15th-century classroom reproduced here
with permission of the Bavarian State Archives, Munich.

(Cremin, 1961). Many calls for reform, even well-documented ones like
So Little for the Mind (Neatby, 1953), *Educational Wastelands* (Bestor, 1953),
or *Why Johnny Can't Read* (Flesch, 1955), or those focusing more specifically on the children themselves such as *The Process of Education* (Bruner,
1960), *How Children Learn*, and *How Children Fail* (Holt, 1967, 1964) may
have affected the local practice of individual teachers, but long-term,

FIGURE 2. Public school classroom, circa 1900 (John N. Teunisson, photographer) reproduced here with permission of the Louisianna State Museum, New Orleans.

systemwide effects are not obvious. Similarly those mandated by governments that are designed to effect pervasive change have left little trace. Indeed, in her recent history of educational reform, Ravitch (2000) concludes that even the most well-meaning attempts at reform have been disappointing if not counterproductive and lays the failure at the feet of a broad set of reforms she labels "Progressivism." Broadening the curriculum and making it more child-friendly and culture-friendly have tended to water down rather than enrich educational experience.[3]

---

[3] Ravitch's lovely book documents the pervasive reforms that swept through education over the last century, but the evidence she provides does little to demonstrate her central claim, namely, that the liberalizing reforms she discusses in fact caused a lowering of standards. The data tend to show, rather, that they had little effect on raising standards. Introducing vocational options, for example, had the effect of accommodating an increasingly diverse population rather than grinding down the disciplinary standards.

I find Ravitch's book remarkably atheoretical. There is no theory of institutions or of persons, perhaps befitting American pragmatism.

Although Ravitch's discussion of the shifts in educational policy over the past century is extremely enlightening, it is not clear that her more general claim is sustainable. It is not clear that standards have indeed fallen or that if they did it was because of the progressive movement. More importantly, it is not clear that the reforms were directed to raising educational standards rather than addressing more pressing social needs such as adapting schooling to an increasingly heterogeneous population of students with increasingly diverse goals and interests. Broadening of school programs was a largely successful solution to the problem of drawing and retaining a vastly increased student population, not an attempt to raise academic standards. Further, progressivist reforms such as those of the child-centered movement, the subjugation of content to method, and the broadening of criteria for judging competence did not necessarily lead to poorer achievement. The best designed and most frequently cited comparison of traditional and progressive schools was the Eight-Year-Study conducted by Ralph Tyler in the 1930s (Cremin, 1961, p. 255; Lagemann, 2000, p. 141). Thirty public and private alternative high schools implemented a progressivist curriculum over an 8-year period that integrated subject areas and encouraged the arts as well as community involvement. The performance of graduates of these programs at college entry was then compared to that of matched samples of students graduating from regular schools. In fact, performance differences were small but in favor of the progressive schools, who, in addition, were found to be more engaged in the social and artistic activities. A decade after the conclusion of this experiment, little trace of these reforms remained (Tyack & Cuban, 1995, p. 100). Yet Ravitch convincingly shows that attempts to make schooling more relevant and child-centered through adding values education and vocational education, and dissolving basic disciplines such as history and geography into "social studies" contributed little to the central mission of the school, that of the "development of children's knowledge and character" (1985, p. 22).

Consider the more recent attempt at reform in science education in the United States that was designed to move science instruction away from the study of books to the hands-on experience in the laboratory. In fact, this proposal duplicates one made almost a century earlier by Boyd Bode, an ardent Deweyan: "Under Bode teachers were free to do what they wanted in the classroom, but they were not free to use a textbook" (Ravitch, 2000, p. 243). Although the recent reform of science education was perhaps better motivated and well financed, by all accounts schools have largely reverted to standard pedagogical strategies based on books (Roth & Anderson, 1988). Ravitch (1995) reported that some 75–90% of classroom instructional time was structured by textbooks. Indeed, some researchers find the return, by and large, beneficial (Mortimore, Sammons, Stoll, Lewis, & Ecob, 1988). It is tempting to agree with Sarason (1990, 1998) not only that attempts at systemwide reform have been failures but also that those failures were predictable. High-level institutional reforms fail because they ignore local conditions and human diversity, imposing rather one norm, rule, standard, or goal on everyone. On the other hand, pedagogical reforms fail because they pay insufficient attention to the special nature of the school as an institution.

Ravitch (2000) has no doubt that the initiatives introduced under the banner of progressivism such as intelligence quotient (IQ) testing, increasing program diversity, and promoting mental health and multiculturalism, all designed to address the diversity of individual needs and interests, were failures. She points out that well-meaning reforms often had the effect of reducing student responsibility and accountability. "Opportunity classes" rather than providing of opportunity simply offered lower standards. Yet there is no doubt that the literature of educational reform had an impact not just on those who read it but on the public at large, raising the concern and efforts of all to make the most of schooling for their students and for their children. Some may recall the interest in the minds of teachers and educational researchers awakened by reading *The Process of Education* and the concern for content stirred by reading *So Little for the Mind* and *The Schools We Deserve*, even if those concerns tended to be buried under the problems of minute-to-minute management of a classroom of children, each with individual interests and agendas. And the public concern with schooling provoked by educational debates may have increased parental involvement in their children's education, making them more willing to help with homework even if that willingness was tempered by rival demands on working families. As March and Olsen (1989) noted in regard to public policy debates, such attempted reforms contribute importantly to the general understanding of the issues involved as well as increasing willingness to participate even if the altered institutional practices themselves change little. Unfortunately, at least to date, these debates have done little to increase financial support for education, the major factor affecting the quality of schooling (Ravitch, 1985).

Similarly for the study of and research on education. Lagemann (2000) notes "the persistent belief that research rarely leads to improvements in practice" (p. 3) and describes that link as "elusive." There is no question that research has been informative even if the links to improvements in practice are obscure. Research is one of those enterprises in which the answer to any question reveals further questions. Hence, research can thrive whether or not it provides definitive answers. Scarcely any aspect of current schooling has been overlooked by competent researchers dedicated to understanding such issues as the nature of classroom lessons, of children's learning and understanding, and of teacher–student relations. Furthermore, there are conspicuous advances in our disciplined understanding of children's thinking and learning as well as of the history, politics, and policies of education that have resulted from systematic research. There is a wealth of information currently available and growing daily, and, while practitioners complain that research findings lack direct applicability, theorists despair of integrating them into any general explanatory framework.

Part of the problem lies in the notion of applicability. Lagemann and Shulman (1999b) recount receiving a call from an executive of a new charter school, who wanted advice, based on research, on how best to operationalize his plans to meet the needs of a diverse student body. Should he segregate ability levels, sexes, or grades? Should instruction be more formal or less formal? Should uniforms be required? These are decisions any administrator is faced with. The expectation that research could decide such questions betrays a degree of naiveté. Lagemann (2000, p. 221) reports that early on "scholars realized that behavior which fostered success in one year or one classroom did not necessarily have the same effect in the following year or another classroom." Tyack and Cuban (1995, p. 138) concluded their history of educational reform by pointing out that "successful reform depends upon adaptability to local conditions." Professional educators who understand and respect the traditions, philosophies, and pedagogies of schooling recognize these as calling for informed professional judgment, allowing for balance, context, and collaboration within the accountability constraints of a bureaucratic institution. Hence, researchers need not feel inadequate in their inability to provide definitive answers to such questions.

In retrospect it seems clear enough that practical questions such as those mentioned are not the sort of question to which research is likely to give a definitive answer. Rather, the design of a school appeals to the evolved traditions of conventional schooling: deciding who may attend; choosing which subjects to include, how many hours they are to be allotted, how many different subjects and classes a teacher can be expected to teach, how many years students are required to face before graduation, the length of a schoolday, the allocation of resources to library, technology, and athletics, and the like. These decisions will be based on tradition, resources, and discussion with those affected. The main limitation of educationally relevant research, in my view, is knowing the sorts of questions to which formal research may be usefully applied. That in turn depends on the groundedness of the theory on which the research is based. Practical questions, often, are not.

But if research does not lead directly to improved effectiveness of schooling, why is research supported at all? Indeed, there are political forces that see research and scholarship in education as part of the bloated bureaucracy that could be eliminated without loss. Instead of research and theory, some governments, including that of Ontario, Canada, would "rationalize" education by mandating goals and assessing outcomes in the attempt to bypass all the mediating professionalism and bureaucracy of education. Such "command and control" thinking is a consequence of a limited understanding of bureaucracies and, it may be argued, is analogous to fundamentalism in law and religion. Why is justice not carried out by listing crimes and punishments and doing away with the cumbersome institutions of courts, judges, and lawyers? Because to do so is to lose the very idea of justice, the concern for a fair hearing of the special circumstances involved. Similarly, to restrict the discourse of education to goals and outcomes is to ignore the importance of professional understanding of personal growth and disciplined understanding in the institutional context of the school.

There is an even deeper problem. The gap between theory and practice, it may be argued, is seriously misconceived. The problem is less that the research fails to be applied to programs and schools and more that practitioners look to research for the latest insight or directive that will make decisions for them. The optimism for general solutions sponsored by the research and development (R & D) movement in the United States in the 1960s,[4] which continues to this day, as the search for the "best practices," blocked the route to more local, in-house improvements in the organization and effectiveness of each particular school with its particular makeup of students, teachers, resources, and community. In a

---

[4] The R & D model underwrote the formation of my home institution, the Ontario Institute for Studies in Education.

word it blocked the evolution of effective local institutional practices. Practitioners were led both by government mandates and by pioneering research to jump from one recommended nostrum to the next – more breadth one year, more depth, the next; more interdisciplinary study one year, more specialized disciplinary study, the next; more emphasis on personal growth one year, more on socialization, the next; and so on (Egan, 1997).

As the recent comprehensive reviews of educational research and educational reform by the historians Tyack and Cuban (1995), Lagemann (2000), and Ravitch (2000) have indicated, the record on school reform is very checkered. Current initiatives including vouchers and charter schools continue to receive, at best, mixed reviews (Fiske & Ladd, 2000; Good & Braden, 2000; Fuller, 2000a; Orfield, 2000; Gardner, 2000).[5] Even in the absence of evidence, private companies such as Edison Schools Inc. aspire to take over school districts such as the Philadelphia school system with its 1.7-billion-dollar budget "counting on a healthy Philadelphia contract to put the company into the black for the first time" (*New York Times*, Feb. 24, 2002, p. 12). But worse, in my view, such general or mandated reforms block the development of local, professional expertise and local school culture, essential ingredients of a successful institution. What research can provide is an elaborated set of options that professionals can combine with the accumulation of local experience as to what works well and what works less well with their students and staff, in their school, in their community to enhance local practice. Schools are learning institutions in the second sense of improving practice through modest, accumulative developments. The accumulation of professional expertise and local knowledge of the characteristics of teachers, students, and the community are undermined by imposing solutions from on high. Their relative stability over a century if not a millennium suggests that schools are more or less optimal solutions to the competing demands of parents, students, the disciplines, and the larger society and are less in need of bold reform than of fine-tuning to local conditions. One serious impediment to improvement is the high

---

[5] I am less optimistic than Gardner (2000) or Fuller (2000b) that further research will show one form of organization to be better overall. Orfield (2000) shows that there are trade-offs; raising standards is as likely to encourage dropouts as to increase performance. Schools differ importantly, not in terms of such macrodimensions, but in terms of how well they get the job done. How they do it can vary enormously. The best that such research can show is that the advertised claims of some reformers are unwarranted. To advance the study of education we shall have to look elsewhere.

turnover of teachers, often one-third of the staff, that makes such attunement difficult if not impossible. States and nations have the responsibility for stabilizing the teaching staff at least as much as for determining programs and assessing outcomes, responsibilities they routinely fail to meet.

Where the discourse on education and educational research goes awry, then, is in the conflation of two very different sets of concerns. Sometimes these concerns are presented as the conflict between theory and practice, sometimes as that between ends and means, sometimes as a conflict between personal and social goals. None of these adequately captures the problem. It is the more general failure to grasp the nature of institutions and their role in public and personal life. Education is an institution created by a society as a means of achieving a set of goals including the preservation and enhancement of its language(s) and culture, its workforce, and its sponsoring institutions, whether governmental, legal, medical, scientific, or economic. To understand this we must have a fuller understanding of the nature of institutions generally and schooling as an institution in particular.

But education as a social institution with its particular agenda must be clearly differentiated from education as a pedagogic process – the active, intentional, social processes of the students who are educated and of the professionals who undertake responsibility for their development. As students, learners are attempting to establish an identity in the new social organization, the school, and to understand the new information for which they are held responsible and accountable. This personal understanding makes up their private and subjective mental life – their beliefs, desires, goals, and intentions – intentional states for which they are responsible and accountable. The fostering of intentionality and responsibility in students is what I describe as the pedagogical problem.

The problem in the discourse on education and educational reform is that the goals of the former, the institution, are addressed in terms of outcomes of the latter, the beliefs, intentions, and responsibilities of the learners. A common case of this conflation occurs when schools are given the responsibility for the actions (the learning and thinking) of the students as if the students themselves were to have no say in the matter. Indeed, in some nation-states, specified "learning outcomes" are government policy. Conflating the institutional and the personal gives no account of how such responsibilities are to be adjudicated, of saying who gets the credit and who gets the blame. The solution, as I see it, is that institutions must be assessed in terms of institutional goals and purposes, whereas children must be assessed in terms of pedagogical goals, including their particular beliefs, goals, and understandings. There are two goals here, not one. This conflation, as mentioned, is a result of the failure to recognize the particular nature of institutions on one hand and the nature of personal growth and development on the other.

INSTITUTIONS AND PEDAGOGIES

The contrast I have been drawing between education as an institutional practice and education as individual, personal development runs counter to a well-established tradition in Anglo-American thought. The liberal tradition of individualism, the philosophy that grew up in the 17th century and underwrote the Enlightenment doctrine of "inalienable human rights," puts an emphasis on personal freedom, privacy, and individual rights. Law and government were seen as legitimate only to the extent that they protect these personal freedoms; bureaucracy was seen as intrinsically evil. Institutions as positive social achievements came to be recognized only in the late 19th and early 20th centuries by the great social theorists who were writing with the Industrial Revolution clearly in the background. Max Weber (trans. by Gerth & Mills, 1948), a German, and Emile Durkheim (Durkheim, 1938, 1961; Lukes, 1973), a Frenchman, accorded institutions an autonomy and causal efficacy previously overlooked or denied.[6] Rejecting the Anglo-American doctrine of individualism, these Continental writers, working independently, attempted to capture important properties of an individual's personal or private life such as beliefs, tastes, and morals in terms of the social institutions in which individuals were embedded. For Durkheim this meeting ground was to be found in "collective representations" of the culture, whereas for Weber, they were found primarily in the roles persons played in such institutions as the legislature, the legal system, the economic system, and the specialist disciplines of the academy. For Durkheim, whose theory we examine more closely later (see Chapter 8), both logic and morality were to be analyzed not as personal psychological dispositions or traits but as procedures lodged in language, in the sciences, and in the courts. For his part, Weber could

---

[6] Or still denied. Recall Margaret Thatcher's famous claim that there was no such thing as society, "just individuals and their families," as if families were not a kind of society.

speak of the "rationality of society" in terms of the systematic properties of bureaucratic institutions. Personal rationality was a product of rather than a precondition for the rationality of social institutions. Again, the growth of institutions, not mental growth, accounted for the advance of rationality. Individuals became rational by induction, through schooling, into these institutional practices. Explanation of behavior focused on collective outcomes and less on private mental life.

Such claims long seemed incomprehensible to psychologists, individualists to the core, who think of logic, morality, and truth as psychological problems, rooted in the basic properties of the human mind (Macnamara, 1986) and subject to the rules of mental and moral development (Piaget, 1932). They are also incomprehensible to most educators and educational theorists, who tend to regard education as directed to developing the full potential of the child rather than to adapting the child to the dominant institutions of the society. Indeed, one of the most serious objections to the social perspectives of Weber and Durkheim was the difficulty of accommodating the personal or phenomenological experience of individuals to the functioning of social institutions. Weber knew and was successor to Wilhelm Dilthey in Heidelburg, and although he adopted a *verstehende* psychology, that is, a psychology of understanding rather than of behavior, he did not elaborate on it or reconcile it with his institutional perspective (Parsons, 1947, p. 25). The consequence was that whereas Weber is seen as the father of sociology, his impact on psychology has been limited. Talcott Parsons (1970), the American successor to Max Weber, restricted his concept of persons to that offered by the psychological theories of the times, namely, personality theory (traits) and public opinion research, rather than to subjective experience and to intentional states of interest to this generation of cognitive psychologists. Consequently, social theories have yet to claim their place vis-à-vis theories of individualism (Giddens, 1987; Heap, 1992).

The problem is not limited to the psychologists; social theorists too have tended to move away from large-scale social theories such as those of Weber and Durkheim. Several writers have noted that beginning in the 1950s and 1960s, theories of politics (March & Olsen, 1989) and theories of sociology (Parsons, 1968; Archer, 1979; Bidwell, 1999); have paid less attention to institutional perspectives. Institutions came to be seen as merely the site for the interplay of more fundamental personal and social factors such as habits and beliefs pertaining to social class, ethnicity, language, culture, economic conditions, technology, ideology and religion, and personal dispositions such as intelligence or achievement motivation (see the chapters in Brodbeck, 1971). In this way institutional structure came to be conflated with the rest of personal and social life. That is, institutional "behavior" came to be seen as simply the aggregation of the behavior of individuals rather than, for example, a consequence of adopting the roles and following the rules mandated by an institution. Again, the self-interests and personalities of the actors were seen as more fundamental than the rules, obligations, and duties imposed by the institution.[7] As Bidwell (1999, p. 92) pointed out, sociologists of education have attempted to specify fully the features of student environment that contribute to educational attainment while "remaining mute about the social structural and cultural systems within which the processes of educational attainment . . . take place." March and Olsen (1989) critically describe the bias of this individualizing tradition thus:

> The central faith is that outcomes at the collective level depend only on the intricacies of the interactions among the individual actors or events, that concepts suggesting autonomous behaviour at the aggregate level [i.e., institutions] are certainly superfluous and probably deleterious. (p. 4)

Indeed, this individualizing perspective has been so dominant in psychological discourse that discourse on culture in psychology is often seen as revolutionary (Johnson & Erneling, 1997). In sociology, only in the last decade has there been a "rediscovery" of institutions (March & Olsen, 1989; Bidwell, 1999). Building on earlier work with Herbert Simon (March & Simon, 1958) March and Olsen criticize the individualist stance, citing a wide array of evidence for the view that social and political life can no longer be seen as simply a function of economic and social conditions but must, rather, be recognized as based on the intrinsic structure of political institutions. Bureaucratic agencies "are arenas for contending social forces," but more importantly they are "collections of standard operating procedures and structures that define and defend values, norms, interests, and beliefs" (p. 17). Only now and only to a limited degree, have institutions come to be seen as capable of coherent and autonomous political action somewhat independently of the personal beliefs, feelings, and intentions of the individuals who make them up.

---

[7] When reporters attempted to accord heroic status to a fireman who had just risked his life to rescue a fellow fireman from the ruins of the World Trade Center in New York, he dismissed such an attribution, saying merely, "It's my job." Thus duty sometimes prevails over self-interest.

These institutions have an impact on the psychology of individuals. The individuals who make up institutions have developed a form of expertise suitable to functioning in those institutions. In so doing they acquire both an identity (e.g., I am a teacher, lawyer, firefighter, professor) and mastery of a collection of rules and procedures for participating in such an institution. March and Olsen (1989) continue:

Although they may be rationalized to some degree, rules are learned by experts as catechisms. Physicists learn what physicists do; lawyers learn what lawyers do. The rules are enforced by the standards of the profession and the expectations of patrons. (p. 30)

Such institutions produce order in a complicated social world. Institutions allow the specialization of function and the differentiated allocation of responsibility. Not everything can be dealt with at once – the world is not so conveniently organized that one can, at once, serve both God and mammon, as Ernst Gellner once cryptically noted. By dividing functions and roles, the prosecutor from the judge, for example, one can, it is believed, reduce errors in judgment. In addition, institutions regulate institutional change. Initiatives to reform any institution, including education, must meet not only an idealistic vision, but also the realities of a historically evolved institutional form with traditions that are difficult to change and perhaps should not be changed. For this reason, broad reforms mandated from above frequently fail to have the desired impact (Fullan, 1991; Wells, 1999). Clearly, proposed change must acknowledge the current knowledge and practices of the existing institution in a way analogous to the way instruction must take into account the existing knowledge of the learner.

There is a price to be paid for the failure to recognize the essential autonomy of institutions. For one, it has led to the interpretation of the need for institutional reform as a need for pedagogical reform, reform in teaching and learning of reading or mathematics, for example. The educational reform movements of the 1960s were based on the assumption that reform of schools as institutions could be reduced to reforms in such pedagogical practices as integrating subjects into projects or tying study to practical experience. Rather than addressing the primary obligation of providing an environment in which teachers and students could take responsibility for teaching and learning, reformers focused on pedagogical practices themselves and the actual learning outcomes of individuals. This sponsored the host of research over the last four decades on factors affecting student learning and performance. Aside from some highlights mentioned earlier, this research, on most readings, has been disappointing.

However, there are some indications that conditions have begun to change in the direction of recognizing the nature and effects of institutions. There is an increasingly rich literature on the relations among culture, education, and development (Vygotsky, 1989; Bruner, 1996; Heath, 1999; Cole, 1996). Mehan (1998, p. 262) examined how the institutional demands of schooling dictate the local interactional practices in the classroom. LeTendre, Baker, Akiba, Goesling, and Wiseman (2001) showed how international comparisons of schooling such as those of the Third International Math–Science Study (TIMSS) are less informative than had been hoped because of the "institutional isomorphism" of schools, that is, the fact that all schools in modern bureaucratic societies are essentially the same; local culture tends to be swamped by the bureaucratic "rationalization of society and the spread of institutions that has taken place over the last century" (p. 12). Bruner (1999, p. 404) pointed out the need for examining the cultural contexts of goal setting apart from the narrower concerns of effective pedagogy. Any analysis of schooling will require carefully drawn distinctions among persons, cultures, and institutions. Bromley (1998) has recently begun this by distinguishing the two broad categories of literature on educational reform, the first rising from the educational community and concerned with teaching and learning, what I have called *pedagogy*, the second rising from the economic community and concerned with the school as a firm, that is, a bureaucratic institution, which can be examined in terms of institutional structure and the relations between inputs and outputs. This second perspective, he noted, brings into relief the absence of efficiency indicators useful for upgrading the institution as a whole. In their absence, reformers have been led to telescope a whole structure of responsibilities into a single bottom line, student achievement.

Most professional educators find the input–output model abhorrent, objecting that children are not widgets. But if the two perspectives, the pedagogic and the economic–institutional, are carefully distinguished, we may find a place for both and subsequently the relation between them. The error, I suggested earlier, is in conflating the institutional with the pedagogic, reducing the former to the latter, thereby ignoring institutional structures altogether. Educational theory is ripe for the rediscovery of institutions.

This sets the stage for the remainder of this volume. I shall attempt to provide an analysis of educational processes and educational change in this framework of education as institution and education as pedagogy. There is a great deal of theory and evidence bearing on both. What has been lacking, as I suggested earlier, is an analysis that shows both how and why they are different and ultimately, how they are related. Distinguishing them is the first step in advancing the study of education.

PART II

SCHOOLS AS INSTITUTIONS

3

Rediscovering Institutions

Social life is a system of representations ... "sui generis," and different in nature from those ... of the individual.

(E. Durkheim, 1982/1901, p. 253)

What is there in social life beyond the hedonistic exchange of two or more parties? Not much.

(G. Homans, cited in E. K. Wilson, 1961, p. xxvii)

The eclipse of institutions in midcentury political and economic discourse noted in the last chapter was accompanied by a rebirth in the social sciences of a concern with persons and populations of persons, with public opinion, and with the actions of voluntary, intentional agents. Bidwell (1999) noted in the social theorizing of the 1950s a shift away from the analysis of institutions to an analysis of the individuals involved. This shift, he suggested, was driven in part by the new methods of public opinion research and in part by the trend in sociological theory to what came to be called "methodological individualism," the attempt to explain the behavior of institutions in terms of the aggregate intentions and actions of the individuals who composed them. Bidwell wrote:

it became a dictum for most empirical social scientists to explain any relationship between social or cultural aggregates in terms of constitutive individual-level processes. ... The analysis of individual action intervening between aggregate social states would explain the nature of those states and their patterns of change. (p. 97)

Nowhere was this more conspicuous than in educational discourse, in which research on schooling shifted in the 1960s from essentially

33

demographic features, such as enrollments, budgets, programs, test scores, and school organization, to a new concern with the cognitive processes of individuals involved in teaching and learning. But this focus on the learning processes of individuals eclipsed the larger institutional contexts in which such learning occurred. Rediscovering the institution of the school, as I proposed in the last chapter, requires that we think about teaching and learning in a new way. Specifically, we cannot answer questions about learning such school disciplines as science, mathematics, or literacy without understanding how the institutional structure of the school imposes its norms and standards on that learning. Nor can we understand such institutional practices as promotion and failure; or such classifications of children as "normal," "gifted," or "hyperactive"; or such putative social problems as "illiteracy," until we recognize them as social categories that are uniquely associated with schooling as an institution. Consequently, we require a much more elaborated understanding of institutions. Only with it can we even begin to address the relations between schools as institutions and schools as pedagogical practices of teachers and learners.

The institutional issue, of course, is as old as the biblical question "Was man made for the Sabbath, or was the Sabbath made for man?" Do institutions serve us or we them? There are two broad approaches to understanding institutions.[1] The predominant one, which I referred to earlier as individualism, the one most of us take for granted, focuses upon the beliefs and desires of individuals and takes its essentially modern form in the writings of David Hume's *Treatise on Human Nature* (1740). Hume, following in the steps of Hobbes, Descartes, and Locke, assumed human beings to be rational actors working from private beliefs and desires who, in order to preserve peace and enjoy a civil life, create social rules and practices, including the market, for exchange of both goods and beliefs. At the core is the individual pursuing his or her own self-interest. Institutions, in consequence, are seen as little more than the sum of the activities of these individual actors. Social structures reduce, we may say, to the actions of individuals. This individualism is the prevailing view in market-economic theory, in which human action is explained in terms of enlightened self-interest (March & Olsen, 1989). Schlicht (1998), an economist, refers to this as the "nominalist" view of

---

[1] American political scientists describe the contrast as that between Jefferson's individualism and Madison's institutionalism. Canadians follow Madison in emphasizing institutions even if he is less admired here because he declared war on us in 1812.

institutions: the view that institutions are little more than names for collections of individual actors. The epigram to this chapter asked "What is there in social life beyond the hedonistic exchange of two or more parties?" George Homans, a foe of Durkheim, answered, "Not much," and thereby expressed a view still widely held by individualists (Wilson, 1961, p. xxvii).

The second view grants an ontological status to collectives whether of informal social groups or of more formal institutions and denies that the actions of the collective can be reduced to those of the individuals making it up. This view takes its modern form, as noted earlier, from the sociological writings of Max Weber, Emile Durkheim, Marcel Mauss, and others who saw not only that society as composed of networks of institutions but further that mental life of individuals is rooted in that social life. Weber (1968) used the term *bureaucracy* to refer to the then increasing importance of large-scale organizations with fixed positions or roles linked in a pyramidal, hierarchical structure with specialization of function and division of labor and governed by fixed rules and procedures. A manager, who was not necessarily the owner, interpreted the rules and applied them systematically. Weber contrasted a bureaucracy with the more traditional person-based, usually patriarchal and tribal, relationships in which authority and legitimacy are based on the sacredness of tradition. Consequently, Weber saw a close relationship between modes of social organization and modes of thought such as the disenchantment of nature, the growth of religious individualism, and the development of more formal modes of thought: "Bureaucratic administration means fundamentally the exercise of control on the basis of knowledge. This is the feature of it that makes it specifically rational" (Weber, 1968, p. 339).

Durkheim, a French sociologist and contemporary of Weber, was less concerned with bureaucratic institutions than Weber but more concerned with the means by which all individual psychological life was shaped by social customs, categories, symbols, and practices. He argued that society cannot be simply reduced to collections of individuals, for a "society is infinitely more vast than our individual being; but at the same time it enters into every part of us. It is outside us and envelops us, but it is also in us and everywhere an aspect of our nature. We are fused with it. [Indeed] it is the most important part of ourselves" (1961, p. 71). Durkheim viewed language itself as a social product, arguing that the very consciousness of individuals takes shape in the language and other "collective representations" of a culture (Lukes, 1973). In his writings on education, Durkheim, as did Weber, thought of education as the "methodical socialization" of the young (1956, p. 71). Moral development, for Durkheim, was the result of the imposition of norms or rules that prescribe obligations or duties and of the formation of social bonds of affection and concern for others. Such development involves the elaboration, across generations, of reasons for moral action: "Science permits us to establish rationally what faith postulates a priori" (1961, p. 115). Thus, education was seen as playing a critical role in advancing this science of reasons. Although Durkheim's thought was reintroduced into psychological and educational discourse through the more psychological writings of Vygotsky, "there is little evidence that [Durkheim] has had any impact on education in the U.S." (Wilson, 1961, p. xvii). There evolutionary individualism continues to reign supreme (Hofstadter, 1945) – only slightly less so, perhaps, in Canada and the United Kingdom and much less so in Europe.

Although human action is situated in social context and in large part determined by social context, actors themselves are unlikely to be aware of those social influences even when they begin to identify themselves with such distinctive social groups as family, religion, ethnic group, or class. Consequently, Moscovici (1993) could describe, somewhat hyperbolically, the development of sociological theory as the *invention of society*. Whereas social life, through language, culture, and custom, may lie at the basis of individual, private mental life, consciousness of the ways in which mental life reflects social structures depends, in large part, on the invention of sociological theories such as those of Durkheim and Weber. That mental life itself is fully dependent on social and cultural practices is a point that has come to the fore in more recent writings in anthropology (Geertz, 1973), law (Amsterdam & Bruner, 2000), economics (Schlicht, 1998), and psychology (Nicolopoulou & Weintraub, 1998; Tomasello, 1999).

The strength of these perspectives is in their attempts, from opposite ends, to bridge from the macro – the society – to the micro – the individual. The central problem for both, in my view, is their tendency to reduce one to the other. The temptation is to reduce or explain the social in terms of the individual or, conversely, to reduce and explain the individual in terms of the social. Neither grants sufficient autonomy to both the individual, even the individual as a social being, and the institutions of the society. The distinction must be redrawn somewhat. It is not that between a Hobbesean individual for whom human life is "solitary, poor, nasty, brutish and short" (Hobbes, 1651/1958, p. 107) and the controlling institutions in which the human being is embedded. Rather, it is to be drawn between persons in culture and society and the same persons embedded in formal institutional bureaucracies of a modern society. Although considerable progress has been made in showing how the social practices, customs, and language of a culture define in large part the mental world of persons (Bruner, 1996; Cole, 1996; Schlicht, 1998; Nicolopoulou & Weintraub, 1998), this work leaves relatively uncharted the important differences between persons in a cultural or social world and persons in a bureaucracy. This point takes on some urgency when we approach the peculiar institution of the school.

Showing how the psychology of an individual is based in social life is the fundamental first step. What is needed in addition is a clearer distinction between the shared social practices of everyday life and the institutional structures of a modern, literate, bureaucratic society (Sawyer, 2002a). Institutions are built upon the customs and traditions of existing culture, but, as we shall see, they possess a life of their own, a life that gives institutions, including schools, their special properties, properties that eventually are reflected in the life and minds of the persons educated in them. Only when we have drawn that distinction will we be in a position to understand the rival claims between schooling as an institution and schooling as a site for experience and learning, between what I have called the "institutional" and the "pedagogic."

In fact, a contemporary of Weber's, Tönnies (1887), proposed just such a distinction, that is, a distinction between two types of social organization, which he labeled as *Gemeinschaft*, social organization based on affection and loyalty such as in a family or feudal society, and *Gesellschaft*, social organization based on more formal roles and rules of a modern state. This distinction was adopted by Weber in what he called social systems as opposed to bureaucracies and by Durkheim in what he called "mechanical" as opposed to "organic" solidarity.[2] Some anthropologists such as Elwert (personal communication) acknowledge the importance of this distinction but add that Gemeinschaft societies have more Gesellschaft properties than usually acknowledged. That is, the differences between traditional and modern societies, Elwert suggests, are less categorical than most "great divide" theorists, myself included, usually acknowledge. Yet, institutional structure, Gesellschaft,

---

[2] Incidentally, this distinction has recently reemerged, although in different terms, as a possible account of gender differences: women more attuned to Gemeinschaft, men to Gesellschaft (Gilligan, 1982). I prefer cultural explanations.

I shall argue, is the central, indeed inescapable, basis for the study of education in a modern society.

What then are institutions? There have always been weird people, but institutions with the power to define these people as "abnormal" (by reference to a norm) date only from the 18th century (Foucault, 1979, p. 184). Ignorance has always been around, but "rustics," that is, those who have not attended an educational institution, date only from the 16th century (Davis, 1975, p. 203). There have always been people who could not read, but "illiterates" date only from the 14th century (Clanchy, 1993), at which time illiteracy referred to the inability to read Latin. Children, especially boys, have often been disruptive, but only in the last few decades have there been "hyperactive children." There have always been those who excel but only in the past century has there been a class of "gifted" children. The same could be said of "functional illiterates," "dysfunctional families," "dropouts," "abused children," "homeless youth," and the like. Institutionalization turns persons, perceptions, and actions into social categories or classes with political implications for allocation of public resources and accountability (Hacking, 1999). Families, communities, play groups, and workplaces are all social organizations that share some of the properties of modern bureaucracies such as firms and schools. The social systems of the former, families and communities, are well characterized as cultures, the complex webs of which can only be characterized by "thick descriptions" (Geertz, 1983). Bureaucratic institutions, on the other hand, are characterized by constitutions, contracts, courts, and officials. Attempts to reduce one to the other eclipse important properties of both.

DEFINING INSTITUTIONS

Schlicht (1998, p. 214), an economist, defines an institution as a social organization with two major properties, structure and control. Institutions exist when the collective exerts some control on the behavior of the individuals making it up rather than merely reflecting the peculiar interests of those individuals. It is difficult to imagine that individuals may compete or cooperate without some superordinate social structure determining the form of action that each individual takes. Durkheim was explicit on this point: Even contracts, the ad hoc agreements between parties, are always subject to "non-contractual elements" or generalized norms. The norms are not open to negotiation and in modern states make up part of the rules or norms of the formal legal system, enforced by the legal sanctions of the state. Even a game of tag or checkers constrains the actions of the individual participants by appeals to the rules of the game.

Second, institutions exist when there is some internal structure or organization specifying the entitlements and obligations of actors in the group and hence the allocation of responsibility and accountability to those individuals. But whereas in small-scale social organizations such as families, communities, and tribal groups both structure and control can be left largely implicit and managed through indirection (Heeschen, 1997), in larger-scale bureaucratic institutions such as business firms or schools, control, responsibility, and accountability become matters of "documentation" including explicit rules and procedures, laws, principles, job descriptions, lines of authority, specialized expertise, and accountability.

Schlicht (1998, p. 206) distinguishes small-scale social interactions or customs from larger-scale social institutions such as law courts and examines the transformation of custom into formal law while acknowledging that the two are never far apart:

Custom provides the basis for the law. The law . . . transforms custom both by delimiting and sharpening customary entitlements and by creating new entitlements and obligations in response to functional or other (e.g., political) demands. [Thus] the formal law may be viewed as a kind of crystallized and systematized custom. [Nonetheless] the administration of law in the courts is brought about by the tacit knowledge, the routines, and the mysteries of the trade, as they have evolved among lawyers and judges. In this the law is entirely a matter of custom. (p. 206)

Amsterdam and Bruner (2000), too, see institutionalization as an extension or expression of the culture's canonical ways of thinking, feeling, acting, and affiliating with others. These "norms" vary in articulateness, some highly explicit and accessible, even inscribed in legal statutes, and others implicit in patterned actions. They go on to acknowledge the role of institutionalization in routinizing action and in offloading some otherwise mental routines into explicit procedures. But because their goal is to ground law in custom, they fail to grant institutions the autonomy that I, following March and Olsen (1989) and Scheffler (1974), think essential to understanding modern societies or the role of schooling in them.

Admittedly, to understand such institutions as law, economics, and schooling, it is essential to see their grounding in custom and culture as Amsterdam and Bruner (2000) and Schlicht (1998) insist. But in addition it is important, in my view, to distinguish cultural practices from the institutionalized practices of modern bureaucratic societies in terms of their documentary base; their links to power; their roles in creation of identities; their explicit norms, rules, and procedures; their responsibilities; and their accountability. Only then, I suggest, will we be able to understand schooling. We must come to see institutions themselves as actors not just as the expressions of persons, even persons in a social world. It is the school as an institution that has the power to label a child *hyperactive* or a *failure*, not the particular agent of the school who conducts the test or enters that label into the permanent record. The agent may have a personal opinion quite different from the entry he or she feels obliged to make as an agent of the institution.

A bureaucratic institution, whether governmental agency, business firm, or school system, is "a system of interlocking social roles embodied in job descriptions" (Schlicht, 1998, p. 223). Job descriptions set out what workers are supposed to know and to do in carrying out a function. No one knows everything that the institution knows or does. Some of the "knowledge" of an institution is in no one's mind but buried rather in an official manual, a set of tables, or computer files. Ascribing beliefs, desires, goals, and intentions to such institutions may, at first glance, seem as misplaced as ascribing them to animals – the problem of anthropomorphism. Indeed, Durkheim was criticized for just this view (Catlin, 1938, p. lii). Others, however, argue that attributing goals and intentions to institutions is no more problematical than ascribing such states to individuals (Kahneman, 1982). We may dispute whether or not institutions have intentionality; it seems clear, however, that they do have agency, that they may be commissioned to undertake responsibilities and be held accountable, and thereby have entitlements and obligations (Schlicht, 1998). A primary difference between traditional modes of social organization, Gemeinschaft, and more formal, bureaucratic ones, Gesellschaft, largely unacknowledged by most theorists, is the significant role played by writing and other documentary practices (Smith, 1990b) that reflect the ways we live in "a world on paper" (Olson, 1994).

Note that this is not merely a conceptual distinction; economic historians describe just such transformations. Kocka (1999) provided an explicit analysis of the transformation of a major German firm from its beginnings as a family business to a modern industrial manufacturing giant. The shift involved the "planned decentralization and delegation of authority" (p. 40), making "top managers . . . free to concentrate on basic policy, the allocation of capital equipment and personnel, external relations, legal topics, patents, overall organization, and labor management." These activities were organized through "regular reports, statistics, charts, and . . . administrative standardization" (p. 41). Owners became distinguished from managers, who operate in terms of formalized roles, rules, and procedures. Despite its negative connotations, *bureaucratization* is just the term for describing these organizational processes.

Some political scientists (Stein, 2001, p. 65) claim that "merit bureaucracies" were more typical of the 19th century than of the present postindustrial society. "Postbureaucratic" organizations focus on agreement on norms and on assignment of decision making to the lowest possible level within the organization. But this requires a higher level of professional responsibility, a clearer specialization of functions, a narrowing of goals, and stricter criteria of accountability. Thus postindustrial societies are just as bureaucratic as – though ideally less oppressive than – industrial ones.

Bureaucracies, then, require a specialization of function that is indicated in modern societies by credentialed expertise. As we noted earlier (Chapter 2), and as we shall examine in more detail later, expertise consists of learning, as if by catechism, the rules, norms, and standard practices as well as the mysteries of a domain of expertise (March & Olsen, 1989). Those for lawyers are spelled out in the primer for lawyers *An Introduction to Law* (Derham, Mahler, & Walker, 1971, cited in Schlicht, 1998, pp. 199–200):

Every trade has its mysteries. Lawyers' sense consists of the rules and conventions that are taken for granted, which "everyone knows." The young lawyer starts to absorb them in the first year of study; he picks up more at lunch tables, legal conferences, general conversations over a drink – and naturally by sitting in court. Sometimes he learns by stern reminders from his senior colleagues.

The legal profession often has strong ideas on the substantive law. Judges may favor a precedent as having "always been approved by the profession." Of some proposed change it may be argued "the profession is against it." But for good or ill, the sense of the craft is powerful.

Professional roles in educational institutions are equally delineated by job descriptions specifying obligations and rights, and they are fulfilled by practitioners specialized in their craft whether as teacher, librarian, counselor, administrator, or even student. Learning the professional expertise involves acquiring the specialized knowledge of the domain and the skills of the craft involved in using that knowledge. As do workers everywhere, educational professionals perform their tasks because they are promised rewards, because they are ordered or requested to by those to whom they are accountable, and, most importantly, because such performance is seen as their professional duty, their allegiance to the standards and ideals of their profession.

A further distinction may be made between such small-scale social organizations as a family or tribe and those of a large-scale or modern bureaucracy in terms of proposals for institutional change. In small-scale social groups, significant institutions such as family or tribe are slow to change in part because the rules and procedures remain largely implicit, that is, not formulated into explicit verbal rules or principles. Change is the product of a kind of evolutionary drift due to more general social change. In more formal institutions where the rules are explicit, change can be produced by debating the rules or simply changing the rules and rewriting the laws. In fact, however, radical change is difficult anywhere because of the weight and strength of custom, on the one hand, and because of a failure to recognize the nature of modern institutional structures on the other (Schlicht, 1998). Institutional practices are more likely to shift because of the accumulation of explicit information on inputs and outputs of the institution as a whole. Such accumulation allows the possibility of "learning institutions" in that the institution, as an individual, gains from experience (Keating, 1996). Such learning can occur either because the professionals engaged develop a greater expertise or because the institutional rearrangements themselves improve performance. But, as mentioned, institutional change is much more difficult than usually assumed (March & Olsen, 1989; Clemens, 1999), and imposed changes frequently have little lasting impact (Linn, 2000). This is not to say that institutions such as schools cannot be more or less effective in achieving their goals (Mortimore et al., 1990) but rather that restructuring such institutions to produce such change is difficult and unless keyed to existing practices has little lasting impact.

In sum, modern bureaucracies are rooted in the customs of small-scale social groups. These customs are made up of standard "scripts" explicating the rights or entitlements that one can normally expect relative to the duties and obligations owed to others. When "institutionalized" or "bureaucratized," these rights and obligations are made explicit, systematized, and written down as laws, contracts, job descriptions, accountability reports, and the like, that are common to both public and private institutions. However, they tend to be written and formalized only when the informal systems come into conflict with other informal systems. Consequently, written law is not identical to earlier custom but more large-scale and inclusive. Schooling, then, is not just an extension of the family; nor is it just a pedagogy, but an institution functioning in a complex matrix of interlocked institutions such as the justice system and the economic system, as well as the knowledge systems represented by the disciplines. These are the structures that formulate and attempt to impose norms, rules, and standards on the behavior of learners. Consequently, they are the structures that we must understand before we can even formulate the questions about whether learning, thinking, knowing, or understanding has occurred.

I have argued that institutions cannot be reduced to the individuals who make them up and further that informal social systems or cultures must be distinguished from more formal, bureaucratic institutions with their explicit norms, roles, rules, and systems of accountability. Both of these issues were attacked by Durkheim in his account of the autonomy of institutions and their internalization in the minds of individuals. His notion of collective representations was an attempt to capture the phenomenon that ideas are both individual and social. Whereas many European academics, some already familiar with the writings of Max Weber on bureaucracies, found Durkheim compelling, many British and American scholars, ideologically committed to individual autonomy and the privacy of beliefs, rejected any talk about "group minds," "zeitgeist," or even social action (Sawyer, 2002a,b). Even social action was, for them, to be explained in terms of the private intentional states of individuals.

When Durkheim was revived in the cognitive sciences in the 1960s it was largely through the influence of the newly translated writings of Vygotsky, which were read as indicating possible ways that participating in social practices and internalizing cultural resources could influence the psychological competencies and makeup of individuals. Thoughts were to be seen less as private mental states than as rule-based uses of "collective representations." "Culture in mind" or "mind in culture" or "culture and mind" became an important theme. However, Vygotsky was assimilated to the tradition of cultural relativity and multiculturalism, thereby emphasizing the differences among cultures and subcultures. It can equally easily be read as a basis of bridging across cultural differences via the construction of larger-scale social, indeed, bureaucratic institutions. That is the perspective required to understand the essentially universal effects of schooling. Thus the more institutional side of Durkheim and Weber, the autonomy of institutions and their causal properties, has remained somewhat unexplored.

Consequently, although the cultural revival has helped to show how our mental lives are shaped by our social lives, it has done less to advance our understanding of the specific effects of institutions, including schools, on minds and societies.

Durkheim's original writings attacked the question of social causes directly. In his discussion of radical educational changes that occurred over historical time, he appealed not to the intentions of reformers but to autonomous social causes: "[When] the Renaissance opposed a whole set of new methods to those that the Middle Ages had practiced," it was not as "a consequence of psychological discoveries . . . [but] because, as a result of the changes that had come about in the structure of European societies, a new conception of man and of his place in the world had emerged" (1956, p. 132). Mary Douglas (1986), in her attempt to revive Durkheimian thought, appropriately emphasized his account of the autonomy of institutions, of "how institutions think" and how institutions affect definitions of self.

Admittedly, explanations of social or educational change in terms of general social causes or the zeitgeist or the "charisma" of its leaders seem vague and unsatisfactory to most modern readers. Further, Durkheim's psychology was that of the early 20th century and limited to voluntaristic concepts such as "tendencies, habits, desires, emotions," and the "diversity of intelligence and character" (1956, p. 130), concepts that limited his ability to defend his most important theoretical claims, namely, that society exists exclusively in the minds of individuals and that social life is "realized only in and by individuals" (1956, p. 129). When we return to a discussion of Durkheim (in Chapter 8), it will be to provide a more careful analysis of intention, responsibility, and accountability in both persons and institutions but without confusing the two. For now, it serves to highlight these two poles, individuals and institutions, and to set the stage for examining schools as institutions with the power to define such major categories as student and teacher, success and failure, and what is known as opposed to what is merely believed. Institutions, we will say, establish the norms or standards against which any personal behavior is to be judged. Only by rediscovering institutions can we address these basic questions of teaching and learning.

4

School as a Bureaucratic Institution

I regard it as a prime postulate of all pedagogical speculation that education is an eminently social thing in its origins as in its functions, and, therefore, pedagogy depends on sociology more closely than on any other science.

(E. Durkheim, 1961, p. 114)

Educational science is first of all a social science.

(J. Dewey, 1976a, p. 131)

It is hard to recall how evil a term "bureaucracy" was among the political left thirty years ago.

(M. Katz, 2001, p. xvii)

Although one can easily grant that educational science is a social science in that it involves the relations between persons and society, it is not so easy to grant that the view of society adequate to the study of education is that of an institutional bureaucracy. For a generation that cut its teeth on Joseph Heller's *Catch 22* it is difficult to grasp the notion that bureaucracies, though often cast as relentlessly oppressive – the heavy hand of bureaucracy[1] – are absolutely central to modern social life. Dickens, Kafka, and more recently the revelations of state control in the former Soviet Union or the former German Democratic Republic all fuel the current strong anti-institutional sentiment. Calls against "big government" and for tax reduction, especially in the United States, less so in Europe or Canada, reflect this anti-institutional stance. Some

---

[1] Even Ravitch (1978, p. 5) links "bureaucratization, standardization, and coercion."

ideologues even imagine a state without taxation and without institutions (excepting, perhaps, prisons, the military, and the market).[2] The
rest, they say, we can do for ourselves. But as we noted in the preceding chapter, no modern nation can function without institutions such
as government, courts, finance, the sciences, and the military, as well as
the schools that are needed to prepare persons for life in a civil society,
that is, to operate and otherwise participate in those institutions.

In educational sociology no less than in other branches of sociology,
bureaucratic institutions are again coming to be recognized as central to
social life. While debate continues as to whether institutions should be
thought of as supraindividual causal agents operating over and above
and controlling persons rather than as expressions of the voluntary actions of individuals (Pope, Cohen, & Hazelrigg, 1975), most agree on the
importance of a large-scale, social, institutional (macrosystem) perspective on social life. Archer (1979, p. 31), an educational sociologist and
a leader in this turn, points out that whereas "large-scale organization
is generated from . . . more primary forms of interaction," it cannot be
reduced to them, and she sets out to suggest how they differ and how
they may be related.

Archer criticizes the dualism that has arisen between macrosociol-
ogy and microsociology, the one examining how institutions set goals,
the other the social factors that contribute to individual achievement,
without a clear understanding of how these two affect each other. She
points out that "much of the sociology of education has been founded
upon an acceptance of dualism" (1979, p. 34). On the macroscopic side,
some educational reformers have argued, for example, that existing definitions of school achievement and awarding of credentials (passing special exams) are discriminatory and ad hoc and should be abandoned. It
is easier and perhaps more fair, it is argued, to change the definition than
to change the children. Such critics argue that educational achievement
should rather be analyzed in terms of privilege, organization in terms of
authority, and curriculum in terms of power (McDermott, 1997). Again,
on this macroscopic side it is argued that the implementation of any
recommendation depends upon the macrosocial processes by which
definitions of success and failure are imposed and the conditions under
which they are changed (Bowles & Gintis, 1976). Only by understanding
the macrosocial structures, Archer agrees, will we be able to understand

---

[2] Some trace the American antipathy to government to the Founding Fathers, Jefferson
and Madison (Ryan, 1995).

the smaller-scale events such as changes in curriculum or methods of assessment. Institutions are products of design and therefore have a degree of autonomy isolating them from local social interaction.

Archer goes on to argue that understanding macrostructures does not necessarily advance understanding of microsocial ones. Hence, it is not simply a matter of finding correlations between selected variables and outcomes: "The search for further correlations with additional variables can continue indefinitely without increasing our understanding of the precise forms of home and classroom interaction, which underlie, produce, and explain the coefficients detected" (p. 34). Neither macronor microsocial interactions can be ignored.

Psychological theories of education face a similar dilemma. A major blind spot in the attempt to create a psychology for education is the reluctance or inability to grasp how social institutions structure the social relations between teacher and student as well as the learning and thinking activities of individuals. One branch of psychology sees education as the occasion for the development or fulfillment of human potential. Psychological theory, accordingly, provides a basis for proposing goals in terms of human potential and exploring means for their optimal achievement. To a large extent and increasingly so in recent times, cognitive psychology attempts to see education from the child's point of view while either ignoring the institutional contexts and constraints of schooling altogether or suggesting that they be revised.

Traditional educational psychology, on the other hand, has tended uncritically to adopt institutional goals, categories, and standards and, through multivariate analysis of variance, has tried to determine the causal relations among them. Thus IQ and social class (socioeconomic status [SES]) are taken as causing (at least predicting) student achievement. Educational psychology also is devoted to isolating causal factors that detract from the achievement of institutional goals; "impulsivity" and "learning disability" are frequently taken as among such causal inhibiting factors. Many cognitivists, I among them, have been critical of this tradition because of its inability to address and highlight the intentionality and responsibility of either teachers or learners. I now add to the list of complaints the fact that it takes its categories such as the "ideal student" as well as "ability" and "passing and failing" as natural categories rather than acknowledging their dependence on a particular institutional structure.

Psychological theories of learning and development that do attempt to take social and institutional factors into consideration trace this dependence in two ways, which differ primarily in emphasis. The first is the attempt to recover basic predispositions to culture that may help to explain such characteristics as the rapid acquisition of language by children or their early recognition of the intentions of others, the sensitivities and orientations that make the acquisition of culture possible and effective. Predispositions to culture are seen as a fundamental, innate form of competence: "Educability is truly a species characteristic of man, *Homo sapiens*," wrote two of the fathers of modern biology (Dobzhansky & Montagu, 1947). More recent writers, including Premack and Premack (1996), Bruner (1996), Donald (1991), and Tomasello (1999), have provided compelling argument and evidence showing how predispositions to social learning make the human species the culture-forming species.

The second plays down the significance of predisposition to culture while emphasizing the importance of "internalization," through training, of conventionalized features of the adult culture. Children are seen as possessing properties they would never have had without immersion in adult culture, a view traceable to Durkheim. The adult culture plays a formative role in the developmental process through providing models for talk, action, and interaction that express the customs, traditions, and practices of the culture as well as providing the appropriate sanctions, prohibitions, and rewards. Children gain their identities, it is argued, through membership in social groups; such membership grants favors and extracts tolls. To earn the privileges one must master the rules for action and interaction. On this view it is the internalizing of these institutional roles that is responsible for the formation of adult character. Education, broadly conceived, is seen as central to this enterprise.

Both views are grounded in extensive research. Sociability, joint attention, reciprocal interactions are well established in infancy. Around the time that children acquire an understanding of their own and other's minds, namely, that thoughts can vary across persons and that they can change independently of things, they also begin to acquire the norms, rules, and standards of correctness that can be used to appraise various performances. To defer to authority, to come when called, to eat with a fork are social competencies picked up without deliberate teaching. To sit still at the table or at a desk, to take turns, to apologize, to make promises and stick to them and sanction those who do and dissanction [sic] those who do not, to comply with the demands of authorities are forms of competence that most children acquire in the preschool and early school years. The acquisition of such norms, rules, and standards depends upon a social system such as a family, a play group, or a school that sets its terms for admission and exclusion as well as rules and standards for performance within. Such rules and norms are so pervasive in social life and so readily acquired by children that it is not an exaggeration to say that children both are innately social and readily acquire the norms of their own cultural and social groups.

These social predispositions and the resulting social competencies set the stage for our inquiry but are insufficient for addressing our primary concern, namely, the problem of understanding formal education and its place in a modern society. Families, communities, farms, and shops are all social organizations, but they differ enormously in structure and control from modern bureaucracies and consequently in the extent and type of training and the specialized forms of competence involved. Whereas in small-scale social organizations both the structure and control as well as the pedagogy can be left largely implicit, in bureaucratic institutions these matters become matters of contracts and constitutions, of explicit rules, principles, norms, standards, documentation, lines of authority, specialized expertise, credentialing, and accountability.

Competence required for participation in these bureaucratic institutions may be widely discrepant from that required for participation in less formalized social organizations. Indeed, the central project of the 18th-century Enlightenment, a project that dominates educational thought to this day, was the attempt to displace the local customs, traditions, and mentalities by a critical and rational social system that could serve as the basis for a universal civilization (Gray, 1998; Elkana, 2000). Although there is an important link between custom and institution, as we saw in the last chapter, it is imperative that we distinguish them; to fail to do so will again hide both persons and schools as institutions from our view.

Return briefly to the social theories of the 19th century, including those of Tönnies, Weber, and Durkheim that made a distinction between informal social organization, what we may refer to as the *culture*, and the more formal, bureaucratic organizations of a modern society. Durkheim (Lukes, 1973), we may recall, distinguished two forms of solidarity or social organization. What he called "mechanical" solidarity described a social system in which social ties are customary, largely implicit, and enforced without the appeal to reasons. Organic solidarity, on the other hand, described a social organization in which the pieces fit together by the explicit rules and formal procedures and lines of accountability characteristic of modern bureaucracies. Indeed, "organic solidarity" was very similar to what Weber called "rationality." A rational social system is, of course, an idealization, more characteristic of a computer program than of any macrosocial structure. Nonetheless, rationality, that is, the basing of judgment on explicit, justifiable principles, marks the direction toward which institutional behavior aspires rather than describing an achieved goal.

A distinction drawn from Wittgenstein (1958) is relevant to the one I have been drawing between cultural tradition and bureaucracy, the local and the "rational." Wittgenstein (1958; see also Kripke, 1982; Erneling, 1993; Harré, 2001) distinguished between functions that could be "characterized" or described by a rule or law, for example, the law of gravity, or the social rule of "tit for tat," from functions in which one actually deliberately and intentionally follows a law or rule, as, for example, in playing chess. In both the cognitive and social sciences, there is a systematic attempt to uncover the "rules" implied in personal and social action; thus, deference to authority, or reciprocity as in tit for tat, may be seen as social rules, norms, or law. Yet, one may defer without deferring because one is following that norm, rule, or law; even animals may be said to defer, and it would be absurd to claim that they are following a rule. That is, action can be premised on a disposition or habit rather than on an explicitly held belief or rule. Indeed some radical sociologists, following Nietzsche, claim that there are no rules or laws in social life; there are only ongoing negotiated practices. In such cases, the action may be *characterized by the rule*, say, to defer to authority, but the action is not the product of *applying the rule* defer to authority. Harré (2001) has elaborated this distinction, applying it not only to unintentional actions such as sneezing but also to the myriad habits of everyday life. Habits, even if learned as a rule, are carried out without deliberately complying with a rule or norm. He adds, "In most cases rules are primarily in the possession of the community or institution and only secondarily taken up by individuals" (p. 165). This is the distinction I want to draw between local or small-scale social structures maintained through unreflective habit and the bureaucratic structures in which schools find their place. In such institutional contexts as schools there really are norms, rules, and set procedures, which are both stated and enforced, and participants must, in fact, know and follow the rules – even, in my time, writing them out 100 times, when violated. The rules and norms apply not only to conduct but to the actual organization of schooled knowledge itself as we shall consider in the next chapter.

It would be wrong to make these categories absolute. Implicit norms can take on a mandatory, rulelike function and even explicit rules and norms require understanding and interpretation in implementing them. Nonetheless, what is optional in the first case is a defining structural property of the latter. Bureaucracies are, in principle, rule-governed institutions. They are not characterized by rules; rather they are created by the very rules specified in establishing them. To participate is to learn the rules and learn how to apply them whether those rules be articles of a constitution, the "rules of order" for a public meeting, the lines of reporting authority, or the documented entitlements and accountability of the organization. All of these functions, importantly, are literate functions; bureaucracies, therefore, are central fixtures of a literate society (Olson & Torrance, 2001).

Even if grounded in an innate capacity for culture, all forms of social organization require some level of "education" to induct individuals into that order, whether family, church, sewing circle, gang, or profession. Differentiation of roles requires some level of specialized knowledge and some granting of credentials as member, journeyman, leader, or follower. Bureaucratic institutions build upon these cultural patterns but add two important dimensions. First, the institution is granted a degree of autonomy with responsibility and accountability to some supervisory entity (once thought to be God) that allows the institution to maintain itself independently of the activities of the individuals making it up; that is why, for example, people get fired or students fail – they fail to fill the roles or meet the demands that allow the institution to prevail. And second, institutional practices are organized by means of documentary or literate activities. Hence, I will use the term *schooling* as a specialist term to mark off the educational processes in a bureaucratic, institutional context from the more general "educational" processes in informal or semiformal social groups. In so doing I intend to minimize neither the importance of informal social systems in daily life nor their significance to the development of the competencies required for participation in these large-scale institutions; it is just that schools cannot be understood in terms either of social competencies or of informal cultural practices. Schools are not merely an introduction to bureaucratic society, but are themselves bureaucratic institutions.

Schools, then, are institutions created by a powerful dominant institution such as church, craft, profession, or state to train novices to function correctly in and perpetuate those institutions (Archer, 1979; Bourdieu & Passeron, 1990). The institution creating the school grants a monopoly over a domain of activity, sometimes acknowledged by a Royal Charter, sometimes only by local politics. That activity is characterized by the expertise of its practitioners and its documentary tradition for organizing its activities and for preserving, and in some cases, adding to its knowledge base. Thus schools reflect the larger institutions in which schools are embedded, whether the church or the professions as in the Middle Ages and the Renaissance (Murray, 1978) or the nation-state as in the modern world (Archer, 1979). This is the subject of Chapter 10.

Understandably, to date, the study of institutions has been the exclusive prerogative of sociology, political science, and economics. Yet institutional functions are carried out by individuals with their own beliefs and intentions. Thus the institutional goals of the school are fulfilled only through the actions and intentions of individuals. The gap between institutions and individuals, the macro–micro problem, is not resolved merely by acknowledging them as different perspectives, as Archer pointed out; a fuller account requires bridging theory, a framework for thinking about the macro–micro problem.

At the macro level we acknowledge that modern nation-states are composed not only of citizens but of networks of institutions such as law, government, economics, religion, science, and literature, each of which has a domain or responsibility, access to public funds, and forms of accountability. Schools are part of this network, and changes in schooling reflect changes in the power and dominance of these institutions. Archer (1979), following Durkheim (1956), showed that many features of modern schooling took their form at the end of the Middle Ages, the so-called early modern period, when the ownership and domination of school shifted from the church – whether the Catholic Church in France and Italy, the Church of England in Britain, or the Lutheran Church in Germany – to the secularized nation-state. In the earlier period, teachers, typically, were "priest–teachers," not professionals in their own right, and graduates were particularly suited to serve the church whether as clergy or as laypersons. In the second, domination by the nation-state introduced not only new sources of funding but new goals and new forms of accountability. And so arose the set of universalized goals, fixed curricula, teacher credentialing, exit examinations, and the like, all of which persist to this day.

In the current school-reform environment, there is again much dispute as to the function of the school. To the extent that schooling is thought of as providing only the basic skills needed for an employable workforce, it seems reasonable to delegate responsibility to any group willing to take it – private enterprise, religious or ethnic group, or home schoolers. For example, in Ontario, Canada, a province that prides itself on its multiculturalism, the provincial government has passed legislation allowing any group to organize a school and have access to provincial funds for running it, a kind of charter school program. But if schooling is seen in a historical context, as a society's way of preserving and reforming itself, then it would be a mistake to farm out education to special interests whether wealthy parents, devout religious groups, or private commercial interests. Schooling serves Canada's multiculturalism, I suggest, not by giving schools to sectarian interest groups but by introducing students to the institutional structures – the knowledge that society deems warranted and an understanding of the rule of law, including the entitlements and obligations of citizens – that allow peoples with widely diverse backgrounds and interests to live and work together productively.

Why do nation-states invest so heavily in schooling? In the first place because many constituencies – various elites, lobby groups, and individuals – insist that government, through the schools, take over the responsibilities that they can privately neither afford nor manage, including the needs of the church for an educated clergy, the needs of the state for an educated civil service, the needs of the military for trained leaders, the needs of scientists and engineers for technical schools, of potential employers for a trained workforce, and, to a lesser extent (M. B. Katz, 2001), of the general public for access to these institutions. Nation-states organize school systems in the attempt to meet the needs of the nation not only for trained personnel but also for stable frontiers, a buoyant economy, informed and willing taxpayers, and soldiers who can be counted on in time of war. The perceived needs of the state can easily trump those of the citizens against which they have to be balanced. Thus, tsarist Russia, faced by "student nihilism and Polish nationalism," sought an educational solution to the problem of social control. It was believed that "schooling should promote the political trinity – socialization, integration and recruitment" (Archer, 1979, p. 154). In such a context education easily turns into indoctrination. Yet it remains a fact that schools are the society's way of preserving and improving itself and not just a means for enhancing the personal fulfillment of individuals.

Schooling, as an institution sponsored by government and paid for by taxes, is equally an institution with its own particular entitlements and obligations. As legally established institutions, schools have access to state funds, but acceptance of those funds entails state control of goals, professional training, and appointments, and accountability to the state for their achievements, their graduates, and their cost-effectiveness. Statewide institutions attempt to coordinate the various components of the educational enterprise through hierarchical organization, thereby extending control, and through systematization, thereby reducing diversity.

As an institution, schooling is subject not only to Weberian rationalization, that is, to making its various activities subject to explicit rules for operation and coordination, but also to tinkering with the structure of the institution under the rhetoric of reform. As noted, the basis for proposed institutional reform is often obscure, and the impact of such reform is often either unknown or ignored (March & Olsen, 1989). Decisions based on tradition, ideology, research, decree, compromise, or sheer whim determine the length of school year, the programs of study, the grouping of children, the setting and monitoring of standards, the retention of students, the granting of credentials, and the design of methods for managing teaching and learning. As Cremin (1965) once pointed out, the continuous reshaping of educational institutions through open debate over issues of content and control constitutes a kind of "genius."

CREATING CATEGORIES, POPULATIONS, NORMS, AND RULES

Several features of schools devolve from their essentially autonomous institutional form. The institution is created to serve a mandate, and it is assessed in terms of its success in meeting the mandated purposes and goals. To meet this mandate, categories are formed, rules and procedures are designed and documented, and specialists are trained to apply the rules specified by their roles. These functions are carried out quite independently of the personal interests and goals of the particular individual involved. The distinction between individual and role is not always recognized, as was indicated by the debates surrounding the Clinton–Lewinsky episode, one-half believing that Clinton adequately served the role he was elected to play, the other half believing that such a person should not be allowed to hold such a role. As Goffman (1961) has pointed out, even if roles are highly circumscribed in a bureaucracy, individuals can fill those roles in somewhat idiosyncratic ways. The classic "bureaucrat" (we are all bureaucrats these days, of course) sorts persons (and other entities) into preformed categories such as teacher, student, counselor, grade, track, each such group constituting a "population." The overall structure of the institution determines the roles and actions of the persons involved. These actions consist in part of applying the norms, rules, and standards for the subject, grade, or school to the thoughts and actions of the learners. These norms determine, for example, who passes and who fails quite independently of the beliefs, feelings, and desires of either the person so classified or of the person making the classification. The teacher as bureaucrat has the duty (failure to fulfill this duty is professional irresponsibility and grounds for dismissal) to put students into the category "pass" on the basis of meeting an explicitly specified criterion and into the category "fail" if they do not (approximately one standard deviation below the national average on a standardized test is conventionally treated as a fail), quite independently of what either the teacher or the student so classified thinks of the decision. Thus the teacher, in this case, plays the role of a bureaucrat. Conversely, the role of the student involves a set of institutionally designated responsibilities: Noncompliance constitutes failure, compliance earns a credential.

School as an institution creates categories to designate functions and goals and to characterize the activities that take place in the institution. Thus the category "student" designates a role in an institution. Only metaphorically can one be a student of the human condition. The school creates the category of, say, "fourth grade" and the categories of "curriculum," "knowledge," "pass," and "fail" to organize activities and standards. The school creates categories of "gifted" or "hyperactive" if such categories facilitate or are believed to facilitate or help to explain the working of the school as an institution. In school, "talking" can be seen either as communication or as disruptive behavior and subject to sanction. The mere functioning of an institution in terms of meeting its mandate, that is, its entitlements and obligations, is the source of the concepts and categories that are then often treated as if they existed in nature. Each institution creates ideal types in terms of the functioning of the institution – the good student – and then differences between individuals are defined relative to these idealized types.

Examinations play an important role in this bureaucratic process. Historically, examinations allowed "the constitution of a comparative system that made possible the measurement of overall phenomena, the description of groups, the characterization of collective facts, the calculation of the gaps between individuals, their distribution in a given 'population' . . . [thus forming] the sciences of the individual" (Foucault, 1979, pp. 190–191). There is a kind of irony here in that it is just assigning individuals to institutionally defined groups, whether as infants or as fourth graders, that created the sciences of the individual! The individual thereby came to be seen in relation to the norms or average of the group. "Individual differences," a fetish in much of educational discourse, are not concerned with individuals at all but with assignment of persons to groups sharing a "cognitive style," an "intelligence," or a level of competence. As we shall see, the study of individuals becomes possible only when we adopt a theory of intentionality and responsibility. The psychological implications of studying persons in terms of "populations" shall concern us again in Chapter 14.

Institutional categories are products of the tradition of schooling, the ongoing revision of practices in the achievement of desired goals. Here grade levels come in; here textbooks, here the "recitation method," group work, written assignments, and the like, adapted to school, grade, and the individual teacher and student. Some are abandoned – until the 20th century, the strap was seen as an effective means of instruction! But schools as local institutions also evolve their own versions of the best means for addressing their entitlements and obligations. As we saw, ignoring those local traditions is one of the sources of confusion produced by the managerial approach to school organization, an approach that disallows the development of a local educational tradition based on experience of what works well for a particular teacher, class, learner, or school (Moore, 1996).

Such categories can be oppressive in that a vast number of persons must fall into a very limited number of categories – basic versus advanced, normal versus gifted, A-level student versus B-level student, enthusiastic versus disruptive, visual bias versus verbal bias, pass versus fail, and so on. Moscovici (1993) pointed out how any institutional role comes to be defined in terms of the "ideal worker," "ideal prisoner," or, as earlier, the "ideal student." Such a worker, prisoner, or student is one who is most suited to the institutionally defined role and goal. The ideal student is one who both allows the teacher to play his or her role and in addition achieves the mandated standards. This student sets the norm by which all the others are judged as "abnormal"[3] with whatever personal effects such judgments may entail. Individual differences begin to be defined in terms of factors accounting for deviance from that institutional norm.

Categories that are not essential to the mission of the school as an institution but that may advance the agenda of a special interest group

---

[3] Hacking (1996) showed that the concept of "normal" person was a by-product of the invention of statistics, whereas Foucault (1979, p. 184) argued that the concept derived from standardized education.

may nonetheless be added to this institutional form. Thus personality types such as "gifted" and "hyperactive" may be introduced either to explain failure or to recruit special resources for groups of individuals so designated. Such categories originate largely in the politics of education, categories for which scientific support is then sought, thereby creating a somewhat dubious science. Hyperactivity is a case in point. Further, special interest groups may seek to gain legitimacy for privately held beliefs by getting them adopted institutionally by the school. Thus the ongoing disputes about "Creationism," "school prayer," and "sex education" arise. Conflict can occur, as Scheffler (1997) pointed out, less on the basis of personal beliefs and preference than on the basis of institutional structures. Whereas everyone is entitled to his or her opinion, conflict occurs between, say, science and religion only when "authoritative religious doctrine [i.e., institutionalized doctrine] clashes with competent scientific opinion [institutionalized science]" (p. 123). And it is at this level that issues are debated and judgments made and rules imposed. That is, the political concern is less with personal belief than with institutional structures, for only the latter have the power to impose categories and norms.

Once the categories are established, it is a straightforward matter to understand why and how teachers sort students into categories. They do so to fill the mandated requirements of the institution, namely, to provide qualified candidates for social roles in the other institutions of the society. To function, the society needs lawyers, teachers, soldiers, and the like, and one function of the school is to provide credentialed candidates. It is those institutions that define what competence is and how competence will be recognized and credentialed. The criteria for these judgments then descend the grade levels, specifying competencies that are assumed by higher-level competencies. Thus, even second- and third-grade children have to know numbers and be able to read and write if they are to reach the goals set for more advanced levels. Few educators object to these credentialing and sorting functions; to violate the norm by, for example, inflating scores or awarding unearned credits would undermine the institution as a whole. As professionals, teachers feel an obligation not only to their students but also to the educational institution that gives them their role and identity, not to mention their salary.

In assigning students to somewhat arbitrary categories, the teacher, as must any bureaucratic professional, must adopt an impersonal or objective stance, that is, a "third-person" stance to the person being judged, in a sense depersonalizing him or her. The individual is treated as a member of a population, a group with a norm or average against which the individual is compared. The institution, through the teacher, decides that one is a failure or a success, ideal or marginal, quite independently of the student's own "first-person" perspective on the matter. Indeed, Durkheim and to a lesser extent Weber took as a founding principle of the discipline of sociology that such first-person perspectives are irrelevant to the functioning of social institutions. Human development, personal growth and personal fulfillment, subjectivity and intentionality, including the feelings and beliefs of those so classified – the very features that are of paramount interest to us as persons, parents, teachers, and developmental psychologists – are of secondary importance to an understanding of schooling. Indeed, as I shall argue later, it is the institutional responsibilities of the school that blunt the impact of the findings of developmental cognitive psychology with its first-person orientation.[4] This research has failed to have the desired impact, I suggest, precisely because it has not come to grips with the peculiarity of the school as an institution with its distinctive entitlements and obligations.

PREDICTING AND CONTROLLING OUTCOMES

Schools as institutions have mandates, resources, and lines of accountability. They receive funding in exchange for achieving some set of goals. When the governments or school districts responsible for schools state goals and demand assessments of children in terms of those goals, psychological theory tends to move in one of two directions, neither of which is satisfactory.

On the one hand, psychology becomes the discipline that attempts to predict and perhaps control those factors affecting output so designated. This is the tradition shared by educational psychology and experimental psychology, a third-person or objective psychology that was uncontested until the 1960s. This psychology continues to thrive, and it continues to have an important place in a certain kind of educational discourse. A century of research in this tradition has more or less established the factors contributing to the designated output of school achievement and

---

[4] A commitment to a first-person perspective is not a commitment to clinical methods or introspection as a method of research. Rather one may study first-person perspectives from an empirical, scientific third-person perspective as, for example, is common in much of Piaget and in current "theory of mind" research.

credentialed graduates. These factors are well known; they include social or class background, entering ability, time and resources dedicated to the particular goal, quality of the teaching, and school climate, all of which have been shown to relate to school outcomes (Rutter, Maughan, Mortimore, & Ouston, 1979; Mortimore, Sammons, Stoll, Lewis, & Ecob, 1988). The variables associated with differences between teachers, programs, and teaching styles, although obviously important, tended to wash out or be swamped by demographic variables such as the social class of the family, as the celebrated Coleman and associates study (1966) demonstrated. Schooling as an institution, that is, school versus no school, of course, did make a difference, as did such factors as the years of schooling or the specialist programs taken. Indeed, differences between program levels such as general versus advanced within a school have far more impact on achievement than differences between schools (Linn, 2000). That is, whether one studied math or not makes a massive contribution to one's knowledge of math, as does whether one took the general or the advanced course; whether one studied it mostly through real or verbal problems, via discovery or expository methods, in a single-sex class or a mixed class, with a teacher with vast experience or with a novice tends to have little systematic impact. In regard to literacy, by far the best predictor of how literate one is as an adult is simply how many years one attended school (Statistics Canada, 1996, p. 23).

The second stance is to reject as inappropriate the goals "mandated from a distance" as themselves contradictory to the higher goals of education, namely, the growth of identity, self-sufficiency, personal understanding, moral integrity, and critical thinking. Fixed, measurable outcomes such as a particular rate of reading or computation or particular bits of scientific or historical knowledge are seen as contradictory to the real goals of education, the integrity, competence, and self-reliance needed to participate in and enjoy life. In rejecting the mandated goals and their "objective" forms of assessment, such reformers hope for political change, believing that a more sympathetic and informed body of policymakers would recognize the error of mandating such narrowly defined competencies, allowing educators to do what they do best, introduce learners to the rich literate and cultural traditions of their society and thereby enhance their understanding and thinking. This is the tradition of psychological reform going back to Rousseau and Dewey, which was given its current shape in the 1960s by such critics as Goodman (1960), Holt (1968), Postman and Weingartner (1969), and more recently by Gardner (1999), Meier (1999), and others.

Ravitch (1978, 2000) in reviewing the wave of reform that took shape in the 1960s concluded that such reforms not only seriously failed to meet the needs of all but the most able students, but also cast the role of the teacher as that of a social reformer rather than as a carrier of tradition, thereby usurping the role of democratically elected politicians. This suggests that the current conflict in education is not the time-worn pedagogic one of how best to teach children but the institutional one: Who has the right to set the goals for the school and who has the right to assess whether or not they have been met? In Canada, the United States, the United Kingdom, Australia, and New Zealand the battle lines are drawn between the educational ministries, which are branches of government, on one hand, and professional educators, representing the institution of the school, on the other. Many governments currently attempt to measure the effects of schooling by setting goals and measuring student achievement, independently of the judgments of the teachers, principals, and students that make up the educational bureaucracy.[5] Some see such assessments as important to refining the system; others, as an incentive to work harder; teachers tend to regard them as yet another level of surveillance. Fixing goals and assessing student achievement of those goals restrict the role of professional educators to that of providing the means for achieving state-mandated goals, rather than allowing educators to serve their more traditional role of reformulating goals to those appropriate to the local context as well as devising means for achieving and assessing them. No doubt the state has the right to assess its institutions, including those of health, science, and education. The question is the degree of autonomy that schools are to enjoy within their specified entitlements and obligations. I return to this problem in Chapter 15.

The balance between mandated goals and individual self-fulfillment is also misconstrued. Schools are institutions in which students earn entitlements by undertaking the responsibility for mastering socially mandated knowledge and habits. The teacher's role is to help students recognize their responsibilities and meet them with, so far as is possible, a sense of satisfaction. Psychology performs a disservice if it diminishes

---

[5] In Ontario, Canada, an independent agency, the Education Quality and Accountability Office (EQAO), is charged with creating tests, administering and scoring them at arms length from the teachers, classrooms, or schools involved. A major concern of the agency is keeping the tests confidential so that teachers cannot rehearse the children for the specific items involved. The tests are designed to reflect the mandated course of study and the stipulated objectives of the curriculum ("Literacy scores," 2002).

those responsibilities by appeal to extenuating factors, whether putative abilities, discrepant cultural norms, or special personality traits. As institutions, schools are contractual arrangements with special roles, norms, and standards that it is their responsibility to exemplify and monitor. Access to education is a right, but credentials are earned. School as an institution is likely to be perceived as satisfactory if it helps students achieve goals that students can identify with. But personal goals, self-esteem, self-fulfillment can never replace those institutionally mandated goals if one hopes thereby to earn credentials.

THE SCHOOL IN SOCIETY

Even if a society, by definition, is composed of a network of institutions, it was the sociologists who first brought those institutions into view (Moscovici, 1993). But with that social perspective, psychological concerns with the acquisition and use of knowledge were eclipsed. Sociologists, from Weber and Durkheim at the beginning, to Parsons in the middle, to Bourdieu at the end of the 20th century, have all insisted that psychological development is essentially socialization, that is, the acquisition of beliefs and habits appropriate to participation in a particular social order. In Bourdieu and Passeron's (1990) formulation, that education is the reproduction of the social order. Most educators despair of such claims because they share the Enlightenment view that education is a process of human perfectibility. These are not the same. Yet, in my view, this is not a disagreement but rather a case of conflating of the personal and the institutional.

Short of revolution and anarchy, school as an institution is here to stay. And even if the term *bureaucratic* bears the taint of opprobrium, it is in the understanding of bureaucracy whether in politics, economics, law, or science that we must ground our study of education. It is the institutional structure of education that puts both constraints and opportunities on developing members of the society, whether they like it or disapprove of it, whether they see it as fulfilling or, perhaps more typically, as a hurdle or obstacle to be overcome.

Sociologists may see nothing unfamiliar here, but in their project, the psychological states of individuals, their subjectivities, tend to be replaced by generalized notions such as "economic man" or the "ideal student." Because their concern is with whole populations, individuals are only positions in a distribution. On the other hand, psychologists and educators, who are concerned with preserving and enhancing the

subjectivities and experiences of individuals, find it convenient to ignore the nature and functions of these social institutions. Indeed, as
we saw earlier, many writers ignore institutions, reducing them to simple collections of individuals. Educational theorists are more concerned
with knowledge, understanding, competence, and human aesthetic ful-
filment – with the good, the true, and the beautiful, as Gardner (1999)
reminds us – than with the structure of school systems or the exercise
of power.

But institutions are responsible for the exercise of power in a complex bureaucratic society. Institutions, whether through the Treasury
or through science or through the school system, are essentially autonomous structures that have access to public funds and that are held
accountable, increasingly so, for the use of those funds. In exercising judgment as to the use of funds, institutions are exercising power.
Legitimate uses of power are assured, as we say, by "the rule of law,"
which is to say, not by the whim of the authority but by adherence to
accepted practice. This is how decisions regarding law, finance, science,
and education are managed, neither by a wise autocrat or by utopian
ideals but by practical, bureaucratic decisions, following accepted, documented procedures. This is not to say that bureaucratic practices cannot
become ruthless and oppressive as they have in totalitarian states. Nor
is it to say that even legitimate institutions may be stifling to productive work and creative involvement, but only to say that bureaucracies
are both a modern social fact and an inevitable component of a complex
society. Even Western economists, normally in thrall to the individualizing ideal of the marketplace, have recognized that markets "can endure
only in nations that maintain . . . the rule of law, a legal system, free media and a social consensus on efficient tax collection" (Attali, 1997) – to
which I would add, and the systems of education and forms of accountability that engender respect for and the ability to participate in those
institutions.

To show that the centrality of institutions to public life is not just a
sociological construction or simply a hobbyhorse, it may be useful to
note that the World Bank, that most conservative of public institutions,
dedicated to loaning money to nations to foster economic growth, has
recently recognized that economic reform and the adoption of capitalist
economics require not just control of money supply and economic stability but also the existence of mediating institutions, which they describe
as "framework conditions." These include not only the stable monetary
policy and liberalized trade, the "trademarks" of the World Bank, but

also the need for reliable institutions and the rule of law. According to J. D. Wolfensohn (1999; see Jakobeit, 1999), president of the World Bank, these include

framework conditions in the sectors of politics (an open legislative and regulatory system, appropriately trained and paid civil servants, and measures to combat corruption); institutions (protection of human rights, legal certainty, respect of private property and supervisory systems for financial institutions and capital markets); and the human and social sphere (social security, education and knowledge, health and population growth); [as well as] infrastructure, including water, power, roads, telecommunications, and culture, including cultural identity. (Jakobeit, 1999)

The importance of institutional structure for creating and operating schools is, perhaps, being learned in New Zealand, where the radical move of disestablishing schools from state controls and allowing them to compete in the open market has led, not to the elimination of the poorest schools, as was promised, but to their downward spiral. This spiral has had to be offset by renewed involvement by government for increased resources and training, that is, for the mediating institutions described (*International Herald Tribune*, Feb. 14, 2000, p. 16; Fiske & Ladd, 2000).

For now we must acknowledge that school is an institution with goals, means, and assessable outcomes that sees individuals in terms of characteristics suitable to, and predictive of, their functioning in that institutional context. Institutions see persons in terms of job descriptions, responsibilities, and accountabilities. Personal subjectivity beyond that is seen as irrelevant, perhaps even distracting. But persons, unlike institutions, see persons as persons with a personal identity, integrity, and responsibility, not merely as impersonal roles in an institutional structure. And educators use this more personal, intersubjective perspective in understanding and educating children. Nonetheless, institutions, including educational institutions, are a legitimate, indeed, inescapable part of modern social life, and neither the understanding nor the education of persons can be advanced unless we see how institutions impact on the mental and social life of those involved.

The goals, programs, and assessments are constructed and mandated by governing bodies; although goals may be lofty, such as critical thinking or good citizenship, the goals assessed tend to be more pedestrian. In Ontario, the goal of mastering basic punctuation, including periods and commas, is to be achieved by the end of Grade 3. By definition about 15% of third-graders fall one standard deviation below the mean on any standardized test of that competence. Yet even such a pedestrian goal as that of learning punctuation is seen by educators as presupposing an enormously deep understanding of literate language, an understanding that is unrealistic for many 9-year-olds; they believe that punctuation may be more appropriately taught as an aspect of competent expression and argument rather than as an end in itself. Despite such ambiguities, legitimate institutions such as the school have the right to set goals and monitor such achievements. Educational theory is needed as the basis for understanding schooling as an institution capable of framing worthwhile yet achievable goals and providing suitable assessments of their achievements.

Both goals and assessments are subject to change and "rationalization." Setting goals and assessing children to see whether they achieve them are fundamental responsibilities of legitimate institutions. Modern states recognize their own entitlements and responsibilities as institutional forms. At the moment, however, governments fail to recognize that schooling, too, is an important institutional form, which through tradition and professionalization is suited not just to achieving state-mandated goals, but also to formulating them more adequately, helping children achieve them, and accounting for their successes and failures.

Education, no less than the justice system or the economy, is an institutional function. To understand education we will have to enlarge our ontology, treating as real both individuals and institutions, if our discourse about learning and development is to advance. Not only will it have to include the more traditional concerns with knowing and understanding, with teaching and learning, but it will have to be augmented by concepts important to any bureaucratic institutions, namely, those of entitlements, responsibility, accountability, roles, procedures, rules, and credentials. We may see more precisely what these are like by examining the case of one class of institutions of particular relevance to education, namely, knowledge institutions. This is the topic for the next chapter.

5

Institutionalized Knowledge and Personal Belief

> Objectified knowledge stands as a product of an institutional order mediated by texts.
>
> (D. Smith, 1990b, p. 80)

> The Party had said that Oceania had never been in alliance with Eurasia. He, W.S., knew that Oceania had been in alliance.
>
> (G. Orwell, 1951, p. 31)

Belief in ordinary discourse refers to the jealously guarded, often religious, commitments one holds personally, often collectively, and often in the absence of supporting evidence. "We hold these truths to be self-evident," begins the United States Declaration of Independence. "I believe in God, the Father Almighty, the Creator of heaven and earth, and in Jesus Christ, His only Son, our Lord," begins *the Apostles' Creed*, a basic document in the Christian church. The creed sets out Christian "orthodoxy," the set of correct beliefs for the faithful. Young children, when asked what *belief* means, appeal to this orthodoxy, replying, "Like, in God?" (Astington, personal communication). In the cognitive sciences, on the other hand, *belief* refers to one's own mental states or mental representations whether private or shared, true or false; to *doxy* rather than *orthodoxy*, that is, to belief, rather than to true belief or knowledge.

Erik Erikson in *Young Man Luther* (1962) attempted to account for the remarkable depth of Luther's faith. The depth, he suggested, arose from two sources, combining a more theoretical intellectual knowledge with a more personal "meaning it." We are familiar with the intellectual part as cognitivists; it is the latter part, the "meaning it," that I want to

65

elaborate by appealing to the notion of subjective feelings and personal belief.[1]

Erikson was comfortable in making a distinction between intellectual knowing and personal meaning, a distinction largely lost in the cognitive sciences, because of his, like Dewey's, familiarity with Continental phenomenology, the tradition concerned with exploring the limits of human consciousness. Edmund Husserl (see Nicholson, 1984), a leader of this tradition, shortly before his death gave a series of lectures in Vienna and Prague on the crisis of the modern era provoked by the "one-sided" objectivist tradition he attributed to Galileo, Descartes, and Newton. He argued that this tradition put outside the boundaries of science the very foundation of all science, namely, our concrete experience of the life-world, what he called *die Lebenswelt*. His student Heidigger referred to this as the world of "being," an expression that strikes Anglo-American readers as odd, but that, when recast by Erikson as "meaning it" or by Dewey as "experience" becomes somewhat more comprehensible. Experience involves not only an interaction with the world but also a subjective experience, the feelings and meanings mentioned earlier. These feelings or meanings for Erikson's Luther coincided with his intellectual knowing.

Fortunate is the man for whom, as for Luther, the two perspectives on belief coincide. For Luther, personal belief and institutional belief, in fact, became congruent not by changing his belief but by creating a new institution, the Protestant church. The new orthodoxy of the Protestant church was then congruent with Luther's personally held, deeply felt beliefs. For most of us, such congruity as comes about results from the acquisition of the institutional beliefs, often at the expense of aspects of personal beliefs and feelings. When these violate personal beliefs and feelings, we may better describe such learning as acquiescence to institutional norms. When personal beliefs are reorganized so as to meet institutional beliefs and norms we may appropriately describe such learning as the acquisition of knowledge. The means, in either case, is education.

No one discipline and no one institution has a monopoly on the concept of knowledge. Philosophers claim it, defining *knowledge* as "justified, true belief." Psychologists define *knowledge* as a cognitive

---

[1] "The poet is perpetually in that common human condition of trying to feel a thing because he believes it, or believe a thing because he feels it" (P. Larkin, 2001, *Further Requirements*).

state, sometimes adding that it is a cognitive state shared by members of a textual community (Feldman, 2000). Sociologists and economists claim it as a commodity subject to copyright, patent, and the rules of the market. Educators view knowledge as a cultural possession, which they are entrusted to pass on to the young. To this pantheon, we must now add a further definition, namely, the product of those national and international institutions with the authorized social role of defining what is "known." These latter are our "knowledge institutions." To understand knowledge institutions we must first characterize the nature of knowledge appropriate to such institutions and delineate precisely how such institutions work. Then we can turn to that aspect of the educational problem that I have labeled the *pedagogical problem*, namely, that of relating that institutionalized knowledge, what is "known," to what a child or anyone else knows. I begin by distinguishing personally held beliefs from "institutionalized knowledge," that is, knowledge with a capital *K, Knowledge.*

BELIEF AND KNOWLEDGE

One domain of knowledge is that represented by the sciences; in fact, *science* is just a translation of the Latin word for knowledge. Institutionalized science, so-called Big Science, what I referred to as Knowledge, is neither nature study nor just what living scientists happen to know or believe. The relation between what anyone knows and the "known" is vexed. There is an appropriate sense in which the reform-minded *Bullock Report, A Language for Life* (Great Britain, 1975, p. 50), could claim, "It is a confusion of everyday thought that we tend to regard 'knowledge' as something that exists independently of someone who knows," but as a general statement it conflates precisely what I am at pains to distinguish. It overlooks the very possibility of institutionalized knowledge, that is, Knowledge. Science is a set of activities formulated, documented, and formatted in a complex social institution. Polanyi (1958) is eloquent on this point:

When I speak of science I acknowledge both its tradition and its organized authority and I deny that anyone who wholly rejects these can be said to be a scientist or have any proper understanding and appreciation of science. . . . I accept the existing scientific opinion as a competent authority, but not as a supreme authority for identifying the subject matter called "science". . . . [N]obody knows more than a tiny fragment of science well enough to judge its validity and value at first hand. For the rest he has to rely on the views accepted at second hand on the authority of a community of people accredited as scientists. (pp. 163–164)

To be a scientist is to hold an allegiance to a common tradition embodied in the institution of science. That institution has legitimacy through its creation and funding and accountability to national (or in the past to religious) authority through its training programs, journals, credentials, editorial procedures, and archival forms, all of which contribute to certifying Knowledge as scientifically valid. These institutional structures are given neither by culture nor by nature but have a particular social history. Those in the West derive in part from the rules worked out in 1660 by the Royal Society of London, which adopted a particular "mathematical plainness" of style of language (Sprat, 1667/1966); sponsored the first English-language scientific journal, *Philosophical Transactions*, in 1665; and developed the conventions of the printing houses for fixing authoritative versions of written texts (Johns, 1998).

Of course, science requires scientists, scientific thinking, beliefs, hypotheses, hunches, discourses, and the like, but science cannot be reduced to the mental lives of individuals or even groups of individuals. That Newton privately believed in the occult in no way compromised his contributions to the completely mechanical laws of motion (Holton, 1973). Although living scientists participate, they do not in themselves constitute the institution of science with its tradition, its rules, and its archives; at best they can participate in and represent that institution. It is of the institution of science that governments, as representatives of taxpayers, can ask questions about what is "known" and its implications for the public good. It is about individual scientists that one can ask whether a belief is imaginative or well thought out or sincere. But questions as to whether it is valid or original appeal not to one's prior thought or even to one's immediate community but to the institution of science as embodied in its methods, procedures, and archives. The point here is that it is a mistake to conflate the mind of a scientist with science as a tradition embodied in an institution. Dorothy Smith (1990b) has captured this relation precisely:

The governing processes of our society are organized as social entities [such as law, medicine, economy, and science] external to those persons who participate in and perform them. [Formal organizations] are objectified structures with goals, activities, obligations, and so on, separate from those of persons who work for them. [Similarly, members of an academic discipline] accumulate knowledge that is then appropriated by the discipline as its own. The work of members aims at contributing to that body of knowledge.... [Thus,] we learn to discard [or subordinate] our personal experience as a source of reliable information ... and focus our insights within the conceptual framework of the discipline. (p. 15)

Smith refers to the knowledge collected and valued in a society as "textual realities," arguing that even if they are far from the initial consciousness of individuals, such realities

are the ground of contemporary consciousness of the world beyond the immediately known. As such they are integral to the coordination of activities among different levels of organizations, within organizations, and in the society at large. (p. 83)

Although knowledge cannot be reduced simply to the psychological states of individuals, she emphasizes the importance of this institutionalized knowledge for the ultimate subjective experience of individuals; the psychological states of individuals have to come around to these "textual realities." These institutional structures put constraints on what is taken as known in a society, and the society has the right and responsibility, through these institutions, to see that these structures are maintained and updated and transmitted to the young. These institutional structures then specify a kind of psychology appropriate to them even if that psychology may have only indirect relevance to the subjective experiences of individuals.

In cognitive theory, as mentioned, there is only one conception of belief, namely, the presently held mental states of an individual, often misleadingly referred to as *knowledge states*. Psychology has less place for beliefs held in common and no place at all for social or institutional beliefs and norms, for orthodoxy. Indeed, for some the problem of "other minds" is acute; how can we be sure that anyone other than us has beliefs, let alone shares them with us? However, social and cultural theories of cognition in the tradition of Weber, Durkheim, and Vygotsky and more recently Bruner (1996) have emphasized how personal cognitions are never private mental states of the sort Descartes and Locke defended but already variations on the socially shared ways of talking, narrating, and acting. People have the concepts, beliefs, and practices they have because these practices are acquired intersubjectively. Short of total isolation, such social networks are inescapable. The sense in which the authors of the *Bullock Report* are correct is that Knowledge is an outgrowth of such social networks of individually held beliefs.

What then is the structure of Knowledge as opposed to personally held belief? In the last chapter I described the relations between informal social structures and institutionalized ones in terms of the explicitness, formality, and documentation. Whereas in ordinary social interactions, to acknowledge authority one may more or less unconsciously and automatically divert one's gaze from the eyes of another, in a bureaucratic organization lines of authority and responsibility are spelled out in explicit rules and documented procedures. Thus the so-called rules of politeness, of games, of deference and authority, of dressing, eating, and shopping remain tied to practice and may remain implicit, used rather than mentioned. As Amsterdam and Bruner (2000) pointed out, such social practices remain embedded in procedures that normally escape comment and attention, although in some contexts some of these rules may become explicit, documented, and institutionalized. Our question is, What are those contexts and what are those processes?

To understand a social practice as an institutional practice, I took the further step of marking the important disjunction between the so-called social norms, rules, and conventions embedded in social practices and the explicit procedures of a bureaucratic document culture. Although bureaucratic practices are a type of social practice, they are distinguishable in terms of their explicit, rule-based, textually fixed, documentary practices. By sharply distinguishing them we may inquire into both their differences and, later, the relation between them. I briefly mentioned the most important difference earlier, appealing to Wittgenstein's (1958) distinction between being characterized by a rule and following a rule. The path of a falling body may be characterized by the rule $s = 1/2gt^2$, but only the bold would say that an object determined its path by calculating the values according to that formula, whereas when doing physics, one may do just that. The equation is a theoretical characterization of motion. Playing chess, filing a tax form, or doing physics, on the other hand, is not merely characterized by a set of rules; the player knows the rules and applies them in determining a course of action.

Social practices, then, may be *characterized* by rules but are not the *application* of rules. Now we must apply the same distinctions to grasping the major difference between belief, that is, personally held mental states, and Knowledge, the body of knowledge taken as true by members of a bureaucratic society. In imitating the actions of adults, even capturing the intentions behind those actions, children build up a body of shared beliefs about the world (Meltzoff, Gopnik, & Repacholi, 1999; Tomasello, 1999). But, because they are linguistic creatures, many of these activities become objects of discussion as well as patterns of social action, and these expressions are expressions of beliefs. However, reference to both the beliefs and activities and their violations may remain indirect (Heeschen, 1997). Such practices and their expressions in language may be, as we said, *characterized* in terms of beliefs, norms, rules, codes, conventions, formulas, laws, structures, but such characterization is somewhat misleading in that it borrows a vocabulary from formal systems and uses that language to characterize less formal activities. It is a kind of anachronism, attributing modern concepts to ancient practices. A social routine is not a "norm," a "belief," a "law," or a "rule"; the practices can be seen as lawlike or as rule-based, but the laws and rules may not be known and followed as such. They may exist primarily in the mind of the theorist. This is why children, when asked about belief, as we saw, refer to orthodoxy, rather than to mere doxy. Anthropological descriptions of codes, norms, and rules have given us a picture of social life, but the descriptions may have given us more than is actually there.

But such categories are far more than characterizations in a modern bureaucratic society. There really are rules, norms, laws, codes, manuals, algorithms, job descriptions, and the like, that are explicit, documented, and sometimes even embedded in computer programs. These are not adequately addressed simply as social structures or social practices, although they are that, but as essential constituents of such formal institutions as the school. Schooling is one of the institutional practices that give us our modern conceptions of what knowledge is, what competence is, and who one is as a person.

The transformation of belief into Knowledge, then, is identical to that we have examined in regard to social rules. Personally held beliefs can be transformed into explicitly held and formally organized Knowledge through the process of explication, formalization, definition, criticism, and, most importantly, the norms of institutional judgment. Even the youngest children believe or at least expect that unsupported objects fall down; for such a belief to become Knowledge requires more than that it be noted or even shared. It must match the norms of formal expression, which is to say, a form from which correct inferences may be drawn. This requires that beliefs comply with a set of institutional norms, including the definition of terms, logical relations between subject and predicate, and mapping of rules between expressions and observations that serve as evidence for the truth of the expression. Beyond that it requires an institution or a "textual community" that knows how to interpret and apply such expressions and, in addition, possesses the legitimated authority to do so. Failure to meet those requirements constitutes what used to be called *heresy*, now more likely to be called *personal opinion* or *pseudoscience*.

Institutionalized knowledge differs for each domain of knowledge, whether law, science, or literature and again for every historical epoch.

It is up to each legitimate, authorized institution to face its own responsibilities for managing the "Known." Yet the simple fact of institutionalization entails such general properties as the adoption of explicit definitions (e.g., who, exactly, is a citizen? or what, exactly, is mass? or what precisely do we mean by knowledge?), formal expressions of relations between entities (e.g., causes versus implications), evidence or reasons for taking statements as true, and frameworks specifying the scope or domain to which the relevant knowledge applies (astronomy versus astrology, for example). The goal of institutionalized knowledge is to provide a degree of explicitness that could be embedded in a computer program, again recognizing this to be an aspiration rather than an achievement.Institutionalized knowledge, even if and when it is implemented in a computer program, has only a degree of autonomy. Such knowledge is based on a set of assumptions, hunches, and feelings that Polanyi (1967) has described as implicit knowledge. There will never be a time when science does itself; it will always depend upon the hopes and beliefs and goals as well as the expertise of the persons making up the institution and contributing to its practices. Thus learning science, that is, acquiring Knowledge, is more than learning the effective procedures of the discipline; it involves, too, learning the feel of the discipline and perhaps most importantly learning how one's personal beliefs and commitments are related to those explicitly expressed in the formal Knowledge of the discipline: shades of Luther's problem all over again.

Public education's commitment to Knowledge is conspicuous not only in its commitment to teaching the disciplines but also in teachers' pervasive attempts to induce children to comply with social norms including to "use whole sentences," to "give reasons for your answers," to distinguish "observations" from "inferences," to "write your report in such a way as to explain exactly what happened"; the general attempt to instill a taste for a "mathematical plainness of style"; and a commitment to socially agreed upon truths. Personal opinion along with alternative modes of interpretation are pruned in the pursuit of the "Known."

The distinction between public, institutional beliefs, embedded in public, bureaucratic institutions, what I have called Knowledge, and personal beliefs held by individuals is sometimes recognized. Indeed Egan (1997) has pointed out that the contrast between Platonic knowledge and personal understanding has long served as one of the tropes of educational discourse. But rather than reconciling them, educational reformers adopt one as fundamental and seek to discredit the other. More conservative critics treat personal beliefs as a manifestation of ignorance that must be eradicated, or as misconceptions that must be revised into correspondence with Knowledge. More progressive, "child-centered" critics treat personal beliefs as privileged and orthodoxy, the entrenched beliefs as needing to be criticized and revised. Thus educational reform movements pull in opposite directions, one emphasizing the importance of personal beliefs and understanding, the other emphasizing the importance of formalized, institutionalized Knowledge. The debate is articulated in many forums including those over the "canon," over the ascendancy of DWMs (a feminist acronym for "dead white males"), over multiculturalism, over child-centeredness, among others. Although such debate raises awareness of the issues involved, it does little to advance the study of education.

KNOWLEDGE: OBJECTIVE TRUTHS OR MENTAL STATES?

There is an important epistemological debate in the sciences and elsewhere as to the status of Truth and Knowledge conducted by such writers as Philip Kitcher (1993), who defends the classical view of the nature of scientific knowledge, and such critics as Barbara Herrnstein Smith (1997), who rejects it. Although the debate is about Knowledge it is at the same time a debate about belief, in that knowledge is seen as a special class of belief, the class composed of beliefs held to be true on the basis of sound reasons and evidence. The classical view, broadly realist but sometimes called *modernist* or *early modern* or *positivist*, is that knowledge consists of beliefs that are in fact ascertainably true of some independent autonomous reality. Advances in knowledge, in this view, result from the formation of statements that are more true of that reality than were earlier statements. As Kitcher (1993) writes: "[S]cientists find out things about a world that is independent of human cognition; they advance true statements, use concepts that conform to natural divisions, [and] develop schemata that capture objective dependencies" (p. 127).

B. H. Smith contrasts the classical view with the one she is attempting to justify, a view broadly constructivist but sometimes called *postmodernist* or *postpositivist* or simply *relativist*, the view that subordinates reality to the theories and models constructed in science, which have the effect of specifying what is to be taken as real. As Smith puts it, "What we call Nature can be seen as the relatively stable product of the ongoing reciprocal coordinations of our perceptual, conceptual, verbal, manipulative, and other practices, formed and maintained through the very processes of our acting and communicating in the worlds in which we live" (1997, p. 130). Nature is the product of our cognitions, not its precondition. On this constructivist view, knowledge is made, not found (Olson, 2001).

Of course, constructivism sounds bizarre to the uninitiated; only God makes nature. That, however, is not quite the point. The point is that *nature* is a word expressing a human-made concept that we find useful for certain purposes. The mistake, the constructivist argues, is to assume that the word simply points to some structure that exists independently of our naming. Only the so-called nominal realists commit that nominalist fallacy of assuming that just because there is a noun, there must be a thing denoted by the noun. Names, rather, are constructions or construals, ways of categorizing and ways of seeing or modeling the world. It is not to say that nothing exists independently of our words but only to say that what we take to be the world is a product of our own linguistic, scientific, and interpretive practices. If we grant that it is people like us who have made up the linguistic categories to serve their own purposes of thinking and acting, it is not too great a leap to acknowledge that people make up our science and that we think the world is just what our theories equip or allow us to think it is. That idea does not seem outrageous to me and there are others, beside B. H. Smith, who favor that view, including Nelson Goodman, Jerome Bruner, Bruno Latour, and Richard Rorty, although others, such as Scheffler (1997) and Hacking (1999), remain more realist in orientation. For me, it seems reasonable to say that we do not construct reality but we do construct our representations. As Korzybski (1933) famously said, "The map is not the territory." We only make maps.

Both views, the realist and the constructivist, allow that there is such a thing as science, including currently established scientific knowledge and practice, in which "established" is understood as "broadly accepted and highly reliably worked with [that is, applied, extended, connected, and so on] by members of the relevantly authorized secular epistemic communities" (B. H. Smith, 1997, p. 151). That is, both views allow that there is an uppercase Knowledge. The difference lies in their assumptions as to how such knowledge comes about. According to the realist view, Truth is absolute and theories are approximations, a view that Smith disparages as "scientific manifest destiny," the story of how truth always comes out in the end (p. 132). Science then becomes the ideal against which everything else, including the views of students, can be seen as misconceptions, ignorance, or irrationality. Indeed, in Kitcher's (1993) view, the advancement of science depends upon "the delineation of formal rules, principles, and . . . informal canons of reasoning, [which] when supplemented by an appropriate educational regime, can . . . make people more likely to activate propensities and undergo processes that promote cognitive progress" (p. 186). Again, "some types of processes are conducive to cognitive progress; others are not," and it is presumably the role of the school to inculcate the conducive processes. The normative properties of the science are just those psychological characteristics that are to be inculcated into developing minds with the effect of rooting out superstition, illusion, and circular thinking. This ideal, of course, goes back to the 18th-century Enlightenment.

The major limitation of this realist view is its failure to acknowledge sufficiently that science is not only certain knowledge but rather a bureaucratic, institutional, indeed political practice. Thus, in Kitcher's view, the way to root out such pseudosciences as Creationism is to improve the critical thinking capacities of students. He writes, "The behaviour of creation scientists indicates a kind of inflexibility, deafness, or blindness" (p. 195). Scientific thinking is seen as a kind of propaedeutic for the development of correct thinking practices. To me, that is to conflate what I have been at pains to distinguish, the thinking practices of individuals and the normative structures of scientific institutions.

In the constructivist view, the norms for valid scientific thought are *not* the psychological abilities and dispositions of individuals but rather the normative properties of institutions, in this case the institution of science and its specialized sciences. It is the institution that upholds the stricture on presuppositions, acceptable methods, valid inferences, replicability, and finally "truth," or more realistically, what is taken as truth. Smith refers to these as "historically and institutionally situated conceptual/discursive practices" (p. 152) and argues, against Kitcher, that disagreements between the Creationists and science cannot be traced to the cognitive peculiarities of the individuals involved but rather to differences in institutional allegiances and practices. In a secular society science is the institution with the legitimacy that allows "it" to speak on certain civic and social issues including the evolution of humankind or the history of the world. Conflict between science and religion arises when the legitimate institutions of a society make rival claims over jurisdiction, that is, over the right to speak authoritatively on the matter, and then it is a job for the Constitution and the courts to decide. Indeed, this is the major complaint of realists against the constructivists: their focus on issues of power, namely, who has the right to speak on matters of science, health, or education. Constructivists, they say, weaken the appeal to the facts or the truth of the matter, substituting power for truth.

Scheffler (1997) has raised the same point in a quite different context. He admits that science depends upon the insights and perseverance of individual scientists but insists that science is a corporate activity: "Despite its individualism, then, science is embodied in institutions serving as arbiters of authoritative scientific opinion"(p. 123). He uses this conception of science to address the question of why science and religion could come into conflict. His answer, not unlike that advanced previously, was not given in terms of the psychological characteristics of believers and scientists or the putative truth of the matter, but rather in terms of their institutional forms. It is because as institutions religion and science claim and attempt to hold a certain monopoly on claims to truth that they can conflict. It was because of these perennial conflicts that the Edict of Nantes, granting freedom of religion, was invented and why most Western states sharply distinguish church and state. That, of course, does not mean that the conflict vanishes entirely, but it does establish independent territorial domains, albeit with leaky frontiers, along which their distinctive entitlements and obligations can be contested and negotiated. The sciences are legitimate institutions in most Western democracies with the entitlements and responsibilities to uphold what is taken as known in their fields, and they pass on these responsibilities to the schools, which, in turn, have a responsibility to teach, that is, to hold students accountable for, that body of knowledge. So students can be required to learn biological, evolutionary theories as part of the mastery of that domain – a requirement often violated in both Canada and the United States. However, students have the right to believe, that is, to hold as true, whatever they like, including Creationism. This is a case in which students may know something that they do not believe! This is not a contradiction so long as we acknowledge the distinction between institutionalized knowledge and personal beliefs.

To understand the relation between the products of science, what I have called Knowledge, and the psychological state of individuals, that is, personal belief, it is necessary to see the former as a social and institutional product. Explicit theories, norms, and rules are created in the service of institutional practices, and it is those institutions that teach the rules, norms, and standards and monitor their adherence. Such norms and rules are not themselves an appropriate characterization of human thought in general. Human thought takes on those properties, and even then only in part, in the course of learning to participate in those institutional practices. Ordinary beliefs are the subjectively held and revisable mental contents that, although expressible in a public language, are personally and privately held by individuals. It is these individual mental states that psychologists are concerned with and that educators attempt to encourage in their students, namely, the growth of a rich mental life in a rich social world. On the other hand, as institutions responsible for preserving and transmitting a knowledge tradition, schools adopt the classical view of knowledge as composed of the truths, norms, and rules that are to be preserved and transmitted across generations.

Recall that we need not claim that the truths so preserved and transmitted are absolutely true so much as that they are what is taken as true by the legitimate institutions of the society, in particular the "taken as truths" embodied and employed in the knowledge institutions, including the school. The concept of taken as true is borrowed from the pragmatists, including Dewey, who claimed that knowledge was always shaped by human concern. As mentioned earlier, in my view the blind spot of the pragmatists was their failure to recognize what we may call the normative dimension of institutions and, consequently, of the distinction between belief and Knowledge. What is taken as known by an individual may be appropriately construed as assumption but when taken by an institution becomes simply Knowledge, that is, what is known in science, law, or any other legitimate social institution, including the school.

Admittedly, institutions do change in both structure and content. What is taken as true by a social institution changes as a result of the private beliefs of individuals but never simply or directly. Beliefs of individuals have to "percolate" up through the institution often taking more than a generation to do so. Just how they do is the subject of the next chapter. For now it is sufficient to note that children and the teachers who teach them have to negotiate the gap between the believed and the Known. Only when one's personal beliefs become sufficiently congruent with the Known can one usefully criticize and add to it. Students are in a different position from scientists on this score. First, they understand less of what is known, and, second, there is less value placed on the discrepant beliefs they personally hold. Student beliefs are frequently seen simply as errors by their supervisors. The school as an institution, not unlike science as an institution, values the Known. But pedagogy is successful only to the extent that it can acknowledge and build upon what is personally felt and believed. This is the topic of Chapter 8.

CONSTRUCTING KNOWLEDGE

So how is knowledge created in an institutional context? Official knowledge is as old as culture itself whether expressed as the judgments of a
wise person or the whim of a tyrant or the judgment of a court. Whole
peoples could become Protestant, Catholic, or Muslim simply on the
basis of the decision of a ruler whether king, emperor, or feudal lord.
The whole Roman Empire became Christian with the conversion of one
emperor, Constantine! But rule by direct authority was gradually replaced by rule of law, by the creation of monopolies over distinctive
aspects of social life such as the church, the courts, craft guilds, and universities. The guilds and the church and the universities had their own
means of educating their apprentices, novitiates, and students. Unlike
the church, universities lacked the power to decree truth, rather, they
were institutions that provided a forum for teaching and debate, and
the evolution or construction of norms, rules, and standards. The entitlement to pass judgment as to the Truth took an important step forward, as
we saw, with the establishment of such institutions as the Royal Society
of London under the royal patronage of Charles I, which provided a forum for the orderly presentation, discussion, and publication of scientific
contributions.

The role of writing and literacy in science via the invention and use
of documentary practices such as articles, books, manuals, formularies,
directories, and guides is critical in all institutional practices including
the sciences (Cochran, 2001). Dorothy Smith (1990b) centers her analysis
of what she calls "textually-mediated social relations" in the literate
practices of reading and writing in bureaucratic societies. Smith argues
that in modern bureaucratic institutions, social relations are organized
around what she calls "textual practices" that give these practices their
normative quality. Writing and printing allowed the development of
new forms of social organization that rely less on personal relations and
contacts than on roles and rules spelled out in documents.

As we saw earlier, formal institutions are characterized by structures
with written constitutions, manuals, and rules specifying the entitlements and obligations of the organization. Responsibilities are assigned
to roles set out in job descriptions, filled by individuals who make decisions based on specified rules and procedures and who account for their
actions via time clocks or written reports to other persons playing other
roles at higher levels in the hierarchy. Thus these are literate or textual
institutions. The rules and procedures are designed in such a way as to

assure, so far as possible, that the actions taken and the decisions made are not derived from the personal wish or belief of the person as a person but as a role within the organization. As long as the role is competently served, the personal interests and beliefs of the person carrying it out are of little relevance.

Not only do knowledge institutions use texts, the texts and textual practices in modern societies determine what is taken as reality. D. Smith provides an interesting analysis of the relation between "lived actuality" and what, in a document culture, is taken as what "really happened." She describes a confrontation between police officers and street people that occurred in Berkeley in the 1960s, which a first-person account given by an eyewitness described as "the brutal and arbitrary use of police force." This version is very different from the official version of the event provided by the police chief to the mayor, which served as the official, impersonal, "factual" view of what happened. At issue is who has the right to say what really happened. As mentioned in the epigram to this chapter, "Objectified knowledge stands as a product of an institutional order mediated by texts, what it knows can be known in no other way.... Objectified knowledge, as we engage with it, subdues, discounts, and disqualifies our various interests, perspectives, angles, and experience, and what we might have to say speaking from them" (p. 80). Put bluntly, if the judge says "Guilty," one is guilty, whether one did it or not. Fortunately, in civil society there are usually strict norms or criteria for evidence, rules for impartial judgment, and possibilities for appeal. But the right to make judgments holds as much for claims of knowledge as for claims pertaining to justice.

Reconciling the discrepancy between the eyewitness accounts and the official account is central to the very aspiration of historiography as a science. High school students tend not to grasp this aspiration. Students tend to rely on textbooks and the reconstructions by historians while ignoring eyewitness accounts because of their obvious bias. Whereas they recognize that eyewitnesses may have a limited point of view, they completely overlook the possibility that historians and textbooks, too, may reflect a point of view (Wineburg, 1991).

THE SOCIAL CONSTRUCTION OF SCIENTIFIC FACTS

Scientific facts, then, in an important sense, are institutional constructions. It is a concern with the institutional structure of science that provides the basis for the recent social studies of science, studies that attempt to capture just how laboratories and other scientific activities are organized within a discipline. Latour and Woolgar (1986) described the long and assiduous route between personal belief and scientific fact as a kind of forgetting of the persons and situations that gave rise to a scientific claim. Scientists working in a laboratory entertain ideas, read and interpret other texts, offer hunches and *conjectures*. Some of these conjectures may turn into testable *hypotheses*, and as evidence accrues, hypotheses turn into *conclusions*. These conclusions are then reported as factual *claims*. This transformation is indicated by the speech act verbs used to express the kernel of an idea. At first, an idea is expressed with a modal: "Maybe *x* has an impact on *y*." After clarification of what is meant by *impact*, the idea may be expressed as a testable hypothesis: "If *x* produces *y*, then *a*, which is known to increase *x*, will cause an increase in *y*." If the results confirm the prediction, the initial idea may be expressed with more certainty: "We have shown that *x* produces *y*": thus the verbs introducing the idea change from, I guess that *p*, to I think that *p*, to I know that *p*. These speech act verbs indicate the degree of status to be awarded to any belief. At the same time these verbs imply the means for revising the status of those beliefs – the provision of evidence, for example, is needed to move a belief from a mere hypothesis to a conclusion. These agreed upon rules and standards constitute the normative dimension of knowledge, and they are rigorously monitored by the knowledge institutions, the disciplines. The product, the "world on paper" (Olson, 1994), is crafted in ways not only to express the beliefs of the authors but also to find an acceptable place in the tradition of which they are a part.

The scientific report tends to obscure or hide the more personal and informal aspects of this process. As D. Smith (1990b) pointed out, the final report removes all traces of subjectivity, that is, of the private beliefs of individuals and of the processes actually employed, in the route to becoming statements taken as fact. Indeed, D. Smith characterizes fact as just the end product of these institutional procedures. "Facts are neither the statements themselves, nor the actualities these statements refer to. They are an organization of practices of inscribing an actuality into a text" (p. 71). And again, "A fact is constituted to be external to the particular subjectivities of the knowing" (pp. 69–70). Return to the example of legal judgment. As we say, a person is innocent until proven guilty. Guilt is not simply a matter of what one "actually" did but rather the output of a court that is following normative practices.

The same is true for fact. Facts are not simply what happened but what the institutional procedures, norms, and structures of the science judge to be fact. There is an evolution and transformation of an idea, not just by internal reflection as an earlier generation of psychologists had argued, but rather by survival of the battle of conjecture and refutation, revision and defense, involving many persons, many laboratories, many tentative formulations and revisions. These involve texts, appropriate methods, and vetting procedures, and an "instrumental and laboratory style of reasoning" (Hacking, 1994, p. 214) in the production of facts. Subjectivity, the feeling of knowing, like the feeling of guilt has little or nothing to do with it. Facts are institutional judgments; they constitute the Known.

Pedagogy is largely responsible for children's epistemological development. Epistemological development is nothing other than learning these normative practices of the disciplines. This consists in part of learning to make systematic linguistic distinctions such as that between theory and evidence and between causes and reasons. Four- and five-year-old children equally agree to such contradictory propositions as

1. He has measles because he has spots.
2. He has spots because he has measles.

It is tempting to see this as a logical failure. Children's utterances such as "It is raining because he is carrying an umbrella" led some to argue that children believed in animism, the superstition that if one carries an umbrella, it is more likely to rain. More careful analysis showed that this was not a failure of logic of causation but rather a failure to monitor and distinguish reasons and causes systematically. "Because" expresses an evidential relation in (1) but a causal relation in (2). Leading children to discriminate between them and to use evidence systematically to evaluate their theories is an important aspect of epistemological development that requires extensive schooling. Kuhn and Pearsall (2000) showed children a picture sequence of a boy getting a new pair of sneakers and a later picture showing him receiving a trophy. When asked, "How do you know he won the race?" children were more likely to say "Because of the new sneakers," a causal answer, than "Because he is holding the trophy," an answer that suggests an understanding of evidence for a belief. That is, when asked, "How do you know?" – a question calling for evidence – they gave an answer more appropriate to the question "Why did it happen?" – a question calling for a cause (Astington, Pelletier, & Homer, in press). Again, if shown a picture of a cow, they have no difficulty in identifying it, but if asked, "How do you know it is a cow?" preschool children, rather than pointing to the evidence such as horns and udder, frequently answer, "Because it says 'Moo' " (Ly, 2001). That is, they share their beliefs rather than providing evidence for those beliefs. Apropos of the pedagogy question, this is not merely a stage of development; it is a consequence of mastering a particular set of concepts, concepts relevant to the normative epistemology of beliefs and reasons for believing. Evidence, as we say, "justifies" or "warrants" a belief. But it does not cause the belief; a conceptual step is involved. Reasoning is called for. This is a move that lower animals and younger children and even to some extent less educated adult humans have limited access to, a move tied to language and schooling as exemplified in the familiar pedagogical injunction "Give a reason for your answer."

A more technical note on evidence may help tie this pedagogical discussion to our earlier discussion of science as an institutional practice and what may be called the *percolation problem*. In ordinary perception, as Rozeboom (1972) points out, the event specifies both a mental content and an "attitude" to that content. One not only sees that the cat is on the mat (content) but also believes (attitude) that the cat is on the mat. Hearing the corresponding statement allows the two to be distinguished; the listener can entertain the thought (content) and independently assign the attitude on the basis of the evidence, to believe or to doubt, for example. If the reasons are overwhelming, one may even deny that "seeing is believing," as most of us do when we see flying saucers. Only language-using creatures can make such a distinction and then do it consciously when they acquire these more sophisticated epistemological concepts and the rules for applying them.

Scheffler (1997) raises a similar point in an elegant presentation of a debate early in the 20th century between Neurath, the physicist, and Schlick, the philosopher, as to the nature of science. Neurath had claimed that science is a body of statements that may be compared to other statements but not to the world or anything else. We now refer to this view as the coherence theory of truth. Schlick thought that scientific statements had to be compared to the real: the correspondence theory of truth. The comparison occurred in observation statements containing such deictic terms at *this* and *here*. Schlick continued, "In the case of observation statements . . . the occasion of understanding them is at the same time that of verifying them: I grasp their meaning at the same time as I grasp their truth" (cited by Scheffler, 1997, p. 174). That is, perception ordinarily collapses evidence and belief, content and attitude. But sophisticated reasoning, the agenda of the school no less than of science, requires that the impulse be resisted.

As Scheffler argues, scientific statements are neither systems of statements nor systems of beliefs but rather expressions of institutional practices, and, as Hacking (1999) points out, they depend on networks of laboratories, published papers, colleagues, and publicly legitimized institutions. Learning science is not only learning certain knowledge but also learning epistemological distinctions embodying the norms of institutional practices; theory and evidence are one such distinction.

Publication and peer review are the occasions for seeing that the norms and standards of the discipline have been met and hence assure the validity of the claims made. A nonscientist may read the claim as a *fact*, whereas a scientist may read the claim as an expression of a particular author's *belief* and again question the validity of the belief, inviting thereby another round of research. Facts are not simply truths, but an institutional product that bears a rather indirect relation to the experiences, hunches, and feelings of the scientists who first gave rise to them.

Even then, the idea believed to be true by the researcher is not added to the stock of the "known" until it has proceeded through the higher levels of the institution, namely, the journals, the peer reviews, the replications, and the revisions. The enduring stock of beliefs, adopted by the institution through the activities of a large number of its members, is granted the status of the known. This status is not that of the philosopher's "warranted true belief" but the more guarded and tentative status "warranted, taken as true, assertion." Becoming a scientist is a matter of learning to participate in this institutional system – one's first publication either criticizing or extending published work, more so than one's credentials, allows one to enter this sacred ground. And schools are where children first encounter these institutionalized normative constraints on their talk, action, judgment, and knowledge.

There are both advantages and disadvantages of bureaucratic science (Geisler, 1994). On the one hand, the apparatus of designing replicable procedures, formats for objectively reporting findings, disinterested peer reviews, and judgments of publishability are ways of establishing legitimacy, indeed, of making modern science possible. This is what gives the sciences the right to pronounce on what is true, what is known, and what is not known and what must be taught and learned if one is to think as a biologist, a mathematician, or whatever. But on the other hand, science becomes an institutional product that in its bureaucratic form loses touch with the beliefs and ideas and feelings of the researchers who are responsible for its advancement and with the general public that finances it. It gives official science a distance and apparent objectivity that in one sense it does not deserve, an objectivity that makes it difficult for students and other readers to criticize. That is, it is difficult to see again the propositions of an advanced science as simply the expressions of the beliefs of the actual people who created the document. It has been argued that scientific statements have to be seen as expressions of the beliefs of others if they are to be seen as open to criticism and revision (Olson & Astington, 1990), activities essential to the advancement of a science. The primary advantage of bureaucratic science is that it provides and monitors the norms and standards that yield certified valid knowledge of use to the society. It gains financial support and political power in exchange for the provision of that certified knowledge.

But the creation of knowledge institutions has a further implication. By creating institutions to carry out rational functions whether in banking, science, or schools, the burden of rationality is lifted from the participating scientists and employees themselves. Scientists as individuals are no more and no less rational than anyone else – Newton, recall, believed in the occult; Descartes believed that his dog was not conscious; and some of my scientific friends claim that they can read the mind of their cat! Rationality is bound up in our institutions, not in our intuitions. If one scientist makes an error, one's peers may detect it and improve on the original formulation. Teams of specialists may comb a report for methodological flaws, for unwarranted inferences, for unacknowledged assumptions, and so on. It is in this elaborate institutional process that warranted knowledge is produced. As scientists become more experienced, they can anticipate their critics to some extent, but it remains the final judgment of one's peers or supervisors whether a claim will be accepted as a fact. I do not wish to imply that thinking is no more than following official rules and procedures. These rather are part of the normative structure of institutions; just how they are related to the cognitive processes of persons remains, for the moment, an open question.

The distinction between belief and knowledge surfaces in an interesting way in the ongoing controversy about rationality (Stanovich, 1999). On one hand, some writers, such as Kahneman and Tversky (1982) and Johnson-Laird (1998), argue that many humans are irrational in that they often make serious errors in reasoning such as ignoring the baseline of basic probabilities or not honoring the rules of the logical conditional. Others argue that rationality is always "bounded," limited to particular contexts and to prototypical cases such as permissions and obligations (Cheng & Holyoak, 1985; Gigerenzer et al., 1999). Stanovich (1999) characterizes these two ways of reasoning as "the fundamental cognitive bias" versus "decontextualized rationality." Pinker and Prince (1999) contrast these as "associative" versus "rule-based" cognitive systems. The argument could be expressed as follows: Personal reasoning is always just that, a perspective on a problem taken by a person with an interest, a bias, or a stake in its outcome. Institutions, on the other hand, have evolved normative or standard ways of interpreting and handling problems, including logical and statistical problems of the sort mentioned, that add value to the perceptions and judgments of particular individuals. Whereas all persons have the cognitive resources both to extract associative patterns and to learn formal rules, some persons have learned how to participate in these institutional contexts as expert and critic and they know how to generate, according to the rules, a range of answers likely to be taken seriously within that institution. It is a mistake to expect any unselected individual to be able to function as rationally as a whole institution or the collection of experts who have mastered those rules. Societies have evolved through creating institutions that can do what no individual, regardless of how endowed, could do in the absence of such institutionally based, formalized rules, namely, reason in a fully objectively rational way. To be an expert is to know these institutional ways of reasoning. Acquisition of this orthodoxy is what is fostered by schooling and what is assessed by formal reasoning tasks.

Now we may see why even the cognitive psychology created by the developmentalists of this generation is of marginal relevance to the problem of understanding either schooling or school reform. How children perceive, explore, understand, and enjoy the world and others, the bundle of concerns defining child-centered education, appears to have little to do with attaining institutional norms and goals. Put bluntly, schools as institutions do not "care" whether students enjoy quadratic equations as long as they solve them quickly and accurately. But schools as environments for human development not only serve the impersonal institutional goal of passing on a knowledge tradition; they also, as do parents, pursue fulfillment, competence, understanding, and enjoyment for their children. A psychology developed to address institutional processes and goals may turn out to be quite different from one designed to address the issues of personal growth and understanding. Those psychologies are the subject of Chapters 7 and 8.

6

Science and Schooling as Documentary Practices

O believers, when you contract a debt
one upon another for a stated term,
write it down, and let a writer
write it down between you justly.

(Quran 2:282, cited in B. Messick, 1993)

That's the age we live in. The documentary age.

(C. Shields, 1993)

Cognitively as well as sociologically, writing underpins "civilization," the
culture of cities.

(J. Goody, 1987, p. 3)

MAKING KNOWLEDGE

Science, as the Greeks used the term, was the name for valid knowledge,
the true. We are no longer so certain that science deserves such a vaunted
status. The radical "constructivist" claim, inherited from Nietzsche, who
wrote more than a century ago, was that "truths are illusions which we
have forgotten are illusions" (1979, pp. 83–84, cited by Ginsburg, 1999,
p. 9). If truth is constructed, invented, or imagined, judgment reverts
to more basic issues of power and the will to power, the right to speak
with authority and to demand compliance. In a modern bureaucratic
society that authority is granted to its institutions, including its knowledge institutions, that is, the disciplines. What we have lost in our faith
in our claims about truth we have gained in a new faith in our legitimate
scientific institutions.

86

Even setting aside the right of legitimate institutions to speak author-itatively on matters of knowledge and truth, the threat to our cherished beliefs by the radical constructivists is not as severe as it appeared to be a mere decade ago (Phillips, 1995). As Hacking (1999) pointed out, even our social constructions are constructions of something. The issue has been recast. The supposed conflict between truth and proof on one hand and social construction on the other is not a conflict between two con-tradictory perspectives, but between two factors at work in any serious study, what Ginsburg (1999) has called "narration" and "document"; narration involves invention, whereas documentation allows proof. All serious study involves both, inventing ideas and criticizing them by ap-peal to the standards of evidence and reason mandated and monitored by institutions. Documentation is involved in this proof process and in admission to the archive – the store of legitimate knowledge. The role of writing in this document tradition is the concern of this chapter.

In his account of how knowledge is constructed, Hacking (1994, 1999) analyzed the way in which science actually intervenes in nature through its laboratory methods. Science does not merely make observations of nature; the laboratory is a device for creating "observables," things that would never occur outside the laboratory – mass without weight, for example, or free-fall without the resistance of air, as in Robert Boyle's (1772) famous vacuum jar. Hacking offers the special name "mixed con-cepts" for concepts that are artificially devised. Whereas Hacking fo-cuses specifically on laboratories as intervening devices, I would add the documentary processes of institutions as examples of such medi-ating structures that have the power to set categories and fix rules for operating with them.

Mixed concepts, then, are concepts that do not merely describe preexisting reality but participate in the construction of that reality. Such concepts, which are especially common in the social sciences, in-clude *repressed memory syndrome, illiteracy, learning disability, helplessness, hyperactivity,* and *giftedness* and have drawn severe criticism from re-formers (Meier, 1999; Winner, 1996). Such concepts hover between being descriptions of a preexisting reality and being normative impositions of a governing institution. But we can no longer see them as natural or innocent.

Hacking (1999) described the way that such social categories affect reality as a "looping effect": Once people are classified by an institution, they may adopt the category as a self-ascription and bring their behavior into line with the classification. Further, they may interpret aspects of their behavior or that of others in terms of that category. He cites the case of "repressed memory syndrome," which when introduced produced a profusion of such memories; when it was subjected to more criticism and subsequently rejected, the symptoms disappeared as well. One may be more sympathetic to such invented social categories as child abuse, child poverty, youth homelessness, categories that characterize problems in a certain way but whose classification invites the reinterpretation of experience and provides a basis for creating laws and initiating social programs. When and why does "illiteracy" come to be taken as a social fact, an evil calling for "eradication"? These categories are institutional inventions, not merely descriptions of a preexisting reality. They involve a particular way of seeing or "taking" reality for some particular social or political purpose whether that of legitimating educational programs or legitimating social inequities – usually both. Such categories, again, are not innocent.

Thus the Enlightenment prospect of describing things just as they are, the "final theory," is a chimera, conspicuously so in the social sciences. Even to participate in current discourse about education and knowledge it is essential to grasp that people make knowledge not only through their experience and their language but also through the documentary practices of their institutions.

DOCUMENTING TRUTHS

As we saw in the previous chapter, only some of the beliefs entertained by scientists become part of science or scientific knowledge, that body of scientific knowledge held as true and secure in the relevant institutions of the society. Popper (1972) postulated a "World Three" to account for such venerable knowledge objects as Newton's theory, which outlasts the mind of Newton and full knowledge of which may lie outside the mind of any currently living scientist, but that, even if forgotten, may be revived generations later.

A small but interesting difference between the views of Popper (1972) and those of T. S. Kuhn (1977, p. 292) surfaced in their discussion of the relation between psychological states of scientists and the "truths" of science. Popper, defending his notion of *objective knowledge*, denied the methodological relevance of idiosyncratic psychological states of individual scientists. Kuhn agreed but insisted on the importance of "rhetorically induced and professionally shared imperatives," what I have called the *norms* of the discipline, to the advancement of science.

Whereas personal beliefs and interests of scientists may be of little relevance to the advance of science, their commitment to the institutional rules and imperatives, Kuhn argued, was of great importance. The institution of a science as a discipline evolves its rules and procedures along with its bodies of accepted truths; participation in these institutions, expertise, requires compliance with these norms and rules. As long as one complies, personal beliefs or values are irrelevant.

The role of formal, written documents is critical in the shaping of truths. The documentary practices of a knowledge institution allow one to reverse the ordinary assumption that statements express beliefs. Rather, the attempt is to formulate statements or theories that are defensible in terms of the canons of the science; if they are defensible, one may adopt them as an expression of one's own beliefs or, as is more often the case, regard those statements and claims as worthy of critical analysis and possible elaboration or refutation.

How, then, does the scientific establishment, a kind of bureaucracy, construct knowledge? Bureaucracies, of course, are just networks of people but people hooked up via specialist roles, accepted procedures, and documentary practices. In the case of science, the institution grants credentials to individuals on the basis of appropriate background knowledge and competence with a specialist methodology and then provides a forum for the expression of their opinions, hunches, and beliefs and, finally, an archive for accumulating warranted contributions. These forums include research groups, international conferences, and publications for validating and archiving claims. The contributions of individuals are adopted by the institution as its own when information has survived all the levels of that bureaucratic process. Three aspects of this process require attention, the expertise problem – who creates this knowledge; the percolation problem – how ideas rise to the top; and the documentation problem – the role of writing and literacy in the process.

THE EXPERTISE PROBLEM

The institutional perspective I have been drawing allows me to distinguish the more common notion of expertise as the cognitive skills of an isolated individual from the expertise implied by the entitlement to speak with authority on issues in a particular domain, the entitlement granted to one by the institutional structures of science, government, the courts, or the like. The expert, for Weber (Gerth & Mills, 1948, p. 216), was the person so specialized as to perform in a way corresponding to a role or place in a rationalized institution. A rational institution "demands the personally detached and strictly objective *expert*," who, unlike "the master of older social structures . . . who was moved by personal sympathy and favour, by grace and gratitude," was moved by the rules of the institution. The expert is the one entitled to speak by an institution on the basis of her or his competence with the roles and rules defined by "the imperatives" of that institution. To use more personal feelings or sympathies or to ask or grant favors is, from an institutional perspective, an irrational action, whereas to follow the explicit procedures and rules established by the institution for assigning and judging cases is an exercise of responsible professional judgment. Expertise, then, is tied less to personal competence than to institutional entitlement, although ideally the two converge. That is, who speaks for science, no less than who speaks for the nation, depends more on institutional structures than on personal brilliance.

In a document culture, expertise consists in large part of competence with creating and interpreting the central documents of the tradition. Correct reading of those documents requires not only a general reading ability but also more importantly a deep immersion in the tradition, including the standards, rules, and procedures of the "textual" or "interpretive" community. The modes of interpretation are often largely implicit, learned as a part of the tradition or the mysteries of the trade, although they have been made more explicit via the discipline of hermeneutics. This interpretive community (Kuhn, 1962; Stock, 1983; Smith, 1990b; Olson, 1994) is the real or imagined group of readers who share a particular and specialized way of reading and interpreting documents, a way that is shaped by the commentary and analyses, the editing and revision of those documents. A commitment to these practices is sufficient to admit or exclude one from membership in such a community. In this way, lawyers know to read briefs, academics to read journals, and teachers, textbooks. This interpretive community is shaped up not only by reading itself but also, as Feldman (2000) points out, by discussion about what is read. It is the subjective agreement among these readers that constitutes the "meaning" of a text, and it is readers' compliance with these meanings that confers membership in the textual community.

Yet it is also the misreadings and misinterpretations of these documents that allow for the growth of new knowledge. If pedagogical efforts were perfect, knowledge could neither grow nor change. Documents may fall into the wrong hands, that is, into the hands of those who do not know how to, or are unwilling to, read in the orthodox manner. Sometimes these misunderstandings lead to advances in knowledge, sometimes to pseudoscience or to heresy. Ginsburg (1982; see also Feldman, 2000) describes the case of Menocchio, a 16th-century miller, an autodidact who learned to read. He encountered some religious tracts to which he gave a "florid and idiosyncratic interpretation," including that God had not put people on the world, but that people appeared spontaneously, just as worms spontaneously formed in unattended cheese. His views led to his being charged with heresy before the Inquisition, and, partly because he would not keep his opinions to himself, he was burned at the stake. Although Menocchio's heresy was of little historical moment, another, by his near-contemporary Luther, namely, that Scripture was self-interpreting and not dependent for its meanings on the authoritative doctrines of the church, survived and produced the massive institutional changes associated with the Protestant Reformation. "Not to interpret is impossible," Italo Calvino's (1985) Mr. Palomar says.

Misinterpretation or reinterpretation by itself is not sufficient for social change, as we saw earlier. One needs, in addition, institutional structures that record, preserve, distribute, and criticize both documents and interpretations and assign them to a place in the tradition or the discipline. Here the documentary tradition is critical; laws and contracts not only have to be written as the Prophet insisted in the epigraph that opened this chapter, but have to be written in a certain way to reflect agreements and minimize misinterpretation by the participants and the courts. Some postmodern writers, grasping the importance of interpretation, have downplayed the importance, or even the possibility, of designing texts to express single unambiguous meanings, whether as legal statements, scientific theories, or mathematical expressions. Everything, they say, requires interpretation.

Other writers impressed with the notion of textual "autonomy" (some readers see me as one of those writers) argue that texts can be written so as to invite understanding while ruling out private interpretation altogether. This is the goal of written laws and contracts no less than of science. The balanced equation, the logical proof, the "final theory" would have those properties. Such a goal is only an ideal; there are always opportunities to take texts in new ways, to see new ideas in pictures, to see sermons in stones, to advance new geometries even if radical shifts are rare. Gödel (Lejewski, 1989) is famous for his proof that every proof rests, ultimately, on one or more unprovable assumptions.

Thus, Euclidean proofs rest on the assumption of a rigid surface; drawing geometrical figures on a rubber sheet yields different properties. So too for written texts; new backgrounds allow new readings of familiar texts. Thus, whereas for the ancient Hebrews, Scripture was history, for early Christians, it was metaphor for things to come (Frye, 1982).

Although debate about meaning is inevitable, texts, some more so than others, wear their meanings on their sleeves. The value of an unambiguous formulation is that if readers disagree with a statement they can have some confidence that they disagree with its author; under such conditions debate is productive and worthwhile. Quasi-scientific fields are littered with prose so vague that it is impossible either to know what is intended or to know whether one agrees or disagrees. For some texts such as horoscopes such ambiguity is a virtue. To read a document outside the intended interpretive frame is to misread the document. Expertise includes not just knowledge of the content of critical documents but also the much deeper and less explicit knowledge of how to interpret the information stated in those documents; this is what requires the extended training and warrants the credentialing of experts. Thus the concept of textual autonomy, texts that are fixed (Johns, 1998) and that can be treated as authoritative, should be understood less as a property of the text itself than as a property of the document, that is, a text embedded in an institutional framework (Geisler, 1994, p. 10).

The apparently coherent official view of the expert spokespersons of a discipline in fact hides an enormous amount of dissent and wrangling within a discipline. Overriding this diversity are the presence and fixity of documents and their canons for reading and interpretation that make possible not only the growth of the discipline but the recognition of that growth. Even following the dictates of the discipline, experts as critical readers may judge that what is advanced in a text as a factual claim may more appropriately be considered as an assumption. Assumptions have to be acknowledged; once acknowledged, they may be read or judged by another as unwarranted. Revisions in interpretation play a critical role in conceptual change and, if adopted by the discipline, in scientific progress.

THE PERCOLATION PROBLEM

The percolation problem has been well described by Latour and Woolgar (1986) and Geisler (1994) and summarized briefly in the last chapter. Undoubtedly some ideas spring, as Athena emerged fully formed from the mind of Zeus. To this day, psychologists know little more about where ideas come from than the rest of us, although the brain seems to be implicated! Most ideas have humble origins, of much interest to biographers and social historians. Did Kekule really dream of a snake eating its tail in imagining the Benzene ring? Did Einstein really imagine relativity theory by thinking of his train's leaving a Berlin station? For what it is worth, in my experience ideas arise from reading, not in the sense of assimilation but rather in the sense of provoking my own ideas.[1]

Rather my concern here is with how ideas take shape in the institutional practices of science. Latour and Woolgar (1986) recount cases of the following, recognizable kind. First of all, the participants are already members of a "textual community" in that they have all read the standard works, the canon. Further, they have discussed those works and have reached an understanding of how they are to be interpreted and what the gaps in those interpretations are. A comment advanced tentatively by one researcher in a meeting may be taken up by a second researcher in a way not intended or even recognized by its originator. That view or interpretation may then generate much discussion and reinterpretation. But this "reclassified" idea may have the advantage of being formulated as a testable hypothesis. The hypothesis is then assigned to a graduate student or another scientist, who, following a set formula for experiments of this type, collects and analyzes the evidence. If it is found to be incongruent with the hypothesis, the hypothesis may be redesigned or, more commonly, assigned to another graduate student in the outside hope of confirmation. If the observations are congruent with the hypothesis, the original statement now is again reclassified, this time as evidence for a theory. In this way ideas percolate up from private hunches, to explicit hypotheses, to claims, and after peer review and publication are adopted by the institution as scientific "facts." Thus the statement is reformulated not necessarily by content but rather by the speech act type in which it is embedded: "I guess . . ." "I think . . ." "I infer . . ." "I conclude . . ." and ultimately completely impersonally as "It follows. . . ." Thus, a scientific fact is an institutional product, not simply the idea in the mind of a great thinker. Experts, of course, are persons, but they are persons possessing the "psychological makeup of the licensed membership of a scientific group" (T. S. Kuhn, 1962, p. 22).

---

[1] I am not alone. William Weaver (2002, p. 34) wrote, "When I read Silone's words, some inchoate, previously unacknowledged emotions of my own came to the surface and began to take shape."

Institutions are not aggregates of individuals but individuals organized by social roles. A role in a bureaucratic institution defines what it is to be a professional. To become a professional, whether as psychologist, scientist, or school principal, is to have both the appropriate credentials and competencies set out in a job description specifying responsibilities and entitlements. In acting and making decisions one attempts to comply with the norms, rules, and standards of the profession. Psychologists who label a child *hyperactive* are following the rules of the profession, and their professional competence will be judged by their superiors on the basis of how well they comply with the "job description" for the profession. But here again, the judgments are not simply individual ones. The practicing psychologist submits a report making a classification, but the recommendation may be implemented only after a final judgment is made by a committee, a procedure analogous to peer review for scientific articles. Thus having vetted the report, the institution has met its responsibility to the larger society that created and continues to support it.

Institutionalized science is carried out by duly vetted, thinking scientists working within an authorized, empowered institutional frame with historically derived tools such as methodologies and approved documentary styles such as memos, research reports, and journal articles. Scientific institutions as social arrangements have entitlements and responsibilities; as long as they meet their responsibilities for the production of reliable knowledge, institutions, through their spokespersons, will be entitled to speak authoritatively on relevant issues and entitled to obtain resources to carry on further research. Learning to be a scientist is learning how to play a role in such an institution; to be a scientist is to take on that set of entitlements and obligations and meet them by following the "imperatives" of the discipline. These imperatives make up part of what children are learning in schools.

THE DOCUMENTATION PROBLEM

In Weber's theory of bureaucracy (Gerth & Mills, 1948, p. 197), with its principles of jurisdictions, lines of authority, roles, regulations, and qualifications, documentation plays a prominent part. A "bureau" is made up of the body of officials along with their "files," their written, processed, and stored documents. Bureaucracy without literacy is impossible.

The ubiquity of documentary procedures is largely responsible for the fact that they are underrated and even overlooked. Documentation is required for specifying the entitlements and obligations of the institution as a whole as well as the specific roles of the individuals constituting it. Documentation is required for preserving and sharing the products of the institution. One is entitled to be a participant in the institution only if one has already been initiated into the fraternity both by mastering the relevant background literature and by possessing the relevant credentials, characteristics usually explicitly formulated in job descriptions of the type routinely found, for example, in the *International Herald Tribune* or *The Chronicle of Higher Education:*

A leading information technology (IT) company requires an experienced project manager. The ideal candidate will have

High honors degree in industrial engineering or IT
At least 2 years of relevant industrial engineering experience
Experience in an international environment
Experience in change management
Excellent interpersonnel skills . . . (*International Herald Tribune,* Jan. 15, 2000)

A person filling the role described by the job description becomes part of the institution whether of science or of business. One's role might be somewhat derisively described as that of a kind of document "shifter," taking documents of one type, combining the information in those documents with preexisting information to form a new document, and passing them on to the next "desk," where the process will be repeated. "There is [a] combination of recording and reformulating that is involved in written composition itself" (Goody, 1977, p. 149). Thus here I sit, at my keyboard, Rorty, Smith, and Hacking at hand; reams of notes and tables of original data on the desk; and I take these documents and translate them into a new document (which you are now reading). You (dear reader) will take this document and, with appropriate reformulation, shift it to yet another desk. Ultimately these documents make their way to the archive, the known, or, God forbid, onto the wayside. What one consults, how one interprets, and what can be used as data are all regulated by the accepted procedures of the discipline that have been mastered by the participants as part of the credentialing process; what survives depends upon the vetting processes of editorial boards.

The form the constructed document can take is also sharply defined. Obviously the days when one was required to express one's scientific ideas in rhyming couplets or other verse forms is far in the past (Olson, 1994, p. 160; Godzich & Kittay, 1987). Scientific ideas must now be expressed in a standard form whether as memo, brief, report, experimental report, research article, book chapter, or book. Within these general categories, writing must draw on an appropriate technical vocabulary; it must take a logical if–then structure in the formulation of a hypothesis and an evidence–claim relation in a conclusion. These documentary forms have the property of a formulary or a template into which one must insert one's ideas. The requirements are just as rigid as those of a sonnet or a sonata, formats with a long history that require considerable investment of time and energy for their acquisition and a high degree of expertise for their successful use.

As we saw, D. Smith (1990b, p. 71) argued, "Facts are an organization of practices of inscribing an actuality into a text." What gets into the document depends on the documentary forms available. A generation ago Gombrich (1960, p. 12) in his history of art argued that art develops by the progressive development of a "vocabulary of forms"; what you can see in nature and "say" in art depends on the limitations of your vocabulary or schemata. T. S. Kuhn made the same point in regard to "normal" science, an enterprise that "seems an attempt to force nature into the preformed and relatively inflexible box that the paradigm supplies" (1962, p. 24). Documentation is just that – creating a document suited to the institutional practices of the discipline. The putative facts taught to children and the facts they are to produce for their reports are critical parts of that institutional practice. Further, the document is composed to match the assumed reading practices of the institution; learning to read is not just learning to decipher; it is learning to adjust to those institutional demands.

Latour (1993) has given an incisive description of these institutional practices as a "skein of networks," which he calls the new Leviathan. He writes:

There is an Ariadne's thread that would allow us to pass with continuity from the local to the global. . . . It is the thread of networks of practices and instruments, of documents and translations. . . . The organization of American big business . . . is not the organization described by Kafka. It is a braid of networks materialized in order slips and flow charts, local procedures and special arrangements. . . . [T]hese "networks of power". . . extend across the entire world. (pp. 121–122)

Although this sounds drearily mechanical, and somewhat demeaning of the activities to which many of us devote our lives, it is important to see that these are rather the social means by which documents finally establish their position in the archive as established science. And whereas many of us aspire to contribute to that archive, even those who do not rarely deny the importance of these documents and these knowledge institutions. Seeing knowledge from an institutional perspective provides a way around the romantic notion of science as the product of heroic genius, the great mind thinking true thoughts, or what my university, in its advertising, calls "Great Minds."

Kitcher, in *The Advancement of Science* (1993), pointed out that scientists with messy habits, grumpy notions, and selfish goals may yet advance their science. Hacking (1994), as did Popper and Kuhn, mentioned earlier, agreed that science cannot be explained in terms of the personal idiosyncrasies of individuals. But he goes on to criticize Kitcher for not taking institutions sufficiently seriously: "Kitcher's vision of a society of scientists is one of interacting individuals. There are no social forces in themselves that are relevant to his analysis, except such as arise from atomic individuals bouncing words, speculations, reports, and phenomena off each other" (p. 214). In its place Hacking offers "an instrumental and laboratory style of reasoning" (p. 214), which took shape in the 17th and 18th centuries with the invention of certain institutionalized practices, primarily laboratories. Thus the very idea of reason in the sciences, he suggests, shifted in the early modern period. Rationality was found in the institutional rather than in individual genius. Individuals may be as subject to prejudices, hunches, bias, and vaingloriousness as the next person; it was the collaborative and documentary activities of the individuals in their institutional roles that was responsible for the cautious rationality we identify with science.

SCHOOLING AS AN INSTITUTIONAL DOCUMENTARY PROCESS

Part of the tedium of schooling is associated precisely with its documentary practices. Not only is schooling a matter of reading and producing standard documents; the daily life of classrooms is dominated by documentation. The production of timetables, enrollment and attendance lists, lesson plans, texts and workbooks; the filing of records; the classification of books and other resource materials; the assignment of seats and work; and the collection of homework are all documentary practices. The school is a flurry of papers, as any teacher or parent can attest. Yet proposals for school reform at least since Dewey, perhaps since Plato, have opposed the overweening influence of books and

other documents in schools at the expense of actual "trying and doing" individually and with one's peers. It is argued that children learn
through talk, not only through reading and listening, and through experimenting, not only through learning formulas. They learn through
seeing what works, through being surprised, through suggesting and
counterarguing, not only or primarily through learning to construe authoritative texts. One hundred years of developmental psychology has
been devoted to showing how creatively and spontaneously children
construct their knowledge of the world – presumably without recourse
to the constraining influence of authoritative texts.

Admittedly, these reforms are often liberating. They are steps toward
putting the learner at the center of learning and making the learner more
responsible for his or her own learning and knowledge. But proposed
reforms are premised on a half-truth. One has only to look a little further
and it becomes apparent that the object of discussion is often a document; that the experiment being tried is scripted by a laboratory manual;
that the report being prepared is a document with a specified format;
that the assessment by the teacher is a note in a ledger used as a basis
for further instruction or filed for future report; that on the blackboard
are posted the duties for the day, the assignments to be completed, the
times and places of meetings. Savvy students entering classrooms first
stand and read the instructions on the blackboard before even taking
their seats. Those who fail to read the messages spend part of the day
asking those who did what they are supposed to be doing (Bell, 1990).
Teachers' manuals determine the syllabus for the courses, the exercises
to be completed, and the grades to be assigned. Textbooks elaborate the
knowledge referred to by the curriculum guide and explicitly express
the knowledge or ideas for which the child (and perhaps the teacher)
is to be held accountable. When students open a textbook, there are instructions as to what is to follow, what is to be required after reading,
where to look up answers. If all else fails the teacher may be consulted
(see Figure 3). Examinations involve questions framed with instructions
such as "Contrast and compare" and "Choose the best answer." Every
activity is grounded in rules, procedures, choices, and decisions explicitly set out in written documents. These specify the normative structures
provided by the society at large in terms of which learning and development is to be judged often by means of a written test.

Because textbooks acknowledge, implement, and encourage the application of the normative standards of the disciplines they represent,
they are sometimes seen as the embodiments of knowledge that should

FIGURE 3. Peanuts cartoon by Charles Schulz reproduced here with permission. PEANUTS ©United Feature Syndicate, Inc.

99

directly be taught and learned by students ignoring the learners' own subjectivities. What do we teach children if not the grand "truths" collected in authoritative texts? Some have thought to replace truth with personal belief, some with truth in one's own primary social group, yet others abandon truth altogether, replacing it with allegiance to methods of inquiry. None of these does justice to knowledge as an institutional, documentary process. Texts are documents, which, as do any other documents, provide normative standards against which beliefs are to be judged. Students learn to cite them, quote them, paraphrase them, and criticize them in developing and elaborating their own arguments and to express authoritative arguments "in their own words" (Horowitz & Olson, in press).

The knowledge that students are to acquire and for which they are responsible in the school takes a documentary form. Experience is to be recast into formulas, whether as narrative or as logical explication, following strict rules of premise and inference, cause and effect, reason and conclusion. Norms and rules replace nonschool habits, conventions, and traditions. Meanings are replaced by definitions;[2] expressive utterances, by explicit statements. Teachers instruct: "Answer in whole sentences"; "Give reasons for your answer"; "Try to find a rule that covers these cases." By the turning of impressions, feelings, and implicit beliefs into explicit propositions, formulated with defined terms and justified by reasons, informal beliefs are converted into legitimate, socially warranted knowledge. Ideally this is an extension of the student's own understanding, but it is also the bureaucratization of knowledge and mind, of learning how to think in socially approved, indeed, mandated, ways. A subjective understanding is important but it is not enough. What is required in addition is the ability to formulate and to interpret explicit written statements or other documents that express that understanding. That documentary tradition is just what a modern society has entrusted to the schools.

Forms determine functions. Teachers and children alike know that a failure to have an entry in the appropriate column in a document can provoke a crisis. Further, they know that only certain actions are eligible for entry into these formularies – the form determines the data gathered. The child either is present or is absent, has completed the assignment or has not, passed the course or did not, behaved satisfactorily or did not. Similarly, magnetism was studied or it was not, fractions were covered

---

[2] Much caricatured by Dickens's fact-loving schoolmaster, Mr. Gradgrind.

or not, and so on. These constitute one's "record," ultimately one's curriculum vitae (CV), itself a document. Teachers are routinely required to "document" student progress, to sort children into somewhat arbitrary categories of passing or failing, a categorization that may be experienced by those so categorized as dehumanizing. Alternatively, such acts can be seen as just a part of the immersion into a bureaucratic world where you are either a citizen or a noncitizen, a salaried or a nonsalaried worker, a university graduate or not, and so on, through the host of categories and judgments made about persons in a bureaucratic society. Assessing and credentialing, developing "objective" forms of reporting, are all aspects of life in an institutional context. Schools as institutions provide a context in which learning and understanding are to occur, but equally importantly, they provide and implement the norms, standards, and criteria for assessing that learning. These norms are impersonal and institutional and consequently may be far removed from the learner's more personal feelings and understandings. Thus, not only are documents economical means or useful tools for schooling, they shape the very procedures and persons involved.

Schools as bureaucratic institutions have goals, plans, and systems of accountability appropriate for judging success and failure, much as individuals do. These are spelled out in terms of entitlements and obligations that apply to populations – enrollments, dropouts, curricula, standards of achievement, percentage passing, and so on. Further, institutions, as persons do, grow and change in ways that can be plotted on graphs. One of the landmarks of modern pedagogy is its ability to take into account children's existing knowledge and beliefs as a basis for cognitive growth or "conceptual change"; institutional change, too, must take into account not only entitlements and obligations but existing structure and tradition. As we noted earlier many attempted reforms fail simply because they do not acknowledge the existing traditions of the local school.

By most criteria, science as an institution is more successful than the school as an institution. Science has generated continuous progress, whereas schools appear, at least to some, simply to maintain the status quo. But school as an institution is older than science. Schools have taken some 500 years to achieve their present structure and are in that sense already reasonably attuned to their social functions. Schools can and do change as societies change and adopt new or altered goals and priorities just as science as an institutional practice does. Important to both are the development of institutional forms with clear entitlements and responsibilities and the development of the professional expertise to meet those responsibilities.

Francis Bacon in *The Advancement of Learning* (1857–74) proposed that writing as a public and communal activity was the principal means for developing a progressive science. Each scientist, he suggested, would observe the natural world and record observations, writing them in short prose pieces, essays, that would then be read, retested, and added to by other scientists, each individual text superseded by the next. The final version would be taken as authoritative. Scientific knowledge was to be document construction in a quite literal sense.

Textbooks play another, generally unrecognized role, that of providing to both teachers and students an updated version of the structure and content of a discipline or domain. Differences from province to province or state to state and publisher to publisher are relatively minor as each text is drafted with the others in view. Reformers in the United States and Canada are tempted to "reinvent" the school with new curriculum and new standards. But because different states and nations use essentially the same documents and texts, students graduate knowing by and large the same things regardless of where they went to school and regardless of what test they are given (Porter & Smithson, 2001, p. 69). Consequently, national tests such as the National Assessment of Educational Progress (NAEP) correlate highly with local tests, although the latter may set higher standards.

What the focus on the knowledge "contained in books" hides is the fact that knowledge is also personally held belief. Schools may be criticized if the "bookishness" leads to memorization of texts at the expense of "meaningful" study. Rather than the disparagement of books and private study what is needed is a better understanding of how personal beliefs relate to accepted knowledge, that is, how persons relate to institutions. The burden of this chapter has been to show that distinguishing these is a necessary prelude to understanding the role of the school in human development.

7

The Psychology of Persons in Institutions

Modern nation states "define the characteristics that would be possessed by a perfect working class."

(S. Moscovici, 1993, p. 339)

If we are required to do certain things, then we are required to be the kinds of people who will do these things.

(T. Nagel, 1986, p. 191)

To embrace a role is to disappear completely into the virtual self available in the situation.

(E. Goffman, 1961, p. 106)

Institutions have many of the properties of persons; both can be described in terms of entitlements and responsibilities. Because of their neglect of institutions in understanding both persons and schooling, theorists have inadvertently attributed to people as part of their human nature characteristics that are attributable, rather, to the institutions in which they find themselves. The burden of this chapter is to show that because the distinction between persons and institutions has been unacknowledged, a psychology has evolved that purports to be a psychology of persons that would be better construed as a psychology of institutions, or more specifically, a psychology of persons in terms of those governing institutions. Correspondingly in contemporary educational discourse, schooling is regarded as a more or less neutral or natural means for furthering human development. In this chapter I propose to turn the tables – to show that schools regard students in terms of their own institutional mandates and that children begin to see themselves in those institutionally based terms. I begin by showing that institutions see people not as persons and not objectively, but in ways congruent with their own mandates.

HOW INSTITUTIONS SEE PEOPLE

Once persons are distinguished from institutions, it becomes possible to examine how institutions view people in contrast to how people view people. Institutional roles are defined impersonally by means of job descriptions, and people are perceived in terms of those descriptions. The role is to be filled by a person having the enumerated qualifications and characteristics. It would be self-defeating to define a role by naming a person; persons are meant to be interchangeable in institutional roles. Hence, the person filling the role has to be identified not as a person, a self with a personal identity and private intentionality, but as a member of a class of persons possessing the collection of credentials and competencies defined by the role. Institutions change persons into roles, a transformation some see as the dehumanizing loss of personal identity, others as providing new identities for ongoing selves. Whether seen as positive or negative, that institutions re-represent persons as roles is beyond dispute.

Institutional roles are defined by competencies, identified with credentials, and attitudes, identified with personality traits. Description of persons in terms of abstracted traits is so commonplace in modern societies that one is tempted to see traits as essential features of human nature either selected or amplified by culture or society. On the one hand, many biologically minded psychologists are attempting to locate such traits as intelligence or criminality in a particular gene or set of genes. Anthropologists, on the other hand, see traits as derivative from social roles, whether roles in bureaucracies or roles in everyday life: King is a role in a kingdom; father is a role in a family; lover is a role in a relationship; "it" is a role in a game of tag. Such roles have rules and accountabilities.

However, it is important to distinguish persons playing formal roles in a bureaucracy from persons playing roles in everyday social life. How one learns to be a son or a father is, of course, as important as how one learns to be a "student" or a "slow learner." The distinction is based on the principle articulated earlier: being "characterized by a rule" versus actually "following a rule." Whereas all social behavior can be characterized by roles and rules, and in some cases, those roles and rules are

actually known and followed, in bureaucratic contexts, the institution intentionally defines the roles and rules and selects and trains the persons
to play them. The role defines the holder rather than vice versa. Consider
the difference between a czar and a president. In the former role, except
in the times of revolution, the czar is like a father figure in that only one
person is entitled to play the role; in the latter role, the position is open, as
we say, to all qualified applicants. Although astronomical expenditure
may be involved in selecting the person to play the role, the actual person selected makes very little difference as long as he or she adequately
fills the role. Games with explicit roles and rules are closest in structure
to bureaucratic systems, and incidentally, unlike play, which is universal, games occupy a more prominent place in bureaucratic societies than
in more traditional ones (Lancey, 1996). Indeed, games have been identified as an important educational form by many educational theorists
from Johann Friedrich Herbart (1776–1841) (1898) to Kieren Egan (1997).

Roles are characterized in terms of credentials and traits of potential
holders. But trait ascriptions play an equally important role in ordinary
discourse. One biographer of John Dewey wrote: "The only personality
traits that distinguished Dewey from the other boys growing up in the
New England town were his shyness and reticence" (cited in Scheffler,
1974, p. 192). These adjectival descriptions modify our representations
of the particular person named by the noun. One branch of psychology,
psychometric theory, has attempted to turn such trait descriptions into a
scientific theory of human nature. Such theory ignores the institutional
basis of trait ascriptions. Institutions define specific roles, for example,
that of "top student" or "slow learner" or "ideal husband," and then
search for traits ranging from introversion to intelligence that predict
performance in those roles.

The point to note is that such traits are not descriptive of human
nature but of one's suitability for an institutionally defined role. Consequently, such theories are blind to the intentionality and subjectivity of
the persons in or out of those roles. For that we need an entirely different
psychology, the concern of the next chapter. For now, my goal is to show
that trait theory is an institutional psychology parading as a personal
psychology.

PERSONNEL SELECTION

The primary use of trait ascriptions is in narrowly defined institutional
contexts. When a role is known but the identity of the person who is to

play the role is not known, these adjectival descriptors may be used to characterize any person, x, who would be ideal for the role whether ideal worker, ideal student, or ideal prisoner. Roles, as we noted earlier, may be set out in job descriptions; the role could be satisfied by any number of persons, and although such descriptions are suitable, indeed essential, for a well-functioning bureaucracy, they are far too abstract to represent a real person adequately. One would ordinarily love a person, not a role, and John Dewey is more than a collection of his traits. But when it comes to filling a role in a bureaucracy, such descriptions, sufficiently elaborated, serve quite well. Indeed, the functioning of a bureaucracy assumes that the slots depend upon the existence of a class of workers, a workforce, any one of whom is capable of fulfilling the role, some more capably than others.

Writing a job description to suit a particular individual is a violation of the purpose of a job description; its purpose is to designate a role and a class of individuals who could play that role. Personal identity, in such a scheme, has nothing to do with the role. One of the standard plots of 17th-, 18th-, and 19th-century theater and opera is the inadvertent or intentional swapping of persons in roles to either the delight of the audience, as in the case of *Twelfth Night*, or the dismay of both character and audience, as in the case of Donizetti's *Lucia de Lammermour*, based on a novel by Sir Walter Scott in which a husband, possessing many of the traits of the beloved, is forced on a young woman who then becomes mad. She, apparently, wanted that particular person, not just someone who fitted the job description. Writers to the Personals column never seem to learn that lesson: You cannot love a role, you can only love a person, and a list of even eminently desirable traits does not give you a person. Psychology as a discipline has also been slow to learn that lesson; traits do not confer identity (Taylor, 1989), although roles do.

What defines an institutional bureaucracy, then, is the allocation of functions to particular roles characterized abstractly in terms of traits and credentials, which may be filled by anyone fitting the job description. That job description is given in terms of abstracted properties of persons, not identities of persons. Selecting persons for roles is the job that the discipline of psychology was largely created to serve. Job descriptions of roles in institutions define the ideal person in terms of credentials and competencies, and psychology was born as the discipline for assessing those competencies and working out the correlations between those features and the success of the person in the role and indirectly the success of the institution. All institutions define persons in terms of their suitability for roles in them. As noted in Moscovici's (1993) epigram to this chapter, modern nation-states as institutions define the roles – soldier, worker, student – and then define the ideal person for each role in relation to the optimal functioning of the institution. Training plans are then devised to transform persons into those ideal types. The traits identified are those that characterize that abstracted person most suitable to the role. In so doing, they identify not only those most suited to the role but also those who fit less well, thereby giving rise in educational institutions to such deviant classes as "slow learner" on one hand and "gifted" on the other.

The history of testing is a history of selecting persons to play roles, with the idea that the one who best suits the idealized version specified by the institution is selected for the role. Tests were used as a means for selecting persons for the mandarinate in China at least from the sixth century (Taylor & Taylor, 1995, p. 149; Coulmas, 2000). As these tests were highly competitive and exhaustive, high scores assured that persons of the highest levels of knowledge and competence obtained positions of power and influence. Since the 13th century in Europe, specialist training and earned credentials have been used for selecting persons for roles in government, courts, and religion. Credentials have betokened competence.

Whereas such selection tests have a long history, psychology as a science primarily took its shape early in the 20th century, when Alfred Binet (Seigler, 1992) designed the test that came to be called the IQ test to discriminate among children who would and would not benefit from schooling. Put another way, Binet designed a test that would select persons who could best play the role of "student" in the institutional context of the school. Among other findings Binet discovered that about 5% of the children had difficulty in school because they could not see the blackboard! But he is best remembered for inventing a test that could predict with considerable precision the outcome of schooling and discriminate bright from dull children even before instruction began. These days no one would claim that there are any children who would not benefit from instruction in some form; even the severely retarded may achieve remarkably if patiently and systematically taught and encouraged (Oe, 1969; Sacks, 1986). But Binet's test served a clear predictive function and consequently has come to be used for selection for various roles in the school, including normal, delayed, or gifted programs. The scientific study of traits has helped to define the "ideal student," that is, the student for whom, on average, the least resources produce the greatest gains. Much of educational psychology is devoted to adding to this list of predictive measures, with the result that "excessive quantification" often eclipses more focused research on the relations between "policy and practice" (Lagemann, 2000, p. xi). Such predictive tests, it should be noted, are of markedly less importance than the credentials earned through proper training and relevant experience, and there is some indication that university admissions are beginning to be based more on secondary school achievement than on the supposed abilities diagnosed by the Scholastic Aptitude Test (SAT) (Cloud, 2001).

Testing as a means of awarding credentials must be distinguished from testing that attempts to provide a psychological profile of persons. Tests of intelligence and other abilities developed rapidly during World War I, when it became clear that such tests were useful in classifying recruits for various military roles. Psychological testing became and continues to be an integral part of personnel management of most large bureaucratic systems including schools. Further, modern assessment devices are used to classify persons for all sorts of roles and entitlements in addition to those of concern to the school. The *Diagnostic and Statistical Manual*, the compendium of mental illnesses known as *DSM-IV*, lists the characteristics and traits relevant to assigning persons to any one of some four hundred forms of abnormality.

Whereas personal identities are not comparative, Bill is just Bill, and by law all persons are equal, the abstracted properties of persons are intrinsically comparative. Consequently, a person may be ranked on any trait or criterion, that ranking characterized by the famous statistical distribution, the "normal" curve. On any abstracted trait, the population will be distributed in a way captured by this curve, a finding originally made by Francis Galton, founder of the biometric school of statistical research (as well as eugenics). He wrote that the chief law of probability "reigns with serenity and in complete effacement amidst the wildest confusion" (cited by Hacking, 1990, p. 2). Indeed, as Hacking showed, the understanding of probability was one of the great intellectual achievements of the 18th and 19th centuries. This "bell" curve captures distributions of any abstracted property. Although the buildings in Toronto are enormously variable, many of them unique, such as the upside-down pie plate–shaped Symphony Hall, on any property such as volume, height, or cost, the variability of buildings on that feature will fall in a normal distribution.

The same is true for persons. Whereas no two persons are alike, as Lucia knew, all persons may be described in terms of varying amounts of the same traits. For any abstracted dimension, whether physical or psychological, the variability among persons on that dimension may be characterized by a normal distribution and individuals at the tails of the distribution as deviant, that is, deviant from the norm or average. Those deeply cynical of the whole undertaking recall the celebrated diagnosis reported in 1851 by a surgeon, S. Cartwright, in the *New Orleans Medical and Surgical Journal* of "drapatomania," an affliction common among slaves, which caused them to run away from their masters! In fact, literacy was a contributing factor in Bahia (Goody, 2000); those more literate were more likely to try to run away! The problem with that diagnosis, of course, is that it points to psychological factors rather than social and institutional ones. Although almost any identified feature may show a normal distribution, those that enter the theory are just those that predict, that is, correlate with, a criterion specified by some institutional function such as school success. What makes it a "feature" of a person is not the variability but the criterion imposed by an institution whether a factory, school, or prison.

Critics of testing and labeling make the same complaint: One should look at social practices that label some people failures rather than at the personalities of those so labeled. Yet the search for psychological explanations of "diseases" as criminality, poverty, illiteracy, and school failure persists. Critics point out that this is simply the mistake of blaming the victim. Minimally, one must scrutinize the institutional basis of the classification rather than attempt only to perfect the measures for assigning people to it. When IQ tests were first shown to be culturally biased, the common reaction was to attempt to construct one that was culturally fair rather than to recognize the impossibility of such a task: IQ, as do other traits, reflects a criterion established by a set of institutions in a bureaucratic society.

Intelligence is the abstracted trait most studied, but any other trait, such as patience, perseverance, punctuality, or honesty, can also be so described as long as one selects an explicit criterion such as grades, recidivism, or income level as the "dependent variable." No dependent variable, no prediction! Institutions such as prisons and schools traditionally have the power to choose the dependent variable. It is both a practical and a theoretical impossibility to generalize such traits to a whole person in all contexts. Nonetheless, one consequence of the discovery of this statistical fact was that it changed the way persons were perceived, and now most of us desperately try to be "normal" so as not to seem pathological (Hacking, 1996). Average scores can serve as "norms" and extreme scores can be taken as indications of deviancy, "giftedness," " an A student," on one hand, and "learning disability" and "attention deficit" on the other. There is a kind of tyranny of the average at work here that we shall consider more fully in Chapter 14.

I have argued that abstracted traits are comparative: They are defined in relation to an explicit criterion, and they are defined in the service of institutional judgments. Institutional judgments and explicit criteria are related in that traits are traits only in terms of a criterion, such as functioning well in a school. It is its relation to a criterion that confers "validity" to a psychological trait. As schools can no longer select their clients but must admit everyone, considerable effort goes into training children to be "ideal students"; that is, the institution sets the norm and children are shaped to fit the institution, to be ideal students. With ideal students the school is more likely to achieve its mandate. This is not as sinister as it sounds; all institutions select or shape their participants to play institutionally defined roles. Even prisons have the notion of the ideal prisoner, namely, the one who is most likely to help the prison achieve its mandate for safety and rehabilitation. Schools have a responsibility to produce and certify competent graduates with the credentials suited to the job market. Educational planners meet that responsibility by designing appropriate programs of study and experience. In this way, such obvious factors as the content of the curriculum, the length of the program, and required background knowledge have long been central to educational planning. But only in the past century have the more subtle factors of IQ and SES, factors essentially beyond the control of either the planner or the learner, been shown to have predictive value. Traits have become part of the theory of education and in some cases have replaced actual earned rights to specialist programs. Thus, in Ontario, "giftedness" is assigned not on the basis of outstanding achievement, something the student has actually earned, but of the supposed ability diagnosed by the IQ test.

Some theorists attempt to push descriptions of persons in terms of traits or characteristics to universality, that is, to create a scientific characterization of a person as a person rather than an account of a person's suitability to an institutionally defined role. A psychological theory that aspires to account for the behavior of persons in terms of traits comes up against two insurmountable objections. The first, already mentioned, is that such traits predict only in relation to a well-defined criterion, say, spelling or algebra, but contribute little to our understanding of what it is to be a human. The second is that persons are intentional creatures whose behavior cannot be explained in causal, that is, dispositional, terms. This was the objection that ended a half-century domination by behaviorism. Trait theories cannot address the intentional states of persons, their beliefs and intentions, goals and satisfactions. Nor can they approach the phenomenology of experience – what it is to perceive, believe, intend, think, or judge – and these are the very processes at the heart of every educational theory from Plato to the present.

Nonetheless, because such traits are abstracted across a diversity of particular contents and particular situations and because they can be measured reliably, they have proved to be useful for some types of inquiry. It remains a fact that trait assessment accounts for some variance in a person's performance relative to that of a population (Stanovich, 1999; Gigerenzer, Todd, & ABC Research Group, 1999) within well-defined institutional contexts such as reading and formal reasoning. They have, in addition, proved to be useful for the science of population genetics. Further, traits such as intelligence, extroversion, and reticence are sometimes usefully applied to characterize persons – one learns something about Dewey when informed that he was "reticent," but the characterization does little to account for the breadth and depth of his thought or for his appeal to a century of readers. Traits are, it seems, here to stay, but their usefulness as psychological theory is limited.

The limitations of viewing the actions of a person in terms of dispositions and habits provided one reason for constructing an alternative psychology, a cognitive psychology, which takes as its goal the understanding of the beliefs, desires, and intentions as well as the emotions and subjective feelings of persons. The Cognitive Revolution saw itself as rooting out the vestiges of a defunct behaviorism (Chomsky, 1957), replacing it by a more generative model of mind. This tradition is represented by the developmental theories of Piaget, Vygotsky, and Bruner that helped to define the Cognitive Revolution of the 1960s (Johnson & Erneling, 1997). This tradition attempts to place the "mind" back in psychology, including the psychology of education. Although this theoretical advance captures cognitive states and structures, it fails largely to capture the first-person experience, including the "felt needs" of the acting subject (Donaldson, 1992).

The problem that has remained unresolved has been how to think about the relations between these two perspectives, one objective and causal; the other, subjective and intentional. And the view I have been elaborating here is that trait psychology, sometimes called *differential* or *measurement psychology*, is a psychology for populations defined by institutional contexts, not for persons with beliefs, feelings, intentions, and responsibilities.

THE TWO PSYCHOLOGIES

I am not the first to propose that we require two quite different psychologies, one for persons as intentional agents and one for persons as defined by institutions. Wundt, who is regarded as the father of experimental psychology, also introduced a cultural psychology, a *Volkspsychologie*. In educational discourse, Cronbach (1957) in his address as president of the American Psychological Association attempted to reconcile what he called the two disciplines of psychology, suggesting that experimental psychology attempts to explain conditions under which a particular pattern of responses would occur, whereas differential psychology attempts to capture the diversity of what individuals introduce to those conditions. The first of these examined the effects of treatments; the second, the effects of aptitudes, and he hoped for a discipline that would unite the two. Indeed, a vigorous program of research (Cronbach & Snow, 1977) set out to capture such aptitude–treatment interactions – assessing children and then designing programs suitable for their patterns of aptitude. Although the ideas that there are "different kinds of learners" and that "some methods are better than others" remain familiar tropes in educational circles, the research program linking them has not been successful. Indeed, in a retrospective article, Cronbach (1975) pointed out the limits of the program, despairing of making "progress toward enduring theoretical structures" (p. 123). Characterizing learners and treatments in general terms fails completely to address the local interactions between the two and ignores precisely what learners believe, want, or are willing to do or trying to do in particular and unrepeatable historical contexts. As an alternative he advocated as a research goal the development of explanatory concepts that "help people to use their heads" (p. 126). Thus the classification of children by aptitude is still too crude to provide specific guidance as to just what should be taught or how. A much more reliable guide as to what should be taught is not a general measure of aptitude or even prior achievements but an exploration of mutual understandings and misunderstandings of the topic under study and the negotiation of achievable goals, a perspective that has proved to be enormously productive (Clay, 1998; Olson, 1999). How to conceptualize such practices will concern us when we turn to the problem of pedagogy.

But the problem runs much deeper. As I have argued, measurement of mental abilities and psychological traits is part of a psychology of persons in relation to specific institutions such as the school. When the institutional function of such psychology is recognized, it becomes clear why it continues to play an extremely important and conspicuous part in institutional practices not only for filling roles in bureaucratic institutions but also for classifying children for special programs, for assigning persons to particular treatments or mental institutions, for admitting applicants to universities, as well as for making judgments of passing and failing and awarding credentials. Measurement summarizes a class of performances in terms of a trait appropriate to some particular institutional frame. As do persons, institutions have responsibilities for which they are accountable, and research on institutions may isolate some of the factors that contribute to their effectiveness. But whereas such theories purport to be about persons, they are more appropriately seen as social or institutional theories in which the causes are social or institutional. It is entirely appropriate to ask whether 5 hours of math instruction per week "causes" more learning than 3 hours per week and, having isolated such a causal relation, use it as a basis for educational policy. What such research does not tell us is anything helpful about why or how learners adopt the mandated curriculum, whether they understand the material taught, how they go about learning, or how such study alters their personal beliefs, desires, feelings, and intentions. It is, therefore, an institutional psychology, not a psychology of thinking persons.

It is well established that the best predictor of future behavior is present behavior, a fact that can be explained by either dispositional or intentional theories. There is no question that the credentials indicative of advanced training are suitable criteria for the assignment of roles in institutional contexts. Not only have training and testing and credentialing been parts of institutional functions since antiquity, earned credentials are considerably more fair than alternative bases for selection such as nepotism, bribery, or purchase of commissions by officers as occurred in the British Admiralty in the 18th century. Measures of achievement as indications of competence are, therefore, relatively fair and objective means of assigning persons to roles.

Just how much the suitability to a role is enhanced by adding psychological variables remains controversial. Thus whereas first-year college achievement is predicted well by performance in secondary school, SAT scores, a proxy for IQ, add little to the prediction (Lemann, 1999).

Because reliable and comparable achievement scores are often unavailable, SAT scores have continued (at least until recently) to play a role in selection. Measures of achievement are useful not only for awarding credentials but also for judging the success of institutional functions. The problem arises only when the assessments and network of correlations built around them are not recognized as what they are, namely, theories of persons in relation to specific institutional forms rather than general theories of human nature. Thus although I do not deny such theories have a role, I am attempting to assign them a particular role.

What Cronbach (1975) appeared to be calling for was just the sort of psychology that was taking shape in the "cultural turn" in psychology, led in large part by the work of Vygotsky discussed earlier that had its roots in the writing of Durkheim and Weber. A parallel turn was made in sociology by Talcott Parsons (1951, 1970), a sociologist and translator of Durkheim who attempted to link the psychological inner life with social, institutional structures. In his perceptive analysis of the school as a social system Parsons argued that the school is "the first socializing agency in the child's experience which institutionalizes a differentiation of status on non-biological bases" (1959, pp. 300–301), that is, on status that is "earned" through performance on achievement tests rather than given or inherited from the family. Thus, he distinguished such "ascribed" factors as social class from such "achieved" factors as school achievement in relation to the functioning of the school as an institution. It is the "achieved" factors, essentially school achievement, that call for an analysis of the intentions and goals of learners as persons – for intentional causes rather than social causes. Like Durkheim, Parsons considered persons to be "volitional," but he contented himself with examining intentional states indirectly through personality tests[1] (Parsons, 1959) and public opinion research rather than what, these days, we would call intentionality. Yet in his empirical work, Parsons found, for example, that medical professionals lived simultaneously in two worlds, the world defined by their professional obligations and the world defined by human intersubjectivity, which is to say, they treated patients both in terms of the rules and norms of the profession and simultaneously as persons deserving of affection and sympathy (Parsons, 1970). Thus, although a sociologist, he worked very much in the tradition of Durkheim in the

---

[1] Parsons had a deep sympathy for his colleague David McClelland's concept of achievement motivation, an entrepreneurial trait deemed lacking in Asian cultures in the post–World War II reconstruction era.

attempt to bridge mental life and social life. His theory of institutions, in my view, correctly describes roles and rules, the normative structures of the society, and the fact that these roles and rules have a role in personal mental lives. But he was less successful in describing the personal, subjective side of mental life or in making the distinction I make here between the generative cognitions of persons and the norms and standards against which those cognitions are criticized, judged, and sanctioned.

Schools as institutions have goals most readily achieved by persons possessing certain traits, and psychologists have been quite successful in identifying such idealized students – high IQ, bookish, middle-class family, and the like – as well as certain races, social classes, and genders relative to whom all other children are considered deviant. Most pedagogical theory is then designed to change the "deviant" students into "ideal" students. Changing the school to fit the children would require a change in social structures generally, an ideal often embraced in the 1960s and 1970s by such social critics as Bowles and Gintis (1976), but rarely seen as a plausible option since.[2]

Bruner (1983), reflecting on the history of Psychology, noted that when psychology embraced sociology to form the Department of Social Relations at Harvard,[3] it became apparent that sociologists such as Parsons envisioned psychology as the handmaiden of social systems. Psychology was to describe individuals in terms of characteristics or traits that would match individuals to ruling social structures much as I have been describing here. Psychology, at least the psychology envisioned by Bruner, rejected that role. Institutions, he argued, must be seen as reflections of human interests, aspirations, and beliefs, not vice versa. Anthropologists, too, criticized Parsonian sociology for its assumption that cultures and institutions are fixed "objective" structures, whereas they may be more correctly thought of as complex systems of social activities (Silverstein & Urban, 1996; Garfinkel, 1967; Brown & Levinson, 1978) reflecting the intentional and interpretive perspectives of individuals, a move that would bring social activities into closer contact with the phenomenological experience of persons.

---

[2] Only in the 1960s and 1970s could teaching be seen as inherently subversive (Postman & Weingartner, 1969).

[3] Forrest Robinson's (1992) biography of Henry A. Murray highlights the conflict between the psychologists who, as did Boring, wanted to study brain and behavior and those who, as did Murray, wanted to study persons.

Although these critics show that personal or social action cannot be reduced to bureaucratic, "structuralist" terms, in my view they fail to acknowledge sufficiently the effect of large-scale bureaucratic institutions such as firms, governments, and schools in which the social structure is much more rigidly fixed through explicit roles, rules, and documentary practices. Hence, as I argued earlier, it is useful to distinguish culture generally from these more formal institutions such as the school, for only then can we recognize the kind of psychology invented for managing, understanding, and assessing those institutions and more importantly for recognizing the limitations of that psychology.

THE PSYCHOLOGY OF SCHOOLS AS INSTITUTIONS

As other complex bureaucratic social institutions do, school systems specify goals, means, and systems of appraisal that, although they depend at every point on the thoughts and actions of individuals, may, nonetheless, be specified and monitored independently of these personal and idiosyncratic experiences of those individuals, indeed may be used to judge the conformity of those experiences with social or institutional norms. Institutions can operate without concern for the experiences of the individuals so long as their performances in specified roles comply with the goals of the institutions. As long as a student's performance exceeds the standard as expressed by the national norms, for example, no one cares what that student really feels or thinks. Compliance with mandated norms and standards determines both whether an individual is judged a success or a failure and whether the institution itself is judged a success or a failure. Indeed, students often express their goals in terms of overcoming of institutional hurdles to their real personal goals rather than in terms stated in the curriculum.

Foucault (1979) examined the origins of such institutions as prisons and hospitals as well as schools in terms of their social function in which power, including rewards and punishments, is exercised. Just as mental institutions create mental patients who can be disciplined and punished, so too schools create students who can be rewarded or punished, passed or failed. Institutions are in the business of creating "normal" individuals where normal is defined by the dominating institutions. Power is exercised in such institutions through their judgments:

The workshop, the school, the army were subject to a whole micro-penalty of time (lateness, absences, interruptions of tasks), and of activity (inattention, negligence, lack of zeal), of behaviour (impoliteness, disobedience), of speech (idle chatter, insolence), of the body (... attitudes, ... gestures, lack of cleanliness), of sexuality (impurity, indecency). (1979, p. 178, cited by Hall, 1999)

Whereas most sociologists emphasize how institutional norms and standards are critical to the effectiveness of an institution, Foucault emphasizes the negative side of these norms, especially the penalties tied to noncompliance. This emphasis takes a sinister turn when we recall that social norms are now defined statistically; by definition one-half of a population falls below the average. For every winner there is a loser.

Many factors are associated with school success, only some of which students have control over and for which they can accept some responsibility. Recall Parsons's distinction between ascribed factors such as ability, race, class, and gender that are essentially fixed by birth and achieved factors such as school success over which one has some control. Attributing success or failure to ascribed factors, although perhaps relevant to equitable social policy, is of little relevance to the learners themselves in that they have no control over such fixed properties. On the other hand, these categories, as do other social categories, confer identity and therefore may not only have political relevance – being dyslexic, learning disabled, or a member of an identified minority may entitle one to special resources – but also undermine learners' willingness to accept responsibility for their own learning.[4]

Schools reward success and punish failure in order to create compliance with social norms. The institution defines the ideal or normal student and then judges everyone in those terms. But this abstracted ideal student is far from any living, feeling person. Moscovici (1993) suggested that there is an unresolvable conflict between personal life and institutional life. Modern bureaucracies classify persons in ways often counter to the wishes and interests of those so classified. An observer at first hand of Soviet repression, Moscovici was extremely skeptical of the move to identify institutional rationality with personal rationality even in modern liberal democracies. As the epigram to Chapter 5 illustrated, what Orwell's Mr. Smith knew contradicted what "the party" said and that difference placed him in serious danger. Moscovici argued that "modernity represents a frantic attempt, doomed to failure, to allow

---

[4] Social theories that attributed human action to social causes instead of "blaming the victim" inadvertently turned whole populations into victims, thereby eroding the very idea of personal responsibility for one's actions.

the rational [normative] pole to assume command" (1993, p. 338). By this account, the enterprise is doomed to failure because it ignores too much of the authentic, firsthand phenomenological experience of the persons who play roles in those institutions. I am less convinced that the enterprise is doomed to failure because, in my view, persons can perfectly well fill the roles specified by institutions without surrendering their personal perceptions and feelings even if, as we shall see, these often come into conflict. Indeed, personal beliefs and feelings are required to reform institutions.

For now, it is important to note only that categories, norms, and judgments are defined by institutions; institutions determine the allocation of resources and privileges; and they have the authority and power to classify people quite independently of the intentions or desires, hopes or dreams of those so classified. This is no less true of being classified as above the norm than of being classified below it. Institutions have the power to tell people who they are. Classifications do more than describe: They carry authority. Teachers, who are required to make these judgments and classifications, are the agents of the school as an institution. But they also know their students as persons and consequently are often reluctant to document failure in report cards. As teachers frequently note (S. Katz, 2001; Olson & Katz, 2001), a child may be succeeding in that she is learning and participating and enjoying her school activities while, in terms of the institutional norms, she is failing. Teachers frequently agonize over whether to honor the objective score or the subjective performance and after much internal conflict, usually compromise, thereby preserving the dignity of the student but lessening the predictive value of the test.

Many of us have thought of education as the honest exchange between a child and an informed, sympathetic adult. My purpose has been to show that this exchange is determined in large part by education as an institutional practice. The school, as do other bureaucratic institutions, creates and applies categories and invites a psychology of persons in terms of those institutional categories. Such categories both organize its practices and explain its success and failure in a distinctive way. Schools, as Schleiermacher (1976) once said, are for turning boys and girls into workers, craftsmen, pastors, and scientists. A century later Elwood Cubberly claimed that schools are factories in which raw materials are shaped into products to meet the demands of life (Bowles & Gintis, 1976, p. 199). Bowles and Gintis offered an institutional perspective on the schools that included a distinctive psychology.

But there is another psychology, a psychology of greater relevance to pedagogy in that it addresses the first-person phenomenological experience of teachers and learners, one part of which derives from the cognitive revolution of the 1960s, the other part of which harks back to the earlier writings of Dewey. That is the topic of the next chapter.

PART III

SCHOOLS AS PEDAGOGICAL ENVIRONMENTS

8

The Rediscovery of the Mind

> Every new idea, every conception of things differing from that authorized by current beliefs, must have its origin in an individual.
>
> (J. Dewey, 1980, p. 305)

Dewey was the first, and perhaps the last, theorist who aspired to address the problems of learning and thinking in relation to social institutions, school in particular and democratic society in general. He posed the problem as the relation between the "child" and the "curriculum," the former referring to the mind, the second to the society, with education the negotiation between the two. Since his time specialization has tended to divorce the social from the psychological. Thus, the sociologists Bowles and Gintis (1976) use a social theory to explain why Dewey's proposed reforms have never been widely implemented – such reforms run counter to social structure; educational reform would require social change, not merely pedagogical change.[1] On the other hand, psychologists such as Piaget chart intellectual growth in universalistic terms while neglecting the impact of social institutions, particularly the school, on that development. Some researchers, notably Kohlberg and Meyer (1972), attempted to extend Piagetian theory to show that the natural product of intellectual growth would, in fact, correspond to the progressive ideals of the normative sciences. Yet the study of human development has not come to terms with society and its institutions. Consequently the attempt to derive educational principles from

---

[1] Bowles and Gintis tie educational structures to capitalist society, failing thereby to notice that schools in socialist societies are essentially the same as those in capitalist societies.

the study of human development is problematic if not seriously misleading. Dewey denied the split; he asserted that learning and development could be understood only in the context of democratic social institutions. Enhancing personal development required appropriate institutional reform. This was the motivation for the progressivist movement. Hence it is not inappropriate to begin the examination of the relation between mind and society with Dewey's theory of education.[2]

Dewey was a product of the Enlightenment with its optimistic view of the future and its belief in the perfectibility of human beings through education broadly conceived.[3] It is tempting, these days, to disparage such optimism; to set goals too high is to guarantee failure to achieve them. It is perhaps Dewey's optimism that allows him to be seen, these days, as the problem rather than as the solution to educational problems, especially in polemics about the basics (Cremin, 1961; Ravitch, 2000). But some such optimism, even in the face of uncertainty, is absolutely essential to developmental and hence to educational theory and practice; if we did not seriously believe that education is the key to both self-fulfillment and social progress, why would we as a society bother? And bother we do.

Dewey well understood the complex relations between government and those governed in a democratic society where institutions, including schools, were seen as expressions of the people rather than as means for social control. And he saw both the process and the goals of education as congruent with those of the society as a whole, namely, the creation and sharing of knowledge for the solution of recognized problems by cooperative means, a process that he took to be more or less identical with that of the advanced sciences in a modern society. Indeed, thinking in the sciences, the experimental method of recognizing a problem, offering hypotheses, empirically testing hypotheses, drawing conclusions, and repeating the cycle, was for Dewey a model not only for thinking but also for education and social change as a whole. And he drew his suggestions for thinking about children, about subject matter, about pedagogy from this general pragmatic model (Dewey, 1980;

---

[2] I myself have made a pilgrimage to the site of Dewey's summer cottage on Sawlor Lake at Hubbards, Nova Scotia, where he spent some months each summer from 1928 to 1948. Ned Norwood of Hubbards Historical Society served as informant and guide.

[3] In this Dewey followed Kant, who wrote, "Man can only become man by education. He is merely what education has made of him" (Kant, 1960, p. 6). Durkheim, too, quoted Kant: "The end of education is to develop, in each individual, all the perfection of which he is capable" (Durkheim, 1956, p. 62).

for recent comprehensive assessments of Dewey's work, see Westbrook, 1991; Ryan, 1995).

As Cremin (1961) has pointed out, much of Dewey's progressivism was a response to the massive industrialization and urbanization that took place in mid-19th century. These social changes rather than ped-agogical ones were the immediate causes of changes in schooling. The changing labor market, increased mobility, and immigration all called for the broadening and liberalization of schooling. Dewey's attempts to "shift the centre of gravity away from the curriculum back to the child" (Cremin, 1961, p. 118) tried to make the schools responsive to the di-verse needs of children growing up in this changing world and taking responsibility for the decisions that affected their lives. His focus on the learner as the agent of social change made his writings central to the progressive movement in education.

Much of Dewey is perfectly compatible with later and more recent work on knowing, learning, and thinking that we associate with such writers as Piaget, Vygotsky, and Bruner and with contemporary research within these traditions. Indeed, his early paper (1972), in which he chal-lenged the behavioristic notion of the "reflex arc" as a model for psychol-ogy, offered in its place the notions of agency and intentionality,[4] can be seen as a forerunner of recent work on cognition. However, two features of Dewey's theory that have been eclipsed by more specialized studies are essential for thinking about education, his emphases on subjectivity, that is, the personal, private beliefs and feelings of learners, and on the social structures and institutions that give mental life its more special-ized and reflexive concepts and procedures. I shall refer to these as the *subjectivity* and *normativity* issues, respectively.

THE SUBJECTIVITY OF EXPERIENCE

Although Dewey was a philosopher largely of the Anglo-American indi-vidualist tradition and, therefore, grounded in the theories of Descartes (Cartesianism), Hobbes, Locke, and Hume, he had also assimilated the Continental influence of Kant and Hegel. The former stressed the me-chanical properties of mind, including the laws of association of ideas and the environmental conditions that caused them. The latter stressed

---

[4] Philsophers since Brentano (1973) distinguish intentionality as "aboutness" from the more limited notion of intentionality as "deliberateness." The former includes such mental states as beliefs and desires as well as intentions.

the nature of the experience itself, its phenomenological feel. Dilthey (Makkreel, 1975; see also Nicholson, 1984) early in the 19th century characterized the Continental view in terms of understanding, *verstehen*, the subjective side of human behavior and culture, and he used this as a basis for distinguishing the modes of explanation of the social sciences from those of the natural sciences. Whereas the natural sciences explain by appeal to natural causes, the social sciences explain by appeal to intention, interpretation, and understanding. Roughly speaking, the distinction to be drawn was that between causes and meanings (intentions), as is vividly illustrated in Anscombe's (1957) contrast between unintentional, that is, causal, statements such as "I am going to be sick" and such intentional statements as "I am going to the movies" (see also Kenny, 1989, p. 143; Davidson, 2001). Psychology as a science studies such first-person mental states from a third-person perspective, thereby treating subjective states objectively in what has come to be labeled the *representational theory of mind* (see Chapter 4, n. 4).

The Cognitive Revolution that essentially put an end to behaviorism introduced rich notions of mental states and mental processes, internal states generated either by external events or by other internal states, often described in computational terms. Whereas all such theories acknowledge that "one learns from experience," experience itself may be thought about in quite different ways. For the behaviorists, experience was simply the initiating stimulus. For the cognitivists, it was the mental state and mental processes initiated by some contingency between internal and external events. The same initiating stimulus could be represented in quite different ways, depending, for example, on one's stage of mental development, on one's purpose, or on one's frame of reference. So experience was seen as subjective. Yet, neither of these conceptions captures what Dewey took to be experience. For him an experience was a conscious mental state, an agent's "doings" with accompanying "feelings," a dimension captured by the expression "what it is like." I know what it is like to be sick, or to fail, or to be surprised, or to understand, feelings presupposed by learning anything at all. The failure to take conscious experience seriously leaves a serious hole in both psychological and educational theory. Neisser (1976) and Bruner (1990, p. 4) both complained that the Cognitive Revolution had lost its direction in that "information processing" had tended to replace the more important topic of "meaning." Donaldson (1996) pointed out that Piaget's concept of experience fell short of capturing let alone addressing "felt" experience – what it was like. And Thomas Nagel (1974), who first used the expression to address the philosophical question of consciousness, contrasted the analysis of a bat's behavior with "what it is like to be a bat." Whereas from the latter we may be permanently excluded, we do have some prospect of knowing something of what it is like to be a struggling student, and modern pedagogy is primarily concerned not just with what students know but also with how they think and feel. Searle (1997), correctly in my view, goes so far as to claim that consciousness is not something to be explained away but rather an ontological given. In this, he is at one with Dewey.

The subjective side of experience thus includes the assessment one assigns to those external events in terms of the emotion or feeling or attitude produced as well as the mental content or belief constructed. The important point to note is that the feelings, emotions, and cognitions are not caused by the environment but rather are produced or generated by the experiencer; we somehow make our own emotions and cognitions. As Keith Oatley (personal communication) pointed out, when we feel an emotion while reading a book, we must recognize that it is we, the readers, who are producing the emotion, not the content of the book or the marks on the page. But whereas in one branch of the Continental tradition the focus on subjective feelings and the structure of consciousness would give rise to phenomenology, for Dewey those feelings were guides to tryings and undergoings, to practical activities in a concrete world.

Consequently, Dewey was not a phenomenologist and he had no sympathy for Hegelian *Geist*, the idealist, nonrealist world of the spirit. Rather he was a pragmatist, which is to say he saw knowledge and experience as the product of practical attempts to do things in the real world. But neither was he an empiricist who saw the mind as a copy or a mirror of nature (Rorty, 1979). Rather he, like Piaget after him, saw the mind as the record or product of attempts to do things. These intentional or deliberate attempts to do or understand things along with the beliefs and feelings that resulted, constituted experience. In this way he adopted the phenomenological concern with the centrality of subjective experience.

Experience, for Dewey, was derived from his conception of experiment, the active attempt to do or make something and to receive feedback bearing on those attempts. "Trying" and "undergoing" as Dewey (1980, p. 146) described them are very much like Piaget's notion of how children go about constructing knowledge; they do not so much become conditioned to stimuli as attempt to control them. A simple Piagetian example is the primary circular reaction in which a child shakes his or her head, notices that a mobile overhead jiggles as a consequence, and then deliberately repeats the head shake in order to restore the jiggling, and so on; control constitutes a kind of understanding. Experience, then, is not something external to the actor; it is not a stimulus, but a response: what the experiencer makes of it in terms of his or her own resources, interests, and predispositions. For Dewey, experience was "more than the passive registering of phenomena; it involved deliberate interaction with environmental coincidents, the consequences of which are critically noted and fed back into the control of future conduct" (Scheffler, 1974, p. 197). Or as Cziko (2000) put it, actions are means for controlling perception.

Dewey highlighted the subjective quality of experience by pointing out that experience was preceded by a feeling of *perplexity* or *puzzlement*, that hypotheses were accompanied by *doubt* and conclusions by *satisfaction* (1978, p. 188), sometimes adding the adjective *felt* to experience. Feelings are produced by the experiencer in the light of what he or she is trying to do; frustration and satisfaction are such basic feelings. Feelings are not simply caused by a stimulus; they are generated as a way of taking or interpreting a stimulus. A milkman in the American writer Thornton Wilder's *Our Town* commands his horse, "Gaddyup, you bleeding cripple," and the horse whinnies, he says, as if he had heard words of endearment, rather than an insult. Even for an old horse there is no identity between stimulation and experience.

Feelings are fundamental to all learning and experience. And although it is unlikely that we could have thoughts that are utterly incomprehensible to others – because all thoughts are formulated in terms of the language and symbols, that is, the "collective representations" of the culture – it is possible that one has feelings, including pains, that are utterly private, subjective, and unknowable by others and yet are real. Thus we can legitimately say, "I can share your pain" only if we, too, have experienced such pain. Feelings constitute a kind of primitive language of experience that provides the basis for the construction of all knowledge. Richard Hughes, the author of the classic *A High Wind in Jamaica* (1928), which contains unrivaled accounts of young children's understanding, commented, "Babies may not have thoughts but they do have feelings." And again, "You can no more think like a baby than you can think like a bee." Feelings, which are sometimes referred to as *emotions* and sometimes as *intuitions*, are the subjective states I am trying to capture here. Babies and other animals, I feel safe in asserting, feel pleasure and pain, desires and satisfaction, puzzlement, and, more controversially, understanding. Without such preconceptual subjective feelings, learning and thinking would be impossible.

Feelings and emotions, of course, are conscious mental states. One cannot be unconsciously frustrated or satisfied. Understanding involves such a feeling; it is the feeling that we have when we solve a problem or feel we have solved such a problem. Without the feeling we would not know when to stop and when to continue. These conscious feelings then lie at the base of experience. Dewey's theory of experience is the core of his theory of pedagogy: "Education might be defined as . . . an emancipation and enlargement of experience" (1978, p. 301). Trying and undergoing with their accompanying feelings and emotions constitute experience and provide the basis for all learning. For Dewey even thinking was a kind of experience, namely, reflective experience. His model of reflective experience was similar to that offered by Bacon's method of eliminative induction, a method "which allows us to transcend our natural cognitive deficiencies" (Gaukroger, 2001, p. 138). And as Bacon did, Dewey characterized them in psychological terms of doubt and certainty:

They are (i) perplexity, confusion, doubt, due to the fact that one is implicated in an incomplete situation whose full character is not yet determined; (ii) a conjectural anticipation – a tentative interpretation of the given elements, attributing to them a tendency to effect certain consequences; (iii) a careful survey (examination, inspection, exploration, analysis) of all attainable consideration which will define and clarify the problem in hand; (iv) a consequent elaboration of the tentative hypothesis to make it more precise and more consistent . . . with a wider range of facts; (v) taking one stand upon the projected hypothesis as a plan of action which is applied to the existing state of affairs: doing something overtly to bring about the anticipated result, and thereby testing the hypothesis. It is the extent and accuracy of steps three and four which mark off a distinctive reflective experience from one on the trial and error plane. They make *thinking* itself into an experience. (1980, p. 157)

As we have seen (Chapters 5 and 6), Dewey's conception of scientific thinking needs to be revised to take into account that science is not only a way of thinking but an institutional practice. Yet Dewey's conception of experience with its marks of intentionality and consciousness, his theory of thinking as a kind of rational problem solving, and his theory of pedagogy as a social or institutional practice are central to an understanding of knowledge, learning, mind, and education as well as of responsibility and accountability. In a sense, the cognitive theories of the past three decades have yet to overtake Dewey. The cognitive sciences have adopted the notion of the mind as a representational system, as we have seen; they have been less successful in addressing the problems of consciousness and subjectivity of experience.

NORMATIVE DIMENSIONS OF MIND

Dewey's conception of mind was tied to his conception of society. In Dewey's theory thinking as problem solving or experimentation was the way that individual minds grew and that social institutions reformed themselves. His theory of education attempted to explain how the social and institutional structures and practices of a democratic society were to be found in and nurtured in the cognitive activities of individuals. He was not only being idealistic in arguing that individuals must learn to accept the responsibilities of living in a democratic society. Rather his point was more general, namely, that minds have the properties they have because of the institutional practices they participate in. Dewey traced the importance of institutions in the formation of mind to a "whole series of German writers" beginning with Kant, who showed that the growth and development of mind derived from "the slow growth of science and philosophy and its gradual diffusion throughout the mass[es] of the discoveries and conclusions" (1979, p. 156). Dewey went on to say, "It was henceforth impossible to conceive of institutions as artificial. It destroyed completely – in idea, not in fact – the psychology that regarded 'mind' as a ready-made possession of a naked individual by showing the significance of 'objective mind' – language, government, art, religion – in the formation of individual minds" (1980, p. 64). That is, people think and act the way they do because they are inheritors of a tradition and are involved in jointly solving practical, social problems. Just how social practices add a normative dimension to the subjective mind remains, shall we say, underdeveloped, both in Dewey and in the cognitive sciences more generally.

Dewey's argument was that democratic institutions are, or should be, expressions of the conscious will of the people as enacted in social practices. Not that Dewey assumed he already lived in a perfectly democratic society; rather education was to equip persons with the capacities and sensitivities that would allow them to create one. Bowles and Gintis (1976, p. 101) point out that Dewey recognized that his goal of education for personal development could be accomplished only if democracy were extended to all parts of the social order. Achieving consensus on social issues, Dewey implied, would advance the giving and evaluation of reasons and allow for the survival of the most valid beliefs, the best actions, and the most promising plans. Dewey seems to have underestimated the difficulties of creating such an environment whether in a school or in the larger society. Moreover, as Ravitch (2000) has pointed out, Dewey perhaps overreached with his educational theory in that he proposed to change both school and society, whereas, in fact, schools do not have the power or authority to change society; social institutional change is a political, not an educational, responsibility.

MIND, SCHOOL, AND SOCIETY SINCE DEWEY

Although Dewey's account of mind and society provides a model for all such theory, three aspects of the account are in need of revision and updating. First, although Dewey recognized the inescapable importance of a personal, private mental life, his account has been greatly expanded in cognitive theories of persons capable of and responsible for their beliefs, intentions, and actions. As I shall say, the mind is real. Second, as Dewey insisted, mind is in some sense a product of social action and interaction. The role of social action in the creation of "collective representations" has been greatly advanced in social-cognitive theory. As I shall say, collective representations are real. Third, for all his concern with assimilating mental activities to social or institutional practices, Dewey underestimated the distinctive properties of scientific thought as opposed to everyday thought and he insufficiently distinguished the school as an institution from society more generally. As I shall say, school as an institution is real.

The Mind Is Real

The rediscovery of the mind is not only an act of rescuing it from behaviorism but equally a matter of defending it from social theories that assimilate minds to social practices on one hand and computational theories that reduce minds to cognitive processes on the other. To say that the mind is real is to embrace a view of persons as individuals capable of performing intentional action and conscious thought and, equally importantly, of accepting responsibility for that thought and action.

It is a view of mind that can readily be traced to Descartes's writing in the 17th century. Descartes's method of "doubt" led him to conclude that the one thing he could not doubt was that he was thinking. He then used this to define the human being as the thinking thing, *res cogitans*:

What then am I? A thinking being. What is a thinking being? It is a being which doubts, which understands, which conceives, which affirms, which denies, which wills, which rejects, which imagines also and which perceives. (1960, p. 85)

What may seem obvious to the modern reader – of course we all think – is important to a cognitive theory that aspires to educational relevance because it dissolves ideas, the stock and trade of all mentalistic theories since Plato, into two parts, the content thought about, and the "propositional attitude" to, that content. The same content or idea can at one moment be firmly believed and the next moment seriously doubted. Beliefs and doubts, as we say, are "attitudes" to content. Thought is allowed by intentionally manipulating such contents and such attitudes. Fodor (1998), a major exponent of this standard view, refers to it as the *Representational Theory of Mind*, adding that beliefs, desires, intentions, and other mental states are computational states that both cause and explain human actions. Learning is updating or changing one's belief, desire, or intention on the basis of evidence. Knowledge is the theory-like assembly of such beliefs into interlocking systems that allow inference and consequently prediction. Furthermore, beliefs cannot simply arise from the outside as Locke might have assumed; beliefs are constructed internally out of the initial states and structures of the mind, hence, the commitment to innate structures as prerequisites for learning and the commitment to hypothesis testing as a means of acquiring knowledge. Aside from its technical precision and its computational metaphor, this view is notoriously close to commonsense or "folk" psychology (Stich, 1983) but, perhaps, none the worse for that.

The main rivals to the form of cognitive theory outlined by Fodor are the theories of Searle (1983, 1997) and Dennett (1978). Searle's contribution to this story is his insistence that one can have a theory of intentionality – that beliefs, desires, and intentions cause and explain behavior – without claiming that the mind is intrinsically computational. He does so by treating intentional states as primary biological structures rather than symbolic structures. Only when put into a public language do they become symbolic and computational. Second, he shows how the states of mind map into the structures of public language. What it is to believe something, a private mental state, can be analyzed in terms of knowing what it is to be in the state of sincerely saying something (see also Austin, 1962; Vendler, 1972). He calls these mental states the *sincerity conditions* for speech acts. To *say* something sincerely is to *believe* that something. To *request* something sincerely is to *want* something. To *promise* something is to *intend* something. Not that sentences precede beliefs; the intentional state, the belief, rather finds expression in the public language. However, to know what a mental state is one must find the linguistic structure that expresses it and then reconstruct the mental state that would make that utterance sincere. There is nothing obscure here; it is simply an elaborated theory of the relation between language and thought. It is merely to point out the close relation between a mental state and a speech act: between *wanting* and *asking*, between *believing* and *asserting*, between *intending* and *promising*. *Want–ask, think–state, intend–promise* are members of a class of speech act and mental state terms–concepts that are absolutely critical to both acquisition of reflective knowledge generally and to critical thinking in particular, topics that we revisit in our discussion of pedagogy.

Dennett's (1978) contribution to this picture is to show that intentional states, that is, beliefs, desires, and intentions, are more appropriately seen as reasons for actions than as causes of those actions.[5] That is to say, like other socially constructed concepts such as the traits we considered in the last chapter, beliefs should be seen as part of social practice, not just as part of the intrinsic biological structure of the brain. Seeing mental states as ascriptions and avowals provides an important route to the normative issues of moral responsibility and free will. Beliefs, like actions, may be expressions of underlying neurophysiological states, but it is only the representations of those neurophysiological states that may be subjected to normative standards of truth and appropriateness, of responsibility and accountability. That is, we can be held accountable for what we choose to do or believe but not for things we are caused to do, even things our brains cause us to do – recall Anscombe's "I'm going to be sick" and the inescapable responsibilities for one's own intentional acts as shown in the Nuremberg trials.

Responsibility and accountability are central to any theory of pedagogy as well as to any theory of schooling. A theory of cognition that

---

[5] Brains cause in some sense but minds provide reasons. In my view the brain events that cause beliefs also cause actions, but beliefs do not themselves cause; rather they provide reasons for actions. This complex topic requires a whole chapter or book rather than a footnote.

fails to address issues of responsibility is of limited relevance to a theory of schooling. The very idea of holding people accountable for their beliefs and for the personal intentionality of their actions in the light of normative standards – the true, the good, the right thing to do – is the universal way that culture impacts upon mind. In some cultures more than others, however: It is a peculiar characteristic of so-called guilt cultures such as ours that we not only value reason giving but create institutions such as schools to see to it that children know and live by the rules, understand that they will be held accountable for violations of those rules, and recognize that there are some excusable ways of circumventing those rules. That is because these rules, known as such, as we saw in the first two chapters, are critical to one's functioning in a bureaucratic society.

Despite these important differences among holders of the various versions of the Representational Theory of Mind, they all equally emphasize the centrality of intentionality to the explanation of language, thought, and action. Furthermore, their analyses provide us with an account of the basic concepts we require for any discourse about education. Indeed, I would be so bold as to urge that if a psychological theory does not address the issues of individual subjectivity on one hand and the normative impact of social standards and norms on the other, it is at best marginal to educational discourse.

Cognitive psychologists, too, are broadly committed to some version of the Representational Theory of Mind and attempt to determine experimentally just what rules and representations children or adults create and call upon in any particular task such as solving the problems routinely given on IQ tests or acquiring the knowledge mandated by the school curriculum. In some cases these rules and representations are attributed to learners to explain their actions; in other cases, the rules are explicitly known and applied by the learners themselves. But in both cases, learning and thinking are characterized in terms of concepts and relations organized in terms of beliefs, desires, and intentions. This is a psychology that addresses persons as intentional, knowledgeable beings who hold the beliefs they do for reasons and who can justify their utterances and actions by appeal to norms of truth, validity, and appropriateness. It is a psychology that sees persons as persons, not as generic roles in an institution.

Whereas the psychologist's vocabulary, then, relies on notions like belief, desire, and intention, children themselves come to apply this set of concepts to their own and others' behavior only when they are

4 or 5 years of age. This acquisition, referred to as children's "theory of mind" (Astington, Harris, & Olson, 1986; Perner, 1991; Astington, 1993; Bloom, 1996; Zelazo, 1999), allows children to see their own and other's behavior in terms of such mental states as beliefs, desires, and intentions. They begin to see themselves, as Descartes urged, as "things that think." The process involves a shift from a situational perspective to a representational one (Perner, 1991). Children begin to assign knowledge to themselves and others on the basis of "informational access" (Wimmer & Weichbold, 1994) and responsibility on the basis of intention rather than observed action (Astington, 1988a; 1988b); to see lies as intended misstatements rather than mere falsehoods (Peskin, 1992); and to keep secrets and play such children's games as hide-and-seek, tag, and Simon says successfully. In so doing they work out the relations among a set of linguistic and mental concepts such as *see–know, intend–act, accident–on purpose, think–know–guess, evidence–reason–inference,* and *say–mean,* all in a short period at roughly 4 to 8 years of age. If schooling is a matter of teaching children to hold beliefs for reasons, it is no accident that school, almost universally, begins around this age.

Such agreement as is found among researchers hinges on the shared Piagetian view that children, as do societies, have to construct their own knowledge on the basis of experience and that those constructions grow in complexity through the process of elaboration and reflective abstraction. Piaget (1962, 1974, 1983) and Karmiloff-Smith (1992) have shown that children's understanding of space, time, causality, and morality can be characterized as a series of progressive cognitive reorganizations that take the child from a narrow, nonperspectival view to a more comprehensive, sociocentric frame of reference.

The Piagetian tradition not only has contributed analyses of how children come to think about a large variety of problems ranging from mathematics to morality, it has redefined *intelligence,* away from the more conventional IQ, a quantitative individual difference notion, to a qualitative account of just what the child or adult is doing, saying, thinking, and feeling. This psychology attempts to reconstruct children's point of view, including why children see things a certain way; give answers of an interesting, if peculiar sort; use language in a certain limited way, ignoring embedding clauses, for example, not only whether, on average, they are better or worse than someone else in a particular domain. Piaget, more than anyone else, changed, I hope forever, the way cognitive psychologists think about intelligence, that is, about how people think. (As we saw in the last chapter, this is not to say that IQ is of no relevance to some impersonal research programs and to some institutional decisions.)

The Representational Theory of Mind shares with Piaget's concepts what we may call an *internalist* perspective on mental development. Cognitive structures are generated by the learners themselves – it is the individual who must build the mental representation out of his or her own cognitive resources. The environment provides only the "nourishment," as Piaget once said.[6] It is agreed not only that there is no way to transmit knowledge to the learner, there may be no need to do so (F. Smith, 1998; see also Chapter 10).[7] It is the learner who has to build his or her own mental structures; learning cannot be simply stamped in by the environment no matter how rich; knowledge is always a product of the learner's constructing models to organize his or her experience. The product of experience is necessarily the child's own, sometimes idiosyncratic, always personal and subjective, at the base of the child's private and personal self. Beliefs are your beliefs, intentions your intentions, goals your goals. Whether you share them with others is, from this perspective, neither here nor there.

In accepting the mind as a real, nonreducible, part of nature, not only are we able to see persons as knowledgeable and responsible and in possession of a private mental life, we gain access to a model of thinking essential to understanding the formation of concepts, beliefs, and belief revision, issues of obvious importance to schooling. However, critics point out that most cognitive theories are blatantly nonsocial: Such theories disregard the role of subjectivity and intersubjectivity in the formation of intentional states (Bruner, 1996); they have underplayed, if not ignored completely, the normative role of culture and its institutions in cognitive growth (Nelson, 1996; Tomasello, 1999); they neglect the ways that public symbols have a formative influence on thought (Nicolopoulou & Weintraub, 1998); and they underestimate the effects of education in general and literacy in particular on cognitive development (Olson, 1970). Such critics insist that whereas beliefs may be private, even private beliefs take their form from the intersubjective agreements, norms, and conventions that constitute a culture.

---

[6] Much to the annoyance of educators who put in many hours teaching just those cognitive structures. But that they are taught is no argument against the view that the learner must construct his or her own representation in response to that teaching.

[7] Frank Smith (1998) pointed out the distortions that occur when policy statements are taken as a basis for curriculum design.

Collective Representations Are Real

Vygotsky (1986) was among the first to raise the alarm about the "internalist" perspective on child development. Vygotsky was a follower of Weber and Durkheim in stressing the importance of society to personal development. Durkheim (1961) argued that society could not be reduced to mere collections of individuals, "that it must constitute a being *sui generis*" (1961, p. 60); that a collective, whether family or nation, could be thought of as possessing a separate level of intention as a "sentient being" (1961, p. 59);[8] and that a person derives humanity from being involved in such social systems. For his part, Vygotsky noted that the cognitive structures supposedly built up in the course of an individual's cognitive development were just those that had evolved historically in a society and either directly or indirectly had been instilled into the minds of growing children through systematic education.[9] There was, so to speak, nothing natural or developmental about cognitive structures! Indeed, he argued that the only reason we can even claim that the development of mind is a matter of increasing rationality is the presence in the environment of the required *collective representations* and institutional structures. What Piaget took to be natural, Vygotsky claimed to be cultural. Vygotsky argued that to account for the importance of such cultural products as language and mathematics, one must appeal to the acquisition and mastery of second-order or cultural modes of representation. Nelson (1996) has extended this line of argument by showing that in acquiring a language, children are learning not only to communicate but to represent the world in a certain, intersubjective way. In learning a language one is learning "the culturally established knowledge systems that she meets through language" (1996, p. 335).

Much cultural knowledge is formalized and taught in school. Bruner (1990, 1996) has long insisted that education is "a major embodiment of a culture's way of life, not just a preparation for it" (1996, p. 13). He sees schooling as an occasion for the meeting of the versions of

---

[8] It was this notion of a "group mind" that got Durkheim into such trouble. If he had distintinguished agency from intentionality, institutions possessing the former but not the latter, he could have escaped much of that criticism.

[9] G. Stanley Hall (1965) is worth a footnote for his attempt to capture in a developmentalist framework the relation that Vygotsky attempted to capture through learning. Hall argued for a theory of recapitulation, namely, that the mind in its internally driven developmental trajectory goes through exactly the same steps that the history of the society had gone through, thus avoiding what for Vygotsky remains a major hurdle, the problem of internalization or appropriation.

the world one builds under the "institutional sway" of the culture and those one builds as a product of an individual history. These versions are elaborated through learning the "toolkit" of the culture, including its linguistic and metalinguistic resources and its devices for "going public," giving one's hunches and beliefs expression in external, formal documents, drawings, texts, and equations. Bruner spells out these forms of expression in terms of modes of knowing – the narrative and the paradigmatic – modes I discuss more fully in Chapter 9. But he also emphasizes the importance of acquiring the skills needed for participation in the major institutions of the culture. As do Vygotsky and Dewey, Bruner sees a continuity between social codes, customs, and practices and their institutionalized forms as rules, laws, and principles with education the meeting ground between the two.

There is a rich literature documenting the ways in which social relations and social activities provide the roles and rules that shape beliefs and confer identity on participants in a culture. Social actions articulate roles that individuals can play: "To embrace a role is to disappear into the virtual self available in the situation" (Goffman, 1961, p. 106). Other cultural psychologists such as Cole (1998), Wertsch (1985), Shweder (1991), Donald (1991), Shore (1996), and Wells (1999) account for the human diversity in terms of cultural diversity, showing that minds acquire their properties by adopting or appropriating the historically developed knowledge systems of the culture. Damerow (1998) offered as a specific case the emergence and evolution of notational systems in ancient Sumeria, arguing that the advanced stage of cognition that Piaget described as "formal" is not a natural and inevitable stage of development but rather the consequence of learning to use the specialized conceptual resources of the culture, including its elaborate writing and number systems. Thus, once a writing system was developed, operating with the symbols of such a system could produce a new level of cognition and with it a new level of social organization. Nicolopoulou and Weintraub (1998) provide a useful summary of this perspective:

> To say that culture plays a critical role in development is to say that systems of collective representations are a reality *sui generis*, and that they play a constitutive role in the formation and structuring of individual representations. This recognition is . . . an indispensable foundation for any serious sociocultural psychology. (p. 220)

Social-cultural theories, including that of Vygotsky, succeed in showing that mental development cannot be thought of outside the cultural patterns and resources of the society. Indeed Vygotskians (we are all Vygotskians these days) tend to regard all learning as social learning through participation in the cultural symbols and social practices of the society. Schooling tends to be seen as just one means among many for influencing social and cognitive development. However, when social–cultural theorists turn their attention to schooling, it is often to accuse the school of an insensitivity to the cultural differences of the children who attend it rather than to recognize the school as a specialized institutional form with its own power, resources, goals, agendas, practices, and professions, all of which need to be addressed in their own right. Consequently, as Dewey did, they have tended to underestimate the school's autonomy, the extent to which it stands apart from local culture and tradition – indeed as providing a bridge across cultural diversity – and the extent to which it has its own patterns of responsibilities and entitlements, as well as its legislated power to execute them. Instead of recognizing schooling as a specialized institutional practice, such theorists tend to see it as continuous with culture (Bruner, 1996; but see Bruner, 2001, p. 201) or as in need of reform so that it becomes more so (Heath, 1999). Neither understanding nor reform is likely to be achieved unless schooling is first recognized as an institution analogous to law, medicine, or science with its own rules, goals, and assessments as we saw in Chapters 2 and 3. Only then, I suggest, will we be able to understand the policies and practices of schooling.

There is one branch of cognitive and sociocultural theory that comes very close to analyzing the cognitive resources central to the peculiar demands of schooling in a modern, bureaucratic society and that is the area referred to by the concept of *metacognition* – roughly, talking and thinking about one's own talking and thinking. In one sense, this is not a new branch of theory. Piaget, through his concept of "reflective abstraction," and Vygotsky, through his concept of "higher mental functions," set the stage for the concept of metacognition, the ability to reflect back not on things, but on one's representation of things. Whereas cognition is "about" the world, metacognition is "about" one's cognition, about one's thoughts, beliefs, reasons for believing, inferences from beliefs, and patterns of beliefs or theories.

Vygotsky was taken primarily with metacognition as a form of cognition "about" language. For Vygotsky, this allowed "conscious control over [one's] own reasoning" (1986, p. 169) and a new level of deliberateness "since the control of a function is a counterpart of one's consciousness of this function. Intellectualization of a function and voluntary control of it are just two moments of one and the same process of the formation of higher mental functions" (p. 167). With deliberateness is a new form of responsibility and accountability, recognized in all the cultures of the world in terms of an "age of accountability," the age at which a child may be held responsible for his or her own misdeeds. The route to this degree of intentionality is what Vygotsky called "verbal thought," the ability to bring our meanings and intentions in line with specific verbal expressions and conversely, the deliberate, planful use of speech. This deliberateness is sponsored by a consciousness of language itself, when, as Vygotsky said, words "become things" (p. 256).

For all his discussion of consciousness of speech, a topic further discussed by Luria (1946, cited by Downing, 1987), consciousness and its cognitive implications remain somewhat mysterious. Vygotsky gives examples of this development and provides an analogy to pinpoint the problem. Vygotsky's examples are drawn largely from Piaget, who reported such findings as the following: A boy of 5 or 6 may be asked whether he has a brother, to which he replies that he does. When then asked, Does your brother have a brother? he denies or perhaps says that they have a sister. Or again, if there are three roses and two tulips, when asked whether there are more roses *or flowers*, the child may "misanswer" that there are more roses because there are only two tulips. When asked, "Do you know your name?" the child provides the name rather than answering, "Yes" (or even recognizing that that is a legitimate answer). When asked which is a longer word, *caterpillar* or *train*, the child chooses the latter, and so on (see Huttenlocher, 1964).

Such tasks require the kind of reflexivity that both Piaget and Vygotsky hoped to explain. Piaget did so by postulating a general shift to "operational thinking," the condition of being able to reflect on such mental operations as class inclusion, a general development not significantly affected by experience or training. Vygotsky argued that what is required is "self-reflective awareness" (1986, p. 170), adding the descriptors "logical" and "voluntary" (p. 166), and argued that such "reflective consciousness comes to the child through the portals of scientific concepts" (p. 171). Scientific concepts are what we may call *taught concepts*. They become special, conscious, and reflective when the learner organizes them into a system of concepts. He saw reading and writing as important to understanding the "influence of schooling on . . . development" (p. 180) by virtue of the "abstract quality" imparted by writing being signs of signs, what he calls the "second degree of symbolization" (p. 181), again claiming that "writing . . . brings awareness to speech" (p. 183). Hence, whereas speech is spontaneous, involuntary, and nonconscious, writing is abstract, voluntary, and conscious.

Vygotsky, here, offers something essential for understanding both development and schooling, but his explanation, namely, that taught concepts have a more articulated hierarchical organization or that they are articulated as "verbal concepts," perpetuates rather than resolves the mystery. A clearer understanding of the normative aspects of formal institutions is critical here. It is the institutions of the arts and sciences as represented in the schools that turn or map the subjective and informal intuitions of the child into the "objective" knowledge of the society. They do so by providing the normative standards and rules in terms of which any informal, intuitive, or subjective belief is judged. Learning these normative standards and rules and applying them are what turn informal knowledge into formal knowledge. Legitimate social institutions judge such knowledge to be sufficiently secure as to warrant its transmission to the young and to hold children responsible for that knowledge. It is the institutionalized forms of knowledge and their institutional norms and practices, including their goals, definitions, explicit methods, and rules for interpretation, that have an impact on children's thinking through the curriculum of school. Teachers literally correct student work. This normative, evaluative dimension is managed through a metalanguage, a language for talking about meanings, assumptions, implications of statements, warranted beliefs, and good judgments; about truth and falsity; about validity and proof. It is here that the metalinguistic orientation to language is called into play. As Donaldson (1978) noted, children in school have to learn to "pay scrupulous attention to the very words," what is said, meant, implied, and entailed. Think again of the primary school game called "Simon says" designed to encourage just that form of attention. It is a form that is massively recruited by writing (Olson, 1977, 1994) in that the written form best exemplifies the normative standard. Learning the normative standard is accomplished only when the child recognizes in the norm something that was already implicit in his or her own practice – when an action that could be "characterized by a rule" is seen as "generated by a rule."

Vygotsky, as did Dewey, provided a comprehensive theory well suited to practical pedagogic thinking. His insistence that the adult mind is the product of social interactions and cultural practices makes education a primary factor in development. But he was less successful in capturing the specific nature of metarepresentations, and for all his concern with schooling, he completely missed the normative functions of the school as an autonomous institution with its own entitlements and obligations, its rules and standards, that give both knowledge and pedagogy its authoritative form.

School as an Institution Is Real

Whereas Dewey linked mind with society, specifically, a mind capable of reflective thought with democratic institutions, he failed to acknowledge that school is not simply continuous with society. Both school and the sciences are institutions in their own right. Scheffler (1974) criticized Dewey as making too easy a link between personal thinking and institutional, specifically democratic, practices. He argued that Dewey's attempt to relate cognition to practice, although salutary, is somewhat misleading in that it fails to make allowance for the autonomy of scientific theories from general problem solving. Whereas theory, like everyday thought, is linked with observation and action, "it is also autonomous; it has a life of its own. Neither the content nor formation of a theory can be fully understood by reference to the resolution of practical problems" (1974, p. 251). There are, Scheffler notes, several traditions of thought that are exemplified in various disciplines, and it is an oversimplification to "filter them through an abstract philosophical schema of thinking as problem solving" (p. 253).

In a similar vein, Scheffler (1974, p. 254) has pointed out an equally important limitation in Dewey's theory. It is a mistake, he argued, to identify the school with the society as Dewey tended to do. Dewey tied the goal of the school to the long-term transformation of the society, whereas, as Scheffler pointed out, the school has an autonomy that allows it "to stand sufficiently apart from the resolution of social problems to cultivate intellectual concerns and cultural standards that have their own worth." In other words, although Dewey succeeded in showing how schooling is related to society, he failed to recognize that schools are autonomous institutions within that society, institutions with their own goals, roles, means, and systems of accountability. So whereas Dewey was completely correct in seeing mind as taking shape in society, he failed to recognize sufficiently the special nature of the school as one institution within the society, an institution that imparts its own peculiar properties to knowledge, language, and mind.

Dewey was not the only one who failed to recognize adequately the autonomy of the school with its distinctive pattern of entitlements and obligations. Not only have cognitive theories and sociocultural theories underestimated the distinctive properties of schools as institutions, much of the current educational reform literature merely takes sides on traditional issues, one side (Ravitch, 2000) attentive primarily to issues of norms and standards of the institution, the other (Meier, 1999) attentive primarily to the subjective mental life of students. In fact, schools have conflicting goals. The school must meet its obligations to the larger society; it must also meet the needs of students as persons with their own rights and responsibilities. The two are not always congruent.

THE WAY AHEAD

Our own subjectivities, our own private as well as shared public beliefs, attitudes, feelings, and meanings not only are important to us as individuals but are at the root of all learning and development, even the learning and development of social routines and of collective representations. Every new idea, as Dewey argued in the epigram to this chapter, must be an idea in the mind of an individual. Collective ideas, in my view, are only metaphorically collective; ideas exist only in the minds of individuals who have constructed their own knowledge and beliefs usually in a social context. What the society does is provide the normative standards whether through social cooperative activities or through the school or other social institutions. These representations become collective to the extent that they are subjected to the same normative criteria, which is to say, evaluated by the same rules and standards.

Mind and society meet, not through any form of identity but through a meeting of subjectivities, including both the ideas and feelings of individuals and the normative standards, including the norms and standards that institutions apply to the products of that subjectivity. Institutions through schools provide or impose standards of correctness, truth, validity, goodness, and beauty on the overt actions and subjective states of individuals. The institutions through teachers indicate those standards for judgments through a metalanguage of truth, validity, and value. Students themselves can acquire this language and the standards expressed by it and in this way become capable of monitoring their own actions and statements. When they can revise their own subjective states to match those imposed by institutions or when they can revise the institutional standards to meet their own subjectivity, they, like us, will be in a position to understand how Erikson's (1962) Luther could not only know the "truth" intellectually but also subjectively "mean it."

9

Understanding and the Growth of Knowledge

> There are two stems of human knowledge, namely sensibility and understanding.... Through the former, objects are given to us; through the latter they are thought.
>
> (I. Kant, 1966, p. 29)

A new conception of mind entails a new conception of learning. In the last chapter I elaborated a conception of mind premised on issues of experience, intentionality, consciousness, and responsibility. I justified this stance on the basis of both its scientific validity and its appropriateness to the educational enterprise. This conception of mind allows teachers to acknowledge their learners as persons with goals, feelings, and beliefs for which learners can take responsibility and, indeed, be held accountable. For teachers, children are not only roles in an institution nor bundles of descriptive traits but real, conscious, intentional, responsible human beings. Nor are they to be described objectively as an entomologist would describe a colony of ants, but rather intersubjectively, in terms of a set of concepts known and shared equally by theorist and subject, by teacher and taught. And finally, it allows one to distinguish the intentionality and personal beliefs of the learner from the normative standards, rules, procedures, and authoritative knowledge represented by the school that are used to criticize those more personal beliefs and that, when mastered by the learners themselves, allow the critical self-reflection we call *metacognition*.

To review briefly this theoretical scheme: We as educators regard learners as being or becoming persons like us, with intentional states – beliefs, desires, and intentions – although for learners, these intentional states remain largely implicit in their perceptions, actions, and speech. These intentional states may become conscious and deliberate with age, experience, and education. Acting intentionally and deliberately entails responsibility and accountability and, hence, entitles one to praise and blame as well as to feelings of satisfaction in achievement and dissatisfaction at failure. Further, acting intentionally is what grants autonomy and freedom to the doer; one is free to the extent that one's own actions are intentional, in one's own control, rather than caused, forced, or prescribed by another. Finally, it is this autonomy that allows the formation of unique personal identity, a self. Thus to be relevant to education, a psychological theory must be centered on intentionality both in the sense of deliberateness and in the sense of mental states composed of propositional attitudes and representational content. The general scheme I have chosen links a set of concepts usually treated separately, if at all: intentionality, responsibility, accountability, autonomy, freedom, and self-fulfillment. As mentioned, this scheme, expressed in a language of action and intention, can be shared intersubjectively by adult and child. That is to say, the learner can come to understand and explain his or her actions in the same vocabulary that the teacher or the theorist uses and thereby take responsibility for those actions. The account will be in terms of what the actors are doing, not what their brains, their genes, their traits, or their background conditioning are doing, but what they are responsibly and accountably doing.

Yet, although such an account is necessary for a general theory of mind, it runs afoul of the entitlements and obligations of schools as institutions. In some sense, schools are responsible for the knowledge children acquire; if children fail to acquire this knowledge, the school is deemed to have failed. By stipulating what must be known the school would appear to deprive the learners of the right to form their own beliefs and to accept the responsibility and autonomy that devolve from that right. This dilemma has been tempered somewhat in educational discourse by replacing the more traditional goal of the school, namely, the learner's acquisition of objective knowledge, with the more subjective goal of his or her increased understanding. Understanding, or apprehension, has become a central concern of philosophical theory at least since Kant (1966) and of educational discourse at least since Dewey. What may be lost in substituting more personal meaning or understanding for objective knowledge are the normative standards of the disciplines. How to incorporate notions of normative standards into a pedagogy of understanding remains to be addressed.

Earlier, I distinguished between personal mental states, what I called *beliefs*, and the knowledge held as valid by legitimate institutions such as science and law. Learners, as have all persons, have the right to believe whatever they like, but institutions such as science, and by proxy the school, have the right to insist that learners "know" the fundamental principles of the discipline whether it be Newton's or Darwin's theory if they desire to be credentialed as physicists or biologists. Hence, one may know the theory of evolution, thereby meeting the requirements of the discipline, and yet not believe it! What "knowing" the theory as part of the discipline entails is understanding it as an explanatory model along with the evidence for and against it and the lines of research sponsored by it, not necessarily believing it. It was recognizing knowledge as an institutional product that gave us the option of strongly distinguishing knowledge and personal belief. But if understanding is to assume a central role in the study of education, it is essential that it have some more adequate theoretical base.

UNDERSTANDING *UNDERSTANDING* AS A SUBJECTIVE MENTAL STATE AND AS AN OBJECTIVE ACHIEVEMENT

The shift in orientation from compliance with an external authority toward that of a more subjective understanding began to take shape in the medieval period when such scholastic philosophers as Anselm and Abelard (Clanchy, 1997) began their debates about action, ritual, and intentionality. Would God forgive one if an act were committed with a good intention but a bad effect? Is a correctly performed ritual efficacious in the absence of the correct intention, if one asks forgiveness without repenting, for example? Abelard went so far as to say that what is in the heart is all that matters because God knows that part even if human observers see only the evil outcome or the outward show. What is in the heart, of course, is one's intention, and it is the intention that counts. Much classic literature such as *The Sorcerer's Apprentice* and much modern philosophy, let alone justice, revolves around Abelard's concern. Searle (1983) relates a story of a man who intended to kill his uncle in the hope of inheriting a fortune and who became so preoccupied with his intention that he drove carelessly, killing a pedestrian, who turned out to be his uncle. Should he be convicted of murder or merely manslaughter? The correct answer: manslaughter, because he did not intend to kill his uncle by running him down. Piaget (1932), too, used such dilemmas to study children's moral development and found that they had an increasing concern with the intentions behind the actions. Whether he would have found the same development in children in the Middle Ages or in children in other societies remains moot.

Understanding, apprehension, and "sense making" have moved onto central stage in much of educational theory, yet the concepts are not well defined. Cognitive theories address understanding as a cognitive state, a matter of assigning new input to a schema, thereby allowing inference; indeed understanding is assumed to occur equally in humans and in computers (Moore & Newell, 1973). Wilson and Keil (2000, p. 97) suggest that understanding is "a cognitive state that remains largely implicit but... entails prediction, inference and memory," which when made explicit constitutes an explanation. But understanding is not adequately described as a mental process for two reasons. It leaves unspecified the normative standards or criteria to be met. Again, how do you distinguish understanding from misunderstanding? Second, the definition makes no explicit reference to the subjectivity of those states, either to their intentionality or to their associated subjective feeling. As we saw in regard to knowledge, both subjectivity and normativity are critical. So if understanding is to have a place in educational theory, we must have a clearer notion of what understanding is and a more explicit account of the criteria one uses in judging one's own or another's understanding. For Abelard this was no problem as God knows the things of the heart. But how are mere mortal educators to judge whether or not someone understands? More serious yet, how do we know we ourselves understand something?[1]

FIVE FEATURES OF UNDERSTANDING

There is a difficult philosophical question that may trip us up at the outset, namely, whether one can understand without knowing or recognizing that one understands. To understand is to meet a social or normative criterion that makes one's mental state understanding rather than misunderstanding. But in addition I would argue that to understand is to know that you understand; understanding, in my view, is reflexive or metarepresentational. This reflexive property is important because how one knows or judges understanding is critical to the school's concern with teaching and learning. The school has responsibility for judging

---

[1] My own view is that we never know that we understand; at best we believe for good reasons that we understand, but we may still turn out to be wrong.

students' understanding and for helping children to judge their own understanding. Judgment of understanding, for both self and other, involves at least four features.

First, norms or standards may be implicit in practice, and such judgment as occurs is based on successful action or successful practice. If you do not fall off your bicycle, you must have mastered the norms of balance; if you answer a question correctly, you must have understood that question. The norm, as we say, is implicit in action or in what Wittgenstein (1958) called a "form of life." Forms of life are more commonly social, that is, practices that we engage in with others.

Consequently, how we judge whether the norms or standards have been met varies from context to context. In regard to language use Wittgenstein (1958, p. 241) referred to forms of discourse as "language games" in which a set of norms or standards have to be in place before one can even aspire to be understood: "That is not agreement in opinions but in forms of life."[2] Of course, these norms and standards need not be explicit; one can understand an utterance without the reflective awareness that one is complying with a set of norms, rules, and standards.

Criteria are not exclusive to using language in a conventionally appropriate way. In some contexts such as apprenticeships, but also in traditional schooling, the criterion for judging competence was a successful performance; the correct performance implies that the subject knows or understands what he or she is doing. A blacksmith's apprentice could shape a rim for a wheel and if it did not fall off, it was successful, and should the question arise, one could say that the apprentice "understands" how to make a rim. The guilds of the Middle Ages added a further criterion. It involved judgment by an expert and granting of credentials. Not only could the rim not fall off, the master had to judge that the so-called masterwork or masterpiece met the standards set by the guild. Similarly, for learning in schools, a correct performance of a memorized text would not in itself suffice; it had to be judged by the teacher as meeting or not meeting the teacher's criterion. Schools, whether through the teacher or through the state, set the criteria that had to be met and student performances were appraised in the light of those

---

[2] Christopher Olsen called to my attention the idea that Wittgenstein's concept of "forms of life" was advanced to cover much the same ground as my concept of "institutional practice." However, I insist that institutions are organized on explicit rules and agreements, whereas forms of life remain relatively implicit, more visible to observers than to the participants themselves.

criteria. Because memorized material is readily judged by the expert, it retains a favored place in the assessment practices of both traditional and modern schooling. Listing, reciting, filling in the blanks, and taking multiple-choice tests are typical practices.

Second, successful performance may be seen not as the goal of education but as an indication of the achievement of the real goal, that of understanding. Understanding, that is, possessing the appropriate knowledge and correct intention, may be seen as more important than the correct action – recall Abelard's emphasis on intention over action. For Kant (1966), as the epigram to this chapter stated, knowledge depends on both sensibility and understanding, the latter required for thought. For Dilthey, early in the 19th century, *verstehen*, understanding, was a kind of empathy or projection of oneself into the characters encountered in history or literature, and for Dewey (1980, p. 343) early in the 20th century, understanding was a matter of "giving meaning" to experience. Understanding not only lay behind correct action; it was to be the real goal of education. Dewey saw understanding as a problem in the organization of one's beliefs: "All knowledge, all science . . . aims to grasp the meaning of objects and events, and this process always consists in taking them out of their apparent brute isolation as events, and finding them to be parts of some larger whole *suggested by them*, which, in turn, *accounts for, explains, interprets them; i.e.,* renders them significant" (1978, p. 272). To understand something, then, is to fit pieces of knowledge into larger, more coherent wholes suitable for further inferences. When the pieces fit, not only do you understand; you know that you understand.

To illustrate the ways in which understanding organizes beliefs consider the case of the European discovery of the New World. When Christopher Columbus realized that the world was round and therefore representable as a sphere calibrated into 360 degrees and that the known world, traveling eastward to Japan from Spain, encompassed 260 degrees, he inferred that sailing westward 100 degrees, some 5,000 miles, should take him to Japan. Of course, we now know that he wildly miscalculated and arrived in Cuba rather than Japan, thereby leading to the discovery of some 120 degrees, one-third of the Earth surface, which had previously been overlooked by mapmakers. Inference as opposed to strict recall is an important indication of understanding available to both teacher and learner.

Third, understanding is a subjective mental state that a learner can experience as a feeling of understanding. That is to say, understanding is an emotion. The learner therefore has access to something largely unavailable to the teacher or judge, this subjective "ah-ha" experience when, as we say, things make sense. Wittgenstein (1980) discounted the importance of these feelings because they can be prompted even when one does not understand but only thinks he or she understands. But Wittgenstein was interested not in experience but in correct understanding, the normative dimension, and feelings are insecure routes to correct or valid understanding. But they are critical to a learner's judgments about his or her own learning. One can have the feeling of understanding prior to actually working out the reasons for a belief, and one can have the feeling of not knowing and be led to make further inquiries. Columbus in fact did not understand, but he *felt* he understood and that was sufficient to set him off on his remarkable voyage.

These feelings, feelings of puzzlement at a problem and satisfaction at its solution, are critical to all cognition. The recognition of a known object is a simple form of understanding manifest in the furrowed brow or the smile of even an infant. These are the feelings that indicate to the learner when to stop or when to continue looking or studying; feelings are not just rewards and punishments awarded after the fact. Rather, feelings provide information internal to those acts (Oatley & Johnson-Laird, 1996; see also Lazarus, 1984; Zajonc, 1984). Feelings are universal, but they are not always acknowledged; nor are children often encouraged to trust those feelings rather than simply capitulate to adult judgment. Much pedagogy goes wrong on this point in that the child is led to take the encouragement of the teacher as the indication of success rather than the feeling of understanding internal to the activity itself. This is, in part, what is involved in what is called *intrinsic motivation*, the satisfaction in completing the task itself, but not only intrinsic motivation is involved but also feelings in general, of being puzzled, of understanding, of certainty, as well as of satisfaction for a job well done. Without attentiveness to these feelings, a learner would lose access to one of the main routes to the control of his or her own understanding and would remain forever at the hands of the judgments of others.

Teachers assume that students can recognize the feeling of understanding when they ask the general and often pointless question, "Do you understand?" In some cases this means merely, "Will you comply?" but in more educative contexts it is intended to appeal to the feeling of understanding. Learning to recognize that you do not understand, especially understand written texts, is an acquired ability, and children often fail to detect inconsistencies in a text (Markman, 1979). Students vary enormously, and many of them have a keen sense of failure to understand. Teachers report of their bright kids, "If they didn't get it, their hands shot up" (S. Katz, 2001). Successful learners, it appears, know when they understand, and that knowledge arises from the feeling of knowing. It is that feeling that leads them either to persevere in their studies or to know when they are finished. Students may need practice and encouragement to learn to recognize and trust that feeling. But, recall, understanding is not only an emotion; understanding has a normative dimension, namely, correctly understanding. In my earlier work (Olson, 1994) I distinguished understanding, with its implication of correctness, from interpretation, with its implication of personal subjectivity. Understanding in an educational context carries this normative standard and implies a responsibility for judging correctness, not only for generating an appropriate subjective feeling, a point that may be lost in inquiry-based pedagogies.

Fourth, understanding involves an appeal to implicit knowledge or intuition; the pieces to be fitted together may not be "at hand" but rather implicit in perception and action. Learning is never simple acquisition but rather the finding of something in one's implicit knowledge or intuition of which the knowledge to be acquired is an expression, extension, formulation, or reformulation. Polanyi (1958), to whom we owe the concept of "personal knowledge," the view that all objective knowledge of the world is grounded in our own interests, perceptions, and actions, wrote, that "In performing a skill we are acting on certain premises . . . which we know only subsidiarily as part of our mastery of that skill, and which we may get to know focally [explicitly] by analyzing the way we achieve success in the skill in question" (p. 162). In Polanyi's examples one learns to ride a bicycle by keeping one's center of gravity within a base described by the displacements of the wheel from the true vertical, a relation not known as such by a rider. Or one learns to swim by retaining in the lungs enough air to displace sufficient water to keep the body afloat, again, a principle not known to most swimmers. Karmiloff-Smith (1992) has called this process of drawing implicit knowledge into consciousness "representational re-description." It is this mapping between intuition and expression in a symbolic form that gives rise to the feeling of understanding. Implicit knowledge or intuition is what provides the "meaning" of a proposition or expression. Learning the formal rules and procedures and explicit knowledge of the discipline does not exhaust or even adequately represent what is implicitly known. To understand an explicit rule one must capture the intuitions, that is, the implicit knowledge and feelings, the "background" (Searle, 1983) that both provides the meaning for the rule and indicates the reason for having the rule.

Wittgenstein (1958, §200), to whom we owe the most careful analysis of what is involved in learning or following a rule, argued, "Knowing how to play a game or being master of a technique does not involve simply knowing rules (if it involves rules at all)," but knowing what the rules are for, what the game *is*, what he called the *Witz* of the game. Strategy in chess, for example, is not just following of rules – a mistake in chess is not just moving a rook as if it were a pawn but of, say, leaving the queen unguarded (Staten, 1984, p. 106). It is that deeper understanding that lies behind, and gives point to, the rules. (I shall return to this point later to comment on the importance of joint intention in pedagogy.)

The critical role of implicit knowledge may be seen in many pedagogical contexts. I shall mention two – learning explicit grammar and learning to read. A grammatical rule such as the use of the objective form of a pronoun after a preposition (e.g., *for you and me* versus *for you and I*) is easy to learn if one has some implicit knowledge of that form (roughly, it sounds right) and difficult to learn otherwise. In regard to learning to read it was long thought, indeed many still think, erroneously in my view, that learning to read could be built up from elementary constitutive elements, the letters of the alphabet and their "sounds," which could then be organized into "syllables" and finally into meaningful units, "words." A more justifiable understanding of learning to read begins at the other end by recruiting the linguistic intuitions that children already possess, albeit implicitly, in their ability to speak. Thus the letter *t* comes to represent the sound that the child can hear – with practice and some instruction – at the end of the word *cat*. It is the implicit knowledge of speech, when analyzed and reorganized into constituents and patterns, such as words and, ultimately, phonemes, that the child contributes to understanding the written symbols.[3] Thus children are not merely being taught to read; they are learning to perceive their own speech in a new way: That is, they are learning how the structures of their speech may be represented by a visual code (Olson, 1994; Homer & Olson, 1999). This important point is summarized by another pedagogical trope, namely, that all learning presupposes prior

---

[3] This insight is captured in "whole-to-part phonics instruction" (Moustafa & Maldonado-Coln, 1999).

learning. In regard to reading, the error has been thinking that the prior learning consisted of the elements of the writing system rather than the knowledge implicit in the prior oral competence of the learner, which could then be subjected to explication, analysis, and reflection, that is, linguistic awareness.

Fifth, understanding involves the holding of beliefs for reasons. Reason giving is the application of normative criteria to the task of judging understanding. In other words, reason giving is the way you know that you understand. Implicit background beliefs constitute a kind of reason for believing, but they are implicit and inarticulate and are more akin to feelings – "The heart has its reasons" – than to genuine reasons. To function as a normative criterion, reasons have to be judged as being valid and as warranting a claim. Only some societies make a fuss about making these reasons explicit in the form of an explanation and subjecting them to criticism. Indeed, the giving of reasons is a peculiarly Western habit (E. Goody, 1978; Greenfield & Bruner, 1966), and a habit important to increasing the "mindfulness" of schooling (Tishman & Perkins, 1997; Tishman, Perkins, & Jay, 1995; Salomon, 1983). Scribner and Cole (1981) in their detailed study of the effects of literacy and schooling among the Vai of Liberia, West Africa, found that schooled children became much more adept at handling metalinguistic discourse, that is, "talking about" and giving reasons for answers to questions, than were their other groups of subjects. Justifying beliefs by appeal to explicit reasons is an important means of certifying those beliefs as valid and for turning informal, commonsense knowledge into what I earlier described as institutionalized knowledge. Equally importantly, it is also a means for holding one accountable for those beliefs. "Why do you think that p?" helps to refine knowledge, but it is also a means whereby the authority can judge and perhaps reject another's beliefs (E. Goody, 1978). This is the key to one of the fundamental revolutions in educational thought, the revolution I shall presently (Chapter 12) describe as the Third Pedagogy, the pedagogy of understanding.

JUDGING UNDERSTANDING

The shift in criterion for evaluating competence from external performance such as memorization to internal criteria such as understanding coincides with a less visible shift in the realignment of authority, responsibility, and accountability that it implies. As we shall see in more detail in the next chapter, this realignment is fundamental to the modern idea of education. It revolves around the question of who is to judge competence. In the classical model of the school, that is, in schools going back to antiquity, it is the teacher who must have both the authority and the responsibility for making judgments about student understanding and student competence. The examination is the most obvious of these means. The school, through its agents, sets the standards and makes judgments about student competence, classifying students accordingly as successes or failures. Foucault (1979, p. 189) has shown how the keeping of the school "register" and the use of examinations not only served the purpose of judging knowledge and understanding but also were important forms of surveillance allowing one "to know the habits of the children, their progress in piety, in catechism, in the letters, during the time they have been at the School" as one 17th-century schoolman wrote. The criteria for judging competence and understanding were in the hands of the educator.

Progressive schooling, on the other hand, rewrote these issues of responsibility and accountability in a fundamental way. Dewey (1980) insisted that it is the student's understanding that is important and that the students themselves must have some means for assessing or judging their own understanding. Progressivism as well as much recent pedagogical writing (Egan, 1997; Gardner, 1999) by emphasizing student understanding has shifted the concern from how adults judge competence to how the learners themselves can judge their own competence and understanding as well as that of their peers. The very point of modern education is to make students conscious of their own beliefs and reasons for believing and acting in order to allow them to be responsible, autonomous performers and ultimately critics of their own and others' knowledge and beliefs. This is especially important in a democratic society, so let us consider this point in more detail.

Progressivism in education is an expression of the democratic goals of freedom of action and expression. It marked an advance over the externalist stance of the traditional school with its emphasis on compliance with imposed adult norms and standards. Yet, progressivism had a blind spot in that it did not seriously address the question of how the criteria for judging a performance were to be set. A pedagogy based on the importance of the students' own judgments must address how students set standards that are both their own and yet acceptable to the goals of the school.

Dewey and the progressives believed that the standards against which performance was to be judged were internal to the practice itself.

To a large extent this is true. Premack and Premack (1996) point out that it is only members of the human species that practice their actions, repeating them over and over until a certain level of performance is achieved, at which point the learner loses interest. Such practice is a form of "play" and may be distinguished from "work," the former involving self-selected standards; the latter, normative standards. To practice implies the presence of a goal or a criterion picked up through observation of others. However, self-selected criteria are highly variable, and students may use ad hoc criteria or relegate the judgment back to the external authority (thus forfeiting the valuable legacy of progressivism). So passing the responsibility for learning and understanding back to the learner, an important and progressive act, poses a dilemma. If it is the teacher's high standard that is involved, it is the teacher who holds the student responsible rather than the student. If the authority is passed to the student, there is no assurance that the student will set a standard sufficiently high to be acceptable to the school or society. Indeed the most common criticism of progressivism is that it sacrificed socially accredited norms and standards on the altar of child-centeredness.

To circumvent this dilemma one may propose that teachers set high standards and students will recruit the energy and resources to achieve them. This is the assumption underlying much of educational policy, especially policy created at sufficient distance from practical contexts of schooling. But if the standard is too high or discrepant from the students' own standard, students will not take it seriously. Students, after all, are not stupid. Alternatively, teachers can set standards that they judge achievable, that is, within what Vygotsky called the "zone of proximate development," but those may fail to meet the state's mandated goals. Neither of these strategies allows the student the progressives' goal of letting the student assess his or her own performance in terms of his or her own standards and goals, the democratic ideal.

I have already pointed to one aspect of the solution to this dilemma in distinguishing between the beliefs held by learners and the knowledge accepted by the society and represented by the school. If the learner is to judge his or her own understanding, it must be against the normative criteria that the learner shares with the teacher. In a word, they must share the norm to be used in judging performance. Knowing and accepting the norm allow the learner not only to experience success or failure but to *understand* the success or failure. Only the latter allows the learner to take responsibility for his or her success and failure.

If students fail to reach agreement with the teacher (or other authority) about the criteria to be used, they may simply ignore indications of failure by labeling the subject or the test as "too hard" or themselves as "not able." On the other hand, if they agree to the criteria, failure may lead to more study, the search for deeper meaning, or the appeal for help from a teacher. Hence, the central question is not whether the teacher monitors standards or whether the learner learns to monitor understanding but rather, how do teachers and learners reach agreement on the criteria to be used and met in making the judgment. This is a matter of negotiating joint or mutual intentions and mutual understanding, a problem that remains largely unexamined in a school context.

Understanding, then, becomes a matter of knowing, and accepting as valid, the social criteria against which any piece of learning or work is to be judged as well as knowing the way to perform an activity in such a way as to meet those criteria. This returns us to our earlier concern with metacognition as an awareness not simply of one's own cognition but rather of one's own cognition *in relation to a norm or standard previously agreed on with the teacher or other expert.* This is the way in which standards become internalized as part of the knowledge and understanding itself. Such joint intention is not easily achieved. Pramling (1996) observed a teacher whose stated goal was to teach children about time. Part of the lesson was spent on making clocks. When asked what they had learned, most of the children claimed that they had learned to make clocks! Unless children and teacher agree on the point of a lesson and the standard to be achieved, learning of the relevant sort is not likely to be achieved. Even to disagree, participants must share some common or joint purpose; otherwise misunderstanding but no communication results. Whether judged by self or other or jointly, different modes of understanding may be appropriate to understanding different things, and it is these ways that I refer to as "modes of apprehension."

MODES OF APPREHENSION

Apprehension, a mental grasping, like the 19th-century notion of apperception, a mental seeing, emphasizes the role of the agent in the uptake and the construction of knowledge. Modes of apprehension are the forms or frames of reference in terms of which children and adults formulate their experience, the major modes of which define the discourses or disciplines that are the concern of schooling.

There are many candidates for the "modes" of apprehension. Academic disciplines are obvious candidates: One learns to think as a physicist or a biologist, and there is some developmental evidence that infants at an early age begin to make the distinctions suitable to these disciplines, distinguishing, for example, between caused motion and intended motion (Carey & Spelke, 1994). Social roles are also candidates: One learns to think as a blacksmith, a manager, a scribe, a researcher, a judge, or a student, and again there is evidence that at an early age children in their pretend play take on different roles they see played out in the lives of adults (Piaget, 1962). Traits, especially primary mental "abilities" or "intelligences" (Gardner, 1999), may be construed as modes of understanding, especially if they are thought of as resulting forms of competence rather than as underlying abilities (McClelland, 1973). Developmental conceptions of intelligence such as that of Piaget offer a series of stages in the growth of competence, each of which dictates a mode of apprehension; one can think in terms of concrete cases or one can think more abstractly and formally. Literary genres such as poetry and prose offer alternative modes of apprehension (Godzich & Kittay, 1987; Feldman, 2000; Bakhtin, 1986; Wertsch, 1991). Donaldson (1992) drew an interesting distinction between intellectual and value-sensing modes, the first dealing with facts; the second, often overlooked, with emotions. All of these conceptions transcend the simple vocabulary of "learning" and "remembering" to address the question of just how learners grasp, interpret, or make sense of the natural and social world generally and, more specifically, of the mandated material and information presented to them in school and for which they are held accountable and, ultimately, hold themselves accountable.

There is an important constraint on the modes of understanding that is dictated by the domain of the discourse or discipline involved. Not any mode will do for any subject. Talk of "learning styles" and of "mental abilities" is sometimes taken as implying that individuals are free to choose a preferred style to address any content. Rather, it is that each discourse or discipline recruits a particular form of learning or cognitive stance appropriate to that domain. This comes to be seen as the method or the mode of thought appropriate to that field. Thus one learns to think as a scientist or a poet or a philosopher or a historian. These modes of thought are an intrinsic part of the domain or discipline and determine in large part what I describe as modes of apprehension.

Within disciplined modes of thought, the latitude that remains is between "content," that is, an emphasis on the "structure of the discipline"

(Phenix, 1964; Bruner, 1960), and "projects," which have an intrinsic interest to the teacher or the students and around which various forms of knowledge can be organized and integrated. Dewey had sought to ground the growth of knowledge in such basic aspects of social life as cooking and gardening: "Cooking becomes . . . a most natural introduction to the study of chemistry" (1976a, p. 84). Gardner (1999), adopting a similar stance, suggests organizing projects around such topics as a Mozart opera or the Holocaust. The integrative and the disciplinary are not alternative methods to the same goal but rather different methods for achieving quite different but equally important goals, and a place for both can be found in schooling. Dewey's contrast between interest and effort should be seen as a corrective to the more traditional view that only effortful learning is educative and not as justification for allowing children to chose their own goals on the basis of personal interest.

But my concern here is not with method (see Chapter 11) but with the primary modes of understanding associated with the disciplined forms of knowledge in a modern bureaucratic society, those modes of apprehension that allow one to organize and reorganize one's understanding in ways that allow inference, that is, allow one to "go beyond the information given" (Bruner, 1973). Bruner (1996) divided these modes into two great classes, the narrative and the paradigmatic. The role of narrative as a mode of understanding has only recently been acknowledged as perhaps the most accessible and most important means of organizing experience into an understandable form (Egan, 1997; Brockmeier, Wang, & Olson, 2002). The narrative mode is an extended version of the intentionalist theory I laid out earlier, the mode that explains in terms of goals, intentions, beliefs, and subjectivity. The wide applicability of this mode justifies the centrality of the language arts and historical studies to the school program. But equally important are the paradigmatic modes of apprehension framed as causal and logical explanations. In the physical sciences these are primarily mechanical causes, in the biological sciences these are functional causes, and in the human and social sciences these are what are misleadingly called *intentional causes*, misleading in that they are less causes than the reasons for believing and acting (Elster, 1983; Carey, 1996).

Whereas these modes may be more or less universal – all human beings have to cope with the personal world, the physical world, the biological world, and the intentional world – these domains are institutionalized as the "sciences" in a modern society, and they pass on to the school the responsibility for preserving, upgrading, and utilizing these sciences. Thus, as we noted earlier, these modes of apprehension are committed to explicitness, to a reliance on evidence, to public forms of expression and evaluation, to openness to criticism and revision, and to maintenance of a close tie to an archival, documentary tradition.

Many of the normative practices of the disciplines are built into the general structure of schooling rather than into its explicit curriculum: its appeal to books; its management of information; its requirement for organizing ideas into logical arguments or narrative structures; its reliance on explicit rules, norms, standards; and its storage of new information in archives, largely notebooks. Other features are built into the course of study, the curriculum, the simplified version of what each of the disciplines takes as essential to performing competently in its domain. But the curriculum often leaves largely implicit the institutional roles (authority, reporter, critic), documentary practices (writing and interpreting of data and reports), and acceptable modes of inference and interpretation (literal, metaphorical) that are critical to these domains. Although these features are embedded in the very nature of schooling generally, I shall consider in modest detail three primary and distinctive modes of apprehension because of their significance to schooling, namely, actional frames, narrative frames, and scientific frames of apprehension.

ACTIONAL FRAMES

Piaget is appropriately credited for showing how action contributes to the formation of knowledge; learning by doing is an exemplification of this idea. Children learn through play and imitation subject to their own goals and intentions. But learning by doing takes on a special form when that learning is under the supervision, that is, subject to the normative standards and authority, of another person. Thus play turns into work when the same activity is subject to the control of an adult. In traditional societies, in what is called the Domestic Mode of Production (E. Goody, 1989), this work of children is supervised by family members. When social structures become more complex, family roles become distinct from occupational roles, and learning those roles, say, learning to be a blacksmith, may fall under the authority of a specialist. When an expert assumes responsibility for such learning, we have the institution of apprenticeships. Apprenticeships differ from play or learning to work within a family context in that they involve a contract that makes the entitlements and obligations more or less explicit. The apprentice complies with the authority in return for credentials. Further, the master is assumed to possess special knowledge or skill that could be acquired neither through observation as a bystander nor through direct practice. Yet the knowledge or competence to be developed is not abstracted from the practice and is largely unverbalized: "Make it sound like this," a music teacher may say to a student as she illustrates the sound on her own instrument. (Ray Jackendoff provided this example.) Although observation and participation are important, knowledge of a specialized craft such as blacksmithing is largely nonverbal and "arises only in the process of work . . . and must be acquired through engagement in that process" (Keller & Keller, 1996, p. 136). Guidance to the apprentice may indicate the criterion to be used such as "That's good" or "It's too cold, Charlie." In learning to make traditional Japanese *mingei* pottery, an apprentice may be told to make ten thousand small sake drinking cups in the exact shape, thickness, and size of the model provided by the master with little advice as to how this is to be done (Coy, 1989; Singleton, 1989).

Although apprenticeships are an important occasion for learning, their relation to teaching is indirect. Few anthropologists report incidents of direct teaching or explanation in traditional societies, that is, nonliterate, nonbureaucratic societies. On the other hand, some writers (Greenfield & Lave, 1982) see apprentice learning as joint activity in which the master progressively transfers increasingly difficult tasks to the learner as he or she becomes competent to do them. Lave and Wenger (1991) and Rogoff (1990) describe the process of learning in apprenticeships less in terms of content transmitted than in terms of the gradual shift of responsibility from master to learner. Other writers (Spittler, 1998; Lancey, 1996) see these informal learning processes as largely self-chosen and self-paced. First, only some children demonstrate the interest and talent that make them suitable for an apprenticeship, and, second, novices take up more and more responsibilities on their own initiative rather than on the initiative of the master. It is the fact that learning is largely self-initiated that guarantees that the learning is attuned to the learner's experience rather than that the master adjusts the tasks to fit the learner's "zone of proximal development." E. Goody (1989) points out that when apprenticeships are institutionalized, that is, turned into explicit practices and procedures, these guidelines rarely mention any teaching but rather specify duties and criteria for promotion. Consequently, traditional apprenticeships provide a limited model for schooling. It appears that little teaching is involved in these contexts;

the learning is largely self-organized and self-paced. When I consider the history of schooling in the next chapter, I will refer to such self-paced learning as *Stage Zero*.

However, even the most bureaucratic forms of expertise such as those required to participate in the institutions of science and law require some familiarity with these actional frames. Learning to be a lawyer, as we saw earlier, is not just learning the formal rules and procedures, that is, reading the law and writing briefs, but soaking up the practices of a law firm and the courts, seeing how things are done, largely by observing and overhearing. Learning to be a scientist is in part learning to judge what is likely to work in an experiment, how long an experimental subject will take to perform a routine task, what kinds of questions are tractable, what is likely to work, what evidence is likely to convince, and many other small details picked up through spending time in a research group or in a laboratory. These competencies are difficult to assess via written tests.

NARRATIVE FRAMES

Martha Nussbaum (1992), in her *Love's Knowledge*, explored the relation between philosophical ethics and the practical judgments of particular individuals as depicted in narrative literature. The philosophical link to literature arises from her conviction that "certain truths about human life can only be fittingly and accurately stated in the language and forms characteristic of the narrative artist" (pp. 4–5). Each human life is lived in its own particular time and place and in its particular relations to other particularly situated individuals. This is the stuff of narrative. Even ethical judgments, which are usually examined in terms of abstract philosophical rules and principles, when explored in narrative may be better understood in terms of the particular feelings and beliefs of unique individuals. Amsterdam and Bruner (2000) examined the relations between the law and the particular cases before the law in terms of constructing a plausible narrative. Narrative, then, is especially suited to capturing and expressing the insider's view, the subjectively experienced life of an individual as a particular if not a special case.

Nussbaum argued that understanding particular individuals, whether in fiction or in real life, is rooted in one's own particular experience of life. We understand others in terms of what it must feel like to be that person. Thomas Nagel's (1974) analysis of "what it is like" argued that we can have no idea of what it is like to be a bat because we have nothing to compare it to in our own experience. Our grasp of what it is like presupposes some experience of ours to which that of the bat could be related. It is the nature of that personal experience, that subjectivity, that can become the focus of narrative. As we read a novel, for example, we sympathize or empathize or distance ourselves from the characters in the fiction. We understand how Dorothea felt when she discovered that Casaubon was a disastrously failed scholar because we have made such a discovery ourselves or can imagine ourselves making such a discovery or, worse still, being discovered.[4] The feelings, as Keith Oatley (2000) has pointed out, are our own. It is we the readers who experience whatever emotions we can generate but we can then ascribe them to characters.

These feelings are our own subjective mental and emotional states that can be occasioned by particular settings. Dorothy Parker's *Big Blonde* (1942), in seeing a horse fall on the icy street, imagines how it feels to the horse because she knows how it would feel to her. Our reading about Big Blonde's seeing a horse fall on an icy street allows us to know how she feels because we, too, have felt lost and alone. In each case our understanding is premised on empathy, our own feelings called out by the narrative. Narrative is well adapted, perhaps uniquely adapted, to the exploration of our own and others' subjective states.

Further, it has been argued that the rich inner lives of individuals are a direct consequence of the invention of narrative fiction. That is, the exploration of feelings by such writers as Stendahl, Proust, Woolf, and James leads us as readers to the clarification and differentiation of our own feelings. Literature thereby contributes to a growth in subjectivity.

As we saw earlier, all learning is based on the subjective feeling states or intuitions that the technologies of the cultures may express. These feelings and subjective states are what the learner contributes to the learning process. Further, certain cognitive structures suitable for the perception of motion, location, number, and identity (Carey & Spelke, 1994) may be based on feelings occasioned by redundancy (habituation), novelty (surprisingness), recognition (familiarity). It is sufficient to note that without some subjectively held feeling we would have no basis for judging or experiencing *what it is like*.

---

[4] Keith Oatley tells me that when George Eliot was asked who the model for Casaubon was, she made a fist and struck herself on the chest.

It is not only narrative that can explore subjectivity. Although as Montefiore (1994) has pointed out, "The full truth of human particularity can never be captured in terms of universal discourse alone" (p. 106), the concepts, by means of which the subjective mental states of individuals are referred to and described, may be made part of the abstract sciences. These subjective states are introduced into the sciences through the theory of intentionality, and when intentionality itself becomes the object of discourse, we refer to it as the theory of mind or *folk psychology*, itself a domain of considerable empirical research.

Egan (1997) has elaborated greatly on this narrative mode, showing that there are at least four distinctive versions of the narrative mode. These versions not only are ordered historically but may be "recapitulated" in the interpretive understanding of children as they grow older. He describes these modes as folk, heroic, romantic, and ironic, and he sets out in some detail how these alternative narrative modes can explain the appeal to young children of, in turn, Goldilocks, Superman, and the *Guinness Book of World Records*. He then elaborates on how these modes can be exploited in educational settings. Spufford (2002) too has advanced a fascinating developmental account of children's reading preferences around such integrating themes as the forest, the island, the town, and the school.

PARADIGMATIC MODES OF APPREHENSION: CAUSAL MODES, FUNCTIONAL MODES, INTENTIONAL MODES, AND THE PROBLEM OF CONCEPTUAL CHANGE

Scientific modes of apprehension have at their core basic conceptual systems, or "theories," composed of sets of concepts representing entities along with causal relations among those entities (Carey, 1996). Conceptual systems are theory-like in that they are composed of a set of categories or concepts with "ontological commitments"; that is to say, the concepts refer to something other than themselves and may be judged true or false of that something. Second, the concepts are related by "causal relations" that may then serve explanatory purposes. Basic types of causal relations were first enumerated by Aristotle; the primary ones were mechanical or physical causes (A causes B), functional causes (A in order to B), and intentional causes (A gives a reason for B). Entities with causal relations among them are known even to young children in terms of expectancies about the permanency of objects, their number, and their causal interactions with other objects. These expectations and understandings then provide the basis for the explicit sciences studied in the school. However, a major problem arises when students are expected to shift from one kind of causal explanation to another as such shifts constitute a shift in frame of reference.

Mechanical Causation (a.k.a. Humean, after David Hume, Causes)

Children enter school with strong intuitions about force, motion, and acceleration, but those intuitions are often nongeneralizable and hence out of tune with the general causal laws taken as known by the adult society. Children think of force as something they can do or apply to a table but fail to acknowledge that the table exerts an equal and opposite force on them (at least so Newton's third law tells us). How children move from one frame to the other is a fascinating and much discussed issue in what has come to be called the "conceptual change literature" (di Sessa, 1996, 2000; Carey, 1996; Schauble et al., 1991; Driver et al., 1994).

An equally puzzling problem for children (and many adults) is the understanding of light. Again the problem is that their intentionalist intuitions lead them astray. Children associate light with looking and seeing and attribute to light the properties they know about seeing. Piaget (1974), Roth and Anderson (1988), and Shapiro (1994) all reported that children think of vision as a passage of light from the eye to the object rather than, as Newton's optical theory postulates, from the object to the eye. Thus, experimenters report that children are quick to volunteer that they "cannot see through a brick wall" but are reluctant to grant that the more correct expression is that "light cannot pass through a brick wall." Similarly, when asked how light permits one to see an object, a tree, for example, children tend to say, "The Sun shines on the tree and we look at the tree." In school, on the other hand, they are taught that the Sun shines on the tree and the tree reflects the light into our eyes. Consequently, they cannot see anything wrong with the possibility, for example, of Superman's X-ray vision. They continue to believe, as do many adults, that the light comes from the eye, not to the eye. This so-called misconception is not simply a developmental one. Historically, there seems to have been a lack of understanding of the role of reflected light in vision. Illich (1994) in his discussion of medieval modes of thought points out that in 12th-century miniature paintings,

the painter neither paints nor suggests any light that strikes the object and then is reflected by it. The world is represented as if its beings all contained their own source of light. Light is immanent in the world of medieval things. (p. 19)

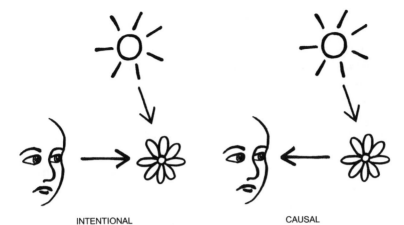

INTENTIONAL   CAUSAL

FIGURE 4. Children think that the light passes from the eye to the object rather than from the object to the eye.

That assumption, furthermore, seems to have carried over into the 17th century. N. Poussin, a renowned 17th-century French painter who in addition wrote about painting, said:

Once you have received your painting...adorn it with some framing, for it needs it; so that when gazing at it in all its parts, the rays of the eye are retained and not scattered outside. (1911, p. xx)

The "rays of the eye" are just what children seem to assume in explaining vision. These "rays" are just what give credibility to Superman's enhanced X-ray vision. Perhaps it is somewhat misleading to call this a misconception. Rather the participants are talking/writing about different things, one about seeing, an intentional act; the other about light, a natural entity. To meet the normative standards of the society, children will have to make the necessary distinction between intentional and causal explanations (see Figure 4). To the extent that educators recognize the problem as one of changing frames of reference, they will be in a position to aid students in meeting the normative standard.

Functional Causes

Biology as a science, too, has postulated entities related by causal laws, although in this case they are functional laws, namely, how certain organs carry out a function. Here a favorite example is how plants "make" food or whether rivers are "living" things. Here, too, fascinating research with school-aged children has revealed the difficulty they have in seeing plants actually make food, especially when, in the garden shops nearby, they frequently see bags of "plant food." Children assume, correctly, that just as they need food to survive, so too, do plants. But they also assume, falsely, that just as our food is supplied from a source outside us, so too is the food for plants, thus not grasping that plants actually manufacture their own food through photosynthesis.

Deciding what objects and events to treat as falling under mechanical, biological, or psychological laws is not immediately obvious; nor is sorting them out, a capacity that develops with age and experience – it requires the mastery of a mature science. In the course of carrying out adult education programs for the empowerment of women in rural India, Ghose (2001) encountered a clash between traditional and biological ways of thinking about living things, a concept central to modern biology. At stake was the women's belief that soil and rivers belong in the category of living things, "Just as human beings require air, water, and food to keep alive, soil too requires the above" (p. 311). On rivers, the discussion ran as follows:

> TEACHER: Which of you think that soil and rivers are living? [All the learners except one raised their hands.] Why do you think they are living?
> STUDENT: They both give life – our grain, plants, forests grow in soil. Rivers give us life-giving water. Our mothers give life.
> TEACHER: It is true that they are life supporting but that does not mean they are living themselves.
> STUDENT: But if soil did not have life it would not produce life. Rivers grow. They grow in the monsoons and shrink in the summers. They do give birth to other rivers. (p. 311)

The teacher soon noticed that the discussion was not fruitful, that the traditional classifications were not the same as the scientific ones. "Learners, 'til the end, were far from convinced that the categorization we were trying to suggest had any value or validity.... Their beliefs that earth and river are 'life-giving' and 'mothers' could not be separated or broken down into components such as 'river is made of water and water is non-living.' Humanizing or giving things human attributes was integral to their language use – branches are children, sap is blood . . . and the rustling of leaves when a tree is being cut, are cries of pain" (p. 312).

What we Westerners call *animism* is a matter of using one kind of cause, intentional cause, where the abstracted science of biology has settled on another kind, namely, functional cause. What is required is a shift in frame of reference, from one kind of cause to another kind of cause, and with it a reconceptualization of the entities thus related by the shift. Again it is not so much misconception as talking about different things, the world one acts on and lives in and the world ordered by distinctive causal principles as determined by an institutionalized science.

Intentional Causes

Intentional explanations have been of interest to a long line of philosophers going back to Aristotle's "final cause." The German philosopher Wilhelm Dilthey (Makkreel, 1975; Nicholson, 1984) used his theory of understanding, *verstehen*, as the basis of the distinction between the natural sciences, which are directed at causal explanations, and the human sciences, which are directed at intentional explanations. For Dilthey (and for me) they are strictly different: Mechanical causes of the natural sciences are subsumable under strictly causal laws: if one, necessarily the other – if pressure increases, volume decreases. The intentional causes of the human sciences are better construed as reasons for acting or reasons for believing. One important reason for believing is the evidence available. Consequently, children's understanding of evidence is one indication of their growing comprehension of explanation generally (Astington et al., 2002; Kuhn, 1991, 2000; Ly, 2001). Beliefs, rather than causing actions, provide reasons or evidence allowing one to decide what to do or what to believe (Norris & Phillips, 1987). Actions, as we say, are considered rather than merely habitual. Consequently, developmental psychology in many cases may have to content itself with the explanation of actions in terms of beliefs and desires rather than in terms of causes (Keil & Silberstein, 1996; Keil & Wilson, 2000). I discussed the gap between causes and reasons in Chapter 8.

Even if behaviorism is dead, empirical psychology remains split between those who search for strictly causal explanations and hence advert to genes, neurology, habits, and dispositions, traits and abilities, and the like, and those who regard people as being rational, who see them as having reasons for acting, as being capable of revising those reasons on the basis of evidence and even of subjugating personal desires to duty. When the latter become teachers, they pass on this acknowledgment of intention and responsibility to the young.

Conceptual Change

The correct diagnosis of the problems facing learners in the preceding three cases has been suggested by Carey (1996), who traces the difficulty to children's difficulty in distinguishing forms of causality and correctly assigning them to their appropriate domains. Forms of causality in turn designate the entities that can enter into those selected causal relations. Water shifts from something to quench one's thirst to a chemical; rivers change from a mode of existence to water in motion; light changes from something we see with to electromagnetic energy. Children's intuitions are often premised on their understanding of themselves as intentional agents, an intuition not easily surrendered even by adults (although the behaviorists succeeded in doing just that). Intentional agents think about things, do things, have reasons, and cause things to happen. Force is the energy an agent applies to open a door; food is a resource an agent prepares and eats; light is what must be present for a person to see. In each case, the solution preferred by the student is an intentional one, relying on intentional causation. In fact, in the history of the sciences one finds similar patterns of conflation of mechanical, functional, and intentional causes – alchemy with chemistry, astrology with astronomy, living things with moving things such as rivers (Toulmin & Goodfield, 1965).

What school requires of children is that they allocate intentional explanation to its correct domain, namely, explaining human action and interaction, and take an objective stance to mechanical and biological aspects of nature. The appropriate stance is defined by the authorizing institutions. How children achieve this understanding is an ongoing scientific question; my hunch is that if the role of intentional explanation became explicit and conscious, children would be in a better position to distinguish such intentional causes from the mechanical and functional causes needed for the natural sciences. To date, neither in school nor in educational theory is the intentionalist theory explicitly addressed to state either its importance for psychological explanation or its inappropriateness for explanations of mechanical or functional systems.

CURRICULUM AND POLICY

Whereas learning, thinking, and understanding are subjective mental states and hence addressable only in terms of a theory of intentionality, institutions such as the school act on the basis of policies that average out these intentional states so as to specify the goals of the institution and the procedures adopted in causal terms. Thus the policy of the school can specify the number of credits required or the years of study or the criteria for admission or graduation; they cannot and need not spell out these goals in terms of the subjectivity of the learners. In this way, the causal psychology I disparaged earlier as inappropriate for pedagogy may nonetheless be useful for general policy decisions. The goal of increasing the number of engineers in the society may be addressed in terms of programs and credentials and the data on the successfulness of 3-year as opposed to 4-year programs without a concern for subjective states such as feelings and understandings of the learners. But in doing so, planners must leave a space for those concerns to be addressed by the schools and teachers who actually work with the students as these are critical to both their learning and their life. This is not to say that policy could not be usefully rewritten in intentionalist terms rather than in brute, causal ones, a possibility pursued in Chapter 14.

10

Some Preliminaries to the History of Schooling

> Every time that the system of educational methods has been profoundly transformed, it has been under the influence of one of those great social currents the effect of which has made itself felt through the entire collective life.
>
> (E. Durkheim, 1956, p. 132)

Once persons and institutions and their respective psychologies have been distinguished, it comes as no surprise that there are two quite different histories of schooling that could be formulated. The first, appropriately thought of as a history of schooling, examines the creation and evolution of the school as an institution in response to large-scale social change. The second, more appropriately thought of as the history of pedagogical theory and pedagogical practice, examines how pedagogical interactions between student and teacher have changed over time. The first history examines the realignment of goals and purposes of the school, whereas the latter tends to take for granted those goals while searching for more effective means for achieving them. The history of schooling in the first sense is the concern of this chapter; pedagogy, of the next two.

School reform is, mistakenly in my view, thought of as primarily a matter of finding improved pedagogical methods or higher standards, mistakenly, because the invention of schooling and changes in schooling reflect the changing conceptions and goals of powerful institutions more than the effectiveness of the pedagogies involved. Consequently, this chapter argues that the very establishment of schools, granting them authority over children and mandating the achievement of certain goals, is by far the most important development in the history of education. Methods are, by comparison, of minor significance for policy although of considerable significance to local teaching practices. Although schooling as an institutional practice has become almost universal, it has received little systematic attention, at least within the reform literature (Tyack, 1995, p. 209), whereas pedagogy as a method for advancing human development has over the past half-century been subject to repeated calls for reform, often with little effect (Ravitch, 2000), as well as to extensive research and theory, again without obvious effect (Lagemann, 2000), as we saw in the first chapter.[1]

As autonomous institutions, schools have entitlements and obligations, often accompanied by a relentless barrage of criticism; as long as schools are seen as meeting those obligations, they continue to receive a steady flow of candidates and resources. Historically, the obligations of the school were defined in terms of larger social needs such as the continued successful functioning of craft, church, or state. Schools were entitled to support as long as they were seen as serving those larger interests.[2] Just what those interests were and how they were spelled out in terms of goals and available resources account for much of the history of schooling.

A HISTORY OF SCHOOLING AS AN INSTITUTIONAL PRACTICE

Whereas pedagogical theory has, over the past century, become more child-centered, schooling as an institutional practice appears to have changed little for a millennium. Schools take learners, usually children, and by hook or by crook (pedagogy) train them for participation, whether as experts or laypersons in the dominant institutions of the society. As those institutions are literate ones, educational activities tend

---

[1] Ravitch's (2000) impressive history of educational reform makes no distinction between the history of schooling as an institutional practice and the history of pedagogical practice, as I do. Consequently, Ravitch concluded that progressivist reforms failed to advance learning, whereas I would interpret it as the attempt to liberalize the ownership and consequently the purposes of education. Further, I am less sanguine than she is that one can infer a close link between the rhetoric of reformers and what actually goes on in schools. Schools are largely impervious to reform.

[2] Winner and Cooper (2000) have shown that education in the arts is often, inappropriately, justified on the basis that it is instrumental in advancing general academic achievement. Rather, they argue, the arts deserve a place because they are an intrinsic part of human culture.

to be organized around reading, reciting, reckoning, and interpreting critical texts, and at the highest levels contributing to a written archival tradition. Such changes as occurred reflected the changing purposes and goals of those who institutionalize, own, operate, or otherwise control the schools. These goals are the obligations taken on by the school as the basis for its entitlements. Realignments of these goals or obligations have produced the major shifts in schooling as an institutional practice. More subtle changes are the result of local knowledge and expertise summarized by the notion of professionalism – knowing what works in the local context. I will sketch in a very preliminary way seven major shifts of schooling as an institutional structure: the invention of schooling, schooling as the training of elites for the society, schooling in the service of the church, schooling in the service of the nation-state, schooling in the service of a democracy, and schooling in the service of the bureaucratic society and global economy. As the very idea of schooling is the most critical of these shifts, whereas the others are expressions of the currently predominant social concern, whether heaven, the nation, the person, or the economy, I shall devote most attention to it that idea of the need for schooling.

STAGE ZERO: THE PREHISTORY OF EDUCATION: LEARNING WITHOUT TEACHING

Schooling is not only a matter of who takes responsibility for learners, whether family, church, or state, for example, but the very purpose of institutionalizing child rearing. The school as an institution takes responsibility for children's learning, a responsibility that entitles that institution to resources such as funds and status. This in itself constitutes the fundamental schooling revolution. Whereas the child's development beyond infancy may have been at one time largely the child's own responsibility, with schooling that responsibility has been co-opted by or assigned to a public institution. Schools take responsibility not only from parents but from the learners themselves. This is best seen by considering teaching and learning in noninstitutional contexts, specifically, among higher primates and in human nonschooled societies. I begin with humans' nearest kin, the nonhuman primates.

Although humans and nonhuman primates are from some perspectives extremely similar, sharing not only some 99% of the genetic code but also many social practices, there are important differences.

These differences are sometimes attributed to the fact that humans have language, certainly an important difference; sometimes to the fact that humans have special social understanding (Byrne & Whiten, 1998); and sometimes to the fact that humans create and transmit an acquired culture, such as tool making and tool using, across generations (Tomasello, 1999). All three, language, social understanding, and tool making, are combined in the systematic influence across generations that we think of as the transmission of culture, roughly speaking, through education.

Whereas some have suggested that primates have an "instinct to teach" (Barnett, 1968), Premack and Premack (1996) have argued that pedagogy, the teaching of one individual by another, is a uniquely defining feature of the human species. It is this pedagogy that is said to make culture and history possible. Through a comparison of many different species, they concluded that teaching, the deliberate attempt to influence the actions of another, along with practicing, the deliberate repetition of an action in the attempt to achieve a certain standard of performance, and speaking a language all occur together. They go on to say that although an anthropology of pedagogy remains to be written, the preservation and transmission of culture across generations are the basic characteristics of humans that explain the origins of culture and the development of a mental life. However, pedagogy, as teaching, is an intentional act by the teacher, and it is possible that culture is preserved and extended generationally not primarily by the actions of the teacher but by the intentional learning of the child. That holds particularly for those aspects of culture of which knowledge remains largely implicit – language, social relations, and practical activities.

Education in the broadest sense is coterminous with human culture – without some means of preserving accumulated knowledge across generations, culture could not exist (Tomasello, 1999). The means of preserving this accumulated knowledge, as mentioned, are conventionally seen as the product of the intentional efforts of the adults to pass this knowledge on to the young. Humans are said to be distinctive in their recognition of ignorance in others and in their competence and willingness to help pass on their more elaborated knowledge. Some have claimed to observe the basic forms of teaching in higher primates. However, although deliberate attempts at teaching are common in institutionalized schooling, they are less common, if they occur at all, in noninstitutionalized human cultures and occur not at all among nonhuman primates. Justification for this claim is based on the now massive work on culture and cultural transmission in nonhuman primates and the equally important work on learning in some traditional human societies.

Consider first the case for teaching among nonhuman primates. Dobzhansky and Montagu (1947, p. 589) argued that "educability is truly a species characteristic of *Homo sapiens*." More recent writers concur, arguing that a major difference between apes and humans is the existence of culture and that teaching is the means of passing it on to succeeding generations (Bruner, 1972). In an authoritative review of this work, Tomasello (1999) concluded that there are important differences between primates and other mammals as well as between nonhuman primates, such as chimpanzees and gorillas, and human beings as well. Mammals, Tomasello reports, "comprehend and cognitively represent spaces and objects," including other individuals of their species and the dominance and affiliative relations among them. As do other mammals, primates understand their relations to others of their species, but they go beyond that to understand secondary relations between those others such as who is the mother of whom. Primates have even been known to retaliate against the relative of an enemy, a kind of vendetta.

The watershed between nonhuman primates and human ones, Tomasello argues, is the unique ability of humans to recognize and impute intentional states to themselves and others and, consequently, to establish joint attention and joint intentions. Nonhuman primates are "intentional and causal beings; they just do not understand the world in intentional and causal terms" (1999, p. 19). Children's ability to recognize intention in self and others would account for the fact that they, unlike other primates, can readily and successfully imitate the actions of adults. Whereas other primates may recognize objects and motions and anticipate what is likely to happen next, they do not see that motion as an intentional action, of someone doing something in order to achieve a goal, and consequently they do not imitate that action.

Again, this is somewhat counter to the commonsense idea "Monkey see, monkey do," namely, the belief that monkeys and apes imitate. In fact, they may copy actions, but they do not, strictly speaking, imitate them. Imitation, the grasp of the relation between the goal of the action and the means for its achievement, escapes all but the most advanced, hand-reared apes, whereas it is trivially easy for 18-month-old children (Meltzoff et al., 1999).

This limitation is demonstrated in several studies summarized by Visalberghi and Limongelli (1996) in which apes, capuchin monkeys, and young children were provided with a desirable object, a peanut in a horizontally fixed plastic tube, and various tools, some of which could be used to poke the peanut from the plastic tube. Some of the available sticks were too short or too thick and so on. In some cases the successful action was demonstrated to the subjects by a human adult. Both apes and capuchin monkeys eventually succeeded in such tasks but with much trial and error and little evidence of imitation. In one task, for example, all four of the chimpanzee subjects, the "cleverest" of all nonhuman primates, behaved at chance levels for 70 or more trials, banging around with a stick in every imaginable way, whereas 2-year-old children seem to grasp the solution from the earliest trials. Tomasello summarized such research by concluding that humans are unique in their ability to imitate the actions of adults because they perceive the actions of adults in intentional terms, that is, as trying to achieve some goal by some means. This understanding is well in place by the time a human infant is 2 years old. And although human children can distinguish goals from means at about 2 years, it will be a further 2 years or more before they understand the prior intentions and beliefs of themselves and others, that is, before they acquire a theory of mind.

The absence of true imitation, imitation in which there is some understanding of goals and means, corresponds to two other characteristics of nonhuman primates, their inability to form joint intentions required for understanding gestures and other symbols, and the almost complete absence of attempts at teaching. In spite of such impressive observations as Jane Goodall's mother chimpanzee's apparently helping its infant to fish for termites with a straw or Kawamura's potato washing by Japanese macaque monkeys, Tomasello concluded that the learning skills of chimpanzees "are not sufficient to maintain . . . cumulative cultural evolution" (1999, p. 36). What permits the latter, he argues, is that "in all human societies there are some things that adults feel they need to help children to learn" (p. 80), and again, "One of the most significant dimensions of human culture is therefore the way in which adults actively instruct youngsters" (p. 80). That is, Tomasello, as did the Premacks and Bruner before him, argued that what makes the accumulation of culture possible are the pedagogical teaching practices of adults.

Here I see the pattern differently. It is not the pedagogy of the adults that makes human culture possible but rather the imitative abilities of the children. True, what makes culture possible is the evolution of means for preserving accumulated experience. But counter to the more widely held view, this preservation of the culture results less from the social or educational practices of adults than from the peculiar and special imitative abilities of children. Responsibility for learning and for the accumulation of culture can in large part be left to the learner. As F. Smith (1998) has emphasized, children are natural learners.

The progressive shift of responsibility from the learner to the teacher, I suggest, is definitive of schooling and consequently of one of the more noteworthy differences between traditional and modern human societies. This is well illustrated in some recent work in cultural psychology. The ways in which children are inducted into the cultural practices in some traditional societies have been described in some detail (Greenfield & Lave, 1982; Lave & Wenger, 1991; Rogoff, 1990; Premack & Premack, 1996; Lancey, 1996), both the attempts by children to learn from observing the activities of adults and also the occasional deliberate attempts by adults to sponsor or guide that learning. Although social groups differ greatly, researchers report a similar pattern of introduction into adult cultural life that they describe as a kind of apprenticeship, the traditional counterpart of more formal schooling.

It is difficult to know where, precisely, to draw the line dividing the child's spontaneous learning in a social context from apprenticeship and again from schooling. These differ primarily in terms of responsibility. The responsibility shifts in degrees from the child to the institution. But the differences are critical. To describe the acquisition of cultural knowledge as a kind of schooling is somewhat misleading. It is an anachronism to use concepts derived from a modern, bureaucratic social order to describe the practices of a traditional society as when we talk about "their" economic system, their science, their justice system, or their educational system. There are discourses about obligations, truths, and knowledge in all societies; these discourses are institutionalized into formal systems primarily in bureaucratic societies. To call initiation rites in a traditional society a "bush school" is a case in point; clearly it is school-like, but that designation gives a picture of a seamless continuity between traditional social life and bureaucratic institutional structures, a continuity that I am attempting to dissolve.

What is often called pedagogy in traditional societies may more appropriately be called intentional learning as it is primarily an intentional act of a learner rather than an intentional act of a teacher. It is the learner who is in control and who is responsible. Lancey (1996) studied the cultural routines employed by the Kpelle, a traditional society in Liberia, through which children were "educated" to become adult members of the society. At about the age of 6 years children were deemed to acquire "sense" and so were allowed to play an increasing role in family routines and in simple household tasks. As adolescents a few took up serious apprenticeships and all underwent the initiation described as bush school. Lancey's important finding was that such education as occurred during childhood was very much dependent upon the initiatives of the learners, who often observed adults work and then attempted to imitate them both in actual productive work and in play. A great deal of learning went on, but the adult interventions were negligible; they simply went on with their work. What little guidance was given was confined to allowing the child to participate and providing sanctions: "The boys are not taught in any formal sense; they learn entirely through observation and imitation" (1996, p. 153). Only if the learner demonstrated intense motivation to learn would an expert agree to act as an expert by correcting mistakes, offering advice, or perhaps demonstrating a procedure. Thus, learning was almost entirely the responsibility of the children themselves rather than of the adults around them. Even storytelling was not pedagogical; children took from the episodes whatever they liked.

Somewhat more systematic training and education were observed around adolescence and young adulthood. Some youths undertook lengthy apprenticeships in complex crafts such as medicine making or blacksmithing for which something more than observation and practice was required and with which some social advantage or credential was associated. Although all adolescent children underwent initiation rites in "bush school," the educational value of such rites is much in dispute. Lancey (p. 178) concluded that for the Kpelle bush school is of little educational value and that "few skills and little information is imparted during this period [of about 4 years]; it is largely indoctrination. . . . It is indeed rare that [such] a society finds it must invent the peculiar routine [namely, a school] that we take so much for granted." In some cases it is more like hazing than schooling.

On occasion adults do accept responsibility for their children's actions, offering praise and blame. But again this has less to do with the flow of knowledge from adults to children than with a form of social control. Responsibility for learning, and hence for the perpetuation and growth of culture, remained very much in the hands of the children!

Consequently, as Lancey notes, adults take no special responsibility for their children's learning and create no institutions for its achievement:

The Kpelle traditional educational system works beautifully without anyone being in charge, without schedules, without parental anxiety. There is no district school board to which to complain, no teachers to "in-service," no superintendent to fire, no curriculum to be revised, no new technology to purchase. No one is in charge; hence no single adult feels the responsibility to say, organize storytelling tournaments to keep the *meni-pele* genre alive. (1996, p. 198)

My point is not that all traditional societies leave the responsibility for learning entirely in the hands of the learner but rather that acculturation is possible with a low degree of adult or institutional control. When responsibility for learning is tranferred to an institution, we have the beginnings of schooling.

STAGE ONE: SCHOOLING

What is distinctive about all schooling is the realignment of responsibility for learning. School, through its agents, determines goals, means, and forms of assessment. The evolutionary basis of human culture, the child's eagerness to manage his or her own learning, is set aside or at least subordinated to the goals and procedures adopted by the adult culture. The child is no longer responsible for what he or she learns even with the somewhat reluctant assistance of the parent; the institution of the school takes over that responsibility. That is just what institutions *are*. When a child chooses to watch an adult weave a mat, he or she gleans whatever he or she is able and willing to take in. Adults may offer praise or blame but the initiative is the child's. All of that changes with school primarily because of the institutional entitlements and obligations of the school. The school promises to achieve a goal, say, make someone able to participate in the religious life, and it sees to the achievement of that goal. This is the fact that makes all schools more or less alike, and it is this institutional fact that deflects proposals for educational reform with the, as mentioned, predictably disappointing results.

It has been suggested that schooling is little more than apprenticeship or perhaps an "apprenticeship in learning" (Rogoff, 1990) in that both involve goals, roles, methods, assessment, and credentialing and take some years of specialized practice. Indeed, any specialized discipline such as law or psychology involves aspects of craft acquired through just such participation in ongoing professional activities. But the alignment of responsibility for learning is quite different. In an apprenticeship the learner may still be left responsible for what and when he or she learns or tries, whereas schools take on that responsibility as a basis for their original entitlements. Indeed, Lave and Wenger (1991) analyzed apprenticeships in terms not just of the changes in activity but also of changes in responsibility, an important factor rarely considered in theories of schooling.

Schooling is peculiar in another way. It is an institutional practice in which responsibility for learning is passed over to adults, who now see their role as "teaching," while assigning the child to the role of "student." The initiatives and responsibilities of the learner take shape within that authoritative structure. The school is authorized to hold the learner accountable by rewards and punishments and, ultimately, the awarding of credentials. The goals of returning responsibility to the learners and recognizing of children's willingness to accept responsibility for their own learning are among the distinguishing features of modern "child-centered" pedagogical theories, but such goals are difficult or impossible to accommodate within the institutional obligations of schools.

Why then were schools instituted? Why not leave responsibility for learning in the hands of the learner if that is how humans have evolved in any case? Many writers, following Weber, noted the relation between schooling and complex social organization. Dewey (1980, p. 230) noted, "[Schools] come into existence when social traditions are so complex that a considerable part of the social store is committed to writing and transmitted through written symbols." But it is more than that. They come into existence when an institution is empowered to achieve a goal, the goal of providing the empowering institution with the competencies needed for its functioning, normally, a firm, a church, a state, or an economy. If the first giant stride in cultural learning were the newly evolved abilities of human infants to imitate and thereby to perpetuate and extend culture, the second stride was the invention of pedagogy, the turning over of responsibilities for learning to adults, a shift more or less coterminous with the establishment of schooling as an institution. Modern societies exist by virtue of perpetuating their institutions. Historically speaking, the invention of schooling appears to be tied to the functioning of the state and the need for an effective civil service. Evolutionarily speaking, schooling is a recent development associated with the invention of writing and the growth of cities in roughly the fourth millennium b.c. in ancient Mesopotamia (Nissen, 1988; Damerow, 1998) and at about the same time in ancient Egypt (Gaur, 1984). In this period writing was used for a variety of royal, legal, and bureaucratic purposes and schools were established to train people to make and read, file and retrieve, such inscriptions. These roles, however, were highly specialized and often marked by official status. Writing was a craft as much as a knowledge code.

A similar pattern is found in ancient imperial China. The Mandarin scholar–bureaucrat tradition was maintained through an arduous civil service examination system initiated in the Sui dynasty (589–618 A.D.). These tests examined knowledge of the classics as well as skills in composition and calligraphy (Taylor & Taylor, 1995). Competition was fierce and failure so damaging that Hong Xiuquan, an applicant whose repeated failure on these examinations led to a mental collapse, began to see himself as Jesus' younger brother charged with the task of eradicating the "demon-devils," the ruling Manchu dynasty. The resulting war, China's Taiping Rebellion (1845–1864), resulted in the loss of some 20 million lives (Spence, 1996).

STAGE TWO: EDUCATION AND THE CHURCH

Once schools were institutionalized they could be readily adapted to serve any empowered authority whether king, church, or nation. In classical Greece specialized professional and craft knowledge gave way to more general education needed to shape citizens to participate in the democratic activities. Such a general education required that knowledge be separated from craft as an entity in its own right. This is an important step but how it came about is not clear. Havelock (1963) suggested that the very idea of knowledge as a kind of commodity separate from the knower was invited by writing. Goody (1977) and Ong (1982, p. 105) tied this distinction to the development of speculative philosophical thought. Ong wrote:

By separating the knower from the known . . . writing makes possible increasingly articulate introspectivity, opening the psyche as never before, not only to the external object world quite distinct from itself but also to the interior self against whom the objective world is set. (p. 105)

Plato's dialogues in the *Phaedrus* emphasized the development of critical thought, and, although he disparaged writing, and indeed perhaps only 10% of the citizens of classical Greece were literate (Harris, 1989; Thomas, 2001), Plato used writing to preserve and spread Socratic thought. Writing and literacy played important roles not only in the bureaucracies of cities and empires but in the construction and transmission, through schooling, of this literate, archival tradition. To be educated was to be learned in this written tradition (Olson, 1994).

With the end of the Roman Empire, the dominant literate institution in the West was the church, which perpetuated itself through its own institutions for schooling. The church used schools to train a literate elite for both religious and administrative purposes. The church set criteria for admission, programs of study, its own pedagogy, and the granting of credentials. Indeed, so close was the relation between clerical functions and literacy that the original meaning of the term *literate* was the ability to read and write Latin. The so-called benefit of clergy, the right to a trial rather than summary execution for severe crimes, was restricted to such literates (Clanchy, 1993). Education of laypersons was essentially a matter of preparation of the population to respect the authority of the church and to participate in its functions. Consequently, being literate for a layperson conferred little status (Levine, 1994).

STAGE THREE: EDUCATION AS TRAINING FOR A SECULAR ELITE

Another major change occurred when the institution of the school shifted from being the servant of the church to preparing a more diverse array of experts for an increasingly secular society. Murray (1978), discussing the growing role of specialized knowledge in the West, cites one 12th-century writer who claimed, "The glory of any kingdom has always grown vigorously so long as schools of the liberal sciences flourished in it" (p. 117). It was an expression of the growing awareness of the "powers of the 'trained' mind for government and the military" (p. 130), a training in which mathematics played a prominent role. Grendler (1989) traced a similar pattern in 13th- and 14th-century Italy: "In 1333 the Commune of Chioggia decreed that judges and other civic officials must read and write to hold their jobs" (p. 12). Secular social roles such as judge or administrator required the special training that was to be provided by the newly established universities. Along with the universities were schools that trained persons so that they would be eligible for admission to and benefit from those universities. Thus grew up the preparatory schools associated with the great universities. To be admitted to Harvard College in 1642, one had to be able to read classical Latin and conjugate in Greek (Ravitch, 1995, p. 168); that training fell to the preparatory schools. The pedagogy that evolved and continued through the 18th century was based on then current assumptions about knowledge:

The subject matter, whether beginning reading, Latin grammar, advanced rhetoric, or abbaco, had to be divided into very small individual bits of knowledge. Teachers and textbooks taught by breaking a skill into its smallest components, drilling them intensively, and then assembling the bits to make the whole. (Grendler, 1989, p. 409)

STAGE FOUR: GENERAL EDUCATION

Another development was the idea of general education for the laity, people who did not aspire to the professions but who still found literacy interesting or useful for daily life in an increasingly urban, commercial culture. This provided the basis for independent fee-charging schools of the 16th century in which students would be assured of learning to read and write and in some cases of having their fees refunded if they failed to learn. These lay schools were closely associated with the invention of the printing press and the abundance of reading materials that became available when printing houses were established in the major urban centers of Europe (Eisenstein, 1979). Northern Europe led the way in part because of the efforts of such humanists as Erasmus, who believed in the importance of a secular education, and because of such Protestant reformers as Luther, who urged individuals to study Scripture in order to embrace the word of God for themselves. Whereas Luther had assumed that everyone would want to read and write for just this purpose, it was not long before he found it necessary to ask the German state to make such learning mandatory. It became "required reading." Grendler notes that "spiritual ignorance and illiteracy [came to be viewed] as two aspects of a deprived condition" (1989, p. 339), thereby providing an additional motive for schooling. Increasingly it was granted, with Richard de Bury (1945), that "the treasure of wisdom is chiefly contained in books" and schooling and reading began to be seen as increasingly important (Hofmeister, Prass, & Winnage, 1998).

STAGE FIVE: EDUCATION AND THE NATION-STATE

The fourth change was associated with nationalism and the development of the nation-state. Anderson (1983) defines a nation as an "imagined community," imagined in the sense that a nation is, as we say, a social construct, and yet imagined in the minds of citizens, as a genuine community for which one may, if need be, go to war. Further, a nation has frontiers with other nations and it has sovereignty. Nation-states, Anderson points out, were born when the Enlightenment and political revolution were "destroying the legitimacy of the divinely ordained, hierarchical dynastic realm" (1983, p. 6). Nation-states picked up for themselves rights or entitlements and obligations that previously were held either by prince, church, or family. Literacy and education were two of these. Literacy was seen as a way of identifying and extending a vernacular language, thereby heightening the identity of the people, and education was seen as a means of filling the new roles of a bureaucratic nation-state and of training the populace to comply with these institutional functions. To meet these goals the state provided funds for the establishment of public schools, which grew as the society as a whole became more literate and reached their present form with compulsory schooling.

Schooled literacy, it appears, has always been an important instrument of national identity. The case of the French Revolution is exemplary. In adopting a republican form of government, the French assumed the need for an informed citizenry, a citizenry who could be guaranteed only through universal schooling in the vernacular, that is, the French language. In the republic, education replaced feudal loyalty as the basis for national identity (Weber, 1976). Other nations were quick to follow. In Russia, the politics of Russian cultural domination led to the imposition of language and literacy policies on the non-Russians of the eastern empire (Dowler, 2001). Even now, literacy in the national language is seen as crucial to national identity. Coulmas (2000) has shown that the collapse of the Soviet Union has been accompanied by renewed interest not only in local languages but in the development of distinctive scripts that then are spread through compulsory schooling. The public debate about a national language and bilingualism shows that this issue remains unresolved.

Although the form of schooling remained much the same over this period, the function of the school changed from serving professional, personal, or family needs to fulfilling national needs. To survive, a nation needs to defend itself from external threat and from internal strife; it needs to foster the welfare of its people, especially the welfare of its wealthy class (who may otherwise rebel or, in Canada, move away!); and it needs to train the professionals needed for public administration and the professions. Further, it needs to educate its citizens so that they see or at least believe that the state serves or at least meets their interests and needs, thereby creating loyalty. Loyalty to feudal lord or king was no longer sufficient. Making education into the instrument of the nation-state involved creating a "system" of education allowing promotion and credentialing as well as upward social mobility.[3] Thus arrived the "big" categories of educational practice including the distinctions between elementary and advanced levels, between education and "basic skills," between grade levels, specialized subject matter, passing and failing, dropouts, standards and a national curriculum – categories now more or less universal.

I believe it was in this period that schools were first recognized as at least partially autonomous institutions. Like the nation, the school, was accorded entitlements (to resources) and obligations (to produce responsible and competent citizens). It was in this period that polemics about educational reform in curriculum, methodology, and standards took their shape, the period when Comenius could advocate a language curriculum that would unite all (Protestant) persons and when Luther's schools could be seen as instruments of state. Ravitch (1995) has described the debates in the United States over the past century as a polemic between dominant institutions seeking to uphold their authoritative positions through the imposition of high standards and the educational elites advocating the rights and interests of diverse learners.

STAGE SIX: SCHOOLS AND DEMOCRATIC NATIONALISM

The sixth change in schooling, a change that continues to reverberate through one strand of the present calls for reform, is tied to the 18th-century notion of the "rights of man" as formulated within a liberal democracy. This was complemented by a parallel concern with the form of education suitable for a citizen with inalienable human rights, the move to a more "child-centered" form of education. Although Kant (1960) was the first modern writer to argue that education was essential to human fulfillment, that is, a goal in its own right, Dewey was among the first to see it as essential to the formation of a democracy. This was an explicit plank in Dewey's early platform for school reform:

The old education [with its] uniformity of curriculum and method . . . [had] its center of gravity outside the child. . . . Now the change which is coming into our

---

[3] The upward social mobility allowed by educational systems as well as the dislocation and disorientation such mobility produces are interestingly handled in Margaret Drabble's (2001) *The Peppered Moth*.

education is the shifting of the center of gravity. It is a change, a revolution, not unlike that introduced by Copernicus when the astronomical center shifted from the earth to the sun. In this case the child becomes the sun about which the appliances of education revolve; he is the center about which they are organized. (1976a, p. 23)

These educational reforms were derived in part from the political reforms associated with the liberalism of John Stuart Mill's *On Liberty* (Ryan, 1987); Mill, as did Kant, saw the state as the great enemy of individual freedom. New boundaries, they claimed, had to be drawn between individual choice and institutional requirements; the Sabbath was to be made for man. Dewey saw that a democratic state was not an enemy of the individual but a means of expression of the individual. But it could be so only if persons were educated to participate in democratic institutions. Such education must allow for individual experience, free expression, and social participation in the democratic processes. Dewey pointed out, "The modification going on in the method and curriculum of education is as much a product of the changed social situation, and as much an effort to meet the needs of the new society that is forming, as are changes in modes of industry and commerce" (1976a, pp. 5–6).

Thus Dewey helped establish the theme dominant through much of the 20th century, that schools are not created to produce persons to meet the needs of the society but rather that the society is required to be the expression of the needs, goals, feelings, and experiences of the people. Not that schools should be play schools of course; they should be "permeated throughout with the spirit of art, history, and science" (1976a, p. 19). By attending to the thoughts and feelings of the child, one would be able to find the pivotal or germinal ideas out of which more elaborated forms of knowledge were to be constructed. In his perhaps best-known book Dewey wrote:

The case is of the Child. It is his present powers which are to assert themselves; his present capacities which are to be realized. But save as the teacher knows, knows wisely and thoroughly, the [knowledge] ... embodied in that thing we call the Curriculum, the teacher knows neither what the present capacity is ... nor yet how it is to be ... realized. (1976b, p. 291)

Thus, the institution of the school was seen, at least by the reformers, as serving the students who attended it. Responsibility for learning and development, as in traditional societies, was expected to revert to the learners, who were to be given opportunity to exploit the resources of the adult culture for extending their own capacities and for achieving their own goals. But for Dewey, this was not some form of ascendant individualism but rather the acquisition of the ability to participate in the democratic institutions of the society, to hold an opinion, to evaluate it, to think critically, and to express opinions and judgments on public issues. Although reform was often justified on the basis of the importance of self-fulfillment and personal experience rather than the set goals and roles of the adult society, the school remained the instrument of the state. Kantian rationality and Deweyan experience were welcomed as long as they were seen as instrumental to the "real" social goals of the school. For Dewey, the purpose of education was to allow everyone to participate in the dominant institutions of the society, not merely to enjoy a full private life. However, as we saw earlier in the appraisal of Dewey's thought, Dewey failed to recognize the autonomy and power associated with social institutions even in a democracy. Schools, even liberalized schools, retain a primary obligation to the state that supports them, an obligation met, in large part, through the awarding of valid credentials. Meeting those obligations puts serious constraints on educational practices and schools accommodate only certain limited reforms.

STAGE SEVEN: EDUCATION FOR A POSTINDUSTRIAL, BUREAUCRATIC SOCIETY AND A GLOBAL ECONOMY

Human development in a bureaucratic society is not like human development in any other type of society. As we have seen, educational theory and practice reflect social structures. In a bureaucratic society students are expected to find fulfillment in terms of the social roles available in adult society and in terms of the disciplinary systems of bureaucratically organized knowledge. In a modern bureaucratic society they do this largely through learning to express their beliefs in explicit, logical form, preferably in terms of sets of explicit procedures relying heavily upon documentary resources and rules of argument and evidence. Personal identity is realized in terms of professions, whether accountant, systems manager, or teacher.

Stated this way, it becomes clear that schooling has long been a globalizing institution in that the forms of schooling are increasingly borrowed and imposed around the world. The rationality of the school is not local or cultural but rather generic and to some extent universalizable. As LeTendre and colleagues (2001, p. 4) point out, "Rationality as a pervasive cultural product (some would say even a hegemonic product) of the historical rise of Western ideas serves to bureaucratize, marketize, individuate, and homogenize the institutions of the world" (see also Gee, 2000). Consequently, schools in the modern world are increasingly alike. Schools are at the vanguard of this universalizing function, not simply as a result of cultural imperialism but because they are effective and economical forms for introducing citizens to the norms, rules, and procedures for dealing with diversity within and between societies by making behavior more or less predictable and understandable. Even local custom is subordinated to the institutional practices of schooling. There are important cultural differences, but they tend to be subordi-nated to universalized practices. A striking example is given by Flinn (1992, p. 51), who reported that in the Pulap Atoll, "female teachers of-ten have to write on the blackboard while sitting on a chair or kneeling on the floor" because of cultural attitudes about women. Thus the con-spicuous cultural differences are subordinated to the inevitable reliance on writing along with a fixed curriculum, attendance requirements, and awarded credentials, all universal aspects of schooling.

Some writers such as Stein (2001), an economist, see the current ini-tiatives for school reform, including parental choice, diversifying and funding of alternative schools and school systems, and increased ac-countability, as marking a shift from a bureaucratic to a postindustrial culture. The hierarchical bureaucracies and meritocratic promotions that characterized the 20th century are being tempered, she argues, by a re-duction in bureaucracy and by an increase in local autonomy for schools. Whereas in the past parents had been willing to trust their children's schooling to the experts, increasingly they want a say. Yet, as we saw in the first chapter, such reforms, advertised as radical and innovative, tend rather to "reinvent schooling" (Tyack, 1995) along very traditional lines, lines determined largely by the very nature of institutions with mandates for which they, like the teachers and students involved, are accountable.

Once the goals are adopted and methods developed for seeing that those goals are met, pedagogical diversity, critical for dealing with the diverse beliefs and goals of individual students, becomes irrelevant as long as the mandated goals are met, thereby initiating the search for causal variables that relate to output, the enterprise that I criticized ear-lier. But the battle over goals shows no sign of abating. Reflecting this bureaucratization of knowledge, adult lobby groups, traditionally from the disciplines but increasingly from business and industry, attempt to shape the curriculum and the standards of assessment to meet their often discrepant goals. Those in the educational academy advocate an inclusive, equitable, general, discipline-based education as a means of human fulfillment and as a basis for democratic reform. Those from business and industry, more concerned with cost-effectiveness, wealth production, and social stability, tend to encourage the preparation of a highly trained elite suitable for managerial roles on one hand and a more basic education composed of basic skills and good working habits for the masses, lavishing funds on elitist higher education while starving public schools. The current impulse to draw public funds for the creation and support of charter schools suited "to the 'tribal' agendas of well-off white parents, faithful home schoolers, La Raza devotees, black nationalists, even Mormons and Muslims" (Fuller, 2000b, p. 4) may meet the needs and interests of special interest groups but at the same time may undermine the traditional responsibility of the public school to advance the more general and inclusive goals of a democratic society.

These conflicting goals play themselves out in the classrooms of the world. Students will participate and apply energy if they believe that meeting social goals is in their personal interest; authorities legislate their values through the curriculum and through assessment while trying to assure students that the rewards merit the effort required. The school, through its teachers, attempts to balance these demands. Researchers seeking the ideal method fail to recognize that these are not different means to the same goal but quite different goals to be achieved by quite different pedagogies. These pedagogies concern us next.

11

Some Preliminaries to the History of Pedagogy

By the turn of the century, Herbartians had turned [this method] into a mechanical formalism, as leaden as the bookish tradition it had meant to replace, and was replaced by a Deweyan emphasis on felt experience.

(H.-J. Ipfling & J. J. Chambliss, 1989, p. 39)

No "method" turns out ... the carriers of art and thought ... like marketable goods.

(J. Barzan, 2001, p. 78)

The history of schooling as an institution, surveyed in the last chapter, illustrates how the school, as bureaucratic institution, takes on the responsibility to produce a certain output or effect in return for its entitlement to funds and social recognition. Institutions, as we saw earlier, are machines or mechanisms designed to achieve certain social effects whether in government, justice, economics, science, or education. As long as they can enlist participation and as long as they are seen as meeting their obligations, institutions are free to evolve any effective procedure they believe will enhance the achievement of their goals. As do other institutions, they do this without regard for the feelings or personal beliefs of those involved. Schools are institutions that have evolved to balance their entitlements with their obligations. However, an emphasis on the input and output functions of the institution as a whole leaves unacknowledged the importance of the personal beliefs, goals, intentions, and responsibilities of the teachers and students involved in those institutions. That is to say, the institutional concerns tend to dominate the more personal pedagogical ones.

In this chapter I examine the relation between pedagogy and culture and the institutionalization of pedagogy in the form of schooling. I then attempt to show that the school as an institution gives rise to the two most fundamental aspects of pedagogy. First, it determines to a large extent the choice of goals and the curriculum as well as the criteria chosen for judging that those goals have been achieved. And second, school as an institution gives rise to the very idea of a group method, that is, the belief in, or hope for, an algorithmic procedure that, if followed, would assure the achievement of those goals by the mass of participants. The history of pedagogy, in large part, is the history of this idea of method.

PEDAGOGY AND CULTURE

Whereas the growth of culture, as I argued in the last chapter, may rely on the imitative capacity of the young rather than on the explicit teaching practices of adults, there is also no doubt that the deliberate attempts of adults to pass on the knowledge and traditions of the society are important and of increasing significance to modern societies. Learning is left, less and less, to the interests and initiatives of the learners. Just what role pedagogy, that is, deliberate teaching, plays in the development of humans and other species is the subject of what Premack and Premack (1996) called an "anthropology of pedagogy."

An important beginning to the anthropology was made by Tomasello and his colleagues (Tomasello, 1999; Tomasello, Kruger, & Ratner, 1993; Kruger & Tomasello, 1996), whose work on the role of pedagogy in the transmission and growth of culture across a variety of species we considered briefly in the last chapter. Culture can grow, they argued, not because of what one generation learns but only because of the capacity for what one generation has learned to be taught to a new generation. As Premack and Premack (1996) had suggested, pedagogy makes the accumulation of culture possible. A variety of species including birds and mammals have remarkably sophisticated systems of adaptive actions and remarkable capacity for learning within those systems; those systems, however, are largely biologically based and are passed on unchanged from generation to generation. Such changes as do occur are Darwinian, which is to say that they can be explained by variability in the population and natural selection. Even if some limited evidence of actual teaching is found in nonhuman primate societies (Whiten, 1999) there is no evidence that what is learned is accumulated and transmitted across generations to allow a kind of Lamarckian evolution of culture. Tomasello (1999) traced the difficulty back to the fact that nonhuman primates seem to have extremely limited resources for detecting the intentions of others. Only humans seem adept in detecting the goal of another's actions and the means used for its achievement, the two constituents that make genuine imitation possible. Thus whereas adult primates may aid the young in the performance of an action, they tend not to recognize ignorance and consequently fail to mount a teaching program. Humans, by contrast, even by 2 years of age, recognize such intentions (Meltzoff et al., 1999), and by age 4, recognize, and attempt to remedy, ignorance.

Some have argued that human parents are particularly sensitive to ignorance as a cause of failed actions and not only help but actually teach their young. Thus, Gopnik, Meltzoff, and Kuhl (1999) suggested that human "parents seem designed to provide just the right sort of information" to their children. Yet, as I argued earlier, it is possible that the accumulation of cultural knowledge is achieved through the intentional learning capacities of the children themselves or rather through the pedagogical, that is, directed teaching, practices of adults. Teaching, I suggest, requires a much higher level of understanding than does learning and a relatively elaborate level of institutional structure. Teaching as a deliberate activity is, to a large extent, a response to the assignment of responsibility for learning to some governing institution, namely, a school.

Once the achievement of some goal is put into the hands of the school, teaching and learning are seen as matters of engineering belief change and theory change in learners. That is, teaching is seen as causing learning. The knowledge children are to acquire, whether about the mind, about society, or about science, exists before the learner, and the school adopts the responsibility for the learner's acquisition of that knowledge. This is, as we saw in Chapter 7, just how institutions see people. But we also saw in Chapter 8 that this view flies in the face of the deeper psychological fact that knowledge is not transmitted but rather constructed or reconstructed by the learner. The role of the school in the learner's acquisition of knowledge does not mean anything as vague as providing "facilitating conditions," as Piaget suggested, but rather involves setting, negotiating, and monitoring the normative standards of the disciplines – the methods, concepts, and rules for appraising and revising personal beliefs and intuitions in terms of some defined standard.

The primary means of achieving these institutionalized goals is through the creation of a curriculum or program of studies – the knowledge and skills assumed to address the goals. Only secondarily do questions of method of organizing or "transmitting" the curriculum arise.

Alternative pedagogical theories, ancient and modern, hinge on basic assumptions about the mind and knowledge. The fact that belief change can be produced by telling or teaching has led to pedagogical theories centered on transmission, communication, and rhetoric, all premised on the notion that knowledge is transferred from the curriculum to the mind. The fact that children have to construct their own understandings has led to pedagogical theories based on discovery and inquiry. The fact that interactions between learner and expert are often involved has led to pedagogies based on discourse. Basic to all is the provision of forums for evaluating and revising personal beliefs in the light of the standards articulated by the controlling institutions of the society.

PEDAGOGY AND THE SCHOOL

It is a mistake, I believe, to see schooling as a mere convenience for child rearing or as an extension of the family. Schooling is an institutional practice that alters both the society and the development of children in distinctive ways. As an institution the school has explicit obligations or goals; it chooses a means, namely, a curriculum designed to achieve that goal, and a method of administering that curriculum. As mentioned, most of these choices are determined by the schools' institutional structure, which is designed to produce certain outcomes. The history of pedagogy, therefore, is a matter of design of curricula appropriate to the goals and the selection of means suitable to their achievement.

The search for optimal means of teaching or for an ideal method has been a shibboleth for well over a century. Reformers with bold ideas have sometimes completely revolutionized pedagogical practice on the basis of urgent social concerns, sometimes on the basis of purely imaginative schemes, at other times on the basis of supposed first principles, and at yet other times on the basis of scientific research. Still the bold advances of one generation often are seen as groundless heresies by the next. As we noted earlier, the child-centeredness that endeared the writings of John Dewey to generations of educators shortly thereafter was seen as the cause of the low levels of discipline-based knowledge (Neatby, 1953; Meyer, 1961, p. 53; Betz, 1940; Ravitch, 2000). The *Hall-Dennis Report* (Provincial Committee, 1968) on early education in Ontario, which was received as bold and persuasive for its attention to the spontaneous learning activities of children, within a generation was considered the cause of falling "standards."

Bold reform initiatives have added little to the growth of pedagogical knowledge because they fail to address learning in its institutional context. The institution of the school reflects the larger society that determines its goals. The goals in turn dictate the curriculum, and the curriculum determines the method. What is taken as or accounted as student learning is determined by this entire institutional context. What the student is actually doing, trying to do, hopes to do, is another matter entirely.

PEDAGOGY AS A REFLECTION OF INSTITUTIONAL POWER

If we see schools as institutional structures that take on obligations to one or more dominating institutions in return for financing and other forms of social support, we may locate some of the sources of pedagogical change. In fact, this is the view elaborated by social historians, particularly those of the Annales school of French historians, concerned as they are with the many social factors impinging on everyday life. A.-M. Chartier (in press), who has done much to spread this research to the English-speaking audience, points out that educational methods are difficult or impossible to compare because they are not addressed to the same goals. The elite schools created for training specialists in religion or law were very different from the primary schools created for the more general education of the masses; different practices ensued.

Those who set the goals for mass education thereby determined the curriculum. Medieval schools that existed for the training of clergy and other church officials focused on religious texts that were taught by the classical methods of lecture and seminar (Clanchy, 1997, p. 85). Both curriculum and methods changed when the linked development of the printing presses and the Protestant Reformation and Catholic Counter-Reformation made schooling for the masses feasible. In the Catholic world, the Council of Trent (1545–1563) decreed that in order to pass on the "science of salvation," it was necessary to ensure that all Christians become literate (Chartier & Hebrard, 2001, p. 3). Chartier recounts the efforts of J.-B. de la Salle in the 18th century to create schools that combined the educational concerns of the Catholic Counter-Reformation with the secular interests of working people by offering lessons in reading and memorizing sacred texts as well as lessons in writing and keeping records and accounts useful for business. Larger numbers of students and new technologies also allowed him to introduce the then-revolutionary group methods of instruction, soon to be taken up with a vengeance by Joseph Lancaster in England, and eventually to be a defining feature of all modern schools.

In the Protestant world, literacy was also primarily a concern of the church. Thus, in Lutheran Germany literacy was seen as a means of giving Christians direct access to the word of God, a fundamental premise of the Reformation. The Protestant ability to read was less a matter of private spiritual meditation than a matter of distinguishing the "truth" from Papist fallacies. As not everyone sought such access, schooling was made compulsory by the state. Under the supervision of the pastors, schoolmasters required children to learn to read Luther's small catechism and the Bible as well as to read and write for secular purposes. In return for state support, the masters taught the students to honor and obey their prince.

Later reforms were increasingly in the service of the nation-state. This showed up first in the shift from education in Latin to education in the national language. After the French Revolution, public education was charged with the task of creating the "French," that is, citizens of a republic with a territory, a language, and a history. The cultural frame became not the history of Christianity but the history of the nation. Thus by April 1867, the examining board would use as an exercise in style "a chronicle taken from the history of France," rather than "a chronicle taken from the story of the Bible" (Chartier & Hébrard, p. 17).

In Germany, these national concerns came to the fore after Germany's defeat at the hands of Napoleon in 1805–1806. Fichte proposed a complete reorganization of the German schools in such a way as to create a spirit of national sentiment and commitment as well as competence that would prevent a repetition of such a disaster. The reform was apparently successful, for within the century, Germany was able to return the favor, humiliating the French in the Franco-Prussian War of 1870 (the monument celebrating the event still stands on the Kaiserdam in Berlin).

However, the lasting consequence of the growth of nationalism was not success in war but rather the growth of vernacular, national languages as instruments both of culture and of schooling. It was schooling in the national vernacular language that not only consolidated the boundaries of the nations but made schooling readily accessible to the masses. A major component of schooling was devoted to study of the language and to mastery of the writing and reading of that language.

Dowler (2001) and Coulmas (2000) have pointed out how written language was used not only as a means of establishment of national identity but also as a means of social control in China, Japan, and Korea as well as in the former Soviet bloc. After the collapse of the Soviet Union, for example, in Moldova, the Cyrillic script, imposed by the Soviet regime to foster ties with the Soviet Union, was replaced by the Roman script, chosen to foster Moldovian identity, and hence taught in the schools.

In all of these cases the "method" was simply "teaching" the curriculum. Method was not seen as relevant; any method would do as long as the goal was met. However, shifts in method that reflected changes in technology did occur. Methods of teaching reading only changed into new methods that combined reading and writing when writing materials became cheap and manageable. Quill pens and expensive paper had prohibited their use by young children so literacy had been tied to learning to read not write. Further, the scarcity of books and the difficulties of consulting a text encouraged the students to memorize the contents of the books studied, thus sponsoring the reading–recitation method. Limitations in memory, in turn, restricted memorization to the most important texts, usually Scripture but also pledges of allegiance and such basic skills as could be not only learned, but overlearned, that is, memorized.

GROUP METHODS OF INSTRUCTION

Perhaps the most important and certainly most lasting shifts in pedagogy resulted from the wide availability of printed materials and the invention of "group" methods of instruction. A pictorial illustration of schooling in the early Renaissance by Ambrosius Holbein, 1516, which served as a sign on the schoolhouse door, shows a teacher teaching one child at a time, the others engaged with their copy books (see Figure 5; see also Figure 1). An even more interesting picture, *A School for Boys and Girls*, painted by Jan Steen around 1670, shows the range of activities apparently typical of a classroom of the period (see Figure 6). J. H. Astington (2002) described in detail the activities depicted in this painting:

[I]n the seventeenth-century classroom shown in the painting a certain amount of chaos and disorder is balanced by evidence of hard work – islands of calm, concentration, and absorbed interest are interspersed among the foolery, laziness, and discord apparent in the other parts of the picture. . . . Two of the boys at the table in the right foreground are absorbed in writing and reading, while a

Wer)emandt hie Der gern welt lernen Diitch schriben und läsen
uß dem aller kürtzisten grundt den Jeman erdencken kan Do durch
ein Jeder der vor nit ein büchstaben kan Der mag kürtzlich und bald
begriffen ein grundt do durch er mag von jm selbs lernen sin schuld
uff schribe und läsen und wer es nit gelernen kan so ungeschickt
were Den will ich um nüt und vergeben glert haben und gantz nüt
von jm zü lon nemen es sig wer es well burger oder hantwercks ge
sellen frouwen und junckfrouwen wer sin bedarff der kum har jn-der
wirt driuwlich glert um ein zimlichen lon · Aber die junge knabe
und meitlin noch den konualten wie gewonheit ist · 1 5 1 6 ·

FIGURE 5. Schoolmaster's signboard painted in 1516 by Ambrosius Holbein, reproduced here with the kind permission of the Kuntsmuseum Basel.

Translation: He who wishes to learn to read and write German by the quickest method, and who does not know a single letter, is informed that here he will be able to learn all that he needs to know of writing and reading. And if anyone is so foolish that he does not manage to learn it, I shall have taught him *gratis* and for nothing and he shall not owe me anything. Whoever you may be, burgesses, artisans, laborers, women or girls, and whatever your needs, he who comes here will be faithfully instructed for a reasonable fee. On the other hand, children, little boys and little girls, will pay every term as is customary.

less industrious group behind them make faces behind the teacher's back, and tease the school mascot, a pet owl. (p. 97)

Of special note for our purposes is that the teacher, or teacher's helper, is engaged in teaching only one child at a time – pure individualized instruction. Contrast that with the photograph from around 1900, that shows what is characteristic of schools in our time, namely, the whole class or group method of instruction (see Figure 2, p. 18). Teaching the whole group or whole class was a radical pedagogical innovation, an innovation based on the use of printed materials, identical copies of which could be given to each student in the group. Employing whole

FIGURE 6. Jan Steen's *A School for Boys and Girls* (1617). © The National Gallery of Scotland.

class methods puts a new demand on learners intentionally to "pay attention," shifts speech and language from a personal to an impersonal level, requires new methods of surveillance and evaluation, and is suitable primarily for children above 5 or 6 years who have an appropriate sense of responsibility (see Chapter 8). The recitation method of question–answer–feedback sequences commonly employed in classrooms to this day is a form of discourse evolved for such group lessons.

Chartier (in press) points out that the group method of instruction was pioneered early in the 18th century by de la Salle in his "simultaneous system," which abandoned individual teaching, which, in his view, caused a lack of discipline and an intolerable level of background noise in the classroom (still a concern). The fact that all the children could focus on one blackboard or consult an identical text allowed for a group focus of attention. Furthermore, group methods become possible only when learners are more or less similar, hence the classification of children into classes, grades, and levels. Group methods of teaching reading, for example, became common as classes increased in size, as attendance became more regular, and when printing presses produced multiple copies of identical texts, which allowed all students to be "on the same page," a necessity for group reading instruction: "Teaching a whole class would require regular attendance and standard books" (Chartier, in press, p. 5). Ironically, the invention of group methods highlighted individual differences and drew attention to the problem of individualizing instruction. Classifying students into types is a response to the school's commitment to group methods; such classifications become irrelevant when individualized methods are adopted (Clay, 1998; Olson, 1999).

Group methods became a fetish, particularly in England, through the adoption of a technology invented by Jeremy Bentham, his Panopticon, for the surveillance of hundreds of prisoners from one fixed vantage point. His method of surveillance found a place in the school in the so-called Lancastrian method by means of which one teacher could teach a hundred or even a thousand children in a single classroom. The classroom was arranged in serried ranks of students, each rank headed by a monitor. The teacher taught a rigidly prescribed lesson to the dozen or more monitors, who then taught his row of pupils the lesson, whether in reading, writing, arithmetic, or spelling. Other monitors saw to the routines of classroom management, taking attendance, passing out supplies, giving tests, and the like. School activity was directed with military precision with an emphasis on drill and memorization (Delbos & Jorian, 1984; Ipfling & Chambliss, 1989, 18:39). "The careful, repetitive, and cumulative drill went on and on," as Grendler (1989, p. 196) put it.

In all of the reforms discussed the focus of attention was on the curriculum appropriate for achieving the goal of creating adults of a certain sort, able to participate in religious life, in national culture, in business, and so on. However, in the 18th century there developed a new concern with pedagogical theory, the theory that would address the question of how to set and adjudicate goals and adjust means to achieve them. The shift originated in the larger social changes, the decline of church and empire, secularism, and new understanding of the "rights of man." Such educational writers as Rousseau, Pestalozzi, and Herbart began to see schooling at least to some degree not just as socialization into adult norms but as an opportunity for human fulfillment. The intellectual content of this pedagogical shift may be traced to Kant's rejection of empiricism. Whereas Locke's "tabula rasa" theory of the mind imposed few constraints on what could be taught to children – children became whatever experience taught them to be – for Kant, what could be acquired was limited or constrained by the initial knowledge pre-dispositions of the learner, the "a priori" that no amount of training could impose, alter, or account for. Thus in regard to education, Kant would claim that "the end of education is to develop, in each individ-ual, all the perfection of which he is capable" (cited by Durkheim, 1956, p. 62). Whatever account of the dawn of the 18th-century Enlighten-ment prevails, writing on education and pedagogy became increasingly "child-centered," reaching its apotheosis in the writings of John Dewey. This is not to say that Dewey simply adopted Herbart's attention to the learner. Whereas Herbart considered the learner only in terms of how best to introduce the society's knowledge to the child, Dewey sought those foundations not in the society's knowledge but in the spontaneous interests and predispositions of children.

Chartier and Hebrard (2001) conclude that the changes in the meth-ods employed in teaching children to read were less a consequence of advances in pedagogical understanding than of the fact that "at each stage, the objectives of teaching have changed" (p. 29). Further, "the constraints set by the format of schooling," what I call its institutional structure of responsibilities and entitlements, determine in large part what goes on in the school and explain why "learning processes that are so effective in the wider social sphere on a one-to-one basis" are impossible to apply to groups in a school context.

HOW EDUCATIONAL INSTITUTIONS PURSUE THEIR GOALS

For much of history pedagogy was identified with the curriculum, with what was to be taught. The shift from the classical notion of education as the means of imposing adult norms, whether those of church or state, to the Enlightenment view of individual rights and human development is visible in the history of teaching particular subject matters. The transfor-mation is summed up in the trope common to most modern pedagogies, namely, that "we teach children not subjects." The fragment of truth in that expression is revealed by the clear contrast between classical and modern methods of teaching reading. Classical methods focused en-tirely on the structure of the knowledge to be acquired. In medieval Roman education, for example, literacy was taught by methods "slow, thorough, and relentlessly pedantic" involving from an early age "the practice of writing and reading out the letters of the alphabet in all sorts of combinations before proceeding to syllables and complete words" (Green, 1994, p. 26). Renaissance learning, too, emphasized repetition and memorization, breaking knowledge into its components and then assembling them into larger units (Grendler, 1989, p. 409).

The practice of analyzing knowledge in terms of its basic concepts and relations may itself have been a product not only of literacy but also of the attempt to teach. Unlike more traditional apprenticeships, in which knowledge is largely embedded in practice and in which the learner is primarily responsible for the management of his or her own learning, schooling is premised on the assumption that there exists a body of knowledge that can be analyzed into parts, and that adults have responsibility for teaching that knowledge in a systematic manner. Indeed, earliest pedagogies were directed almost exclusively by assumptions about knowledge, its structure and its basic elements. Knowledge was thought to reside in books, especially in Scripture, the most respected of books, and instruction then proceeded by analyzing that knowledge into its elements and building up knowledge in the learner by assembling those elements into higher levels of structure. The pedagogical methods appropriate for the building up of knowledge involved "rigid method and severe discipline to achieve uniformity in cultural transmission" (*Encyclopedia Britannica*, 1989, 18:2).

The teaching of English grammar in England from 1640, when it first became a subject, was examined in detail by Cohen (1977). Prior to that time Latin had been the language of learning. Cohen was able to distinguish three periods and three stances in the teaching of language: language in relation to the world, language in relation to the mind, and language in relation to language itself. In the earliest period, pedagogy was informed by the assumption that words mapped to things; pedagogy articulated that mapping. The important knowledge for students to learn were the details of the thing so that words could have their correct meaning. Comenius (1968) was a central figure in this pedagogical development, urging that "the school would indeed become a School of things [at least the pictures of things, which his *Pictus* provided] obvious to the senses, and an Entrance to the School intellectual." Words were broken into their constituent parts, ultimately the letters of the alphabet, and then knowledge was assembled from these constituents, of which words were most important. Indeed, Comenius was a 17th-century J. D. Hirsch (1987), compiling word lists "containing all things which are necessary to be knoune . . . with an exact Index" (preface), which were to be used as a basis of instruction. And as Hirsch came to do, Comenius saw in the learning of the correct meanings of words the basis for a universal, or at least national, brotherhood. On the positive side, Comenius took as his mandate all knowledge, not just basic training, and it provided a technology, printed books, that made education available to the masses rather than only the elites.[1]

Organizing and ordering knowledge for teaching language were seen as no different from teaching anything else. Teaching language required that the knowledge be analyzed into its basic parts and then built up in the learner, beginning with the basic parts, in this case the letters of the alphabet. When the child had memorized the letters of the alphabet, these could be organized into syllables, and finally into words. One grammarian recommended dividing all words into syllables "be-cause long Words are ea-si-ly read, when right-ly di-vi-ded" (cited by Cohen, 1977, p. 9). I have seen school primers printed in 1920s Germany that employed this procedure, breaking words into syllables rather than presenting whole words. Such methods are currently under suspicion in that they underestimate the central importance of meaning.

In the second period, language was seen as mapping to ideas, not things, a view defended by Locke (1961). Grammarians of this period emphasized syntax rather than word lists, thereby emphasizing sentences and paragraphs as well as longer units, including poetry, narrative, and plot. Drill and memorization in the mastery of adult norms remained the primary means of education.

The third period, which Cohen identifies with the 18th-century dictionary of Samuel Johnson but that we may see as a more general expression of the Enlightenment, scaled back the aspirations of grammarians from their former pedagogical aspirations to reform either knowledge or the mind of the user to treating language as a complex living system and a possession of its users. Instead of attempting to "fix" the language in a firm set of rules and meanings, Johnson documented its richness, its shifts in meaning, and its progress. Nonetheless, assumptions tying language to its written form persisted. Cohen cites the 18th-century *Introduction to Languages* as claiming that Egyptian hieroglyphics, like Chinese, "cannot be considered as a language because . . . they denote not single Letters and Words, but Things themselves" (1977, p. 97). That is, the language was identified with its written form.

All of these widely different views of the subject entailed widely different pedagogies for reading and writing including some that look

---

[1] That Hirsch's lists are limited by their ad hoc nature becomes apparent when one searches in vain for the concepts critical to advanced, metacognitive thought such as *assume, infer, conclude,* and *hypothesize.*

very similar to those being experimented with to this day. These include analysis into basic constituents versus larger narrative structures, emphasis on code versus use, emphasis on learning rules versus learning self-expression.

Perhaps the most decisive shift in pedagogy occurred in the third period, when reading and writing became divorced from knowledge of the world and began to be treated as basic skills. This split the meaning of literacy into two parts, one thought of as a basic skill useful for everyday working life, and one thought of as the means to a liberal and general education, the former for the masses, the second for the elites. This separation did not occur in either the classical period or the early modern period but rather seems to be an invention of our own industrial era with its need for literate workers. Whereas literacy was in the past taught to give access to the truths of the church or the strength of the nation, the literacy of greatest concern to the modern industrial economy is that of "functional literacy," the competence to deal with modern bureaucratic institutions. The history of the concept of "basic skills" remains to be written.

Although education in its most general sense may be viewed as any process or activity that allows the young to benefit from the accumulated knowledge and experience of the old, the very idea of pedagogy is based on the premise that it is the adults who are responsible for children's learning anything worthwhile. This is not an assumption shared with members of traditional societies, as we saw in the last chapter. But with the institutionalization of schooling, pedagogy began to be seen as essential. It is not that the pedagogical responsibilities of parents are off-loaded to the school; rather, with the institutionalization of education through the school, parents begin to see themselves as "educators" and to treat their own children as students (Olson, 1984).

Methods derive from goals, and goals, I have argued, derive from obligations to sponsoring institutions. To understand methods one must uncover more fundamental questions about these obligations and responsibilities. First, is learning the responsibility of the learner or the responsibility of the adult? Second, is education restricted to a professional elite needed to run the powerful institutions of the society, or is a mass education required to participate in and foster allegiance to that society? Third, what is the dominating institution (including lobby groups) of the society that the school is being shaped to serve? Is it the church, the nation, the economy, special interest groups, or something more general such as civil society and human fulfillment? Fourth, how is the knowledge to be acquired conceptualized by the adults? Is it a skill, a set of good habits, or a body of specialized knowledge? Is it composed of elements that can be assembled into wholes? And fifth and most important, is pedagogy thought of in terms of the structure of knowledge itself or the modes of apprehension that the child brings to the encounter?

Thus, pedagogy is rarely a question of choosing the optimal method to achieve a single goal, but rather one of changing goals, which entail different curriculum content. Churches want compliance in beliefs so they encourage memorization; nations want loyalty and civic order so they encourage a devotion to national culture and respect for authority. Specialized professions want expertise and employers want trained workers who know how to follow explicit procedures and accept responsibility for their actions.

To understand pedagogies, therefore, we must first understand the nature of the institution of schooling and the larger social systems of power that create, fund, and hold schools accountable. Pedagogical theories are often little more than rationalizations of this arrangement of power and authority. Current debates about whether children learn better if they understand or better if they have extensive drill and practice are not primarily pedagogical issues but rather institutional ones, namely, who has the power to set the goals, design the curriculum, and monitor its achievements. This principle is more easily stated than applied. In a democratic society, who is in control is not a straightforward question, as it is neither the religious interests of the church nor the national interests of the state nor the aspirations of the parents nor the spontaneous interests and talents of the children. Rather it is an ongoing political debate among a number of special interest and lobby groups, and the schools are shaped and reshaped as they attempt to address the interests of these groups. Contemporary educational theorists, who, understandably, put the child at the center, tend to overlook the fact that the church, the nation, the sciences, and the economy all have claims in addition to those of the parents or the children themselves. Conversely, political reformers who put the interests of national competition at the center tend to overlook the aspirations, abilities, and varied intentions of the students as well as the ethos and varied traditions of the schools involved. These are political concerns, which is to say, matters for ongoing debate that are eventually decided by elections. Educational theory has the job of setting out the dimensions on which such debates play out, dimensions that include the entitlements and obligations of states, school systems, individual schools, teachers as well as students, rather than settling on best methods for achieving specific goals.

Schooling, in both traditional and modern forms, survives, because schools serve a multiple set of goals and consequently pedagogies are largely compromises among interests. If one narrows the goals sufficiently, one may design an efficient method for their achievement, ignoring all other considerations (Satz & Ferejohn, 1994, p. 72). Narrow goals, however, do not constitute an education in the modern sense. Once those goals are broadened, pedagogy becomes a matter of judgment: of balancing the welfare of the individual with the demands of the society. Ways of balancing these factors make up much of what we may think of as pedagogy. Specifically, how does one balance concerns for persons versus roles, for personal beliefs versus objective knowledge, for personal freedom versus social norms, for interest versus discipline? There is no "method" for achieving contradictory goals; professional competence and professional judgment are called for. For this reason modern states display wisdom in stating goals and aspirations rather than mandating specific outcomes, and leaving to the judgment of professionals whether or not an individual has met the norms and criteria that indicate achievement of those goals. This wisdom seems to be lacking in the current drive for strict accountability to the state.

THE SEARCH FOR THE BEST METHOD

The mere fact that schooling as an institutional function has survived, let alone become universal, suggests that it is successful. Institutions that fail to meet their goals tend to disappear. Schools manage their responsibilities and entitlements and to that extent constitute an adequate system. In schooling, as in science, the justice system, and business and industry, there are both an aspiration to and a place for the design of a system for achieving educational effects. Indeed, professional schools have been training people for such institutions for decades if not centuries. Education is a systematic enterprise and to that extent at least employs an explicit system analogous to, say, the justice system. The justice system can be revised, improved, and evaluated, but one would be naive indeed to believe that the ideal justice system would eliminate crime. Similarly, an educational system can be evaluated and reformed, but one would be equally naive to believe that the ideal educational system would eliminate ignorance.[2] Tyack (1974) points out the fallacy of thinking that there is one best educational system, indicating rather the need for adapting any educational system to local conditions. Hence, despite considerable diversity, schools are systems for meeting goals, which goals, as argued previously, are matters of power and influence and means must be adjusted to circumstances.

Pedagogy traditionally has been a matter of choosing goals and designing curricula or programs for achieving them. The method of teaching was not differentiated from the curriculum. Methods were distinguished from content only with the development of pedagogical theory in the hands of such 19th-century writers as Herbart. Methods are specific procedures for producing effects; methods assume causality. There are methods for making ice cream, for bisecting a triangle, for tempering steel, for weaving a mat. Why not a method for teaching? Certainly finding an effective procedure for producing knowledge in learners has been the goal of educational researchers for almost a century. Policymakers, too, assume the efficacy of a method, for example, in mandating the "phonological method" over the "whole word method" or sponsoring research to choose between them.

The search for discovering the best method has not been encouraging. Despite all the differences in pedagogy discussed, children have learned. Historically, no reform had a dramatic effect on attendance or levels of achievement. The sociological analysis presented in the *Coleman Report* (1966) found little effect of particular types of schools or particular forms of pedagogy on student achievement. When variability across schools was examined more fully by Rutter and associates (1979) and Mortimore and coworkers (1988), the factors that mattered were not explicit pedagogical factors but rather matters of school climate or ethos including the use of praise and punishment, degree of classroom organization, clarity of goals, teacher preparedness, and the extent to which the school was a well-functioning social community.

But that does not mean that pedagogy is unimportant. Recall the distinction between the institutional and the intentional. The empirical search for the best method has been the search for factors that affect performance of the group; as such these are institutional facts, not personal, intentional ones. Such pedagogical factors as whether teachers use small

---

[2] I once wrote a review for the U.S. National Academy of Education of a proposal to eradicate illiteracy by the year 2000. The point of my review was that in implying that they could do it for some 10 billion dollars, educators were disingenuous: "They should have told the truth because they did not get the money anyway" (1975, p. 172).

versus large groupings or text book versus inquiry methods, or provide a summary before or after the content, factors that may be manipulated or controlled at the group or institutional level, have turned out to be of little significance. But pedagogy at the personal intentional level such as whether a teacher actually succeeds in explaining Ohm's law in such a way that one student understands is of enormous significance to both *that* teacher and *that* child even if no causal factor can be isolated and no method is strictly applied. Method and pedagogy may be quite different. Recall Cronbach's (1975) concern about the limitations of applying general models to particular learning situations; all learning is local.

Such considerations suggest that the whole enterprise, the search for "method," is seriously misconstrued. It is worth retreating a step and examining the fate of the search for method in some other domains. The early modern, that is, 17th-century, scientists, led in part by Francis Bacon, believed that they had discovered a new *method*, a "new organon," for the advancement of learning, a method based not on deduction from first principles but on observation and experiment. Bacon's method required one to set aside the usual habits of mind, what he called *idols*, and adhere mechanically to strict rules. He required "that the entire work of the understanding be commenced afresh, and the mind itself be, from the very outset, not left to take its own course, but be guided at every step, and the business be done as if by machinery" (Bacon, 1965, p. 327). The laboratory, a critical part of the method, allowed one to exclude extraneous factors and isolate the causal ones in an open, public, and nondisputatious way. Robert Boyle (1772), a leading early modern scientist, developed laboratory methods for the study of a vacuum, what he called "the spring of the air." The laboratory method scrupulously followed would allow one to obtain the same results each time the experiment was repeated. Repeatable results assured that one had hit upon the causal factors. Further, the method involved inductive rules for going from repeated observation to general laws. The early successes of early modern science led to the belief in a universal method of determining truth, the scientific method. This method for producing reproducible effects has become a major part of the natural sciences and is taught to every schoolchild as the scientific method.

The success of Method, set out in rules and procedures, was widely applied to other aspects of social behavior. Erasmus (Rummel, 1990), between 1500 and 1530, published a number of manuals setting out the rules for correct behavior in church, at the table, in bed, and at play that included how to dress, act, gesture, and display feelings. These measures were seen as creating an ethos of responsibility for previously sponta-neous actions. Just as one could follow correct procedures for discovery of truth, one could follow correct procedures for social conduct. Both conferred a new level of responsibility on persons (Gaukroger, 2001).

Although Method, that is, routine, explicit formal procedure, is a crit-ical feature of institutionalized science, much more is involved in pro-ducing original knowledge than following explicit procedures (Latour & Woolgar, 1986). Conant (1964, p. 18) pointed out the concepts and the-ories of science have originated in many different ways: "That is why it is worse than nonsense to speak of *the* scientific method." Conant found two quite different styles, if not methods, of doing science, which he called the *rational deductive* and the *inductive empiricist*. He took them to be tied to the domains of inquiry as well as to the psychological charac-teristics of the scientists themselves while emphasizing the importance of cooperation between the two modes.

The belief in method as explicit procedure that if followed would yield an assured outcome was not restricted to science. It was, if not believed by, at least attributed to, the followers of John Wesley, who came to be called *Methodists*. Methodism was distinguished, at least to bystanders, by the belief that if only one followed the correct procedures, one would necessarily arrive at a state of grace; its laudable aspiration was the design of an assured method for achieving salvation.

Although skepticism remained about the possibility of a method to assure salvation, with the development of psychology the possibility of a method for assuring learning drew the interest of many reformers. Primary among them was the German philosopher Johann Friedrich Herbart (1806), who set out to define philosophy not by its content but by its method. The method consisted of analyzing concepts, form-ing judgments, and justifying inferences. He then applied this philos-ophy to education. Unlike de la Salle and Lancaster, whom we met in the last chapter and who saw education as simply imposed on the young through training, Herbart, following Kant, believed that learning was a change in the learner's system of beliefs or "apperceptive mass." Nonetheless, he advanced a systematic method of constructing correct idea masses in the mind of the student, what today we would perhaps call engineering belief change. Herbart's method, modeled on his phi-losophy, had four stages: first, clarification, that is, turning experiences into clear concepts; second, associating these new concept with old ones; third, organizing these concepts into systems; and fourth, methodiz-ing the concepts into useful practices. Hence, clarification, association, systematization, and methodization. Anyone who has taught elementary school is familiar with this expository method. Although Herbart advised against too rigid an imposition of this method, within a generation it became as formal and mechanical as the classical methods it had sought to replace and would later become the object of much of Dewey's criticism (Dunkel, 1970).

Pedagogy has, from the outset, been concerned with how to teach a class and therefore tied to group methods and to the learning of the class rather than of individuals in the class. This is what makes it a part of educational psychology rather than human development. Thus pedagogy has been an aspect of the institution of schooling. Schools are institutions designed to produce a certain effect or product, and research and theory have been devoted to isolating causal factors that affect that outcome. Pedagogical methods are the product of that inquiry. But as institutional facts they have little or no bearing on the personal intentional states of the particular teachers and learners involved. Pedagogy, in other words, has tended to be concerned with objective outcomes rather than with subjective intentional states. Consequently, one can seriously question whether or not a specific method, that is, a set of formal procedures, exists for altering the intentional mental states of an individual. Indeed, such an imposition may be seen as an infringement of a fundamental human right.

Yet psychology, for much of the 20th century, beginning with Thorndike (see Lagemann, 1997), has employed scientific methods in the attempt to isolate the factors that cause learning. Thorndike reduced them to biological predispositions and laws of learning, and a century of research has located patterns of relations among such factors in the search for the causes of learning with implications for teaching. Gage and Berliner (1975), in a comprehensive textbook that when it was published well represented the discipline of educational psychology, provided an exhaustive examination of all the factors known to or thought to affect learning. Their analysis included objectives and assessments, traits of learners, and the methods of instruction that may affect student learning and other factors important to educational practice. They provided a clear analysis of how educational goals could be translated into behavioral indices – how you could know whether a child had indeed learned how to tell time, for example. They provide a full discussion of what was known about abilities, conditions of learning, transfer of learning, and, new for the time, discussion of methods of teaching and their implications.

Gage and Berliner summarized the results of hundreds of experiments comparing method A with method B for students of type X as opposed to students of type Y. Although the book remained decidedly upbeat, a more objective appraisal would see much of the research on methods of instruction as diligent but unpromising. For example, they cite a review of nearly 100 studies over a 40-year period of the lecture method as opposed to alternative methods including the discussion method. The score? 51 to 49! "The overall verdict is that the lecture method is just about as effective, by and large, as the other methods" (1975, p. 465). Such equivocal results reflect not merely the difficulties of ruling out the interactions with other variables such as the competencies of the learners or the placement in the curriculum but the much more serious problem, namely, that methods are seen as causes of learning. The intentionality of the learner is completely overlooked.

Here again we encounter the conflation of institutions and persons. The theory attempting to account for student learning on the basis of causal factors such as those considered by Gage and Berliner is appropriate to the description of institutions, not individuals. It is a search for causal variables – programs, traits, and treatments – that affect an outcome. An intentionalist theory, on the other hand, appeals to an individual's beliefs and reasons for believing in relation to his or her goals, obligations, roles, or even whims. Pedagogical theories veer between these two sets of aspirations, both of which are important but when conflated become trivial.

Institutional factors that contribute to learning are subject to policy; they include the choice of goals, the invention of programs, the establishment of criteria for successful achievement, the allocation of time and resources for their achievement. Further, they include such classroom issues as orderly management, clear goals, engagement, and the like, factors that tend to show up in large-scale analyses (Mortimer et al., 1988). Method is a concept suitable for describing a causal, institutional bureaucratic procedure but is largely misleading when applied to the intentions and responsibilities of teachers and learners (Mills, 1959, pp. 100–118).

Pedagogy of teaching and learning is intentional rather than institutional: What are learners thinking, doing, or trying to do? How are they interpreting what they are seeing or hearing? Can they assimilate what they encounter with what they already know or believe? Do teachers and students share a joint intention and a common goal? A person gives a good answer to a question because he *knows* the answer; she *thinks* the question called for, say, a logical rather than an empirical answer; he *understood* the framework from which the question arose; and she *intended* to express her knowledge. Such an intentionalist account does not trade in "traits" or "methods" but rather in cognitions, beliefs, meanings, understandings, and intentions. These are much more intentional or "first-person" questions that are not addressable in terms of institutional characterizations of populations, programs, and methods.

To summarize: Educational psychology has been in the grip of a causal theory of behavior with traits and treatment methods as the variables under consideration. This empirical research tradition reflects an institutional perspective to pedagogy with the limited results we have reviewed. The more individualized cognitive question, But what is the child actually thinking? or, What is the child trying to do? was not asked. These questions call for a first-person perspective and a quite different approach to a theory of pedagogy. When individual learners are addressed, it is more appropriate to acknowledge that there may be many paths to the same goal (Clay, 1998). The flaw was in addressing institutional goals in terms of personal, intentional activities of teachers and learners; in confusing populations with persons. As pedagogical theory aspired to become an objective science, it drove out the analysis of first-person intentions, emotions, and goals, and with them the educator's concern with experience, identity, responsibility, autonomy, and fulfillment.

Thus, the search for the method for arriving at truths, as with Bacon, or for salvation, as with Wesley, or for school learning, as with Thorndike, and his followers, is neither appropriate nor productive. There is no way to ignore the goals, beliefs, and intentions of the teachers and learners; there are no shortcuts to learning or to gaining an education. Pedagogy, then, must be distinguished from methodology; pedagogy, as we shall see in the next chapter, is the professional competence involved in making timely, informed decisions about drawing minds and cultural resources together; it is not the discovery of a method for turning lead into gold.

12

Pedagogy as a Bridge from the Subjective
to the Normative

> Under the old method law is taught to the hearer dogmatically as a com-
> pendium of logically correlated principles and norms, imparted ready-
> made as a unified body of established rules. Under Langdell's method
> these rules are derived, step by step, by the students themselves by a
> purely analytical process out of the original material of the common law,
> out of the cases.
>
> (J. B. Conant, 1964, p. 48)

In the Latin West, traditional methods of teaching included a Ciceronian
method of authoritative and comprehensive declaiming of the major
ideas of a subject and a Socratic method of discussion between teacher
and student. Most teachers through the ages used both, setting out the
truths of their subject and then discussing them with the learners. Some,
such as Abelard, combined lecture and discussion by composing lectures
in which he argued with imagined interlocutors, "But perhaps you will
say ... " (Clanchy, 1997, p. 90). But a concern with what exactly students
were learning and how that learning might be enhanced developed only
in the 18th and 19th centuries with the great pedagogical theories of
Kant, Rousseau, Pestalozzi, Froebel, and Herbart. The effort, primarily
that of figuring out how to get information into the learner's mind, was
also an attempt to show how the learner's own predispositions, interests, activities, and efforts gave rise to knowledge and understanding.
Thus by the early 20th century, Dewey developed a pedagogy focused
almost exclusively on how the learner's experience led to intellectual
growth. Whereas Dewey's theory reflected the social changes we associate with the Enlightenment, his more specific theory of experience

as a source of knowledge required a radical rejection of the concept of the "reflex arc," a mechanical, causal connection between stimulus and response. In its place he revived an earlier intentionalism, the view that knowledge was the product of the "tryings" and "undergoings" of a conscious, intentional agent (shades of Abelard). These revisions reflected in a general way the changing conceptions of persons as individuals capable of the independent and responsible actions that are essential to life in a democracy.

Dewey's attempt to design a psychology appropriate to the actions and intentions of the learner had little effect on the discipline of psychology. Although psychology as a discipline grew out of pedagogy, it was and in large part continues to be a "third-person" objective science designed to isolate the factors that explain the extent to which children benefit from schooling. Concepts such as intelligence, dyslexia, hyperactivity, and motivation are advanced to explain why instruction succeeds or fails. The agency or cause of learning is seen to be in the hands of the institution of the school. The teacher causes the learning through taking certain actions. This approach has hindered the development of a more adequate theory that would put the agency into the hands of the learners. The first-person subjective nature of experience, what the learners are doing, think they are doing, hope to do, judge themselves as doing, were set aside in the attempt to create a natural science of learning.[1]

From an institutional perspective it is not inappropriate to view the school as a causal system so organized as to produce a kind of product. The causal system is the curriculum and the method of instruction is designed to produce a desired effect or goal just as in any plant or factory. As mentioned, the more narrowly and precisely the goals are specified and the more powerful the institution, the more likely it is to achieve its goals (Satz & Ferejohn, 1994).

Three characteristics make this simple bureaucratic model inadequate. First, educational goals are never narrow and human development is not a precisely defined notion. Second, the rights and freedoms of persons, enshrined in most charters and constitutions of the modern world, limit the right of any institution to impose its version of the good on anyone, including children. Children, too, have beliefs and goals

---

[1] To be more precise, I am advocating a scientific or third-person perspective on first-person experience; that is, the scientific theory I propose takes agency and intentionality as scientific concepts that the theorist uses to understand or represent what the child learner is doing. Eventually, this theory is to be shared with the learners themselves.

and intentions that must, by law, be respected and not simply revised or eradicated. And third, the "intentionalist" psychological theory that I set out in detail in Chapters 8 and 9, implies that neither children nor adults are simply trained into compliance with externally imposed norms but learn by accommodating their own earlier ideas to those to which they are exposed. Thus, any pedagogy, at least pedagogy in a modern democratic society, must be based on or at least account for the personal subjectivities and intentions of the learners. Pedagogical theory must account for the way teacher and student achieve a matching of minds. In such a case, content and method cannot be easily separated. As long as pedagogical theories are frozen in the causal mode of determining the method or calculating the factors that contribute to the success of the institution, pedagogical theory will continue to ignore, and in fact discourage, the growth of the subjectivities and understandings of the learners. Once we give up the causal notions implied by the notion of method, we find that there are at least three ways of thinking about the relation between teaching and learning. I refer to these ways as *folk pedagogies*. To these three, a fourth, which is based on the subjectivities of the learners but views them within the normative structures of the society, may be added.

FOLK PEDAGOGY

The concept of a folk pedagogy (Olson & Bruner, 1996) was advanced to characterize the link to folk psychology. *Folk psychology* is a somewhat dismissive yet apposite way of referring to commonsense, intentionalist psychology, that is, the psychology of beliefs and desires, as currently employed in mainstream cognitive science. The notion of a folk psychology was introduced by Wundt (1916), to contrast with the scientific psychology. Whereas the latter would set out the universal properties of the mind, folk psychology focused on everyday commonsense, culturally diverse psychological views of interest primarily to anthropologists. The Cognitive Revolution of the 1960s (Johnson & Erneling, 1997, 2002) drew many of the features of folk psychology, including consciousness and intentionality, into an enlarged scientific psychology.

The cognitivist claim is that we are directed in our practical and social behavior by a set of beliefs or assumptions about our own and others' mental lives, that we explain actions on the basis of beliefs and desires, and that we organize our interactions in terms of joint projects and collaborative discourse. But the cognitivist claim also specifies a set of assumptions about how children learn and how they are drawn into adult society. It is these latter beliefs that have been dubbed *folk pedagogies*. The attempt was to formulate an account of how different assumptions about mind, the folk psychologies, are related to different assumptions about teaching and learning, the folk pedagogy. The theory allows one to trace any pedagogical move of the teacher to the assumptions about knowledge and mind, responsibility and accountability, held by the teacher. These beliefs and assumptions, like any other set of beliefs and assumptions, are largely formed historically and, as we noted, are reflections of the larger institutional structures of the society. The diversity of these many possible relations between teaching and learning allows for variability from person to person and from context to context, thereby relaxing the constraints of a fixed methodology. On the negative side, the folk pedagogy already in the teacher's mind may limit his or her understanding of or sympathy for alternative conceptions of pedagogy. Thus, for example, novice teachers are taught to replace a traditional model of the mind with a more constructivist one.

There is a close tie between the ways of understanding another person, particularly a child, and the ways of going about attempting to influence or teach another. Thus, any attempt to teach someone something assumes that the learner is ignorant of the information to be taught. By definition you cannot teach a person something he or she already knows. Conversely, to learn from another assumes some ability to recognize the actions, meanings, and intentions of another. In an important paper, Tomasello, Kruger, and Ratner (1993; see also Tomasello, 1999) identified three basic types of social learning, imitative learning, instructed learning, and collaborative learning, each of which is premised on a specific way of understanding the actions of others. First, in order to imitate an adult or other child, the learner must see not only the motion but also the intention behind it. Put another way, the learner must recognize the goal of the actor and the means chosen to achieve it. Second, in order to learn from adult instruction, the learner must recognize the adult as a knowledgeable agent and himself or herself as ignorant of that knowledge. Third, in order to collaborate in learning, the learner must see the other as an intentional agent having beliefs, opinions, and a point of view that may be understood and perhaps shared. Those authors showed that nonhuman species differ from each other and from humans in their understanding of intention. Learning by recognizing and sharing intentions is essentially unique to humans, and whereas 18-month-old humans can imitate the actions of another person (Meltzoff et al., 1999), only when they are around 4 years can they grasp the knowledge or ignorance of another, and only at about age 6 or 7 can they fruitfully cooperate around the rules of a game (see also Chapter 8).

Building on this lead, Olson and Bruner (1996; Bruner, 1996; Olson & Katz, 2001; see also Olson & Bruner, 1974) set out three folk pedagogies that they found exemplified in the social interactions between the naive and their caregivers, between child and parent or child and teacher, for example, that could be taken as having a pedagogical intention. The three folk pedagogies were distinguished in terms of their differing conceptions of competence and the pedagogical moves aimed at altering or enhancing that competence. If competence is regarded as skill, an appropriate pedagogy might call for demonstrations and practice. If competence is regarded as possession of knowledge, then an appropriate pedagogy might call for transmitting that knowledge through telling or teaching. If competence is regarded as dependent on appropriate shared beliefs, then reasons and explanations may be an appropriate pedagogy.

This theory was used to explain not only teachers' choices of pedagogical strategy but also some aspects of the evolution of culture. Following Premack and Premack (1996), it was argued that pedagogy makes culture possible; without means for preserving and accumulating competencies, culture could not evolve. However, as we saw in Chapter 10, the growth of culture may depend less on the pedagogical intentions of adults than on the imitative powers of children, a kind of learning without teaching. Schooling is peculiar, it was argued, in that it turns over responsibility for learning to an institution. The teacher, in an institutionally defined role, interacts with the learner in a variety of ways, depending upon the adult's conception of the child, of knowledge, and of learning.

THE FIRST FOLK PEDAGOGY: IMITATION AND LEARNING TO DO

Imitation is far less common in nature than has often been assumed. Monkeys do not imitate, and only home-reared chimpanzees acquire the ability to imitate an action. To imitate successfully, as mentioned earlier, it is necessary for the learner to see another person not only as an object but as an intentional being who is carrying out some particular activity in the attempt to achieve a goal. Imitation requires the recognition of that intention. Human infants become adept at imitation in the middle of their second year, and imitation continues to be an important means of learning right through adulthood, although as we saw, imitation frequently occurs independently of the pedagogical intentions of the model. Even in cultures with little explicit teaching (Spittler, 1998), adults note their children's competence and sense of responsibility as well as the differences in talents and interests. Rather than the adult shaping the child to a preformed role, the interests, dispositions, and inclinations of children themselves are allowed to determine who will become, for example, a camel herder.

In some contexts and some cultures adults are recruited as experts who can give advice and provide demonstrations of a skilled performance, breaking up the complex act into simpler acts and providing commentary on successful actions. Here there is clearly a pedagogical effort, that is, the intention to alter the practices of the learner through an intentional demonstration. Such teaching bears the features noted by Lave and Wenger (1991), namely, that the teaching is embedded in practice, that is, it is highly contextualized, and, further, that it rarely involves linguistic or other symbolic forms of representation. Knowledge is taken to be embedded in activities; identified with particular holders, experts, or authorities; and acquired through practice.

Learning through imitation and participation is not limited to non-schooled societies but is a critical ingredient of all early learning, as Piaget demonstrated, and of many forms of sophisticated competence – the feel for the law courts or for the running of a laboratory, the implicit knowledge celebrated by Polanyi (1966). In most practical activities as well as in some crafts, such as blacksmithing, much of this knowledge is implicit in the sense that it cannot be readily expressed or explained: "You have to feel it yourself." Although much of this is acquired through observation and participation, observing and practicing are not sufficient for many advanced forms of competence. Studies of expertise demonstrate that just knowing how to perform skillfully requires not only skill but also knowing in some conceptual, reasoned way why one performs as one does (Chamberlin, 2002). Gardner, Torff, and Hatch (1996) point out that pianists need more than to have clever hands; they need to know as well something about the theory of harmony, about scales, about melodic structure, phenomena that rely heavily on scripts and scores and that require a much more explicit form of teaching.

Overall, the first folk pedagogy makes clear that learning is not reducible to teaching, that learners take responsibility for much of their own learning, but also that they learn by seeing how things are done and then imitating, playing, and practicing the routines they have observed around them.[2] Imitative, hands-on, and participatory forms of activity are central to learning in the preschool years and it is an error, I believe, to regard these years in terms of the standard schooled or instructional model. Young children need opportunities for experience, recognizing intentions in others as well as formulating intentions, acting on them, and noting the consequences; they do not need the explicit teaching that I shall describe in the second folk pedagogy.

THE SECOND FOLK PEDAGOGY: THE ACQUISITION OF KNOWLEDGE

The second folk pedagogy is best exemplified in didactic teaching in which pupils are presented with facts, principles, and rules of action that are to be learned, remembered, and applied. Such teaching assumes a sharp distinction between the knower and the known (Havelock, 1963); the known is seen as a commodity that can be shaped, stored, and transmitted quite independently of any particular knower. This was the dominant view in the West prior to the 17th century. As Hacking (1975a) has pointed out, there was thought to be an unbridgeable gap between knowledge, the true, and opinion, the beliefs of ordinary humans. Humans were not thought of as creating knowledge; at best humans preserved it and teachers and the clergy transmitted it. This pedagogy also assumes a strong distinction between culture and mind; the mind must incorporate the norms and standards of the culture through education. This pedagogy, too, assumes a certain theory of mind, that the mind is a kind of container – memory is the chief faculty, a blank slate to be written on by experience and teaching. The learner, prior to being taught, is seen as ignorant: "He does not know" indicates a defect to be remedied by passing on the critical knowledge through teaching, showing, or telling. What is to be learned by the student is just that which is presently "in" the mind of the teacher supplemented by books, maps, charts, computer databases, and the like, which can be written into class reports and ideally into the learner's mind. This knowledge is represented by the "canon," the standard works of the culture, which

---

[2] Yogi Berra is famous for saying, among other quotables, "You can observe a lot by just watching."

it is the responsibility of the teacher to present and the responsibility of the learner to assimilate.

Whereas knowledge is seen as existing external to the mind, the mind has to be seen in a particular way. Knowledge can be acquired only because the mind is composed of faculties, of special "learning abilities," abilities to learn, to remember, to infer, to paraphrase, and the like, which were then measured by IQ and other diagnostic tests. Thinking of the mind as composed of such faculties offered as well a commonsense explanation of the differences among learners: Some are brighter than others, some are at a later stage of development, some have special talents, some have special interests, and so on. This "transmission" model of pedagogy has, of course, been the object of scorn for generations of educational theorists, but an obstinate fact in its favor remains: that the best single explanation of a student's failure to know, for example, that bats are mammals, is that he or she has not yet been taught. Either it was not in the curriculum or it was being saved for the next grade. Yet, teaching is not the same as telling. Both assume ignorance in the learner, but whereas telling simply provides information, teaching also implies the notion of uptake, some standard or criterion for judging that learning has occurred. That is to say that in teaching, the teacher takes some responsibility for the student's learning.

When knowledge is considered to be a commodity, an object to be conveyed, the pedagogical problem is one of deciding how to break the knowledge into assimilable chunks. These chunks are then taught, beginning at the beginning. This would explain the traditional forms of instruction that date back to the classical period.

As noted in chapter 10, in 15th-century Italy all forms of subject matter were divided into individual bits of knowledge that were drilled intensively and then assembled into wholes, much like a bricklayer, building up knowledge block by block (Grendler, 1989). This authoritative knowledge was literally installed into what was taken to be a blank but respective mind.

And although the frequent object of scorn, this conception of teaching and learning is the folk pedagogy adhered to by most policymakers and curriculum designers and many practicing teachers and students, especially in the higher grades whether in history, literature, science, or mathematics. Its principal appeal is that by virtue of its clear conception of what is taken as known and its orderly procession through it, it offers an equally clear analysis of what is to be taught as well as a clear criterion against which competence is to be assessed. Even more importantly, it allows an unequivocal assignment of responsibility for coverage by the teacher and for mastery by the learner – hence students' questions before exams as to what they are responsible for knowing. Finally, it is the conception most compatible with objective statistical analysis that has provided the field with a set of factors that account for the variance in performance of students – when knowledge is regarded as a commodity, the factors affecting its transfer may be measured and rough predictions of outcomes calculated. Although such a folk pedagogy is appropriate for thinking of the school as an institutional function, it is less appropriate for the analysis of the learning and thinking of individual children in particular learning contexts. This lacuna is filled by the third folk pedagogy.

THE THIRD FOLK PEDAGOGY: THE ACQUISITION OF BELIEFS AND THE SHARING OF INTENTIONS

The traditional transmission model of education was under harsh criticism by the end of the 19th century. Writers such as Dewey (1976b) criticized the emphasis on the dead weight of isolated facts; more recently, Freire (1972) criticized the "banking" model of education, insisting rather that learning is always contextual and that learners must construct their own understandings and take responsibility for their own experience. The cognitive theory that attempts to come to grips with the understanding of mind and other minds, the so-called theory of mind, attempts to recover the learners' perspectives rather than simply imposing authoritative knowledge on them. The teacher, according to this view, is concerned with what children think, how they arrived at what they think, and how they could be led to think in a more precise, responsible, and accountable way. Learners are seen as constructing models of the world by using narrative and paradigmatic frames in order to interpret their experience and plan their actions. These models are elaborated through experience, discussion, and collaboration as well as through the explicit representational forms such as texts, diagrams, and working models. Each child is expected to represent developing ideas in several ways, depending on the task at hand and the need to share that understanding with others.

This pedagogy premised on discussion and collaboration is based on the assumption that the human mind is the repository of subjectively constructed and privately held beliefs and ideas that, by means of discussion and cooperation, may be incorporated in a shared frame of reference with others. Children, no less than adults, are thought of and treated as having a point of view that they are encouraged to recognize, to express, to compare to alternative points of view, and to revise on the basis of new forms of evidence. Knowledge is no longer seen as the objectively given and true but rather as human invention, the revisable product of human endeavor. This is the sense behind the *Bullock Report*'s assertion (Great Britain, 1975, p. 50) that "it is a confusion of everyday thought that we tend to regard 'knowledge' as something that exists independently of someone who knows." As long as knowledge was seen as an eternal, unchanging gift from God rather than the product of human inquiry, the gap between knowledge and belief remained unbridgeable. The third pedagogy closes that gap.

"Knowledge exists only in the activities and participation of subjects as knowers," as D. Smith (1990b, p. 66) has pointed out. Knowledge is of a piece with the thoughts and beliefs of learners. In this third folk pedagogy, children, as are adults, are seen as constructing and entertaining "theories" that may be revised on the basis of new experiences, including the explicit lessons of a teacher. These bodies of beliefs, these theories, when subjected to the processes of discussion, revision, and collaboration, constitute their knowledge. Thus the learner is invited to form his or her own understandings rather than merely recite those of the authority but then to go on to examine those understandings in the light of further evidence, possible implications and the like. This pedagogy is child-centered not in that it stoops to the child's level but rather in that it treats the perceptions and explanations of the child seriously while attempting to build an understanding that can be shared by teacher and child. It is an attempt, as Dewey said, to find in the intuitions of the child the roots of systematic knowledge (1976b).

Considerable psychological and educational research in the past three decades has contributed to the development of this third folk pedagogy (Bruner, 1960; Donaldson, 1978; Strauss, 2001). Research on children's theory of mind in relation to learning suggests that only when children recognize beliefs as beliefs and beliefs about beliefs are they able to understand basic epistemological relations between theory and evidence, contrary beliefs, implied beliefs, and the assorted concepts important to metacognition (Kuhn, 2000). Further, studies of learning in particular cognitive domains have indicated the importance of collaborative learning and metacognition, and of treatment of children as thinkers (Brown,

1997; Bereiter & Scardamalia, 1993; Bransford, Brown & Cocking, 1999) in fostering their learning and development.

One advantage of such folk theories is their accessibility to ordinary language, a language that can be learned and shared by the teacher and student. Whereas scientific psychology often introduces explanatory concepts that remain opaque to laypersons, every teacher and every child can come to understand what it is to know, to believe, to have a reason, to judge truth and falsity, to recognize contradictions, to have a theory, a hunch, a piece of evidence, and so on. Further, these concepts are conscious and intentional and one can be held responsible for them. Folk psychology is democratic.

THE TROUBLE WITH FOLK THEORIES

Much pedagogical theory for the past century is at worst a battle and at best a discourse between the second and the third folk pedagogies. Teachers know both theories and are forced to switch between them with little to guide them beyond their own experience and judgment. S. Katz (2001) asked teachers to describe how they approached teaching a mandated curriculum. They reported deep conflict about "drumming in" testable facts at the expense of a deeper understanding as well as a conflict about honoring the mandated standards rather than the individual's progress. One teacher reported:

The Ministry documents say "the student will independently . . . " [write a report on Louis Riel]. [One child] might only be a level 2 but I'll give him a 3 plus because he has come so far. The guy next to him who has all the grey matter upstairs and is just lazy, he gets a 2. So sometimes I just toss what the Ministry says aside; I'm working with this kid's self-esteem and he has put in hours on it. (p. 76)

Another teacher wrote:

Oh, I'll go through [the assignment] the first time and see where he stands according to everybody else [the norms]. Then I'll go back and look at where he is himself [relative to] what I know he has done in the past. (p. 75)

That is, the teacher tries, often unsuccessfully, to mediate between the rigid standards of the published curriculum and the feasible achievements of each child. In so doing the teacher switches between these two pedagogies, often feeling guilty about either ignoring the ministry guidelines or accommodating the special needs of the child.

The teacher's attempts to reconcile the mandated criteria with the personal needs of students remain a matter of hunch, intuition, and professional judgment. No theory guides them in reconciling these conflicting aspirations. Rather, they have available two pedagogies, one emphasizing compliance with a fixed external curriculum buttressed by a psychology that explains performance in terms of impersonal, causal factors such as abilities and treatments, the other emphasizing personal growth and understanding buttressed by an intentionalist psychology that explains performance in terms of concepts, beliefs, theories, and conceptual change.

In one sense, the three pedagogies reflect advances in our understanding of human cognition and human development (Case, 1996). But in another, they reflect advances not simply in the philosophy of knowledge or the psychology of understanding, but rather in the social changes discussed in Chapter 10. Folk pedagogies are orientations to knowledge and minds that in a larger sense reflect social practices. Durkheim (1956, p. 120) pointed to these dependencies, arguing that education was "ascetic in the Middle Ages, liberal in the Renaissance, literary in the seventeenth century and scientific in our time." We may refine these stages as follows. Nonbureaucratic, nonliterate cultures with low degrees of bureaucratic organization leave learning largely to the innate imitative and agentive resources of children, allowing them to have whatever beliefs they find interesting and useful so long as they comply with the largely implicit social norms of the society (J. Goody, 1986). Classical or transmission pedagogies took precedence when large-scale dominating institutions, whether the church or the nation, took certain beliefs and forms of action as central to their growth or survival and created institutions, primarily schools, to see that these patterns were preserved. Child-centered pedagogies flowed from republican and democratic nations in which the individual was granted the right to play a role in the formation and control of the state. It was seen as necessary to develop the competence needed to participate in these institutions but also to play a role in inventing and reforming them: ideally, to make institutions serve the people rather than control them. Dewey's proposed reforms of the school were intended to make people able to criticize their institutions rather than merely conform to them.

It is doubtful that schools have ever seriously pursued the democratic ideal. We must acknowledge, following Scheffler (1974), that Dewey overestimated the freedom of the school to pursue progressive goals and underestimated the school's dependence on the other institutions in the society. That is another reason for setting out a fourth pedagogy.

A FOURTH PEDAGOGY: CONNECTING THE SUBJECTIVE WITH THE NORMATIVE

Suppose we grant the central premise of the third folk pedagogy, namely, that learners must construct their own beliefs and take responsibility for their own learning. What assurance do we have that the beliefs that they construct are true, at least true in the limited sense of "taken to be true" by the larger society? What is the basis on which we judge children's understandings to be understandings rather than misunderstandings? Without a standard for truth, the very idea of a misconception is impossible; it entails that there is a truer conception against which a person's current conception may be judged. The child-centered pedagogy, with its emphasis on understanding and collaboration, fails to specify how a learner is to judge the truth or validity of any acquired belief and understanding beyond his or her own feelings of understanding.

The two familiar avenues of escape more or less define the discourse of educational reform. One is to deny explicit standards, a relativism that denies the possibility of misconception (they are just differences of opinion) and satisfies itself with the centrality of meaning making. This option is appealing to revisionist educational theorists but appalling to current policymakers, to some historians (Ravitch, 2000), and, admittedly, to me. The other is to abandon child-centered pedagogy and revert to traditional pedagogy with its canon and its externally imposed criteria for judging knowing. This course is appealing to policymakers but appalling to most educators and, admittedly, to me. This polarity provides us with a ground for inexhaustible debate.

Alternatively, we could attempt to formulate a view that escapes that polemic by setting out a framework for relating private, felt understandings with explicit, objective criteria specified by the institutional forms, the disciplined knowledge. This was a project undertaken some three decades ago by Kohlberg and Meyer (1972), who noted that the developmental stages set out by Piaget tended to converge on the institutionally sanctioned disciplinary view. More recently Kuhn (2000) noted the convergence between intersubjective understanding and epistemological development. This convergence is the basis of the fourth pedagogy.

This fourth pedagogy, then, would acknowledge the existence of a cultural store of socially sanctioned knowledge that has been constructed by means of accepted procedures and monitored by the knowledge institutions of the society, roughly "what is taken as known." But at the same time it would acknowledge the experiential skills, knowledge, and beliefs subjectively held by the learner. As noted, the problem is that acknowledging the "taken as known" tends to collapse onto the second pedagogy, the view that knowledge existed and it is the role of pedagogy to convey or transmit that knowledge. On the other hand, granting priority to the personally known or understood collapses onto the third pedagogy, the pedagogy of subjective mental states and communicative discourse. The "known" in the third pedagogy is little more than the set of agreements attained. Aside from acknowledging that any modern pedagogy has to come to terms with what is known and the importance of connecting what is known with the learner's own abilities, knowledge, and experience, pedagogical theory has remained largely silent on how to reconcile the two. A promising alternative is to be found in the concept of pedagogy as the management of joint intention, what Bruner (1996, p. 182) described as "the close-textured pattern of reciprocity about the intentional states of one's partners."

Joint intention transcends the recognition of an intention needed for such more humble activities as imitation and the interpretation of action, to include the formation of a joint project (Oatley & Nundy, 1996). As we saw earlier, humans are innately social (Bruner, 1996; Tomasello, 1999) beings. Cognition is constructed around shared intentions and intersubjectivity, a social understanding that allows the learning of language, the formation of joint activities, and ultimately, the setting of joint goals, plans, and projects. Joint attention is a familiar topic in early child development, the ability of an adult and a child to coordinate their perspectives such as following the direction of gaze and pointing to interesting objects and events. Joint intentions provide the basis for co-operative activities such as turn taking, game playing, and holding of conversations.

Clark (1996) examined such joint communicative activities as greetings, marriage ceremonies, and buying and selling. He offered as an appropriate analogy for communicative action two persons' playing a duet. It is not sufficient that each have an intention to play the notes indicated by the score; each must also recognize that his or her single part is part of a larger enterprise, the duet. This larger intention is the joint intention. To state this another way, the recognition of parts as belonging to the duet is the point, the *Witz*, of the activity. Within this joint activity, individual actors may entertain quite different intentions and beliefs – they may be playing quite different instruments or singing different parts. Young children chase each other around a park, each with a personal intention; only later do they fuse these private intentions into a joint intention, say, to play a game of tag. The game or the communication defines roles, possible actions, implicit rules, expectations, entitlements, and obligations while allowing some scope for individual actions.

The teacher and learner form a joint goal or intention that specifies a criterion for achievement, perhaps through a demonstration of competent performance or correct action or through consideration of the proposed outcomes. Wells (1999) has pointed out the importance of discourse in the formation of these joint goals and understandings. Once a shared goal is established, explicit teaching, reading, experimenting, talking, writing, and listening may all find a place within this joint activity. The teacher neither completely accepts responsibility for student knowledge, as in the second folk pedagogy, nor simply turns over responsibility to the learner, as in the third folk pedagogy. Rather it is a pedagogy of arriving at a joint goal, both shared and public, against which either teacher or student can assess his or her performance and take corrective action. All teaching and learning take place within these joint projects even if at each point the beliefs, intentions, and meanings may be quite discrepant – recall the children making clocks while the teacher thought they were learning about time. Nor are these joint projects adequately described as a conversation in that they are formulated not on a one-to-one basis but on a one-to-many basis – one teacher to a whole class – with the teacher envisioning one goal and each of the students somewhat free to formulate his or her own. Whereas the teacher takes the project to be that of learning math, some students may take it to be "getting a needed credit." To the extent that the projects overlap, joint efforts will be productive.[3] What the fourth pedagogy may alert educators to is the fact that the pedagogical exchange may be divided into two phases, first, agreeing on the criterion, certainly the more difficult part, and second, choosing means for reaching that criterion, much of the responsibility for which may be left to the learner. Joint intentions are the basis for the fourth, to a large extent a future, pedagogy.

---

[3] The latitude in the formation of joint activities is interestingly shown in an autobiographical note by Andrea di Sessa (2000, p. 70): "I was . . . minimally interested in learning for its own sake . . . my social [educational] goals were either mildly subversive or intended to co-opt institutional goals by substituting what I wanted to do for what teachers thought I should do."

Each of these four pedagogies may also be seen as appropriate to particular goals. For the learning of classroom rules, for example, the first and second pedagogies are most appropriate. Anyone with experience in a classroom knows that "off-loading" matters of classroom routines to the rules of the classroom is a massively labor-saving operation. In learning to comply with rules for orderly classroom management children learn both the nature of rules and their duties. As well these impersonal rules save the teacher from endless explanations and justifications for every action. The teacher who says, "I hear talking" acts as one who is monitoring a given, impersonal norm rather than as one who is trying to impose a personal intention. The second pedagogy comes into play when the teacher discovers conspicuous gaps in knowledge or understanding that may be filled by reading a text or hearing an exposition. One teacher reported that although her focus was on students' expressive writing, when she discovered that children had no idea about the use of the comma, she called the class together and explained its basic functions (S. Katz, 2001). Ultimately, the third pedagogy comes into play when the knowledge to be acquired runs up against the beliefs already in place in learner's minds. Recall the difficulties involved in understanding "plant food" or why one cannot "see through" a brick wall, or whether rivers are alive, or, for that matter, whether the theory of evolution is true. Not only is the giving of reasons useful for purposes of evaluation and accountability, the validity of knowledge itself is taken to be dependent on the quality of the reasons and evidence supporting that knowledge. Durkheim's distinction between faith and science is just that one that I have made between the second and third pedagogies: "Science permits us to establish rationally what faith postulates a priori" (1961, p. 115).[4] That is, schooling in a modern society is a matter of rationalizing, giving reasons for, everything that had previously been learned as a matter of faith, rule, or tradition. Pedagogy is explicitness.

This fourth pedagogy rests largely on the elaboration and use of just those epistemological concepts and distinctions with which I have described the pedagogies themselves because these are precisely the concepts needed for establishing the joint learning projects and goals. First,

---

[4] Both Durkheim (1956, p. 72) and Vygotsky (1986, p. 94) saw development as a shift from a biological individualism to a cultural sociality, arguing that the internalization of the culture was responsible for making persons into social beings. Current theory insists that children are innately social. Hence, I argue that development is a matter of going from social commitment to the local culture to commitment to the formal, explicit, institutionalized society.

it requires that a clear distinction be made between knowledge and belief: the former being what is "taken as known" by the disciplines and institutions of the society, the latter what is personally held by the individual. The fourth pedagogy involves an intimate contact with the written, documentary tradition. It involves knowing what a document says and the form of the evidence on which it is based as well as what "scientists believe" and their reasons for so believing. These are held in relation to what "I believe" and allows for some discrepancy between the two. It involves the ability not only to express those beliefs in a variety of representational formats but also to recover and manipulate the "attitude" or commitment to those beliefs – whether as tentative conjecture or firm belief – as well as a robust concept of understanding appropriate to each domain. The fourth pedagogy, finally, provides a basis for an extensive reanalysis of responsibilities for learning that shall concern us in the next chapter.

PART IV

PROSPECTS FOR THE STUDY AND REFORM OF EDUCATION

13

Responsibilities for Teaching and Learning

> The social arrangements that produce responsibility are arrangements
> that create coercion, of some sort.
>
> (G. Hardin, 1968, p. 1247)

So how can an understanding of institutions allow us to think about
education in a more enlightened way? First, we may see that education
is organized as a set of agents in special roles each with a different set
of entitlements and obligations, rights and responsibilities. And second,
we may see that each of these agents has a special and essential type of
tradition, competence, and expertise. Let us first examine the levels and
then the competencies involved in executing them.

A modern nation-state is entitled to tax in return for taking on the
obligation of providing a particular kind of education for the young.
This obligation is normally met by delegating this responsibility to the
class of professional educators, sometimes disparagingly referred to as
"educrats," who then set more specific goals, select and train the professionals required, and provide the needed resources, ranging from
buildings to curricular materials. This professional class in turn passes
the responsibility for the actual operation of schools and the teaching of children to a second level of professionals, including administrators, principals, and teachers, who are entitled to resources with
the obligation to provide students with appropriate opportunities for
learning. This professional class in turn delegates, so far as possible,
the actual responsibility for learning to the learners themselves, who,
if they accept those responsibilities, are entitled to graduate. At each
level, the acceptance of responsibility entails accountability; if one does

not fulfill the specified responsibility, one loses the entitlement. If students do not pass their examinations, they are not entitled to graduate. If teachers do not meet the requirement of providing appropriate instruction, they are not entitled to a salary and resources. If bureaucrats do not provide appropriately trained professionals, programs, and resources, they stand to lose their funding. And if states do not provide credentialed graduates, they are not entitled to tax. And so on.

Whereas there is a long, well-established tradition of assessing whether students have met the obligations that entitle them to grades and credentials, as Bromley (1998) noted, there is an absence of "efficiency indicators" useful for assessing the institution as a whole in terms of inputs and outputs. Institutions such as the legal, health care, and education systems are extremely difficult to assess for efficiency and in the past have settled for a series of reviews by panels of experts who consider a broad range of summary statistics such as cases handled, patient recovery rates, and graduation rates. But in education in the past decade there is a new optimism that these levels of accountability can be telescoped such that the state can directly determine the effectiveness of the entire enterprise by examining student performance. Student performance is then used not only to determine whether students have met their obligations but whether all the other levels of the system have met theirs. That is, state, national, and international testing programs aspire to measure student performance and on that basis judge (1) whether students are meeting their obligations, (2) whether the teacher in the classroom is meeting his or her obligations, (3) whether the school as a unit is meeting its obligations, (4) whether the district containing the school is meeting its obligations, and (5) whether the professional educational bureaucracy is meeting its obligations. The obvious problem here is that success implies that all are doing their duty; failure points nowhere in particular. If everyone is guilty, no one is guilty. Most seriously, responsibility for learning is deflected from its primary focus, namely, students' responsibility for their own learning.

In the past each of these entitlement–accountability levels was assessed in distinctive ways that acknowledged their special responsibilities and their special expertise. States could assess relations between enrollments and graduates, extend or reduce programs according to perceived social needs, examine comparability of graduates across schools via criterion-referenced and norm-referenced standardized tests,[1] and delegate to professional educators the task of working out optimal programs and organizational structures and the allocation of funds. Educational professionals take responsibility for advancing specialized knowledge and establishing programs for teacher training and certification and are assessed, in turn, in terms of the academic quality of their programs and the competencies of their graduates. Schools and school systems take responsibility for providing programs of study and a supporting environment, that is, the ethos of the school, that allow teachers and students to meet their more specific goals. Whether teachers met their responsibilities has been assessed in terms of student satisfaction, contribution to the teamwork and ethos of the school, as well as student learning. Whether students did learn was assessed by tests, performances, and other productions. As we saw earlier, testing has always been a central part not only of teaching but of judging competence as a basis for awarding credentials.

What the recent concern for school effectiveness has done is seriously telescope these levels of responsibility, thereby assigning responsibility to the most vulnerable, the students and teachers, while eliminating responsibilities from the highest levels of the educational system. Thus instead of governments' blaming themselves for the failure to provide adequately trained professionals or the job satisfaction required to reduce the rapid turnover and loss of staff – features essential to a well-functioning school – they tend to focus exclusively on student performance and assign credit and blame to teachers and students. Telescoping assessment by appeal only to the bottom line of student achievement, rather than separately judging the quality of various components of the system, not only inappropriately displaces responsibility but also tends to eclipse the importance of professional judgment embedded in the various levels of the institution of schooling. What a professional class of educators can do is mediate between the aspirations and goals of the state and the personal lives of the learners. Whereas the state may want, and through assessment determine, an increase in piety, participation in civil society, or graduates who read better or calculate faster, professionals play a critical role in embedding those aspirations within the broader context of the community, school, and individuals involved.

---

[1] A move that, when examined in detail in Ontario, Canada, was shown to be no better than more local teacher-based assessments (Traub, Wolfe, & Russell, 1976–1977).

They embed these mandated goals within a network of often conflicting concerns such as health, safety, and the mental and moral well-being of the learners involved, including their general satisfaction and their willingness to participate. The goals selected by the state may be entirely legitimate, but if they are implemented mechanically, that is, as if they were all that mattered, and, further, that success in attaining those mandated goals determined such related considerations as school ranking or teacher salary, the special individual nature of the learner or the class would necessarily be ignored. *Moby Dick* and *The Turn of the Screw*[2] are fictional accounts of what may happen when a goal turns into a fetish; people may resort to desperate means with neglected but foreseeable consequences. In fact, failure to impose measurable goals relentlessly may result in loss of entitlements. What educational professionals can do is assist in the formulation of worthwhile goals as well as mediate between the general institutional goals mandated by the state and the special needs, interests, and talents of the class or learner. Professionals do this in two ways. First, teachers, schools, and entire school districts evolve an ethos, a tradition of practice and understanding of what works and what does not for their students and their community. Second, teachers and schools temper the stated goals to the special needs of the learner. Teachers know when to apply pressure and when to relax it and when to commend a student for effort even if performance is below the norm or standard. These activities call for professional judgment.

The issue of "social promotion" is a case in point. A state, wishing to increase standards, may legislate against promoting a child if he or she does not fully meet the stated target. Although well motivated, such a policy, applied blindly, may in many cases do considerable damage; decisions in education often require professional judgment based on the particular properties of the school, the program, the teacher, and the student. Analogies are close at hand: Medical professionals are required to judge whether the benefits of a procedure outweigh the possible costs.

---

[2] Canadian history, too, has its examples of the effects of "orders given from a distance." The expulsion of the Acadians from what is now Nova Scotia was a brutal act that was carried out in compliance with an order given by an officer residing far away, who, therefore, had no inkling of the suffering inflicted. A second example is the Franklin Expedition to northern Canada, in which Franklin, in the attempt to comply with an order given in Britain, perservered in conditions that caused the death of the majority of his men. On the other hand, failure to comply with such orders exposes one to the charge of insubordination. Such are the risks entailed in issuing orders from a distance.

Economic specialists are required to judge whether tax reduction benefits average citizens more than the loss of services costs them. So too educational professionals do not simply carry out the activities set by the state but judge or mediate between those goals and the needs and interests and talents of the students and resources available. This is not to say that they may not err on the side of charity as often as they err on the side of standards, but it is unlikely that they err in their judgments more often than do judges or umpires or the rest of us, for that matter.

The professional serves one other, often neglected, purpose. He or she interprets and translates the goals of the institution into classroom activities in such a way that students can themselves take responsibility for their learning. In part they do this by helping students translate mandated goals into personal ones. Just as courts have to interpret law by fitting it to the local case, so teachers help students to interpret the goals of the school as personal ones. Successful teachers, as we say, put themselves out of a job.

Thus it is, therefore, incorrect to say that the state mandates the goals and the school devises the means for achieving them. Rather, the school provides an interpretation and adjustment of those goals to local standards and individual learners in such a way that responsibility for their achievement can be negotiated with and passed on to the learners. The conclusion is that the responsibilities of the school cannot be assessed by the single criterion of student achievement of specified norms. As we shall see, norms and standards are important but for a somewhat different purpose.

The so-called market approach to education, an approach that attempts to relate outputs in terms of student learning to costs, may provide new and useful data about schooling. But even firms such as banks that have a single criterion such as earnings recognize the importance of an institutional structure and professional expertise to set a goal in its immediate social context. More so, schools with their multiple goals, goals that are often in conflict, require a profession and an institution with the knowledge and power necessary to exercise judgment in an informed way.

TEACHERS' RESPONSIBILITY FOR STUDENTS' LEARNING

In thinking about education from an institutional perspective, then, one encounters a cascade of intentionality and responsibility, of rights and obligations (Jackendoff, 1999). The state is entitled to collect taxes and it is obligated to provide good education for its citizens. It delegates its obligations on down through the bureaucracy of professionals, including curriculum designers, assessment specialists, and professional educators. School faculty are entitled to receive salary and status in return for taking on the obligations of teaching a body of agreed upon knowledge and mandated skills to the learners. Students are entitled to graduate if they meet the obligations of attendance and test performance.

Schools routinely fail by accepting responsibility for the achievement of goals that lie far beyond their own powers to achieve. This is obviously true for such lofty goals as reducing crime, violence, unwanted pregnancies, or even unemployment. But in any ultimate sense, teachers cannot even take responsibility for student learning because such learning is the intentional product of the learner's own activities. In the first place if the teacher were to take over such responsibility, it would deprive the learner of responsibility for his or her own knowledge and action. At least at some point the learner is responsible for his or her own intentional states. Colonizing minds, making another person think one's own thoughts, is the stuff of science fiction, not education. In the second place, the limits of responsibility of the teacher can be seen in terms of limits of accountability: Who is at fault if a student incorrectly answers a question or fails a test? The student or the teacher or the school district or the state? Phrasing the question in terms of fault allows us to think in terms of possible litigation; in a court of law, who would be found negligent in the case of a failed test or a serious mistake? Ultimately, the actor is responsible for both beliefs and actions even in cases that result in, say, injury on a playground. All the supervisor can be responsible for is context; negligence is failure to provide or manage context, the provision of the necessary resources.[3] The teacher can hope for or have the goal of eliminating accidents but cannot so intend and so cannot accept ultimate responsibility.[4] But at least in the case of physical action, supervision may include restraint or forcible confinement. That is not the case for mental actions, for thinking and believing.

---

[3] The Toronto School Board, fearing litigation, removed playground equipment from schools, after an internal report indicated that it may not meet the highest standards of safety – much to the annoyance of the parents and disappointment of the children.

[4] You can no more intend that a child will learn something or do something than you can intend that it will rain tomorrow.

When it comes to learning and thinking, the obligations of the teacher are further reduced, for it is the child who must not only have the correct beliefs, but have them as his or her own and be responsible for them. Being responsible entails being accountable in the further sense of being able to justify them by appeal to reasons. Beliefs, as we saw earlier, are intentional states; beliefs are intrinsically personal, and the holder is responsible and accountable for those beliefs. What then is the educators' responsibility here? It cannot be the instillation of correct beliefs because then the beliefs are not the child's responsibility at all but the teacher's as we saw earlier. The learning is the child's own and the child's responsibility, a manifestation of the child's own intentionality. And further, the failure of the child to learn certain skills or acquire certain knowledge could not be blamed directly on the teacher by a court unless negligence, that is, failure to provide opportunity for learning, were demonstrated.

As an aside, we may note here the somewhat limited scope of the concept of socialization. If construed too broadly, it makes into a social responsibility the intentional states of individuals. It may be the goal of the school to produce pious churchgoers, willing workers, or law-abiding citizens, but the school cannot accept responsibility for actually achieving that goal. Thus, if workers go on strike or resist the draft or deny a theory, this act cannot be simply ascribed to a failure of schooling. The school has responsibility for provision of conditions for learning not for the intentional states of individuals. Consequently notions such as socialization are appropriate only in institutional discourse, that is, in characterization of entire populations, not the thoughts and actions of individuals.

Both teachers and states grant entitlements in exchange for taking on obligations. Teachers may grant a passing grade if a student accepts responsibility for learning certain content and meets the corresponding obligations. Failure to learn may be met with sanctions just as failure to comply with the law of the state may be met with a fine or imprisonment. In this way societies, including teachers, discharge their responsibilities. States cannot eliminate crime as crime is an intentional act of a perpetrator; similarly, teachers cannot eliminate ignorance because beliefs are intentional states of learners. But as states can, teachers can provide opportunity and apply sanctions. Indeed, failure to provide the resources needed for individual learners to discharge their responsibilities may lead to a charge of negligence by the state. Thus the teacher or the state may be found at fault in a court of law. Under what conditions?

Whereas teachers are not responsible for student learning, they are responsible for the provision of reasonable opportunity for learning. Here the notion of "coverage" emerges; teachers are at fault if they have not, as we say, covered the relevant information, the information mandated by the course of study. The so-called recitation method in which a teacher describes the content to be learned and asks students questions about it is ideally suited to this responsibility. The method is criticized because it leads teachers to ignore all the answers offered until the correct one emerges, when the teacher tends to repeat that answer, perhaps writing it on the blackboard. But if it is coverage for which the teacher is held responsible, this technique becomes perfectly understandable. The correct answer demonstrates that the appropriate information was available to the learner and the teacher has discharged one of his or her responsibilities. The teacher cannot be held responsible for "uptake" as that is the learner's responsibility. Making manifest the norms and standards against which student understanding is to be assessed is a responsibility of the teacher, a responsibility discharged through his or her response to the students' offerings. Some child-centered discourse methods may be criticized as leaving those norms and standards implicit and unremarked.

Taken too far, this would seem to absolve teachers from any responsibility for student learning. The recognition that children are responsible for constructing their own knowledge may lead some to suggest inappropriately that conventional teaching is impossible and that teaching must be revised accordingly. I believe this to be a non sequitur; expository instruction is perfectly compatible with a constructivist view of mind. The learner must make up his or her own representation, whether on the basis of telling or of exploration. Debates regarding the efficacy of discovery versus expository learning revolve not around knowledge representation, but around contradictory claims of responsibility. Discovery aims at inducing children to take responsibility for learning how to find out; expositiory teaching aims at inducing children to take responsibility for specific content. Even in the former case, however, the teacher is responsible for providing whatever help is needed to preempt the charge that the student "was never taught that" or "never shown how to," both of which would constitute negligence. Conversely, expository teachers would be vulnerable if they never taught children "how to find out for themselves" if that were a stated and assessable goal of education. To date, most states content themselves with mastery of the accepted conventional, so-called basic forms with a corresponding loss in depth of understanding.

STUDENTS' RESPONSIBILITY FOR THEIR OWN LEARNING

Responsibility for learning, therefore, devolves ultimately to the learner. If the teacher and school system have met their obligations for providing suitable opportunities for learning, it is the responsibility of children to learn, or, as we say, to construct their own understandings. As it is their responsibility, they can be held accountable and assessed through tests, assignments, projects, and the like. Our central pedagogical question then becomes, What precisely is involved in children's taking responsibility for their own learning? I am not here thinking of the radically individualized and self-directed activities so valued by Dewey and other liberal educators, but rather of the mundane responsibility for learning, say, that light travels in straight lines or that 13 is a prime number. What has a learner to go on?

Educational theory has relied upon two conditions, meeting the public criterion of performance and the private one of understanding. As to the first, teachers can articulate the criteria that have to be met and then help students appraise their performances in the light of those criteria. What learners can do is rely on their own successes and failures to assess whether or not they have met that criterion. "Trying" and "undergoing" accompanied by feelings of puzzlement and satisfaction were central to Dewey's description. Performance allows a child to recognize whether he or she has the required knowledge. Since its beginnings, education has employed tests in some form or another not only to judge learners' performances but to provide learners with information about their own performance. Here the teacher is required if the child fails to recognize either the adequacy or the inadequacy of a solution or the rational basis for its adequacy. If a child spells *arctic* as *artic*, the teacher may by pointing to the standard to allow the learner to revise both pronunciation and spelling. In fact, students may radically overestimate their ability to recall information (Flavell, 1985) and consequently underestimate the need for study or reflection.

But equally important, especially if the learner is to take responsibility for his or her own learning, are the internal criteria for understanding that I discussed more fully in Chapter 9. To understand is to grasp the meaning, and as Dewey (1978, p. 273) pointed out, "All knowledge, all science . . . aims to grasp the meaning of objects and events, and this

process always consists in taking them out of their apparent brute isolation as events, and finding them to be parts of some larger whole *suggested by them*, which, in turn, *accounts for, explains, interprets them; i.e.,*
renders them significant." Such mental grasping is a subjective experience. What is left unexamined in Dewey's claim is the issue of the social
norms or standards that are to be used in judging that understanding. If
understanding is an emotion or feeling, what is to prevent learners from
feeling they understand when in fact they misunderstand. As important
as the feeling of understanding is, it cannot preempt responsibility for
arriving at the correct understanding, and here again the role of the
teacher is essential. The teacher, backed by an authoritative textbook,
represents the society's knowledge, norms, and standards; the teacher
is not simply another person with an opinion.

Nor is this just a matter of passing responsibility for understanding
from the learner back to the teacher; it remains the learner's responsibility, but now a responsibility to understand the standard, orthodox
version and to assess his or her personal understandings and beliefs
in the light of these norms and standards. Pedagogy readily errs on
this point. Either it allows the students' feelings of understanding, their
own "made meanings," to predominate at the expense of the norms and
standards of the discipline, or, conversely, it allows the learners to take
encouragement from the teacher as the criterion for having understood,
thereby abandoning their own feeling of understanding. As the former
is the more or less inevitable consequence of progressive methods, the
latter is the almost inevitable consequence of mandating of external criteria for achievement – the goal becomes passing the test rather than
grasping the meaning. How can a learner take responsibility for the
beliefs and theories that are imposed through standard curricula? This
may not be as impossible as it seems on the surface.

STUDENT RESPONSIBILITY FOR INSTITUTIONALIZED KNOWLEDGE

In order to participate in a modern society, learners have to take responsibility for the knowledge embedded in the public institutions of science,
law, literature, economics, and the like, and the route is through the statement and evaluation of reasons for holding beliefs or for taking certain
actions. Whereas all human beings are rational in the sense that they
act for reasons, institutions articulate, elaborate, criticize, and provide
evidence for and against the beliefs, principles, and knowledge that are

embedded in their domain. Courts develop expertise in assessing claims about responsibility, mathematicians about mathematical proofs, and so on. As I pointed out earlier it is a mistake to identify the "thinking"of an individual with the "practices" of a whole institution, yet to participate, either by using the resources of experts or by becoming expert onself, involves learning how to make explicit and public the reasons for believing and acting. There is a close relation between *understanding* and *explanation*, a relation similar to that between *believing* and *asserting*. That is, explanation is a public, explicit expression of one's understanding. But further explanation may be used as the normative criterion for judging whether or not understanding has occurred, a criterion available to both the teacher and the student. Teachers can assess students by asking them to give reasons for certain claims or beliefs, but students, too, can assess their own understanding by seeing whether they can justify their beliefs by giving reasons. Reasons, too, have to meet normative criteria; there are good and bad reasons, and learning to distinguish them is an important part of understanding.

The normative practice of reason giving and metacognition run together. Explanation, the giving of explicit or public reasons, is not only an important route to assessment, but the route to metacognition, that is, cognition about cognition. It is not enough that a learner have reasons – even the heart has its reasons – those reasons must be recognized as reasons and therefore public and open to scrutiny. Recognizing a belief as a belief and recognizing valid reasons as the grounds for holding a belief are just those actions that make up metacognition, the ability to think about belief, theory, hypothesis, and evidence. Metacognition involves the practices that when explicit make up an epistemology. As a normative criterion it allows assessment to be based on the quality of reasons for a belief rather than on the exact belief held, allowing for judgment and assessment to be based on more than mere compliance with the authority or with the facts. In this way the norm moves from the currently accepted theory to the quality of evidence – the reasons for believing – that the theory is true. Assessment practices must reflect both the theory and the reasons for holding such a theory.

The giving of reasons is a universal feature of schooled knowledge and a reflection of literate, bureaucratic culture generally. Explicit reasons are so central to institutionalized knowledge that schools sometimes make a fetish of them. "Give reasons for your answers" appears at the top of many examination sheets. Beginning mathematics students are often annoyed by the request to provide the explicit steps that lead to their answers; they claim to simply see that if $2/3$ of x is 6, x must be 9. Here the learner has the right "feeling of knowing," a necessary ingredient but not an explicit method for calculating the answer and consequently no way of knowing how to proceed to find x if $3/7$ of x is 21. Conversely, a child who simply slavishly follows a formula, arriving at the correct answer but not obtaining the feeling of knowing, of recognizing the necessity of the answer, is also missing an aspect of understanding. Recall Wittgenstein's *witz*: There is little value in following a rule if you do not know the point of the rule, what the rule is for. Schools may as often fail to help students in grasping the point of the rule as in grasping the rule itself.

We encountered the concept of public knowledge in our earlier discussion of knowledge institutions. It is not enough that a child has beliefs or that the child speaks a language; he or she must have justifiable beliefs and must speak correctly, as we say, grammatically. These standards are prescribed by the legitimated institutions of the society. Law courts determine what the law "No left turn" means; specialist disciplines determine what density is; what science is; what truth, proof, validity are; and what a host of concepts and theories entail. Societies, through their teachers and tests, hold children responsible for this legitimate and institutionalized knowledge and practice. Learners may reject that responsibility, but in so doing they lose the credit and entitlements that accompany it.

However, there are circumstances that limit student liability and accountability, including such causal factors as sickness or brain damage and situational factors as lack of opportunity. But psychology errs when it attributes to causal factors behavior that could be explained by intentional ones. Diminished responsibility is important, but part of the mission of the school is to induce students to take responsibility for their actions, not to justify or rationalize them on the basis of some causal factor. When students take responsibility for their actions they are also responsible for succeeding or for failing and for diagnosing the reasons for that success or failure – a lack of study or a failure to understand and to take appropriate corrective actions. Learners, whether subject to courts or schools, are responsible for constructing their own beliefs, and it is the learners who, ultimately, will be held accountable for earning or failing to earn credit and thereby access to other opportunities for learning or employment. But is it enough to pass off all responsibility for institutional beliefs such as the theory of gravity or evolution to the student alone? To do so ignores a critical feature of teaching.

JOINT INTENTION AND JOINT RESPONSIBILITY: TEACHERS' RESPONSIBILITY FOR STUDENT LEARNING

To this point I have explored the relation between intentionality and responsibility of the teacher and the student as if they were independent, as they often, and perhaps ultimately, are. However, the essential feature of pedagogy, it may be argued, is combining the intentions of the teacher and learner in a joint intention. Dewey (1980, p. 30) made shared activity the basis of common understanding, but left unanswered the question of responsibility. Although schools aspire to make students responsible for their own knowledge, the route to acquiring new knowledge via teaching depends upon the formation of joint intentions to which both teacher and learner can contribute and for which they can accept some responsibility. We should not take for granted that this is plausible, let alone easy – few people, certainly not my friends, agree on much of anything. How are teachers then to achieve joint intentions and undertake joint responsibilities with learners? As we noted, teachers and students have different responsibilities; can they be expected to agree on a shared purpose?

Forming a joint intention involves discovering a common frame of reference, a common goal, or a common ground with the learner. The importance of finding common ground is acknowledged in all theories of pedagogy whether expressed in terms of getting the learner's attention, speaking at the level of the child, respecting the child's stage of development, respecting the learner's patterns or levels of ability, or working within the learner's "zone of proximal development." It is not only that the learner has to attempt to come around to the intention of the teacher to establish a joint intention, say, to recognize the point, the witz, of the classroom activity; it is also necessary that the teacher come around to, and capture, the initial intentions of the learner. Both are involved in a joint intention. But something more is required for a joint pedagogical intention, namely, a clear criterion that may be used to judge whether the joint activity succeeds. It is this last point that has remained unexamined in pedagogical theory. The teacher's first responsibility is to establish with the learner what will count as satisfactory performance, as success. Once this is established, considerable latitude exists for helping students reach that criterion – reading, didactics, discovery, research, group discussion, homework, and so on.

Lave and Wenger (1991) advanced the concept of "limited peripheral participation" to account for the possibility that there are a diverse set of goals and intentions at play in any social practice, including an educative one. Children may learn from teaching even if what they learn is not exactly what the teacher had in mind. But of course the teacher cannot let the matter rest there. The teacher has an obligation to construct with every learner a set of achieveable and recognizable goals and criteria for recognizing achievement.

What the child does to form a joint intention is better understood than is what a teacher can do. The learner's ability to form joint intention is no doubt premised on strong innate social predispositions. Imitation that acknowledges both the goal and the means is well established in 18-month-old children (Moore & Dunham, 1995; Barresi & Moore, 1996; Tomasello, 1999). Joint intentions are manifest not only in pointing out and naming objects, in sharing "knowing looks and glances," but also in participating in adult routines and in playing (Lancey, 1996). Conversely, adults attempt to find common ground by reading intention into unpremeditated behavior, thereby leading children to see acts *as* intentional (Bruner, 1996).

But it is not until around 4 or 5 years of age that children begin to see not only the intentions in an action but also the intentional state, the belief and desire, that lies behind those actions. This allows the child not only to interpret others' behavior in mentalistic terms but to think of his or her own beliefs and actions in these terms. It is at this point that children are equipped to think about not only the world but their beliefs about the world and, even later, their reasons for holding those beliefs or initiating those actions. Now they not only act in ways that may be described by a rule but may intentionally comply with a rule and, further, understand its purpose. This is the point at which we say of children that they are capable of taking some responsibility, what the Vai called "getting sense" (Lancey, 1996). It is this development that makes the age of 5 or 6 an almost universal age for the onset of more formal, group-based education. We could say that this is roughly the age at which most children begin to act voluntarily and on demand can take on the task of constructing joint attention with a teacher or with a group of other children. Only then can school lessons become an object of joint discourse.[5]

---

[5] Preschool education could usefully teach children the rituals of joint attention, rule following, turn taking, role playing, and the like, rather than focusing on any particular content.

But are joint intentions anything more than two individuals each with a private intention? Return to Clark's (1996) account of such joint communicative activities as greetings, marriage ceremonies, buying, and selling. Each must recognize his or her single part as a component of a joint project, the expression of a joint intention. Such joint activities, whether in performing a duet, playing tag, or talking, involve a number of participants, a fixed set of roles such as a buyer and seller, a set of rules for organizing the interaction, and a shared criterion for success. Joint projects entail entitlements and obligations. In addition there must be a common ground or mutual knowledge on which the exchange is premised and to which the joint activity contributes.

The notion of shared or joint intention derives in part from the theory of speech acts (Grice, 1989; Austin, 1962; Searle, 1983; Clark, 1996), in which utterances are seen as narrowing a larger cooperative joint activity to more specific ones – greetings, for example, precede requests. Grice expressed this undertaking as the Cooperative Principle, which enabled participants to make their own contributions relevant and perspicuous to the joint activity. In Clark's words, "Participants use utterances and other signals to increment their current common ground" (1996, p. 132). To this end, they make statements, ask questions, give orders, and so on. Utterances are not merely added to the common ground; listeners have to decide how to take those contributions, as suggestions, for example, or as orders, as statements of fact, or as mere conjectures. These "ways of taking" are represented by the speech act and mental state concepts that make up the language of epistemology that we examined in the last chapter.

We may think about teaching, then, as a species of joint communicative activity. We can identify participants, roles, rules for coordination of action, boundaries for episodes, and the importance of a common ground. In fact, recruiting, elaborating, and explicating that common ground in terms of conventional knowledge norms and standards are the point of teaching. Joint communicative activities include not just lecturing and question asking but also reading, preparing reports, and participating in class discussions. The teacher's special role in these activities is coordinating these diverse elements into a "lesson," a lesson that jointly fulfills the teacher's responsibilities and allows the students to fulfill theirs.

There are limits to taking conversation as the model for the joint activities of a classroom because both teachers and students differ in their authority and responsibility. Further, the school class as an institutional structure (as do the textbooks they study) requires that language be directed not to an individual but to a group, a class. Thus classroom discourse differs in important ways from the conversational discourse examined by Clark (1996). The whole class is addressed as a group, and both teacher and students are required to formulate their joint projects in this group context. Whereas conversation cannot proceed with the inattention of one of the participants, teaching frequently does. Each learner formulates a somewhat unique version of the point of the discourse and the norms and standards that are relevant. Tolerable range and diversity of these personal versions remain largely unexplored. Sociologists sometimes complain about the artificiality of classroom discourse and especially of the recitation method involving question–answer–confirmation sequences when in fact they are a feature of group discourse and are seen as artificial only because of the application of an inappropriate model, namely, ordinary conversation. Classroom discourse evolves its own procedures for establishing joint intentions and monitoring joint outcomes.

Nickerson (1993, p. 248), in his discussion of Cole and Engestrom's (1993) distinction between the goal-directed actions of individuals and collective activity, pointed out that coordinating the two is fundamental to the functioning of any corporation, as, I would argue, of any classroom. He argued that if a corporation is to be successful, it must be organized in such a way that "when individuals work to achieve their own goals they will in fact, albeit perhaps incidentally from their point of view, be furthering the goals of the corporation as well." So too for joint intentions in a classroom; it is optimistic to hope for an identity of goals. More realistic is the aspiration to allow students to formulate goals that the teacher can accept as contributing to his or her mandated responsibilities.

As this is the heart of the pedagogical process, it deserves far more attention than I have given it here. Indeed, I see it as a domain where important and relevant educational research should be done but has not been done because of the emphasis on teaching and learning as independent intentional actions rather than as joint ones: How do children learn to shift personal goals and intentions into joint ones? How do they make the move from one-to-one to one-to-many interactions? How do they come to take on the more specialized roles that joint intentions require? What do they know about the rules for participation? What skill do they have in recognizing teacher intentions? Do they recognize common ground and the ways in which it is augmented in talk and reading?

And for teachers: How do they set boundaries for judging relevance to the joint activity? How do they recruit children's experience into a joint activity? It is even plausible that learning occurs when teachers and learners have widely discrepant plans and intentions, the teacher intending to promote understanding and the learner intending to overcome yet another arbitrary hurdle. In large part these are questions for the future.

The analysis of discourse advances us only partway to our goal. Although it provides a promising account of mutual understanding, it still fails to address the asymmetric discourse between the beliefs and intentions of individuals and the more or less nonnegotiable demands of official, socially sanctioned knowledge, for it is this latter knowledge that teachers and students are responsible for. Again, how do we approach the public knowledge that is the goal of schooling? Whereas conversation assumes a kind of equality among participants, teaching privileges the official knowledge of the culture and the authority of the teacher. As we have seen, some theories of pedagogy simply ignore the issue of common background and attempt to "transmit" the official knowledge directly. They leave it to the learner to scrabble together whatever he or she can to make sense of what he or she is told or they encourage the learner to memorize the relevant information in order to pass the mandated examination. Other theories, recognizing the centrality of understanding, sacrifice the official knowledge of the discipline, supplanting it with personal opinion and inquiry skills. Neither adequately addresses teaching as a nonsymmetrical, joint activity.

Acknowledging the role of authoritative institutions whether in law, economics, science, or the school allowed us to distinguish official knowledge from personal belief. Teachers have some hope of establishing with learners the joint intention to understand the official knowledge of the society by relating it to the personal beliefs and intentions of the learners. What they cannot aspire to is to induce learners to adopt as personal beliefs the knowledge officially sanctioned by the society. There is somewhat more hope that they can share a metacognitive epistemology for evaluating and judging the validity of beliefs by appealing to the reasons behind those beliefs and the validity of those reasons themselves. Although both teacher and learner have some responsibility for achieving this understanding, each remains responsible for his or her own privately held beliefs and reasons for holding them.

THE LANGUAGE OF SCHOOLING

Forming joint communicative intentions does not translate easily into joint responsibilities; each partner has his or her own responsibilities. The agreements reached are that each will do his or her part. The teacher offers to show how to divide fractions and the learners agree to do the assignments. Joint intentions may become mutual through the invention and acquisition of a shared public language, in particular, a language for talking about beliefs and reasons for believing. This is in part the language of ascription, the language parents and teachers use to characterize the actions and expressions of children, as when they say, "You *think* it is in the cupboard" or "I said I thought I would; I did not *promise* to take you to the zoo" (Astington, 1993). Or "Is that a fact or just your theory?" This is the language of epistemology, that is, the language of how we know; of reasons, of validity, and of truth. Saying and thinking are just the most basic examples of this intentionalist language; it is also the language of speech acts and mental states more generally. The language of schooling builds on and greatly extends devices for the public display and evaluation of knowledge.

The formal language of schooling proceeds by distinguishing what philosophers call *content* from *attitude* to that content, roughly, what is learned from the propositional attitude to that content. Thus, to entertain a proposition is not necessarily to believe that content; belief is an attitude to a content. Primarily because of the resources of language and other symbols, a child may entertain, say, the proposition that the Earth is round, without actually believing it or perhaps by only believing that the teacher believes that the Earth is round. Even to entertain such a proposition requires that the learner have some background knowledge and some stock of concepts. The teacher's responsibility is not to convince the child but to form a joint intention to entertain the proposition and, second, to examine evidence, that is, reasons, for the belief. It is the quality of these reasons that determines the attitude one will take to the proposition, that is, whether it will be believed or doubted or merely entertained.

The beliefs in question and the reasons for holding them are precisely those that are at play in the relevant institutionalized forms of knowing. I vividly recall knowing a lot about evolutionary theory and the evidence bearing on its truth/validity but yet not actually believing it;[6]

---

[6] My biology professor, to whom I submitted a final essay on this topic, gave me an A but added, "Ah, sweet reason."

that occurred later. If evolutionary theory is a dominant theory in the institutionalized science of biology, then the responsibility of the teacher is to induce the students to entertain the theory and entertain the reasons for holding the theory that are at play in the field of biology. For this, teachers may reasonably be held accountable by the state, and the student, in turn, by the teacher; for actually believing it or doubting it; on the other hand, is the learner's own responsibility. What one actually believes is a personal matter. Indeed, thinking in any science is precisely a matter of thinking about the relation between what is believed in the institutions of science and what one believes personally. This provides the space in which the sciences may grow.

Linguistic discourse is critical here. Although one of Dewey's ideals was to ground knowledge in experience, that is not enough. Seeing how things work or what happens provides perceptual knowledge. But perception as we saw (Chapter 8) fixes content and attitude at a stroke, whereas language permits the distinction between beliefs and reasons for believing. Discovery permits one to learn how to find out, but, unless coupled with linguistic discourse involving hypotheses and guesses, it does not allow the separation of content from the attitude that would make knowledge reflective. Serious thinking, as we saw in our discussion of the work of Latour and Woolgar (1986), involves not only the formation of new propositions but also the revision of the status accorded to those propositions, from guesses, to testable hypotheses, to factual claims.

Institutionalized knowledge and beliefs are not reducible to private mental states but states given expression in the public language of *state*, *assert*, *claim*, and *theory*. These are all elaborated versions of the verb *say*, and consequently they are all expressions of the mental state of believing. A statement reports, thereby making public, a belief; a theory expresses a network of beliefs. *Reasons* and *evidence* provide grounds for holding and expressing such beliefs. Other ways of expressing a belief as a *hypothesis* or *guess* or *conjecture* indicate the attitude to the belief, in this case one of noncommitment or suspension of judgment. *Assumption* and *conclusion* differ in their requirements; if an assumption, it needs to be acknowledged; if a conclusion, it needs to be warranted. An *inference* is either warranted or unwarranted, and so on. In learning this language the student is acquiring some of the tools needed for forming higher-level joint intentions.

Nor is this just a language for public expression; it is also a language of thinking. This is one way perhaps to make good the vague concept of language as a "tool for thinking." When thoughts are expressed as public statements, they may be scrutinized, criticized, and revised either by oneself or by others. An assumption, once recognized as an assumption, may turn into a hypothesis, as, for example, when Pasteur questioned the assumption that the containers he was using were actually clean and went on to discover microbes. With consciousness comes voluntary control, as Vygotsky suggested. The language about language and thought is a metalanguage, the conceptual resources that make metacognition possible. Metacognition is not, in this view, cognition about mental processes or about introspection, but rather the concepts carried by a language for talking about how we think and why we believe. Such talk is what allows students to accept responsibility for their own beliefs, now held independently of the joint intentions that gave rise to them.

Proposals for educational reform and the psychological theories that sustain them have been of limited value, in part, because they have failed to provide a vocabulary that can be shared by the teacher and the learner. Reformers tend to think causally and "institutionally," that is, in terms of programs of study and modes of appraisal designed to produce a certain effect much as an entomologist regards a colony of ants or a biologist regards a field of grain. An analysis in terms of beliefs, intentions, reasons for believing, responsibility, and accountability not only provides a language for thinking about learning, but provides a set of concepts that can be equally shared by educators and the educated, the theorist, the teacher, and the learner and can thus serve as the tools for the formation of joint intentions.

Dewey's child-centered pedagogy fully recognized the importance of the learner's own intentions, goals, and understandings and acknowledged that the only knowledge worth having was one's own. Such knowledge is composed in terms of intentional states, beliefs, desires, and intentions; doing things, wanting things, and knowing things. The motivation for learning is just the intention to learn, an intention that must originate in the learner. What I have added to that conventional child-centered view is an analysis of how joint intentions, carried in a shared vocabulary, provide a bridge between the official and formal knowledge of the society and the beliefs and intentions of children that allows the learner, ultimately, to take responsibility for his or her own learning of the society's legitimated knowledge.

14

The Achievement and Assessment of Intelligence, Knowledge, and Virtue

> Actually it is a moot question whether the science of psychology has any use for ability concepts at all, any more than advanced chemistry needs to talk about minerals.
>
> (W. Rozeboom, 1972, p. 32)

> I suggest that we stop the endless search for better methods of estimating useless quantities. There are plenty of real problems.
>
> (R. Lewontin, 1976, p. 192)

Schooling is not inappropriately thought of as the development of intelligence. Unfortunately, intelligence has become a loaded concept, linked to a postulated trait underlying actual forms of competence, let alone competence defined, without acknowledgment, in relation to the institutional practices of a bureaucratic society. My concern in this chapter is with the achievement of actual forms of competence, whether construed as intelligence, knowledge, or virtue, that allow one to do things, rather than with the postulated underlying abilities that have captured so much of the attention of psychologists and public alike. Nonetheless before I can advance what I take to be a more realistic analysis of the acquisition and assessment of competence in a bureaucratic society, it is necessary to clear the decks of residual beliefs in the explanatory value of traits in general and the concept of intelligence in particular.

No topic polarizes both academic and public opinion more strongly, more ideologically, and more routinely than intellectual ability or "intelligence." Typical of the previous decade was *The Bell Curve* (Herrnstein & Murray, 1994), a book that summarized a vast amount of correlational data to support the traditional view that IQ is a basic, innate, inherited, and causal quality of the mind that correlates with, and thereby accounts for, not only school success but also success in later life. IQ is taken to be a special property of mind that, through natural selection, could plausibly account for the evolutionary advantage of humans over other species and of some individual humans over others. Other theorists, Howard Gardner (1999) in particular, have advanced the view that intelligence is an important human trait expressed through the evolution of the cultural, symbolic forms of such relevance to education. Still others, more radical, see IQ as a socially constructed concept invented by the advantaged to justify their monopoly of access to the goods of the society and devoid of explanatory power (Meier, 1999). Critics point out that we, the high IQ advantaged, not only consume the largest part of the energy resources of the world but also, through our voracious appetite for reading materials, contribute to the denuding of the planet far more than do the laborers who scratch farmland out of the tropical forests.

Educational discourse about intellectual competence is, of course, inescapable in the sense that the obligation of the school is to develop just such competence (Kohlberg & Mayer, 1972; Edelstein, 1999). But it is an open question whether or not educational discourse about the development of intelligence benefits from a theory that reduces intelligence to the trait or set of traits selected by evolution and assessed by IQ tests. One alternative would be to discard the trait conception of intellectual ability and replace it with more limited notions of achieved competence; one either can solve equations or cannot – no appeal to some supposedly underlying trait called mathematical ability is required to explain why one can. Except for one fact: There is now an abundance of compelling evidence that traits such as intelligence are rooted in our genetic codes and our neurophysiological characteristics. Such traits cannot simply be ignored. But how are we to think about them?

A puzzle analogous to that of traits rises from the appeal to other traitlike categories that are used to explain variability in human performance, namely, class, race, ethnicity, and gender. These categories vie for explanatory power with those of IQ, impulsivity, dyslexia, giftedness, and the like. Class, race, and gender are social categories and, as do giftedness and dyslexia, have a political as well as explanatory use in that they are relevant not only to the identity of the persons so classified but also to issues of power and the allocation of resources. These categories cannot be ignored, but neither can they replace the concepts we have developed to this point, namely, persons as intentional beings with beliefs and desires, and persons as roles with entitlements and responsibilities in an institutional system. The question is, What place do we give to class, race, and gender, as well as dyslexia, learning disability, hyperactivity, and the like, in an educational theory? Here, the contrast between institutions and persons may be relevant.

One possibility is to think of a three-level ontology of persons instead of the two I have defended to this point. Persons are intentional beings as I have set out in my discussion of pedagogy. Second, persons are defined by the roles they play in a bureaucratic system such as the school. But third, persons are "kinds": They are boys or girls, European or Asian, rich or poor, normal or dyslexic. These social categories in part define personal identity as well as rights and obligations. "Kinds" are of enormous political importance and tend, especially in the United States, to dominate discourse about equity in education. Although important, kinds of persons determine neither intentional states of persons nor, at least in a just society, the roles to be played in knowledge institutions, including the school. Nonetheless, they clearly interact with both intentional states and institutional roles to the extent that resources of time and money are not fairly distributed to boys and girls, rich and poor, the disabled, or ethnic minorities.

Because of the failure to come to terms with institutions generally and with the school as an institution in particular, it has become routine to explain school success and school failure in terms of class or gender, ability or disability, that is, the social and psychological characteristics or traits of individuals. However, as argued earlier, to attribute success or failure to such causal factors is to dilute the responsibility of the actor for his or her own achievement. It is an entirely different thing to explain achievement by appeal to social class or IQ than to explain that very achievement by appeal to having taken a course, read a book, or studied for an exam. Only intentional efforts earn credits and entitlements. Education may be a birthright, but credentials are not.

PSYCHOLOGICAL AND INSTITUTIONAL EXPLANATIONS

Let us begin with the simple case of attributing "student failure" to the empirically well-established factor, the lower than average IQ of the learner. Clearly, other considerations may be at play. To begin with, student failure may be a consequence of either (1) a lack in the learner, as described earlier, or (2) a failure of the institution to set an appropriate standard. Setting and raising standards, as currently mandated in all but one of the United States (Fuhrman, 2001), in several provinces of Canada, as well as in the United Kingdom, are not simple matters. On any test given to a group or class, 50% of students will fall below the mean or average *by definition*. Few would impose the harsh standard of failing 50%, so by convention one standard deviation below the mean, some 15%, is often chosen as an acceptable failure rate and two standard deviations, some 2%, as the definition of disability.

Recognizing the relativity of such norm-referenced assessments has led to the development of criterion-referenced tests in which a standard can be set and, if necessary raised, that must be achieved in order to pass. Setting high standards as a basis for achievement, a current fetish, has thus far yielded unimpressive results. In Ontario, Canada, the standards-based tests in literacy and mathematics proved that almost half of Grade 10 students tested had not reached the necessary level of competence (*Toronto Star*, March 9, 2001). Shortly thereafter, however, the same cohort of students was subjected to comparable international tests given to students in 30 other countries – the 2000 Program for International Student Assessment conducted by the Organization for Economic Cooperation and Development (OECD). This test showed that the Ontario students were second only to Finnish students (*Globe & Mail*, December 5, 2001). Clearly, the standards set for Ontario were inappropriately high.

A similar pattern was reported for mathematics achievement in California (Ridgway et al., 2000, cited by Schoenfeld, 2002, p. 21). A standards-based achievement test designed to meet the new, higher standards of the mathematics curriculum, the Mathematics Assessment Resources Services (MARS) test, was given to children in Grades 3, 5, and 7 along with the more traditional norm-referenced Stanford Achievement Test (SAT-9). The correlation between the two tests was relatively high ($r = 0.65$); some 75% of the children who scored either high or low on one test did so on the other. Yet, three times more students scored high on the SAT-9 than on the standards-based MARS, again suggesting that the standards-based test is simply too difficult, producing not raised standards but an inappropriate number of failures. In Australia, too, a standards-based literacy test declared some 30% of Grades 3 and 5 children to be failing, precipitating a literacy "crisis," whereas the traditional norm-referenced tests had earlier shown them to be performing suitably (Hammond, 2001). Even with criterion-referenced tests all cutoffs are essentially arbitrary (Gronlund, 1973, p. 49). Criteria are compromises between judging the difficulty of the test and judging the competence of the student. The arbitrariness of setting absolute standards provides considerable freedom that may be exploited for rhetorical purposes.[1]

Or consider a child's need for individual attention. The lack of sufficient individual attention may be due either to the child's unreasonable demands, as in attention deficit hyperactivity disorder (ADHD), or to the inadequate supply of adult attention available in a class of 30 children. So if some children need additional individual attention, we have two ways to think about the problem: wean the children off the necessity for attention (punishment or a drug may help) or provide more occasions for individual attention by an institutional rearrangement such as one-to-one tutoring. The first sees the problem as a social or psychological one, the second as an institutional one. Proposed solutions in psychological and educational theory have tended to focus on the former. Just how the institution sets the standard for what is considered normal is ignored while the dispositions of individuals relevant to achieving that standard is the object of considerable research. That is, the role of the institution in the creation of the very norms against which behavior is evaluated is largely ignored.

Psychological and social problems are always defined relative to institutional norms. Prior to the establishment of school populations or classes, competence could be judged by the somewhat arbitrary criteria adopted by an individual judge. A blacksmith may, at some point, say that his apprentice was competent to work alone. This changes when competence is judged relative to a population or group. Now the criterion becomes a relative one, relative to the comparison group.

Thus although psychological manuals attempt to define *dyslexic* in categorical, absolute terms, in fact such a child is among the worst readers in the comparison group, roughly *in the class*; the child who has an attention deficit is among the most disruptive *in the class*; the gifted child is among those with the highest tested IQs *in the class*; and so on. As these categories become more scientific, the comparison group increases in size but the relative basis of the judgment remains a relative

---

[1] In Ontario, Canada, the arbitrariness of the cutoff is routinely ignored by the Ministry of Education and by the popular press, thereby giving inflated figures for the percentage of children who are below "grade level" or for the percentage of adults who are "functionally illiterate." In fact, such estimates are meaningless. Tests indicate performance only relative to the mean and standard deviation for the populations tested, which by definition put 50% below the mean, 12% one standard deviation or more below the mean, and 2% two standard deviations or more below the mean.

one. The fact that it is virtually impossible to make absolute judgments of competence has driven institutions such as the school to the more routine and more manageable basis of relative judgments. Thus, IQ scores and achievement scores are assigned relative to the norming population. It is a straightforward matter to say who is worst or best reader but impossible to state in any objective way who can read or who is literate.

Absolute standards-based criteria or "benchmarks" are impossible to establish, whereas comparative judgments – which answer is better and which is worse – are relatively straightforward. Ontario's *Common Curriculum* (OME, 1995, p. 13), for example, distinguishes Levels 3 and 4 of sixth-grade skills as follows:

> Level 3: asks and responds to questions on a clearly defined topic; comments on what has been said.
> Level 4: asks and responds to questions to acquire and clarify information and comments constructively on the contributions of others.

Clearly the wisdom of Solomon would be required to make such a distinction. On the other hand, most judges can rank performances reliably. The conclusion to draw is that whereas one may attempt to specify an absolute standard, in fact, judgments are comparative and relative, hence, the universal reliance on relative rather than absolute judgments. In school contexts, the performance of individuals is defined relative to a norm derived from a population whether class or age group. Further, it is clear that employers want not only someone who has appropriate credentials but if possible someone who ranks among the highest of the group, and above all, a choice among qualified applicants. What is disconcerting to employers, including universities, is to choose from too small a group of applicants. Judgments of individuals in a defined group are inescapably relative.

The class, school, or national average provides the norm for a population relative to which a particular child is considered normal or anomalous. Psychologists for the past century have attempted to isolate the special cognitive properties of those anomalous individuals – limited memory, verbal skills, or whatever – that may explain, for example, poor reading ability. However, some reading difficulties are rooted in the social and linguistic practices of the home, some in the mass teaching practices of the school, and yet others in the idiosyncratic goals, beliefs, and intentions of the learner. Yet if appropriate individual instruction is provided to poor readers, reading difficulties often disappear

(Clay, 1998). Further, with appropriate systematic instructional practices, such reading difficulties rarely arise (Ehri, Nunes, Stahl, & Willows, 2001). Dyslexia is only one case in which a social, institutional problem may be misdiagnosed as a psychological one. This is not to deny that some cases of poor reading ability are traceable to specific brain anomalies but rather to point to the difficulty, bordering on impossibility, of attributing particular cases of reading failure to an underlying psychological trait or disposition. Perhaps dyslexia as a brain disorder may be diagnosed with certainty only by an autopsy, as is Alzheimer's disease.

Second, it is the description of an individual relative to a statistical norm derived from a population that gives rise to the trait descriptions used to explain the variability in the population. As we saw in Chapter 8 that description is incommensurable with an explanation in terms of intentions and responsibilities, the goals, beliefs, and understandings of the individuals making up that population. (Note the important difference in the meaning of the term *norm*. In this case, it means simply "average." In other chapters *norm* or *normative* is not an average but an expected rule or obligation with a moral force. These two meanings are sometimes conflated as when one feels obliged to be nondeviant, that is, to be average in order to be "normal.") Here my concern is explaining not only reading failure but more generally the use of nonintentional factors such as traits or abilities to explain diversity in the acquisition of knowledge, ability, and moral virtues.

This is not to say that causal traits such as intelligence or introversion have no place in the sciences. Statistics is geared to the study of populations. Evolutionary genetics as well as medical epidemiology are based on the theory of the distribution of a causal trait in a population. Evolutionary theory applies to the selection over generations of traits that are distributed variably in a population. The cornea of the frog's eye, biologists tell us, was shaped evolutionarily over some 30,000 generations by natural selection based on that variability in the quality of visual information detected. However, not every selection in each individual case is based on an improved cornea; some with a good cornea fail to reproduce and some with a poor cornea succeed; selection applies only at the level of the population as a whole. The same applies to any human trait or competence. Whereas for the population as a whole the trait may be selected, selection does not apply in each individual case. One may or may not survive to reproduce for any number of reasons, yet evolution may stealthily select for a trait such as language or rationality, thereby producing an effect over many generations.

Epidemiology, too, works with populations. Physicians can increase the life expectancy of a population by encouraging the substitution of fat-reduced milk for whole milk in the diets of millions of people, thereby reducing the incidence of heart disease in the population as a whole. But in so doing they cannot predict whether an individual milk drinker will have heart disease. Epidemiology, as evolution does, works on populations and explains shifts in the population, not the properties of individuals. Indeed, there is no accepted statistical device for moving from frequencies in populations to probabilities in the individual case even if this translation is routinely made. One is twice as likely to win the lottery if one buys two tickets, yet, as we know, the odds of winning are still negligible. "Probability is about frequencies, not about single events" (Gigerenzer & Todd & the ABC Research Group, 1999, p. 170, citing the mathematician Richard von Mises). The correlation between smoking and lung cancer is sufficiently high that one is justified in combating smoking in general even if one cannot predict the likelihood of disease for an individual smoker. Similarly, IQ predicts achievement in general, but one cannot make predictions for an individual child because his or her goals, beliefs, and intentions may take precedence. Only if the correlations are sufficiently high and other factors are excluded, are they taken to have "clinical relevance."

In a cognitive intentionalist psychology, behavior is seen as caused not by either genes or conditioning but by individual rationality, the reasons accepted and acted on by the actor. Recall Anscombe's (1957) contrast between statements implying cause such as "I am going to throw up" and those implying intention such as "I am going to lie down." A psychology appropriate to education has at its core the attempt to explain the latter. This, of course, is not to deny that genes and neurons underlie even our rational behavior. Even our reasons are couched, in ways still largely unknown, in our genes and our neurophysiology. This important point is eloquently stated by Cummins (2000, p. 128) as Liebniz's gap, so called because it was Leibniz who was first to point out that there was, and is, no "precise suggestion about how beliefs, desires, and intentions are instantiated in the brain." We admit both neurophysiological factors and intentional states but also acknowledge an unexplained gap between the two.

Furthermore, even if not all school-relevant behavior is rational, it is the goal of the school to make it so. Intentionality, rationality, and responsibility cannot be finessed. This, of course, is the standard defense not only of education but of free will more generally; we are free to the extent that we are free to decide what to believe and to decide what to do. It is this freedom that precludes the prediction of behavior in the individual case even if such behavior is predictable in a population. Thus, through sampling a population, pollsters can predict the outcome of an election or the choice of a commercial product with astonishing accuracy but not the action of any particular individual. Knowledge of genetics and a causal trait psychology, as does knowledge of evolution and epidemiology, allows one to make causal predictions for whole populations but not for individuals. To the extent that we as educators or as educational theorists are concerned with individuals we cannot innocently generalize from populations to individuals; from behavior relative to a statistical norm to the internal state of an individual in that population, that is, we cannot attribute traits, such as dyslexia or any other disability, to individuals *even if they fail a test*. We may know someone cannot read well but we do not know why, whether poor teaching, misunderstanding, lack of practice, or brain malfunction. When one does not know the cause, the recommended procedure is to teach the learner what he or she needs to know (Clay, 1998).

ABILITY AND DISABILITY

"To be able" has both a competence interpretation and a comparative interpretation; the first is an individual characterization in relation to some achievement, the second by reference to a norm established for a population. In ordinary language, ability is just the possession of the knowledge and skill required for the correct performance of an action to achieve a goal. Yet, as we saw, because theories of schooling have yet to rediscover institutions, they have been blind to the consequences of the fact that institutions create the population norms against which individuals are judged and educators have developed a technology, that is, tests, to aid in that judgment. Frequency in the population provides a norm in terms of which an individual is characterized as, say, two standard deviations below the norm, that is, the bottom 2%, and therefore, "dyslexic." In so doing the psychologist has jumped from a population distribution account to an individual attribution, treating measured ability relative to a population norm as if it were an absolute characteristic of an individual that can be used to explain poor performance. Performance is assessed not in terms of reaching a particular criterion but rather in terms of being better or worse than some percentage of the population. Hence, the lowest 2% of the population may in fact be able to read;

they may simply be the poorest readers in the group. Even advocates of criterion-referenced tests acknowledge that, by definition, tests yield scores interpretable only relative to the statistical norms for a population (Gronlund, 1973). By definition, as mentioned, 50% necessarily fall below the mean and 2% necessarily fall two standard deviations below the mean. If tests are employed, they create failures in the sense that 50% fall below the mean. Raising the mean score does not alter the fact that 50% will still fall below it.

This is not to say that such tests are not useful. They are extremely important for assessing individuals and institutions relative to others in the population. Schools as institutions may appropriately use such descriptions of populations as a basis for altering curricula, programs, admissions, and so on. And they indicate to the student how he or she is performing relative to the group and perhaps suggest corrective measures. Finally, but equally importantly, they specify an objective criterion for the earning and awarding of a credential. It is up to the student and the teacher to take responsibility for the performance and to choose appropriate action on the basis of those test scores. But testers should acknowledge that relative judgments necessarily create failure.

HERITABILITY

The inappropriate extrapolation from descriptions of populations to individuals is not uncommon in the search for causes of low achievement, school dropouts, even criminality. Just as the variability in school achievement in a population can be explained by appeals to neuropsychological and ultimately genetic variability, the performance of individuals is commonly and mistakenly similarly attributed. Almost everyone, except the geneticists themselves, assures us that "half of your IQ was inherited" (Ridley, 1999). Similarly, "scientists now estimate that ADHD [attention deficit-hyperactivity disorder] is about seventy percent heritable" (Gladwell, 1999), implying that if one is diagnosed as having ADHD, the problem probably has a genetic origin. This attribution conflates population descriptions with individual, personal ones. As difficult as this may be to grasp, intelligence may be heritable, but one's own personal intellectual competence, also referred to as intelligence, is not.[2]

---

[2] This is not to argue that it is acquired, of course. All our competencies are biologically, genetically based, but not on those particular genes isolated in population genetics.

Geneticists such as Lewontin (1976) and psychologists such as Coyne (2000, p. 13) tell us that claims about any individual person's intelligence (or an individual's dyslexia or ADHD) confuse valid claims made by population geneticists about *heritability*, a technical notion, with popular notions of *inheritability*, the effects of an individual's genes on his or her behavior. Heritability can be measured: For a given trait in a given population, it is the proportion of the total observed variation among individuals attributable to variation in their genes.[3] Inheritability, on the other hand, the role of the genes in the development and behavior of an individual, cannot be measured – it is not merely not known but unknowable. Interest in heritability among the public arises primarily from confusing these two notions; laypersons reading about "heritability" think, as does Ridley, that they are talking about why some particular people do well in school or in business. In fact, there is no way to determine whether an individual's successful performance on an IQ or any other test is due primarily to the genes she inherited from her mother as opposed to the advice she got from her mother. Again, this is not to deny that the genes determine properties of the nervous system and bias the acquisition of knowledge. If there were no relation, it would not be detected in studies of populations. It is just that it is unknowable in the individual case. As we saw earlier, there is no known basis for inference from populations to individuals.[4]

Just as there is no direct relation between genetic explanations and intentional ones, there is no direct relation between intentional explanations and social ones. Durkheim argued that social facts are not reducible to individual facts. In his (1952; originally published in 1883) famous theory of suicide he argued that anomie, the mental state produced by conflicts between personal identity and social roles, was a cause of suicide. Indeed, he found that suicide was more common in northern European than in southern European countries, and more common in social groups characterized by organic solidarity (what we would call "modern") than in social groups characterized by mechanical solidarity (what we would call "traditional"). In fact, his theory nicely corroborated the relation between individuality and guilt that Max Weber (1930)

---

[3] Even then, located genes account for few of the observed cases. Researchers who located the ELAC2 gene for prostate cancer say that "variations in the ELAC2 gene are probably only responsible for two to five per cent of cases of the disease" (Easton, 2001).

[4] A recent comprehensive review of this literature concluded, "The picture that emerges suggests a powerful role for environment in shaping individual IQ" (Dickens & Flynn, 2001; see also Block & Dworkin, 1976; Sternberg, 1997).

described as a consequence of the Protestant ethic. But Durkheim was insistent that his theory was not a theory that applied to the individual case but rather to a population. Wilson (1961, p. xxiv), who wrote the introduction to Durkheim's *Moral Education*, pointed out, "[Durkheim] would disagree, of course, that suicide as he studies it is individual conduct. He studies suicide rates, and rates are not individual but collective measures." In my judgment it is inappropriate for psychologists to predict which individuals will be successful, commit suicide, or commit a crime on the basis of statistically derived traits that hold only for populations as a whole. Profiling is just as misleading as other forms of stereotyping. Classifying children on the basis of ability rather than achievement is, in my view, unwarranted.

If it were merely a gimmick for stimulating interest in one's theory, one could simply ignore the conflation of heritability with inheritability. But such conflation is pernicious in educational theory. First, it leads one to think of inadequate performances as indications of some deep, perhaps unalterable, defective trait rather than the product of some remediable situational or intentional factor. Second, attributing behavior to some underlying trait advances a causal explanation rather than an intentional one, thereby blurring the issues of responsibility.[5] These issues have been addressed earlier (Chapter 5). Here I add two further objections: The first issue questions the reality of the defects so labeled, and the second argues that even if traits are real, there is the problem of knowing who has the defect. Let us consider these in turn.

THE "NO THERE" THERE PROBLEM

For most psychological traits there is no way of distinguishing the observable symptoms from the underlying trait, disposition, or disability. No one really knows for sure who is genetically intelligent, for example, because there is no independent criterion other than the tests themselves. In the case of real things, such as the disease of cancer, subjects who test positive on a screening test really do or do not have cancer, and the predictive value of the symptom in relation to the disease may

---

[5] It would be possible to revise the concept of trait from that of a causal disposition to a descriptive category that summarizes across intentional states. The goal of character education assumes that one can cultivate the beliefs and habits appropriate to showing mercy or loving justice. Lynd Forguson brought this point to my attention.

be calculated. That predictive relation between symptom and disease determines the validity of the test. For psychological traits such as IQ, dyslexia, and ADHD, and for many other diagnostic categories, there is, at present, no real thing that the screening test diagnoses; there is no cancer that can be determined independently of the symptom. There is no "there" there, as Gertrude Stein famously said when asked about her visit to Oakland, California. So psychological tests do not predict a criterion but rather predict each other; all the tests are correlated, but there is no "thing," no criterion, that they are predictive of. I call this the "no there" there problem.

In some cases researchers have succeeded in going from a set of symptoms, those associated with autism, for example, to an underlying neurophysiological anomaly, and one cannot rule out the possibility of similar success for some other psychological categories. At present, however, the ability or disability is not a discrete anomaly but rather the tail of a normal distribution of the diagnostic test. As we saw in Chapter 4, tails of distributions may be highly misleading. Such categories warrant research, but their use in educational discourse is at best a vaguely descriptive shorthand for commonsense expressions such as "bright," "disruptive," or "poor reader." Such labels do not explain, and to make them educationally relevant the behavior would have to be translated into intentional terms, namely, what the learner's goals, beliefs, desires, and intentions are, so that the problem may be addressed by the student, teacher, parent, or school district.

Calculating the relation between symptom and disease is possible, as mentioned, in the case of genuine illnesses. In an interesting series of studies, Hoffrage and Gigerenzer (1998) showed that the predictive value of such diagnostic tests as the mammogram for the diagnosis of breast cancer is, in fact, quite limited. That predictive value is grossly overestimated by most people, even doctors, because of the tendency to ignore the relative infrequency of the disease in the population as a whole, a factor taken into account in Bayesian statistics. Thus, for example, for a woman at age 40 who participates in a routine screening, the chance of having cancer is 1%. If she actually has cancer, the probability that she will have a positive mammogram result is about 80%. Hoffrage and Gigerenzer show that most physicians report to an individual woman with a positive mammogram finding that the probability she has cancer is about 0.8, 80%, highly likely indeed. In fact, if the appropriate Bayesian probabilities are calculated, the probability is only about 0.08, or 8%, quite unlikely. The flaw in reasoning arises from ignoring what is called the *base rate*, the prevalence of the disease in the population as a whole. This may be presented as follows:

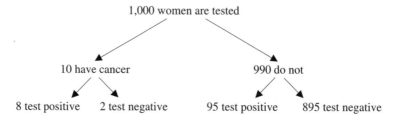

The Bayesian calculation may be approximated by computing with the actual frequencies. Of the $8 + 95 = 103$ people who test positive, only 8 have the disease. Hence, if one tests positive the probability that she has the disease is approximately $p = 8/8 + 95 = 0.08$; 0.08 is, as we say, an order of magnitude lower than 0.8, the probability commonly reported. The presence of the symptom is no sure sign of the disease, although, in matters of this significance, it is clearly worth looking into.

Thus, even when symptoms or tests are highly predictive of a disease, the predictive value in the individual case is modest. But the disease is "there," and the test does indicate its presence to a calculable extent. To date, in the case of psychological and educational diagnostic categories there is no "there" there and such categories are at best convenient summary descriptions of problems, not real, causal traits.

THE "WHO HAS IT?" PROBLEM

The second problem is that even in the case of using tests for diagnosing a disease the predictive value of diagnostic tests is far less than usually assumed. What about the case of predicting performance on the basis of psychological scales and diagnostic tests? Given a diagnostic test, who will perform as predicted?

Relations between predictor variables, such as IQ, and achievement hold, as we say, ceteris paribus, all other factors equal. But other factors are notoriously not equal; they vary widely across individuals, times, and contexts and include whether or not one was taught, practiced, studied, cared, was dared, and a host of other possible considerations. Indeed, as we saw earlier, Keil and Wilson (2000) argued that psychology may have to content itself with explaining performance rather than predicting it. We can often find out why someone failed even if we could not predict it. Consequently, many students do much better or much worse than predicted by an IQ test, and their success or failure depends on just such situational and intentional factors. In part it is this variability that makes it difficult to predict in the individual case from correlations that hold across whole populations.

The task is to infer who really has "it" from the test score that serves as a symptom of "it." But keep in mind that in this case we have no independent evidence of who really has "it," whether we are discussing an outstanding intellect or a deviant personality. All we know is how well he or she performs on the tests that we take as indicating a symptom for having it, this special trait. Who (really) has the remarkable intellect, who (really) has dyslexia, or who (really) has ADHD? Here I am fortunate to have access to the large corpus of data collected by my colleagues Renata Valtin and Oliver Thiel (personal communication) of the Humboldt University, Berlin. Using the data from 416, sixth-grade Berlin students for whom they had both ability scores and achievement scores on a number of language-composition tests, they were able to examine the predictive value of ability measures for academic achievement. Not surprisingly they replicated the well-known correlation between IQ and achievement, in this case, $r = 0.51$. More interesting is the attempt to predict the performance of individual children on the basis of this aptitude.

Overall, the prediction in individual cases is just what we would expect. For the tests combined, about two-thirds of the "gifted" children do well and only one-third of the nongifted do. Yet because the gifted are only 10% of the population, more than twice as many nongifted as gifted children achieved top scores. This fact is the logical outcome of the fact that there are far more nongifted than gifted children. When the correlation is less than 0.5, the ratios are even larger. The point is that if a teacher anticipated outcomes on the basis of "giftedness" she or he would overlook the majority of good performances.

Suppose we take into our calculations the fact that there are, by definition, many more nongifted children in the class than gifted (the top 10% on the ability test). Suppose we look only at the top 10% of achievement test scores in German composition and English composition and ask how well the ability test scores predict performance of the top 10% of achievement test scores. If the correlations were perfect, of course, the top ability students would be the top achievement students. Again Valtin and Thiel's data can answer the questions. Here, on average one-half of the high achievement scores are obtained by the high-ability students. Conversely, on average only one-half of the high-ability students obtain

TABLE 1

		Intelligence	
		Gifted	Nongifted
Class 41			
German	Good	2	1
	Worse	1	15
English	Good	2	1
	Worse	1	15
Class 36			
German	Good	1	2
	Worse	2	16
English	Good	1	2
	Worse	2	16

high achievement scores. Even then, one cannot predict which of the high-ability students will be the ones who do well on the achievement test. Table 1 presents the data for two typical classes.

So, to summarize, although a correlation in a population may be sizable, in this case around $r = 0.50$, it does not allow one to anticipate who will achieve well. Attention to those diagnosed as gifted would lead teachers to overlook the majority of children who in fact do well, namely, those diagnosed as nongifted. Even of the gifted only about half achieve top scores, and even then, one cannot anticipate who of the gifted will be the successful achiever. With such low levels of prediction, the predictive factors are of little or no value. Of course, the teacher has many other pieces of evidence to use to predict who will do well. These include knowledge of what was taught, who was paying attention, who did the homework, who tried harder, and so on. In the lottery of achievement, these intentional factors greatly outweigh the factors that are derivable across populations. Note, too, that the suggestion is not that "doing homework" be made into a trait – studiousness – but rather that the student's intention and goal in the particular case determine the outcome. My goal is not to multiply traits with predictive value but to propose an alternative, intentionalist approach to achievement.

ADHD is a much more problematic case. According to the *Diagnostic and Statistical Manual-IV*, a child *has* ADHD if, for a period of 6 months, he or she exhibits at least six symptoms from a list of behavioral signs including "often has difficulty organizing tasks," "often does not seem to listen when spoken to directly," "is often distracted by extraneous stimuli," and "often blurts out answers before questions have been completed." Clearly every classroom and every school constitute a population in which such behavioral patterns are normally distributed, which is to say, by definition, some three or four children will fall into the unwanted tail of the distribution, one or two conspicuously so. That is what a normal distribution means. This "tail" of the distribution, of course, is the bane of every schoolteacher.

Here again the "no there" there problem arises: There is no known method of distinguishing the symptoms from the disease; all one knows are the correlations among the symptoms. Second, once the deviant group is identified, still more of the disruptive behavior will be produced by the nondeviant group simply because there are so many more children in the nondeviant group. An equally serious problem arises in that these outliers are routinely prescribed the narcotic drug Ritalin, which is said to have been proved effective by some (Gladwell, 1999) but whose efficacy is doubted by others (Schachter, Pham, King, Langford, & Moher, 2001). The use of Ritalin has provoked widespread criticism for a variety of reasons: that such behavior is not a disease but simply a sign of boredom (DeGrandpre, 1999); that it is a symptom of our age, our relentless pace, our parenting practices, and the like (Walker, 1998); that treating misbehavior by drugs removes that behavior from the responsibility of the actor (Diller, 1998). As mentioned, this last point is critical for an educational theory. If performance is attributed to some causal factor such as a gene or a drug, the performer cannot be held accountable for his or her actions and does not merit either praise or blame. Nor can poor performance be an inducement to further study or practice or self-discipline. The causes of behavior are seen to lie outside one's own intentional control. Education, on the other hand, is committed to putting behavior under rational, intentional control.

My argument, then, is threefold. First, as mentioned, there is "no there" there. Second, the use of drugs undercuts the intentionality of the actor. Third, the claims for effectiveness of the drug Ritalin are claims about its effectiveness only in controlling the symptoms, that is, altering the child to fit the class. No evidence exists that it is effective in enhancing school performance, the basic reason for the treatment. Although Ritalin has been found to affect behavior, there is also evidence that it does not improve student achievement even if taken over periods of months and years (Detterman & Thompson, 1997, p. 1088). And finally, given the relatively low correlation between symptoms and disease, the drug may be given to many children who do not even have the syndrome. Legal and moral issues abound. Is it legitimate to recommend that a child take a prescribed drug for a disease he or she may or may not (really) have, let alone a drug that does not enhance performance but simply reduces the symptoms? Such considerations may prompt parents or the subjects themselves to bring a class action suit against the manufacturers, the physicians, and the schools that prescribed them. The basis of the claim, in Canada, would be the violation of the Charter of Rights. More importantly, they would put pressure on governments to provide resources for social arrangements that do enhance performance, primarily individual or small group tutoring, and that reassign responsibilities for behavior and learning.

The general moral of the story is that although heritable traits are valued concepts for studying the diversity and variability in populations, they are of little use and subject to large misuse in the diagnosis and treatment of individuals. The commonsense solution for education is obvious – judge competence on the basis of performance, namely, achievement tests, and analyze performance in terms of the teachable intentional states that gave rise to it. And leave the speculation on the causal roles of mental abilities or disabilities that may underlie performance in the population as a whole to the disciplines for which they are relevant, evolutionary biology and epidemiology, and to a lesser extent to the design and evaluation of institutions. One can determine, through the analysis of performance of defined populations, the major factors that are at work in producing effects and are relevant to institutional design and reform. Poor performance in mathematics in a state provides a basis for revising the program, altering admission and graduation standards, recruiting better trained teachers, and the like. But those revisions have little or no reference to the cognitive processes of individual teachers or learners in concrete settings. Leave pedagogy to the experts who know something about teaching and learning, about understanding and misunderstanding, about negotiating goals and plans. And assist educators in developing assessment devices that are useful in articulating the goals of programs and the extent to which their students are achieving them.

Viewing traits in this way provides a means of getting around the fetish of IQ in Western society. There is no need to attack or disparage IQ tests as critics tend to do; rather they should be seen as what they are. IQ is an institutional characterization of persons in a population distribution in terms of some criterion, including suitability to an institutional role. Institutions find some predictive advantage of such traits for roles in the institution, as did the military in World War I, but their role has declined dramatically. By World War II educational credentials were far more important in assigning roles than were general traits. Although individuals shape the roles they play in distinctive ways, the primary basis for assignment to roles in a bureaucratic society is through earned credentials, not through putative traits. Credentials enumerate the responsibilities one is capable of assuming. As credentials gain in importance, assessment as a basis for granting those credentials also gains in importance. Hence, the recent drive to accountability.

Nonetheless, ever since the *Coleman Report*, which showed that variability in achievement is more strongly affected by nonschool factors such as IQ, family, and SES than by school factors, many writers have inferred that schooling has little impact on achievement. This, of course, is a simple confusion. Nonschool factors outweigh school factors only if the content, grade level, and program – the principal ways that school affects achievement – are controlled for. There is no need to do an experiment to see whether children who studied chemistry do better on a chemistry test than those who did not. What Coleman found was that once one controlled for program, grade level, and the like, then the residual variability between schools accounted for little of the variance. The proper conclusion is that Grade 11 chemistry, for example, is quite similar from place to place. In a similar way, from the fact that it is difficult to trace variability in achievement to differences among teachers, some have inferred, incorrectly, that teachers do not make a difference. Rather, the correct inference is that they all make a similar difference. The correct experiment would be to compare those taught with those not taught, but the outcome is so obvious that no one would recommend such an experiment.

The best predictor of how well one does on an achievement test is whether or not one has taken the appropriate course. It is only when one equates for the course and level that IQ and SES have explanatory value. But here the issues of intentionality and responsibility again enter the picture. Choosing to take or not to take a course is something one does and for which one can accept responsibility and earn entitlements or privileges. On the other hand, IQ, like SES, is not under voluntary control – one does not choose or decide those things – and hence is not something for which one can accept responsibility or earn entitlements. Justice enters the system through the implications of what one does intentionally and responsibly, that is, as earned access to earned privileges. Injustice enters the system when privilege is tied to any putative trait such as IQ or SES (although they predict achievement) for which one cannot accept personal responsibility nor earn entitlements.

ANOVA models of achievement, therefore, fail to discriminate these two types of explanatory cause and hence fail to address the issues highlighted herein, namely, responsibility and accountability. More appropriate models of learning and achievement will have to be invented, and we may make some tentative steps in that direction by revising our conceptions of knowledge, ability, and virtue.

TOWARD A NEW CONCEPTION OF KNOWLEDGE, ABILITY, AND VIRTUE

To this point I have argued that a psychology that attempts to explain behavior by appeal to underlying traits and dispositions is the result of a particular methodology for studying diversity in populations. I promised that having put traits in their place, I would offer the sketch of an alternative approach to understanding knowledge, ability, and virtue. This new perspective arises from seeing the diversity of persons in terms of the intentional states – goals, beliefs, and plans – appropriate for their performing particular roles in more specialized institutional contexts.

Diversity in what individuals know, how original their thoughts are, or how moral their actions must be considered, I suggest, in terms of the diverse roles persons can play in knowledge institutions. Institutions have entitlements and responsibilities that are carried out through defining roles for individuals, each with its own entitlements and responsibility. In science, these roles may include reading, inventing, testing, reporting, and criticizing a set of ideas. An individual may be successful in one or more of these roles, and the institution as a whole is successful to the extent that it can effectively coordinate these roles. Rather than addressing knowledge, ability, and virtue in terms of psychological traits intrinsic to the individual, then, it may be possible to reconceptualize them in terms of the nature of the institutions in which persons are involved.

Knowledge

I have already extensively analyzed knowledge in terms of institutions (in Chapter 5). There I showed that knowledge is not reducible to the beliefs of any working scientist but rather to the set of beliefs, procedures, and norms that have been adopted and vetted by the institutional structure of the disciplines. What students learn is how to relate their own perceptions, favored interpretations, and intuitions to the canons and established knowledge of the discipline. Less critical is actually agreeing to the established knowledge than knowing how to read, interpret, and eventually contribute to the archive of the field. No scientific work is ever an expression of the genius of an untutored individual; no genius can boldly offer new truths. All knowledge builds on and finds its place in a tradition, even if that contribution consists of inserting a *not* into the previously accepted factual claim. Emphasis on personal understanding is of course critical, but it is always in relation to understanding the standard traditions, rules, and norms embedded in the practices and documents of the discipline. The ability to read, understand, and criticize these documents remains a fundamental form of competence. This should not be confused with so-called basic literacy. It has much more to do with understanding critical texts and arguments within a tradition, a kind of societal literacy (Olson & Torrance, 2001). The student's goal of acquiring knowledge, then, is less a matter of stored knowledge than of ability to engage productively in the knowledge tradition of a discipline.

Ability

Ability in an institutional context, too, is not simply the genius of an individual or even the summed brilliance of individuals but the capacity to contribute to the success of the institution that has the responsibility for coordinating its personnel, its informational and technological resources, to achieve a goal. Two groups of scientists, equally gifted, one with knowledge of Newton's theory of optics the other with Poussin's, will make very different predictions about the possibilities of Superman's X-Ray vision. Similarly, the one with a concept of and/or the resources of a laboratory will subject ideas to critical tests rather than allow them to remain as vague beliefs. Intellectual ability, in this view, must be seen not as an individual's measured IQ but as achieved competence with and intentional management of cultural resources. Ability is less an abstracted, intrinsic property of mind than a competence with the intellectual and cultural resources of the culture. In a school context, tests of ability give way to tests of achievement, the understanding and use of the concepts, notation, systems, and theories of the culture. These abilities are to be seen as intentional characterizations of the rationality of actors, that is, as the beliefs and reasons for believing the theories and practices of a discipline.

Science as an institution is successful because it involves a structure in which persons can do original and comprehensible work. It has mechanisms for allowing good work to thrive beyond the limits and prejudices of the individuals making it up. Carlyle's (1901) view of the great man as embodying the scientific ideal is seriously out of date; science is the collaborative product of individuals working within a documentary tradition of a scientific institution. The search for the most "able" is, therefore, not the search for the "best minds" as colloquially stated, but rather the search for the best record of successful participation in the institutional practices of science, the ability, say, to criticize existing work, advance relevant hypotheses, devise or recognize appropriate methods, write concise reports, draw on the expertise of others, and the like. One need not be able to do everything, but one must be able to contribute to the overall enterprise. In part this involves knowing both the forms and the lore of the discipline; such knowledge confers a new identity on its participants.

Virtue

In the traditional individualizing scheme I have criticized, virtue is the property of the mind or character of an individual and is premised on the feelings and emotions of empathy and humane concern. A just society, in this view, is composed of morally virtuous persons. This is precisely the goal Plato envisioned and the goal to which educators frequently aspire. Virtues such as fairness and regard for others, as well as patience and perseverance, are seen as traits characteristic of persons, and the goal of education, in this view, is to instill those virtues.

This sets the goal of the school far beyond what it can realistically aspire to. Moral virtues are acquired primarily in the family and in one's primary social group, that is, one's local culture; these may be thought of as one's implicit entitlements and responsibilities. What the school can do is teach children to participate in the larger-scale institutions of the society that are designed to regulate social interactions not only among friends but also, importantly, among strangers. These include an understanding of and ability to take advantage of the judicial system, to respect the rule of law and the workings of courts – but in addition, an understanding that courts are of little value unless there are instruments of power to enforce their judgments. Moral knowledge and moral action are then organized not by habits and traits so much as by the structure and sanctions of the legal system. When a system of laws is not established, behavior becomes largely unpredictable, as Montaigne (1580/1958) argued when he claimed that public law was even more important than private virtue, such as a sense of justice.[6] Durkheim, too, noted that if there is no public order and no respect for law, private virtue tends to disappear. Moral development, rather than an autonomous form of development as sketched by Piaget, is rather to be seen as learning socially sanctioned ways of dealing with others. These ways include knowledge of the norms, rules, and sanctions the law applies, and the contexts for applying them. Education's concern for the development of private virtue could more appropriately be seen as the development of respect for public order and admissible ways of expressing dissent. Moral competence is just the ability to act intentionally and responsibly in a world characterized by "the rule of law, not of man," as John Quincy Adams once urged.[7]

The school has a special responsibility for moral development. However, schools can do little to instill empathy, attachment, allegience, patience, endurance, or any other virtue acquired in one's primary social group. But schools can do a great deal to instill recognition of rules, norms, and standards and the reasons for the existence of such rules. They can teach and exemplify the entitlements and obligations of children as citizens of classes, schools, and societies. They can learn how to achieve goals they personally value and how to negotiate compromises with people they scarcely know or may even dislike. As I argued earlier, schools are not merely extensions of the family or primary social group but somewhat universalizable institutions for learning to deal with the complexities of a bureaucratic social world. Long before children begin school they become proficient with the implicit rules and roles of their primary social groups. They know who their friends are, how to play with them, and how to exclude others. "You cannot play," they say to strangers or enemies. What school adds is the universalizing dimension: higher-order rules that allow one to interact peaceably with strangers and others with quite different cultural allegiences by learning the rules

---

[6] I believe that this is an issue that in the United States separates Republicans, for whom law seems primary, from Democrats, who make justice primary. In Canada Conservatives are somewhat like Republicans; Liberals and New Democrats are somewhat like Democrats.

[7] In this, Adams was quoting Hume's *Of Civil Liberty* (1987, p. 94): "It now may be affirmed of civilized monarchies, what was formerly said in praise of republics alone, that they are a government of laws, not of Man." I am indebted to Frits van Holthoon for calling this to my attention.

and laws of institutions – "You can't say, you can't play," as Vivian Paley (1992) tells the children in her school. These rules are not merely encouraged: They are sanctioned as legitimate or illegitimate actions by the powers invested in the school.

The negotiated rules and laws established and enforced by the bureaucracies of state make moral behavior possible (Elwert, 2001). If these rules and laws are transparent, if there are clear procedures for dealing with special cases, if the rewards for complying with them and the sanctions for violating them are predictable and justifiable, students will both trust the institutions and also adopt them as a guide to their own moral behavior. Whether all morality is grounded in such institutions is an open question. But the moral development of students for which the school has clear responsibility is that grounded in the knowledge of and respect for the public institutions of the society. Personal virtue is grounded in civic virtue.

Diversity, then, is to be accommodated in terms of institutional roles and the credentials required for occupying them. One earns, through one's achievement, access to particular roles. And with the role are not only rights and responsibilities but also an identity. Living up to that identity may go far beyond the more immediate needs and interests of the individual to include new responsibilities inherent in that role and that identity. "Dooty is dooty" was Long John Silver's way of justifying his responsibilities as a captain.

15

A Framework for Educational Theory

[Educational policies] cannot be resolved without our first achieving some deeper understanding of the culture of education.

(J. S. Bruner, 1996, xvi)

Schools are institutions that reflect the needs of the primary economic, political, legal, and scientific institutions of the larger society. Schools have traditionally assumed the task of devising, assessing, and improving the means for fulfilling these institutional needs. But more recently, schools have been reconceived as instruments for human development and human fulfillment, that is, as institutions for the elaboration of intentional, subjective experience and responsible moral action. The absence of a bridging theory, I have argued, has fostered a polemic between traditionalists and reformers, the former blind to the intentional states of teachers and learners with their subtly negotiated plans and goals, the latter blind to the roles and norms of the school as an institution. To close the gap I have set out a framework for examining both the agency of institutions and the intentionality of persons in terms of responsibility and accountability, entitlements and obligations. The norms and standards of the society as represented by the school meet the subjective experiences of the children through the formation of joint plans and goals with their distinctive patterns of responsibility and accountability. I have offered this as a framework or theory for examining the relations between the institutional demands of the society and the psychological interests and concerns of the teachers and students involved.

Educational discourse and educational theory are polemical rather than constructive to the extent that they fail to distinguish these two quite different agendas, the causal analysis of the factors relevant to the functioning of school as an institution and the intentional analysis of the processes relevant to teaching and learning. Conflating the two has resulted in a model of the causal "factors," whether in the person or the environment, that contribute to school achievement. Although such factors may be relevant to institutional policy decisions, they are largely irrelevant to the deeper understanding of the pedagogical issues of intentionality and intersubjectivity.

To distinguish the institutional and the personal is not to invoke the traditional distinction between the disciplines of sociology and psychology but rather to merge them in a more comprehensive theory of persons in institutions, specifically, children in schools. But neither is it to reduce the psychology of schooling to an aspect of cultural psychology. Rather it is to grasp the peculiar nature of schooling as a literate, bureaucratic institutional practice with its own specific roles, rules, obligations, and entitlements and its own peculiar demands upon mind. To address the relations among society, schools, and minds has required major revisions both in the goals of such a theory and in the methods of inquiry, the epistemology, appropriate to each.

As to the goals, the traditional goal of pedagogical theory has been to explain and improve the acquisition of knowledge and skill, the mastery of what is taken as known. Its goal is primarily cognitive. I have argued that pedagogical theory must take as its goal the explanation of intentionality and accountability for learning, that is, who is responsible for what. In this way its goal is primarily moral. Thus, in the framework I have proposed, the cognitive is secondary to the moral.

As to the epistemology, theories of schooling have shifted without acknowledgment between explanations based on mechanical causes, what von Wright (1971) called "Humean causes," and those that appeal to intentional causes, the deliberate, reasoned choice of means to achieve anticipated ends. I have argued that institutional explanations that appeal to the factors affecting success by explaining "some percentage of variance" are mechanical causal accounts and incompatible with the intentional explanations required for examining and improving teaching and learning, understanding and reasoning.

In fact, the epistemological puzzle of "causes" versus "reasons" riddles the social sciences. Neither sociology nor psychology has been consistent in its choice of what constitutes an explanation. "Rational choice theory" assumes the intentionality of actors but then treats actors collectively, expressing their choices in statistical, that is, causal, laws,[1] ignoring the fact that what enters into the decision varies with the institutional role one is playing. Thus, as Mary Douglas (1986) has noted, rational choice theory has grave difficulties in coping with institutions. Theories of social causation, on the other hand, such as "Literacy causes economic growth," imply a causality that disregards the intentions, beliefs, and goals of the actors altogether. In psychology, behaviorism, with its habits, dispositions, and traits, is a causal theory, whereas representationalism, with its intentional states, is an intentionalist theory. Yet, even representational theories are sometimes reduced to causal, computational models (Fodor, 1998). Both Marx and Freud offered causal theories of behavior that led people to distrust the explanatory value of their own conscious, rational, intentional states while inadvertently diminishing their responsibility for their own actions. Indeed, it is to the discredit of modern psychology that it directs most of its resources to providing explanations that diminish intentionality and responsibility. On the contrary, I have argued that both individuals and institutions may be viewed in intentionalist terms with rights and responsibilities, entitlements and obligations. Whereas the actual working within an institution such as a school is to be explained in terms of the intentionality and subjectivity of the individuals involved, the policy and organization of a bureaucratic institution are carried on more or less independently of the subjectivity of the individuals involved. Consequently, different methods of analysis are required. Analysis of the school as an institution focuses on the causal factors relevant to the optimal functioning of the institution as a whole, whereas analysis of pedagogy focuses on the intersubjectivity and intentionality of the teachers and students involved.

By distinguishing between persons and institutions, it was possible to show how schools as institutions, far from the social practices of everyday life, define new sets of roles, rules, norms, entitlements, and obligations that are attuned to the structures of a modern bureaucratic society. Further, it allowed the possibility of addressing the fundamental concern of modern critics of education, namely, the issue of accountability of the schools as institutions to the citizens who pay for them – schools are not only environments for growth and development; they are environments for mastering the norms and standards set by the dominant institutions of the society whether law, science, or literature. On the other

---

[1] Thagard has argued that causal powers are theoretical entities that are inferred on the basis of finding correlations and eliminating alternative causes (2000, p. 261).

hand, it allowed the pedagogical issues of development and learning to be approached in terms of such intentional states as beliefs, desires, and intentions as well as the joint intentions of teacher and learner. These states are important because they can be held consciously, they can be the subject of discourse, and ultimately, they can be held deliberately, responsibly, and accountably by individuals.

Furthermore, in pedagogical contexts, intentional states can be shared, at least to some extent, by teacher and student. This is not simply the sharing of intentions as may occur in a conversational dialogue but rather an achieving of joint intentions by teacher and student in which the beliefs of the student are formulated and evaluated in terms of the norms and standards represented by the beliefs and intentions of the teacher. Revisions of beliefs in terms of these norms and standards constitute conceptual change in the learner. The child meets the curriculum, not only as Dewey argued, by finding in the intuitions of the child the basis for the advanced knowledge represented by the curriculum, but rather through providing a forum for the formulation of joint or overlapping intentions in which private intentional states may be judged and assessed in terms of the standards and norms of the society. In this way we may honor both the integrity and the autonomy of the learner and the standards and norms of the society. Schooling is both development and socialization.

Casting a theory of schooling as a moral theory with an intentionalist epistemology allowed me to address the pedagogical issues of teaching and learning in terms of setting and achieving of goals rather than of a nonintentional characterization of the particular cognitive structures involved. Further, it permitted me to address the modern concern with the school's institutional responsibilities for knowledge without overlooking the intentionality of individuals. I did so by arguing that both individuals and institutions can be brought into parallel moral frames, frameworks of entitlements and responsibilities, with teaching as a type of joint intention and shared responsibility.

Two qualifications are necessary. In emphasizing the moral dimension of my proposal, I do not wish to minimize the cognitions of learners or the accumulated knowledge of the society. In fact, intention and responsibility assume beliefs and knowledge; one can intend an action and be held accountable for achieving it only if one has the requisite beliefs, desires, and goals. Most of the psychology of the past half-century has been devoted to characterizing these knowledge structures – the works of Piaget, Vygotsky, Bruner, Donaldson, and Nelson are exemplary.

I myself have devoted much of my career to understanding just what children think when they are confronted with visual displays, oral utterances, or scholarly texts. But such theory has yet to address the peculiar normative nature of schooling as an instrument of human development – peculiar in that schools are created not simply to enhance development but to serve and preserve social, bureaucratic, national institutions; indeed, to see development in terms of these intitutionally defined roles. This lacuna may be filled by viewing both personal competence and institutional success in terms of their different but related goals, responsibilities, and accountabilities. The school as an institution fulfills its obligations by providing graduates who meet a certain fixed level of achievement defined by the powerful institutions of the society, including the justice, economic, and scientific institutions. These institutions retain the power to prescribe the norms and standards against which behavior and cognition are to be judged. But the teacher and the child have obligations not just to the society but to themselves and to each other as autonomous persons with jointly and individually constructed goals and intentions. Students not only are shaped by institutions but aspire to their own goals and to goals shared with the teacher. To the extent that goals are shared, the teacher can recognize those achievements and students can be credited and credentialed for responsibly achieving them.

Nor do I wish to imply that the schools or other institutions of a society are completely unalterable or that they provide fixed molds into which malleable youths are poured. That is, education is not merely socialization, the means by which a society maintains itself, as Durkheim seemed to suggest (1956, pp. 118, 122). Indeed, Kant (1960) believed that the state should not control education because of the danger of subverting its humanistic goals for narrowly military or economic ones. Although teachers and children are accountable to the state, education is also the basis for personal growth, which may require the revision of institutions to meet a more democratic ideal, as Dewey persuasively argued. Both persons and institutions have responsibilities and entitlements; the mistake, I argue, is conflating them.

Stating the educational problem in terms of responsibilities and accountabilities gives a new shape to the pedagogical problem of how learners agree to the norms, goals, and standards of the school. Basic operating norms and rules may be embedded in such institutional practices or pedagogical routines as recognizing and completing assignments by specified dates, taking turns in talking, and consulting documents. By embedding these norms and rules in classroom practices, teachers can prevent treating classroom discipline as matters of personal authority or a confrontation of personal wills. But more cognitive goals of the school cannot be simply imposed and monitored by rewards and punishment if the goal of personal autonomy is to be achieved. Rather, by formulating joint intentions or goals, students can monitor their own performance relative to that agreed upon with the teacher and at the same time gain credit from the teacher for their work. Thus goal setting and achievement monitoring become the heart of the pedagogical theory. It is not to be assumed that this is an easy task; students have their own agendas, so to speak.

Joint pedagogical intentions, that is, the intentions shared by teacher and student as to what constitutes appropriate norms for understanding and standards for performance, build upon the more general competence involved in formulating joint intentions in conversation, work, and games. Conversations often have a shared point, such as deciding what to do or what to play. Less often they have a pedagogical point, namely, understanding what is required for a skillful performance or an appropriate understanding. "Skillful" and "appropriate" are normative concepts that imply the standards to be used in making judgments. These have to be worked out largely in a school context in which the teacher as a representative of the norms and standards of the larger society negotiates appropriate goals with individuals or with a class. Once the criteria are agreed upon, students can take responsibility for their own achievement, and, in principle, any means will do as long as the agreed upon standard is achieved. Even that standard may be viewed quite differently by teacher and student; whereas for the teacher the standard may be an appreciation of literature, for example, for students it may be simply a matter of obtaining a credit. In spite of such differences, some common criteria may be achieved.

Putting responsibility into the hands of the learner is the route to personal autonomy. The concern with intentionality, responsibility, and accountability provides a meeting ground between the student as a person with rights and responsibilities and the school with its mandates and accountability. Recall that it was necessary to distinguish the school as an institution for human fulfillment from the school as an institution responsible for preserving the traditions and standards of the society. But here we find a way of synthesizing them. The student in accepting the norms of the larger society is no longer to be thought of as an object to be shaped by a powerful institution but rather as a person who by forming intentions jointly with the teacher can accept personal responsibility for goals and a degree of autonomy through their fulfillment.

The importance of joint intentions and actions in human development is presumably what Durkheim had in mind when he wrote, "The best of us is of social origin" (1956, p. 133). Personal autonomy is achieved by understanding the workings of the world and its institutions sufficiently well that one can assume responsibility for the beliefs one holds and the actions one takes while collecting the credit and blame that the society offers. It is this autonomy that gives rise to the sense of personal efficacy, identity, and ultimately, an enlarged sense of self.

By distinguishing the personal from the institutional we can also address the questions of institutional functions and institutional effectiveness. Understanding institutions allows us to recognize that school reform is not to be identified with pedagogical reform. Historically, the transformation of the school was not a result of better pedagogies but of new social arrangements, with pedagogies' tending to reflect these changes. The school as an institution contracts its own responsibilities from other, more powerful institutions in the society – religious, political, economic, or academic – and it requires the means for assessing its functioning as an institution in meeting its obligations.

Epidemiological research on schools by Coleman, Rutter, and others has shown that some schools and school systems are better than others in achieving their goals. What matters is not a specific pedagogy or a specific method or routine (recall Tyler's Eight-Year Study, Cremin, 1961) but rather a much more general "ethos" conducive to teaching and learning. These characterizations are institutional rather than individual or pedagogical and as such may be relevant to the formation of policy. That is, the research tells us that some environments are conducive to good teaching and learning – a degree of order, of clearly defined goals and clear criteria for success (cf. Mortimore et al., 1988) – and policy directives and resource allocation are important to creating such environments. But such research does not tell us what actually goes on in a successful pedagogical exchange. That must be worked out at the intentional rather than the institutional level.

National and international assessments are of some value in communicating goals and standards and a metric against which teachers can judge their own assessment practices, but they are of limited use in understanding or guiding pedagogical practices, which, as mentioned, rely on the subjective mental states, the goals, desires, and beliefs, of individuals. Similarly, bold reform initiatives such as the charter school movement or a voucher system leave completely unexplained how such a reform could actually alter the educational exchange between teacher and student. Any reform that helps a teacher do his or her work well enough to allow students to do theirs is worthwhile, but such reforms tend to be local and direct – better resources, clearer criteria, appropriate degree of orderliness, and the like.

Several decades of educational research directed to understanding teaching and learning explored the characteristics or traits of populations of persons in the attempt to relate them to student outcomes. Such patterns of correlation between input and output variables have then been extrapolated, inappropriately in my view, to explain the learning and thinking of individual teachers and students and in some cases to prescribe pedagogical practice. I have argued that such patterns of correlation do tell something about institutions' norms and standards and about the ideal student required to maximize the output of the institution but very little directly about the learning, planning, or thinking of individuals. Whereas IQ, for example, is distributed in a population and can be related to an institutional goal, school achievement, it cannot explain achievement in the individual case. As I put it, if a student does well in school there is no way to tell whether this is the result of the genes or the advice she got from her mother. This is because institutional factors are treated as causal factors in the statistical model derived for populations as a whole, whereas a person's behavior is intentional, a product of beliefs, desires, goals, and intentions, and pedagogy must address those intentional states. It is an excuse not an explanation to report that a student has failed geometry because he or she has limited spatial ability. I have emphasized that achievement is more important and more diagnostic than putative underlying abilities and traits.

Only confusion results when research on institutions is then interpreted as if it were appropriate grounds for pedagogical decision making. At the personal level, teachers have the professional responsibility for finding the meeting ground between the beliefs and intentions of the children and the norms and standards represented by the curriculum, and they appropriately describe learning in terms of changed understanding or conceptual change. Teachers analyze learning in terms of what they can assume was learned in a previous lession, what they have taught or failed to teach in relation to the goals and standards specified in the curriculum or textbook. They then negotiate this gap in terms of both class and individual responses in the attempt to construct joint goals and intentions, leaving room for individuals to achieve these joint goals as best they can by using the resources of texts, lectures, discussion, or reflection. They then assess the individual product in the light of the norms and standards specified in the initial shared goal or intention.

But teachers and planners are hampered by a bad psychological theory, a causal theory based on populations as a whole, that attempts to mandate a uniform method that sorts children by race, sex, personality type, trait, or mental ability as the basis for assigning a form of instruction. These categories are too distant from personal goals, beliefs, intentions, and responsibilities to be of any more than minor pedagogical value. Furthermore, mandating methods or prescribing practice limits the options available to a teacher for finding common ground with learners, and it limits the teacher's responsibility and accountability for his or her actions. Classification of students by sex, ethnicity, or other trait may be important for issues of equity but not, I suggest, for issues of pedagogy.

School assessment is not the same as student assessment. Schools are assessed epidemiologically, that is, in terms suitable for characterizing a population, and the treatments proposed are those suitable for populations. As we saw, increasing the tax rate reduces consumption in the population but not necessarily in the individual case. Similarly, on the basis of research, schools may decide to increase the teacher–student ratio overall but that research is not directly relevant to the decision about any particular class, teacher, or student; that must be left to local professional judgment that takes into account the teacher, the children, the school, the resources, the timetable, the subject taught, and so on.

Student assessment, on the other hand, is important for two reasons, one institutional the other pedagogic. The institution may use assessment as a basis for granting access to higher levels of study and for the granting of credentials, but it can also be used for indirectly monitoring the system in comparison to other systems or subsystems. Thus, if failure rates on a common test are poorer in one country, state, or province than another, that may be grounds for changes in goals, programs of study, funding, teacher recruitment, and the like. It is never obvious what to do in the case of a "failing school." Whereas New Zealand threatens to withdraw funding from failing schools, California grants them increased funding. Neither strategy is very promising because the problems are rooted in the deeper problems of poverty and inequality. Pedagogically, assessment is important for informing both teacher and student of the type and level of performance required for success. This criterion can then serve as the basis for a joint intention of teacher and student. Second, and more conventionally, assessment provides information to both student and teacher as to the success or failure to achieve those agreed upon norms and standards. Consequently, it indicates what needs to be studied and reviewed, taught or retaught. Conflating evaluation of students with assessment of schools, I believe, is expensive mischief.

The proposed framework offers an alternative way of approaching the problem of human diversity. Schools, at least since Kant's *categorical imperative* not to see people merely as means, have been charged with contributing to human fulfillment and, more recently, to the recognition and appreciation of the possibility of different forms of fulfillment. Diversity seems at odds with the regimenting functions of the school as a bureaucracy with its fixed goals, roles, rules, and mandated curricula. Diversity has been recognized primarily in terms of the possibility of diverse routes to the same goals, hence, the popularity of trait theory and other psychological classifications of students into "kinds" whether on the basis of race, class, gender, learning style, or disability. In fact, there are as many types of learners as there are individuals in a classroom, and classifications have to be seen as contingent and local, reassigned by role, discipline, level, task, and goal. Basic classifications are in terms of the multiple roles offered not only in the school but in the society – doctor, lawyer, beggarman, thief. But possible roles in adult life are not easily anticipated in childhood; schools can only keep options open by giving children opportunities to try aspects of a number of them in the school years and providing the opportunity to acquire the competencies needed for admission to the advanced-level programs leading to those roles. The job of the school is less to assign roles than to let children explore them before they are forced to choose. When they do choose, it is their responsibility to achieve the standards set jointly with the teacher; taking on such a responsibility is an expression of their own intentionality.

Viewing persons as intentional carries with it an enriched conception of a person as an agent of his or her own actions rather than as the product of a collection of causes. The view of the person that is central to education and schooling is, as I have urged, an intentional conception, of the person as an agent of action who acts knowingly and who is responsible for his or her actions. Intentionality is at the base of a series of related concepts beginning with intentionality and including responsibility and accountability and progressing to identity of the person as a self with rights and obligations. Eventually one's identity is the invariant across the various roles that one plays or is allowed to play in the institutions of the society, and it is this new set of possible roles that children explore in the course of schooling.

This framework is an elaboration of theories that have explored the relation between minds and cultures. "Thinking," as Mary Douglas (1986), following Durkheim, argued, "depends upon institutions," in that those governing institutions have the right, power, or entitlement to say what is real, what is the same as what, and what rules apply in particular cases. Cultural psychology in the Vygotskian tradition (Wertsch, 1985) has addressed the relation between mind and society in general terms but has been less explicit about institutions; hence, as the individualist psychological theories that preceded them, such theories have had little to say about the entitlements and obligations of the school as an institution in relation to those of the learner. As has Deweyan progressivism, Vygotskian psychology has yet to address the special nature of the school as an institution, a formal institution that mediates between the formal institutions of the society – law, government, economy, science – and the interests, beliefs, and intentions of persons. Cultural theory has, however, taken us part of the way by showing that persons are not isolated individuals but members of social groups with roles and norms that remain largely implicit and transparent and that confer identity as some "kind" of person.

Thus, it is important to grant that the mind is in some sense deeply social. But discourse on the social nature of mind cast in terms of culture and society tends also to hide the issue of personal agency – who exactly is doing what and why. This was the basis for an earlier large-scale rejection of both Durkheim and Weber. Durkheim wrote, "The man whom education should realize in us is not the man such as nature has made him, but as society wishes him to be; and it wishes him such as its internal economy calls for" (1956, p.122). Durkheim's critics (Wilson, 1973) were soon to ask, Who is doing this "wishing"? When societies "want" to reproduce themselves, who is doing the "wanting"? Durkheim was seen as ascribing agency to a mythical entity, a group mind, the society. Even Vygotsky is vulnerable to this criticism in that he was sometimes willing to attribute "thinking" to groups as well as individuals (Wertsch, 1985, p. 61). However, by invoking institutions as the mediating factor, the questions of agency, responsibility, and accountability become tractable. Even informal institutions, such as families, have entitlements and responsibilities, implicit rules, and sanctions that are implemented through the intentionality of personal agents playing specific roles. Formal institutions, including schools, hold these rules deliberately and publicly in contracts and constitutions that specify the goals for which they are responsible and obtain resources on the basis of their promises to achieve them. Only by distinguishing the entitlements and responsibilities of institutions from those of persons can we transcend general notions such as mind, culture, and society and begin to formulate a theory of schooling as an institutional practice as well as a forum for personal experience.

Compared to theories of "social causation" common in some branches of sociology, theories of rational choice look pretty good; at least they acknowledge intentionality, responsibility, and accountability: We know who the actors are. And compared to an individualist causal (trait) theory of human behavior, theories of sociocultural cognition that show how individual cognitions reflect social practices look pretty good. The weakness of both is their inability to reckon with institutions. But if both the rational choice of individuals as persons and the rational choice of the same individuals playing a role in an institution can be granted, and if the entitlements and obligations of the two can be distinguished, we may have the framework needed for the study of education.

The framework offered here allows us some understanding of institutional change including the failures of earlier attempts at educational reform. The progressives at the beginning of the 20th century correctly identified the pedagogic problem as the failure to recognize the competencies and initiatives that children took to school that would make the acquisition of knowledge possible and that would allow children to take responsibility for their own learning. Agency was to be returned to the hands of the learner. The reforms failed in large part because of a lack of recognition of the school as an institution tied to the other institutions in the society. Consequently, the progressives found no adequate means to address the possible discrepancies between the achievements that students were happy with and those that the publicly funded institutions were willing to accept. The problem was diagnosed by critics as one of falling standards.

Durkheim was correct, I believe, in his analysis of the history of schooling as a rather direct reflection of larger-scale social organization and social change. As he argued, in the Middle Ages when the church ran the schools they wanted to make everyone a dialectician; after the Renaissance, the university wanted to make everyone a humanist (1956, p. 140). The Industrial Revolution provoked public, mass education as a means for producing a trained and responsible workforce, and *Sputnik*, some say, provoked the modern concern with raising educational standards. The concern could more correctly be attributed to a blind spot in progressivism.

But if social change is the engine for educational change, we may reasonably ask what if anything has happened or is happening to our schools since the Industrial Revolution and the rise of bureaucratic forms of social organization. Social critics since Sinclair Lewis have worried about "Babbitry," about personalities characterized by flexibility rather than character. Thus Reisman, Glazer, and Denny (1950) worried about the "other-directed" personality, and William Whyte (1956) worried about "organization men," those without souls who can be bought for a price. Character, they argued, was more important than the roles one played. In my view, they are right in their perceptions but, perhaps, wrong in their prescriptions. Rather than emphasizing character, they may, more appropriately, have urged more responsible and accountable roles in our institutions.[2] Much of modern life is organized around roles in the form of paid employment offered to us in the economic, governmental, and nongovernmental institutions that essentially rule the modern world. But counter to the worries of the prognosticators, it seems that the route to self-expression and human fulfillment lies more in exploiting the resources of those institutions than in avoiding them altogether. Recognizing this as the age of bureaucracy would help to explain the new concern with realigning issues of entitlements and responsibilities in all institutions including public ones such as the schools. If bureaucracies are inevitable, we can at least work toward making them transparent and more responsive to our personal needs and identities.

But an age of bureaucracy also entails serious limits. The rules, norms, and "formal procedures" that allow for fairness and objectivity may stifle initiative, limit freedom, and hide diversity. Conversely, a bureaucratic perspective may invite the institutionalization of cultural, ethnic, age, and gender differences in ways that undermine fairness and objectivity. Further, it may invite the belief that governing institutions can mandate a set of procedures, a method, that will reliably deliver equivalent products whether in science, government, economics, or education. School is a bureaucracy, and some social reformers naively believe that

---

[2] Even with the demise of the U.S. energy giant Enron, pundits bemoaned the decline of ethical standards rather than recognizing the importance of formal rules and severe sanctions.

what can be done for manufacturing or even for science can be done for schools. Schools as institutions are improvable, but, as for knowledge institutions, their improvement is to be judged in terms of their success in allowing teachers and students to take on and meet their responsibilities. Scientists cannot be told what to do, but institutions can provide, and are responsible for, the necessary framework in which good, reliable work may be done. The same should be true for schools. The role of government is not to micromanage teaching and learning but rather to provide the framework of plausible goals, the resources needed for teachers and learners to achieve them, and clear criteria for assessing success or failure.

In a modern bureaucratic world, knowledge, virtue, and ability take on new form. Institutions such as science preempt knowledge, justice systems preempt virtue, and functional roles preempt general cognitive ability. Thus, ability, knowledge, and virtue are construed and pursued less in the form of private, mental states and moral traits of individuals than in the form of competence in the roles, norms, and rules of the formal bureaucratic institutions in which they live and work. If these institutions fall apart, personal competence and private virtues tend to vanish with them. Consequently, general education is in large part learning to understand and respect these institutional forms – to know, for example, what is taken as known in the sciences, to be able to interpret and construct the documents on which such knowledge relies, and to understand how justice is managed through the legal system. Privately or communally held beliefs and moral and aesthetic intuitions are essential both to learning and to reforming institutional practices but in no way replace them. Acquiring disciplinary knowledge is learning to cope with and participate in the powerful institutions of the society through understanding the basic theories of those disciplines and the reasons and evidence on which they are based, even if they are somewhat discrepant from one's own privately held beliefs and commitments. Although a personal and private subjectivity and intentionality are at the base of all learning, it is not inappropriate that schools reflect in a massive and dramatic way the institutional structures of the larger society with its emphasis on rules, explicit explanations, the rule of law, and the reliance on documentary practices. School is less a preparation for adult life than an early version of it.

Schooling is a bold and risky means of pursuing education. It preempts in a major way the intentionality and responsibility of the learners themselves by turning over those responsibilities to an institution. But schools are successful to the extent that they, through their teachers and programs, return these responsibilities to the learners by negotiating goals acceptable to both and by allowing students to recruit the resources and energy to achieve them. Understanding how persons and institutions negotiate these responsibilities for learning may be the first step in explaining what schools are, what they do, why they are virtually universal, and why they are resistant to fundamental change.

I have done little more than try to explain why educational theory and educational research are largely at loggerheads with each other. I have made a few suggestions as to how our efforts may be better directed and suggested some specific lines of research that are required. These issues for research are equally relevant to policy decisions. The central problems are sorting out issues of responsibility and accountability across states, districts, administrators, teachers, and students and then devising means so that each level can know when it has met their obligations. Those for the teacher define the pedagogical problem as one of engaging the learner in such a way that he or she will accept responsibility for constructing a level of understanding that meets the goals, norms, and standards of the society.

Even if my primary goal is to create a useful description, it is impossible to escape the hope that a better description could lead to a better prescription. In the place of advice, however, I would offer a plea for respect. Respect implies intentionality, responsibility, and autonomy. Children can earn respect by accepting and meeting their responsibilities. Institutions can earn respect by setting worthwhile goals and meeting their obligations. In the attempt to improve the institution, there is always the temptation to specify in great detail the actual pedagogical practices and formal curriculum of the school, and impose them with more powerful methods of surveillance, in order to meet narrow and quantitatively defined goals. The price to be paid for this increased accountability is the decline in the responsibility and autonomy accorded to both teachers and students. No person, profession, or institution can accept responsibilities unless he, she, or it is also granted the autonomy needed to exercise individual judgment in meeting them. Teachers and students can earn respect only by setting and meeting obligations that they can recognize, at least in part, as their own. The role of the institution is to provide the resources and the framework in which teachers, and students too, can set and achieve socially valued goals, and thereby earn respect. This, I believe, is the way to make schools efficient and at the same time make them democratic and humane.

16

Coda

Psychological Theory and Educational Reform

Dewey's *Democracy and Education* remains a founding document in the ongoing attempt to formulate a "science" or theory of education, a framework for relating the policy, research, and practices of education. With its enlightened conception of the child, of knowledge, and of society, it served both to organize much of the discourse about education as well as to suggest directions for reform. The dreary monotony of traditional memorized lessons was to give way to more integrated, meaningful, interesting, cooperative activities and projects of the progressive school. Although there is little doubt that the progressivist reforms did much to make the school a much less forbidding and oppressive place, in the past two decades Dewey's liberalizing agenda has been seen not as the solution to the achievement of high educational standards, but as the problem. Ravitch (2000, p. 309) points out that Dewey was "locked in his dualisms": the school and society, the child and the curriculum, interest and effort, experience and education, siding in each case with only one side of the dualism, namely, the society, the child, interest, and experience. In Ravitch's view this weakened the traditional commitment to serious scholarly academic learning with often disastrous effects, especially for the disadvantaged and less able students, who tended to be shunted into banal and unchallenging programs.

My inquiry is a kind of reprise on this now familiar theme. I asked why the advances in our understanding of children's minds, their language and culture, and their learning has yielded so little to the improvement of learning, schooling, or education more generally. Discoveries about mind, knowledge, and social understanding that explain in some detail the predispositions for learning, the processes involved in forming and revising concepts, the intersubjectivity involved in learning language would seem to hold great promise for improving both knowledge about and the practice of schooling. But psychological discoveries are easily misapplied. The discovery that children learn so rapidly in the early years, learning some dozen new words every day of their lives for the first 10 or 12 years, leads some to infer that the labor of study can be replaced by engaging social experiences. The discovery that knowledge is constructed by the learner leads some to disparage the importance of teaching and explaining; that knowledge is "socially constructed," to disparage private study; that knowledge is subject to constant revision, to an unwarranted respect for the ideas of learners at the expense of the society's established knowledge.

The argument through the book is that the modern advances in the study of the minds of learners, as did the liberating perspectives of John Dewey, go awry not because they are invalid but because in both cases they fail to recognize the institutional nature of schooling. These child-centered initiatives treated and continue to treat learning and development as if they were matters of the learner's coming to terms with the world and with the local culture. Neither of these assumptions is appropriate for understanding schooling. School as an institution takes over responsibility for the student's learning and knowledge, and because the school is responsible to the state or nation that created it, it sets the standards, procedures, norms, and rules in terms of which this learning, thinking, and knowing are judged. Failure to come to grips with the normative standards and procedures of the institution of the school makes much good research and theory marginally relevant, if not actually misleading.

Schools are public institutions that, unlike local and family cultures, exist by virtue of explicit contracts, charters, or constitutions that detail the entitlements and obligations of the participants. They are rule-based, bureaucratic, documentary institutions in which correct procedures matter and in which judgments must be rationally justified in terms of formalized criteria. The obligations are met by delegation to professionals, such as teachers, and then in turn to students, who take on the responsibility of certain courses of study as the basis for entitlement to credentials. It is this interlocking set of responsibilities and entitlements that gives schools the more or less fixed and universal properties they have exhibited for the past five centuries. Almost any means will do as long as the institution meets its mandate. The child-centered programs advocated by Dewey and by many modern reformers are mistakenly seen as providing a superior route to a fixed goal, whereas, in most cases, they are directed to a different set of goals – human fulfillment, satisfaction, initiative, self-esteem, and the like, goals that, although important, are secondary to the obligations of the school to the intellectual, legal, economic, scientific, and political institutions of the larger society. No society educates its young to live in a different society.

The institutional nature of the school has remained largely invisible, not only to Dewey (Scheffler, 1974) but to the discipline as a whole. Schooling as an institutional practice bequeathed to the discipline of psychology the basic categories of both ability and learning. Ability was, and continues to be, largely the study of the ability to profit from schooling, and learning, the study of the factors that contributed to the enhanced performance on a criterion specified by academic disciplines. The split between knowledge and everyday local practice is legislated into the very institution of the school. Congruent with the scientific aspirations of the field both learning and ability were addressed in third-person objective terms as part of a causal theory of behavior. These assumptions have generated a vast body of research devoted to isolating and examining the factors that cause or, stated more modestly, account for the variance in achieved performance of institutionally defined populations.

To a modest extent, this research has contributed to the rationalizing of education as an institutional practice. Factors that contribute to aggregated student performance may be taken into account in the design and reform of institutions. The fact that reading ability, for example, is highly related to achievement in almost any field warrants an emphasis on reading in the early grades and warrants the provision of a wide variety of readable and interesting books and good libraries. The fact that children from literate homes find school more accessible warrants programs encouraging family literacy and so on. Research that indicates how to attain fixed goals is readily taken up; that which attempts to redefine those goals is set aside because it entails more radical social change.

But that tradition of isolating causal factors that contribute to achieved performance, that is, adherence to a causal model, has little to contribute to pedagogy, the understanding of the subjectivity and intentionality of the persons involved in teaching and learning. Intentional states such as beliefs, goals, desires, and plans are essential not only to explaining what people do, learn, or learn to do, but to addressing issues of responsibility and accountability, fundamental concerns of the school as an institution. Indeed, the causal models embraced by behaviorism blinded psychologists for more than a half-century to such an alternative first-person or intentionalist psychology.

An intentionalist psychology is, in part, a revival of the psychology of John Dewey, concerned as it was with experience and intentional action. The revival has provided us with new insight into learners' understanding of both minds, knowledge, and thinking and, equally important for my purposes, responsibility and accountability. The link is simple. One is responsible for one's intentional actions. An account of action in terms of intentions and responsibility is crucial for addressing the nature of schooling insofar as schooling is seen as an attempt to help students accept responsibility for putting their thought and action in line with the accepted practices of the society. The effects of schooling are not to be seen as simply the result of a series of causal factors, whether IQ or social class or personality trait, or peculiarities of institutional arrangements, but rather as a consequence of setting goals, working to their achievement, and judging that achievement in terms of normative standards.

Both cognitive psychology and sociocognitive theory contribute to the required psychology for education while failing to achieve it in their own particular ways. Cognitive psychology remains largely in the causal mode of explanation, isolating the causes of action while regarding with some suspicion the subject's own reasons for believing and acting. Yet these reasons for believing and acting and their evaluation in the light of normative standards are at the heart of the educational process. Because subjectivity and consciousness remain at the margins of cognitive psychology, it consistently fails to address issues of responsibility and accountability. That branch of cognitive psychology that does take into account the actor's own point of view, that inspired by Piaget, marginalizes the role of the social and cultural in the formation of mind.

Social–cultural theorists inspired by Vygotsky, on the other hand, have shown how even infants are not simply cognizers but intrinsically social beings who pick up the ways of thinking, talking, and acting from those around them. Social practices such as games, family routines, mealtimes, bedtimes, and so on, provide occasions for the development of linguistic and cognitive competencies, and the basic habits of social life. However, social–cultural theories fail to distinguish the informal modes of social and cultural action from the more impersonal, formalized, and universalized rules, norms, and standards of modern bureaucratic institutions including the school. By identifying culture with the locally lived social environment – the family, the peer group, the workplace – cultural psychology has done much to understand the variablity of local cultures but very little to understand how schooling in a bureaucratic society serves less to enhance local culture than to bridge across family, religious, ethnic, or gender groups. As are the legal system and the political system, the school system is directed to the development in children of the competencies needed to understand, respect, and participate in the bureaucratic institutions of the larger society, the nation-state, and, more recently, the global environment. Failure to recognize the school as an institution in its own right leads some writers to criticize the school for its bookishness, its focus on assessment and credentialing, and its remoteness from everyday life and from minority cultures. Rather, what needs to be recognized is that schools are institutions with their own evolved language, rules, and procedures as well as largely nonnegotiable norms and standards. Only in the romantic idealism of the 1960s could teaching be seen as "subversive" to the institutions of the larger society.

Schooling is misconceived when it is thought of as providing an initiation into adult culture, in that all culture is local culture. Rather, schooling is the initiation into an explicit, negotiated, transcultural institution based on the explicitness of roles and rules, norms and standards. An institution such as the school is successful only to the extent that it succeeds in helping persons to see themselves as the institution sees them. It is therefore a mistake to make the school more like the home or to see the school simply as an extension of the home. Rather, school is more correctly seen as resembling courts of law with their statutes, laws, credentialed expertise, modes of discourse, and reliance on documentary practices. The charges that some school tasks are artificial or that the classical tutorial mode called the *recitation method* is "infelicitous" are misguided in that they fail to acknowledge that the school has evolved its own special forms of discourse more or less congruent with its institutional form. Similarly, "Give reasons for your answer" is not just a school ritual but part of the introduction to the general project of the rationalization of knowledge and society. Schools, I have argued, owe their allegiance to the society that creates, funds, and monitors them and therefore have to be understood in their own right not just as an extension of local culture.

Schools provide a meeting ground between learners' subjectivity, local culture, and institutional normativity. The learner has a right to his or her own belief, but society retains the right to judge whether or not that belief is valid, true, or worthwhile. To understand learning it is necessary, and it has become possible, to make psychological studies of how children set goals, construe situations, interpret texts, and plan their actions. At the same time it has become possible to make explicit the norms, rules, standards, and procedures that authoritative institutions, such as the sciences, employ in their respective domains. The role of the teacher is then to help learners appraise their hunches, impressions, beliefs, and projects in terms of those institutional norms and standards. Such a view would do much to erase the criticism that schools have neglected the issue of standards. At the same time it provides a framework for examining how those norms and standards are negotiated by teacher and learner such that impossible goals may be averted and unconsidered performances validly criticized. Teachers are responsible not only for monitoring standards but for helping students see them as attainable and worthwhile so that they become joint goals, plans, and intentions. To elaborate on a frequently recited commonplace, students learn to take responsibility for their own learning, which is to say, students progressively learn how to appraise ther beliefs, actions, and texts in terms of the normative standards of the relevant institutionalized discipline. The authority and responsibility turned over to the school when the students enter are returned to them as they gain in understanding.

But revising our conceptions of schooling not only reconfigures how we shall examine the educational process, it provides us with a new conception of the fundamental notions of competence, knowledge, and virtue. Rather than being seen as psychological traits, invariant across time and space, they are to be seen as competence with the rules, norms, and standards of the social and institutional forms in which persons are embedded. Thus ability is not a general "mental ability" but the capacity to play one or more of the roles articulated in the abstract sciences or in other institutions. Virtue is not to be described in terms of a personal trait or even a sentiment so much as a respect for and understanding of the institutions of law and government, the rule of law, and one's entitlements and responsibilities as a citizen, as a teacher, as a student, or as a businessperson. And knowledge is not to be seen as the collection of remembered ideas, theories, and facts but rather as the competence to interpret and inscribe the documents that make up the archival resources of disciplined knowledge – to know the rules, norms, and standards of the discipline as well as its authoritative content. If one can only recall but not also understand the arguments and interpret the central texts of a discipline and, ultimately, contribute to them, one has a limited mastery of a discipline. This is why the frequent criticism of the school as "bookish" is somewhat misdirected. Although children do learn from experience as Dewey insisted, it is also essential that they learn how to read, interpret, and criticize the texts that make up the tradition or discipline involved. An emphasis on computers or other technologies may even detract from the importance of reading, studying, and interpreting these texts. Sustained reading and study, effort perhaps more than interest, are required for any deep understanding. To view ability, moral virtue, and knowledge this way is quite different from achieving the idealized goals expressed in most educational theory. Although humane feelings and personal morality are important, they are not, in my view, the primary concern of the school; people have a right to think and feel as they like. The goal of the school is much more limited, namely, teaching students how to participate in the bureaucratic institutions of the larger society. Thus, students must be taught how to engage with systematic, disciplined knowledge; to understand how the rule of law imparts both entitlements and responsibilities; and to recognize how the public institutions of the society allow them to pursue and achieve their own personal or local cultural goals. Whether or not they love knowledge and empathize with others is, perhaps, less important than that they know their duty and the rights and privileges that are earned by living up to it. Schools cannnot and need not reform human nature. They have a more limited responsibility, namely, teaching the young how to live in a complex society composed of institutions for knowledge, justice, the economy, and the like. In the urban, multicultural societies typical of much of the world, conspicuously so in Canada, the goal of education is not to teach children to love their neighbors, an impossibly idealistic goal, but more simply to teach them to recognize the social arrangements that make social life possible. Education teaches one to live with and interact productively with others one may never have met but who share competence with a common set of institutions and a common committment to explicit norms and standards and the rule of law.

That the school as an institution has evolved into a form sufficiently adequate that it has survived for centuries and is increasingly adopted throughout the world is not to say that it is not in continuous need of ongoing reform. Certainly schools are more hospitable and friendly places and more diverse than they were a century ago. As many recent critics have, I have argued that wholesale or radical reform is inappropriate. The maturing of educational theory as a discipline could help to shield us from the flood of single-minded wonders and earth-saving nostrums that frequently capture the headlines. Revolutionary reforms, whether dissolving disciplinary boundaries, classifying students into types or streams, dramatically liberalizing the curriculum, adding bouts of testing, or computerizing the classroom, have been either disappointing or counterproductive. What is required, I have urged, is a respect for the variety of roles that make up an educational system in a modern society. Let each level of the bureaucracy be clear on its own responsibilities and be held accountable for meeting them. But at the same time grant the other levels the freedom they need to earn the credit for meeting their own responsibilities. This includes both teachers and their students. In so doing, educational theory, far from failing to meet the century-old goal of creating a science of education, will have taken an important step in that direction.

References

Amsterdam, A. G., & Bruner, J. S. (2000). *Minding the law: How courts rely on storytelling, and how their stories change the ways we understand the law – and ourselves*. Cambridge, MA: Harvard University Press.

Anderson, B. (1983). *Imagined communities: Reflections on the origin and spread of nationalism*. New York: Verso.

Anscombe, G. E. M. (1957). *Intention*. London: Blackwell.

Archer, M. S. (1979). *Social origins of educational systems*. London: Sage.

Astington, J. H. (2002). Letters and pictures in seventeenth-century education. In J. Brockmeier, M. Wang, & D. R. Olson (Eds.), *Literacy, narrative and culture* (pp. 97–109). Richmond, England: Curzon Press.

Astington, J. W. (1988a). Children's understanding of the speech act of promising. *Journal of Child Language, 15*, 157–163.

Astington, J. W. (1988b). Promises: Words or deeds? *First Language, 8*, 259–270.

Astington, J. W. (1993). *The child's discovery of the mind*. Cambridge, MA: Harvard University Press.

Astington, J. W. (1996). What is theoretical about the child's theory of mind? A Vygotskian view of its development. In P. Carruthers & P. K. Smith (Eds.), *Theories of theories of mind* (pp. 184–199). Cambridge: Cambridge University Press.

Astington, J. W., Harris, P. L., & Olson, D. R. (Eds.) (1988). *Developing theories of mind*. Cambridge: Cambridge University Press.

Astington, J. W., Pelletier, J., & Homer, B. (in press). Theory of mind and epistemological development: The relation between children's second-order false-belief understanding and their ability to reason about evidence. *New Ideas in Psychology, Special Issue on the Development of Folk Epistemology in Children, Adolescents, and Adults*.

Attali, J. (1997). The crash of Western civilization: The limits of the markets and democracy. *Foreign Policy, 107*, 54–64.

Austin, J. L. (1962). *How to do things with words*. Cambridge, MA: Harvard University Press.

Bacon, F. (1965). *Francis Bacon: A selection of his works* (S. Warhaft, Ed.). Toronto: Macmillan.

Bakhtin, M. (1986). *Speech genres and other late essays* (V. W. McGee, Trans.). Austin: University of Texas Press.

Barnett, S. A. (1968). The "instinct to teach." *Nature, 220,* 747–749.

Barresi, J. (1999). On becoming a person. *Philosophical Psychology, 12,* 79–98.

Barresi, J., & Moore, C. (1996). Intentional relations and social understanding. *Behavioural and Brain Sciences, 19,* 107–154.

Barzan, J. (2001, September). The tenth muse. *Harper's Magazine,* 73–80.

Bell, K. (1990). Children's understanding of procedural texts. Toronto: Unpublished MA thesis, Department of Education, University of Toronto.

Bell, T. (1993). Reflections one decade after "A nation at risk." *Phi Delta Kappan, 74,* 593–597.

Bereiter, C., & Scardamalia, M. (1993). *Surpassing ourselves: An inquiry into the nature and implications of expertise.* Chicago: Open Court.

Berliner, D., & Biddle, B. (1995). *The manufactured crisis: Myths, fraud, and the attack on America's public schools.* Reading, MA: Addison-Wesley.

Bestor, A. E. (1953). *Educational wastelands: The retreat from learning in our public schools.* Urbana: University of Illinois Press.

Betz, W. (1940). The present situation in secondary mathematics with particular reference to the New National Reports on the Place of Mathematics in Education. *The Mathematics Teacher, 33,* 339–360.

Bidwell, C. E. (1999). Sociology and the study of education: Continuity, discontinuity, and the individualist turn. In E. Condliffe Lagemann & L. S. Shulman (Eds.), *Issues in education research: Problems and possibilities* (pp. 85–104). San Francisco: Jossey-Bass.

Bloch, M. (1998). The use of schooling and literacy in a Zafimaniry village. In B. Street (Ed.), *Cross-cultural approaches to literacy* (pp. 87–110). Cambridge: Cambridge University Press.

Block, N. J. & Dworkin, G. (1976). *The IQ controversy: Critical readings.* New York: Pantheon Books.

Bloom, L. (2000). Intentionality and theories of intentionality in development: Essay review of *Developing theories of intention* edited by P. D. Zelazo, J. W. Astington, & D. R. Olson. *Human Development, 43,* 178–185.

Bourdieu, P., & Passeron, J-C. (1990). *Reproduction in education, society and culture* (2nd ed.). Newbury Park, CA: Sage.

Bowles, S., & Gintis, H. I. (1976). *Schooling in capitalist America.* New York: Basic Books.

Boyle, R. (1772). New experiments physico-mechanical, touching the spring of the air. In T. Birch (Ed.), *The works of the Honourable Robert Boyle* (Vol. 1, pp. 1–117). London: J. & F. Rivington.

Bransford, J., Brown, A., & Cocking, R. (1999). *How people learn: Brain, mind, experience and school.* Washington, DC: National Academy Press.

Brentano, R. (1973). *Psychology from an empirical standpoint* (O. Kraus, Ed). London: Humanities Press.

Brockmeier, J., Wang, M., & Olson, D. R. (Eds.) (2002). *Literacy, narrative and culture.* Richmond, England: Curzon Press.

Brodbeck, M. (Ed.) (1971). *Readings in the philosophy of the social sciences.* New York: Macmillan.

Bromley, D. W. (1998). Expectations, incentives and performance in American schools. *Daedalus, 127,* 41–66.

Brown, A. (1997). Transforming schools into communities of thinking and learning about serious matters. *American Psychologist, 52,* 399–413.

Brown, A. L., & Campione, J. (1996). Psychological learning theory and the designing of innovative environments: On procedures, principles and systems. In L. Schauble & R. Glaser (Eds.), *Contributions of instructional innovation to understanding learning.* Hillsdale, NJ: Lawrence Erlbaum.

Brown, P., & Levinson, S. (1978). Universals in language usage: Politeness phenomena. In E. N. Goody (Ed.), *Questions and politeness: Strategies in social interaction* (pp. 56–289). Cambridge: Cambridge University Press.

Bruner, J. S. (1960). *The process of education.* Cambridge, MA: Harvard University Press.

Bruner, J. S. (1972). The nature and uses of immaturity. *American Psychologist, 27,* 687–708.

Bruner, J. S. (1973). *Beyond the information given.* (J. Anglin, Ed.). New York: Norton.

Bruner, J. S. (1983). *Child's talk.* New York: Norton.

Bruner, J. S. (1990). *Acts of meaning.* Cambridge, MA: Harvard University Press.

Bruner, J. S. (1996). *The culture of education.* Cambridge, MA: Harvard University Press.

Bruner, J. S. (1999). Postscript: Some reflections on educational research. In E. C. Lagemann & L. S. Shulman (Eds.), *Issues in education research: Problems and possibilities* (pp. 399–410). San Francisco: Jossey-Bass.

Bruner, J. S. (2001). In response. In D. Bakhurst & S. Shanker (Eds.), *Jerome Bruner: Language, culture, self.* London: Sage.

Byrne, R. W., & Whiten, A. (Eds.) (1998). *Machiavellian intelligence.* Oxford: Clarendon Press.

Calvino, I. (1985). *Mr. Palomar* (W. Weaver, Trans.). New York: Harcourt Brace Jovanovich. Original work published 1983.

Carey, S. (1996). Cognitive domains as modes of thought. In D. R. Olson & N. G. Torrance (Eds.), *Modes of thought* (pp. 187–215). Cambridge: Cambridge University Press.

Carey, S. (1999). Sources of conceptual change. In E. Scholnick, K. Nelson, S. Gelman, & P. Miller (Eds.), *Conceptual development: Piaget's legacy.* Mahwah, NJ: Erlbaum.

Carey, S., & Spelke, E. (1994). Domain specific knowledge and conceptual change. In L. A. Hirschfeld & S. Gelman (Eds.), *Mapping the mind: Domain specificity in cognition and culture* (pp. 455–473). New York: Cambridge University Press.

Carlyle, T. (1901). *On heroes, hero-worship, and the heroic in history.* Boston: Ginn.

Case, R. (1996). Changing views of knowledge and their impact on educational research and practice. In D. R. Olson & N. Torrance (Eds.), *The handbook of education and human development* (pp. 75–99). Malden, MA: Blackwell.

Catlin, G. (1938). Introduction to the translation. In E. Durkheim, *The rules of sociological method.* New York: The Free Press.

Chamberlin, J. E. (2002). Hunting, tracking and reading. In J. Brockmeier, M. Wang, & D. R. Olson (Eds.), *Literacy, narrative and culture* (pp. 67–85). Richmond, England: Curzon Press.

Chartier, A.-M. (in press). Teaching reading: A historical approach. In P. Bryant & T. Nunes (Eds.), *International handbook of children's literacy.* Dordrecht: Kluwer.

Chartier, A.-M., & Hébrard, J. (2001). Literacy and schooling from the cultural historian's point of view. In T. S. Popkewitz, B. M. Franklin, & M. Pereyra (Eds.), *Cultural history and education: Critical essays of knowledge and schooling* (pp. 263–288). New York: Routledge.

Cheng, P. W., & Holyoak, K. J. (1985). Pragmatic reasoning schemas. *Cognitive Psychology, 17,* 391–416.

Chomsky, N. (1957). A review of B. F. Skinner's *Verbal behavior. Language, 35,* 26–58.

Clanchy, M. (1993). *From memory to written record: England 1066–1307* (2nd ed.). Oxford: Blackwell.

Clanchy, M. (1997). *Abelard: A medieval life.* Oxford: Blackwell.

Clark, H. H. (1996). *Using language.* New York: Cambridge University Press.

Clay, M. (1998). *By different paths to common outcomes.* York, ME: Stenhouse.

Clemens, E. S. (1999). From society to school and back again: Questions about learning in and for a world of complex organizations. In E. C. Lagemann & L. S. Shulman (Eds.), *Issues in education research* (pp. 105–120). San Francisco: Jossey-Bass.

Cloud, J. (2001, March 12). Should SATs matter? *Time, 157,* pp. 62–70.

Cochran, T. (2001). *Twilight of the literary: Figures of thought in the age of print.* Cambridge, MA: Harvard University Press.

Cohen, M. (1977). *Sensible words: Linguistic practice in England 1640–1785.* Baltimore: Johns Hopkins University Press.

Cole, M. (1996). *Cultural psychology.* Cambridge, MA: Harvard University Press.

Cole, M., & Engestrom, Y. (1993). A cultural–historical approach to distributed cognition. In G. Salomon (Ed.), *Distributed cognitions* (pp. 1–46). Cambridge: Cambridge University Press.

Coleman, J., Campbell, C., Hobson, J., Mood, A., Weinfeld, F., & York, R. (1966). *Equality of educational opportunity.* Washington, DC: Government Printing Office.

Comenius, J. A. (1968). *Orbis Pictus: Facsimile of the final English edition of 1659.* London: Oxford University Press.

Comer, J. P. (1988). Educating poor minority children. *Scientific American, 259,* 24–30.

Conant, J. B. (1964). *Two modes of thought: My encounters with science and education.* New York: Trident Press.

Cook, T., Habib, F., Phillips, M., Settersten, R., Shagle, S., & Degirmencioglu, S. (1999). Comer's School Development Program in Prince George's County, Maryland: A Theory-Based Evaluation. *American Educational Research Journal, 36,* 543–597.

Coulmas, F. (1989). *The writing systems of the world.* Oxford: Blackwell.

Coulmas, F. (1996). *The Blackwell encyclopaedia of writing systems.* Oxford: Blackwell.

Coulmas, F. (2000). *The nationalization of writing.* Mimeo. Department of Speech and Language, Gerhard-Meriator-University, Duisberg, Germany.

Coy, M. W. (1989). Introduction. In M. W. Coy (Ed.), *Apprenticeship: From theory to method and back again.* Albany: State University of New York.

Coyne, J. (2000, April 27). Not an inkling: Review of Matt Ridley, genome. *London Review of Books, 22,* 13–14.

Cremin, L. A. (1961). *The transformation of the school: Progressivism in American education 1876–1957.* New York: Alfred Knopf.

Cremin, L. A. (1965). *The genius of American education.* New York: Random House.

Cronbach, L. J. (1957). The two disciplines of scientific psychology. *American Psychologist, 12,* 671–684.

Cronbach, L. J. (1975). Beyond the two disciplines of scientific psychology. *American Psychologist, 35,* 116–127.

Cronbach, L. J., & Snow, R. E. (1977). *Aptitudes and instructional methods.* New York: Irvington.

Csikszentmihalyi, M. (1998). Society, culture, and person: A systems view of creativity. In R. Sternberg (Ed.), *The nature of creativity* (pp. 325–339). New York: Cambridge University Press.

Cummins, R. (2000). "How does it work?" versus "What are the laws?" Two conceptions of psychological explanation. In F. Keil & R. Wilson (Eds.), *Explanation and cognition* (pp. 117–144). Cambridge, MA: MIT Press.

Cziko, G. (2000). *The things we do.* Cambridge, MA: MIT Press.

Damerow, P. (1998). Prehistory and cognitive development. In J. Langer & M. Killen (Eds.), *Piaget, evolution, and development* (pp. 247–269). Mahwah, NJ: LEA.

Davidson, D. (1963). Actions, reasons and causes. *Journal of Philosophy, 60,* 685–700.

Davidson, D. (1997). Seeing through language. In J. M. Preston (Ed.), *Thought and language* (pp. 15–27). Cambridge: Cambridge University Press.

Davidson, D. (2001). *Subjective, intersubjective, objective.* Oxford: Clarendon.

Davis, N. Z. (1975). *Society and culture in early modern France.* Stanford, CA: Stanford University Press.

de Bury, R. (1945). *The philobiblon of Richard de Bury.* New York: Duschnes. Original work published in 1345.

DeGrandpre, R. J. (1999). Ritalin nation: Rapid-fire culture and the transformation of human consciousness. New York: Norton.

Delbos, G., & Jorion, P. (1984). *La transmission des saviors.* Paris: Editions de la Maison des Sciences de l'Homme.

Dennett, D. C. (1978). *Brainstorms: Philosophical essays on mind and psychology.* Montgomery, VT: Bradford Books.

Derham, D. P., Mahler, F. K. H., & Walker, P. L. (1971). *An introduction to law* (2nd ed.) Melbourne: Law Book Company.

Descartes, R. (1960). *Discourse on method and meditations* (L. J. LaFleur, Trans.). Indianapolis/New York: Bobbs-Merrill. Original work published 1637–1641.

Detterman, D., & Thompson, L. (1997). What is so special about special education? *American Psychologist, 52*, 1082–1090.

Dewey, J. (1972). The reflex arc concept in psychology. In J. A. Boydston (Ed.), *John Dewey: The early works, Volume 5: 1895–1898* (pp. 96–109). Carbondale: Southern Illinois University Press.

Dewey, J. (1976a). The school and society. In J. A. Boydston (Ed.), *John Dewey: The middle works, Volume 1: 1899–1901* (pp. 1–109). Carbondale: Southern Illinois University Press.

Dewey, J. (1976b). The child and the curriculum. In J. A. Boydston (Ed.), *John Dewey: The middle works, Volume 2: 1902–1903* (pp. 271–291). Carbondale: Southern Illinois University Press.

Dewey, J. (1978). How we think. In J. A. Boydston (Ed.), *John Dewey: The middle works, Volume 6: 1910–1911* (pp. 177–355). Carbondale: Southern Illinois University Press.

Dewey, J. (1979). German philosophy and politics. In J. A. Boydston (Ed.), *John Dewey: The middle works, Volume 8: 1915* (pp. 135–204). Carbondale: Southern Illinois University Press.

Dewey, J. (1980). Democracy and education. In J. A. Boydston (Ed.), *John Dewey: The middle works, Volume 9: 1916*. Carbondale: Southern Illinois University Press.

Dewey, J. (1984). From absolutism to experimentism. In J. A. Boydston (Ed.), *John Dewey: The later works, Volume 5: 1929–1930* (pp. 147–160). Carbondale: Southern Illinois University Press.

Dewey, J. (1986). Logic: A theory of inquiry. In J. A. Boydston (Ed.), *John Dewey: The later works, Volume 12: 1938*. Carbondale: Southern Illinois University Press.

Dickens, W., & Flynn, J. (2001). Heritability estimates versus large environmental effects: The IQ paradox resolved. *Psychological Review, 108*, 346–369.

Diller, L. H. (1998). *Running on Ritalin: A physician reflects on children, society, and performance in a pill*. New York: Bantam Books.

di Sessa, A. A. (1996). What do "just plain folk" know about physics? In D. R. Olson & N. G. Torrance (Eds.), *Handbook of education and human development* (pp. 709–730). Oxford: Blackwell.

di Sessa, A. A. (2000). *Changing minds: Computers, learning, and literacy*. Cambridge, MA: MIT Press.

Dobzhansky, T., & Montagu, A. (1947). Culture: Man's adaptive dimension. *Science, 105* (2736), 587–590.

Donald, M. (1991). *Origins of the modern mind: Three stages in the evolution of culture and cognition*. Cambridge, MA: Harvard University Press.

Donald, M. (2001). *A mind so rare: The evolution of human consciousness*. New York: W. W. Norton.

Donaldson, M. (1978). *Children's minds*. Glasgow: Fontana/Collins.

Donaldson, M. (1992). *Human minds: An exploration*. New York: Allan Lane, Penguin.

Donaldson, M. (1996). Humanly possible: Education and the scope of mind. In D. R. Olson & N. Torrance (Eds.), *The handbook of education and human development* (pp. 324–344). Malden, MA: Blackwell.

Douglas, M. (1986). *How institutions think*. Syracuse, NY: Syracuse University Press.

Dowler, W. (2001). *Classroom and empire: The politics of schooling Russia's eastern nationalities, 1860–1917*. Kingston, Canada: McGill-Queen's University Press.

Downing, J. (1987). Comparative perspectives on world literacy. In D. Wagner (Ed.), *The future of literacy in a changing world* (pp. 25–47). Oxford: Pergamon Press.

Drabble, M. (2001). *The peppered moth*. Toronto: McClelland & Stewart.

Driver, R., Asoko, H., Leach, J., Mortimer, E., & Scott, P. (1994). Constructing scientific knowledge in the classroom. *Educational Researcher, 23*, 5–12.

Dunkel, H. B. (1970). *Herbart and Herbartianism: An educational ghost story*. Chicago: University of Chicago Press.

Durkheim, E. (1915). *Elementary forms of religious life*. (J. W. Swain, Trans.). New York and London: The Free Press.

Durkheim, E. (1938). *The rules of sociological method*. New York: The Free Press.

Durkheim, E. (1952). *Suicide*. New York: Routledge. Originally published in 1883.

Durkheim, E. (1956). *Education and sociology* (S. Fox, trans.). Glencoe, IL: The Free Press.

Durkheim, E. (1961). *Moral education: A study in the theory and application of the sociology of education* (E. Wilson & H. Schnurer, trans.). New York: The Free Press.

Durkheim, E. (1982/1901). The psychological conception of society. In S. Lukes (Ed.), *The rules of sociological method* (pp. 253–255). New York: The Free Press.

Easton, M. (2001, February 12). Prostate cancer gene found. *University of Toronto Bulletin*, p. 3.

Edelstein, W. (1999). The cognitive context of historical change: Assimilation, accommodation, and the segmentation of competence. In E. Turiel (Ed.), *Development and cultural change: Reciprocal processes* (pp. 5–17). San Francisco: Jossey-Bass.

Egan, K. (1996). The development of understanding. In D. R. Olson & N. Torrance (Eds.), *The handbook of education and human development* (pp. 514–533). Malden, MA: Blackwell.

Egan, K. (1997). *The educated mind: How cognitive tools shape our understanding*. Chicago: University of Chicago Press.

Ehri, L., Nunes, S., Stahl, S., & Willows, D. (2001). Systematic phonics instruction helps students learn to read: Evidence from the National Reading Panel's meta-analysis. *Review of Educational Research, 71*, 393–448.

Eisenstein, E. (1979). *The printing press as an agent of change*. Cambridge: Cambridge University Press.

Elkana, Y. (2000). To rethink – not to unthink – the Enlightenment. Unpublished Working Paper. Berlin: Wissenschaftskolleg zu Berlin.

Elkind, D. (1999). Educational research and the science of education. *Educational Psychology Review, 11*, 271–293.

Elster, J. (1983). *Explaining technical change: A case study in the philosophy of science*. Cambridge: Cambridge University Press.

Elwert, G. (2001). Societal literacy: Writing culture and development. In D. R. Olson & N. Torrance (Eds.), *The making of literate societies* (pp. 54–67). Malden, MA: Blackwell.

Erikson, E. (1962). *Young Man Luther.* New York: Norton.

Erneling, C. (1993). *Understanding language acquisition.* Albany: State University of New York.

Feldman, C. (2000). The construction of mind and self in an interpretive community. In Astington, J. (Ed.), *Minds in the making: Essays in honour of David R. Olson* (pp. 17–28). Oxford: Blackwell.

Fiske, E., & Ladd, H. (2000) *When schools compete: A cautionary tale.* Washington, DC: Brookings Institution Press.

Flavell, J. H. (1985). *Cognitive development* (2nd ed.) Englewood Cliffs, NJ: Prentice-Hall.

Flesch, R. (1955). *Why Johnny can't read and what to do about it.* New York: Harper.

Flinn, J. (1992). Transmitting traditional values in new schools: Elementary education of Pulap Atoll. *Anthropoloogy & Education Quarterly, 23,* 44–58.

Fodor, J. (1998). *Concepts: Where cognitive science went wrong.* Oxford: Oxford University Press.

Foucault, M. (1979). *Discipline and punish: The birth of the prison.* New York: Vintage.

Freire, P. (1972). *Pedagogy of the oppressed.* New York: Herder & Herder.

Frye, N. (1982). *The great code: The Bible and literature.* Toronto: Academic Press.

Fuhrman, S. (2001). Conclusion. In Fuhrman, S. (Ed.), *From the capitol to the classroom: Standards-based reform in the States* (pp. 263–278). 100th Yearbook of the NSSE. Chicago: University of Chicago Press.

Fullan, M. (1991). *The new meaning of educational change.* New York: Teachers College Press.

Fuller, B. (Ed.) (2000a). *Inside charter schools: The paradox of radical decentralization.* Cambridge, MA: Harvard University Press.

Fuller, B. (2000b). Introduction: Growing charter schools, decentering the State. In B. Fuller (Ed.), *Inside charter schools: The paradox of radical decentralization* (pp. 1–11). Cambridge, MA: Harvard University Press.

Gage, N. L., & Berliner, D. C. (1975). *Educational psychology.* Chicago: Rand McNally.

Gardner, H. (1999). *The disciplined mind: What all students should understand.* New York: Simon & Schuster.

Gardner, H. (2000, October 19). Paroxysms of choice. *New York Review of Books, 47,* 44–49.

Gardner, H., Torff, B., & Hatch, T. (1996). The age of innocence reconsidered: Preserving the best of the progressive traditions in psychology and education. In D. R. Olson & N. Torrance (Eds.), *The handbook of education and human development* (pp. 28–55). Malden, MA: Blackwell.

Garfinkel, H. (1967). *Studies in ethnomethodology.* Englewood Cliffs, NJ: Prentice-Hall.

Gaukroger, S. (2001). *Francis Bacon and the transformation of early-modern philosophy.* Cambridge: Cambridge University Press.

Gaur, A. (1987). *A history of writing.* London: The British Library. Original work published 1984.

Gee, J. (2000). Communities of practice in the new capitalism. *Journal of the Learning Sciences, 9*, 515–523.

Geertz, C. (1973). *The interpretation of cultures.* New York: Basic Books.

Geisler, C. (1994). *Academic literacy and the nature of expertise: Reading, writing and knowing in academic philosophy.* Hillsdale, NJ: Erlbaum.

Gerth, H., & Mills, C. W. (1948). *From Max Weber: Essays in sociology.* London: Routledge & Kegan Paul.

Ghose, M. (2001). Women and empowerment through literacy (pp. 296–316). In D. R. Olson & N. G. Torrance (Eds.), *The making of literate societies.* Oxford: Blackwell.

Giddens, A. (1987). Weber and Durkheim: Coincidence and divergence. In W. Mommsen & J. Osterhammel (Eds.), *Max Weber and his contemporaries.* London: Unwin Hyman.

Gigerenzer, G., Todd, P., & the ABC Research Group (1999). *Simple heuristics that make us smart.* Oxford: Oxford University Press.

Gilligan, C. (1982). *In a different voice: Psychological theory and women's development.* Cambridge, MA: Harvard University Press.

Ginzburg, C. (1982). *The cheese and the worms.* Harmondsworth, England: Penguin Books.

Ginzburg, C. (1999). *History, rhetoric, and proof.* London: University Press of New England for Brandeis University Press.

Gladwell, M. (1999, February 15). Running from Ritalin. *The New Yorker Magazine*, pp. 80–84.

Godzich, W., & Kittay, J. (1987). *The emergence of prose: An essay in prosaics.* Minneapolis: University of Minnesota Press.

Goertz, M. (2001). Standards-based accountability: Horse trade or horse whip? In S. Fuhrman (Ed.), *From the capitol to the classroom: Standards-based reform in the States* (pp. 39–59). 100th Yearbook of the NSSE. Chicago: University of Chicago Press.

Goffman, E. (1961). *Encounters: Two studies in the sociology of interaction.* Indianapolis: Bobbs-Merrill.

Gombrich, E. H. (1960). *Art and illusion: A study in the psychology of pictorial representation.* New York: Bollingen/Panthenon Books.

Good, T., & Braden, J. (2000). *The great school debate: Choice, vouchers, and charters.* Mahwah, NJ: Erlbaum.

Goodman, P. (1960). *Growing up absurd: Problems of youth in the organized system.* New York: Random House.

Goody, E. (1978). Towards a theory of questions. In E. N. Goody (Ed.), *Questions and politeness* (pp. 17–43). Cambridge: Cambridge University Press.

Goody, E. (1989). Learning, apprenticeship and the division of labor. In M. Coy (Ed.), *Apprenticeship* (pp. 233–256). Albany: State University of New York.

Goody, E., & Bennett, J. (2001). Literacy for Gonja and Birifor children in northern Ghana. In D. R. Olson & N. G. Torrance (Eds.), *The making of literate societies* (pp. 178–200). Oxford: Blackwell.

Goody, J. (1977). *The domestication of the savage mind.* Cambridge: Cambridge University Press.

Goody, J. (1986). *The logic of writing and the organization of society.* Cambridge: Cambridge University Press.

Goody, J. (1987). *The interface between the oral and the written.* Cambridge: Cambridge University Press.

Goody, J. (2000). *The power of the written tradition.* Washington, DC: Smithsonian Institution.

Gopnik, A., Meltzoff, A., & Kuhl, P. (1999). *How babies think: The science of childhood.* London: Weidenfeld & Nicolson.

Gray, J. (1998). *False dawn: The delusions of global capitalism.* London: Granta Books.

Great Britain, Committee of Inquiry into Reading and the Use of Language. (1975). *A language for life: Report of the committee of inquiry appointed by the Secretary of State for Education and science under the chairmanship of Sir Alan Bullock (The Bullock report).* London: Her Majesty's Stationery Office.

Green, D. H. (1994). *Medieval listening and reading: The primary reception of German literature 800–1300.* Cambridge: Cambridge University Press.

Greenfield, P. M., & Bruner, J. S. (1966). Culture and cognitive growth. In D. Goslin (Ed.), *Handbook of socialization theory and research* (pp. 633–654). Chicago: Rand McNally.

Greenfield, P., & Lave, J. (1982). Cognitive aspects of informal education. In D. Wagner & H. Stevenson (Eds.), *Cultural perspectives on child development* (pp. 181–207). San Francisco: Freeman.

Greeno, J., McDermott, R., Cole, K., Engle, R., Goldman, S., Knudsen, J., Lauman, B., & Linde, C. (1999). Research, reform and aim in education: Modes of action in search of each other. In E. Lagemann & L. Shulman (Eds.), *Issues in education research: Problems and possibilities* (pp. 299–335). San Francisco: Jossey-Bass.

Grendler, P. F. (1989). *Schooling in renaissance Italy: Literacy and learning 1300–1600.* Baltimore: Johns Hopkins University Press.

Grice, P. (1989). *Studies in the way of words.* Cambridge, MA: Harvard University Press.

Gronlund, N. E. (1973). *Preparing criterion-references tests for classroom instruction.* New York: Macmillan.

Hacking, I. (1975a). *Why does language matter to philosophy?* Cambridge: Cambridge University Press.

Hacking, I. (1975b). *The emergence of probability: A philosophical study of early ideas about probability, inducton and statistical inference.* Cambridge: Cambridge University Press.

Hacking, I. (1984). The nature of mathematical knowledge. *New York Review of Books, 31,* 36–38.

Hacking, I. (1990). *The taming of chance.* Cambridge: Cambridge University Press.

Hacking, I. (1994). Review of P. Kitcher, "The advancement of science." *Journal of Philosophy, 91,* 212–215.

Hacking, I. (1996). Normal people. In D. R. Olson & N. Torrance (Eds.), *Modes of thought: Explorations in culture and cognition* (pp. 59–71). New York: Cambridge University Press.

Hacking, I. (1999). *The social construction of what.* Cambridge, MA: Harvard University Press.

Hall, D. D. (1994). Literacy, culture and authority. In D. Keller-Cohen (Ed.), *Literacy: Interdisciplinary conversations.* Cresskill, NJ: Hampton Press.

Hall, G. S. (1965). *Health, growth and heredity: On natural education* (C. Strickland & C. Burgess, Eds.). New York: Teachers College Press.

Hall, K. (1999). Understanding educational processes in an era of globalization. In E. C. Lagemann & L. S. Shulman (Eds.), *Issues in Educational Research*. San Francisco: Jossey-Bass.

Hamilton, D. (1989). *Towards a theory of schooling*. New York: Falmer.

Hammond, J. (2001). Literacies in school education in Australia: Disjunctions between policy and research. *Language and Education, 15*, 162–177.

Hardin, G. (1968). The tragedy of the commons. *Science, 162*, 1243–1248.

Harré, R. (2001). Norms in life: Problems in the representation of rules. In D. Bakhurst & S. Schanker (Eds.), *Jerome Bruner: Language, culture, self* (pp. 150–166). London: Sage.

Harris, R. (1989). How does writing restructure thought? *Language and Communication, 9*, 99–106.

Havelock, E. A. (1963). *Preface to Plato*. Cambridge: Cambridge University Press.

Havelock, E. A. (1991). The oral-literate equation: A formula for the modern mind. In D. Olson & N. Torrance (Eds.), *Literacy and Orality* (pp. 11–27). Cambridge: Cambridge University Press.

Heap, S. H. (1992). *The theory of choice: A critical guide*. Oxford: Blackwell.

Heath, S. B. (1999). Discipline and disciplines in education research: Elusive goals? In E. Lagemann & L. Shulman (Eds.), *Issues in education research: Problems and possibilities* (pp. 203–223). San Francisco: Jossey-Bass.

Heeschen, V. (1997). *Change and talking about change among Eipo and Yalenang (Central Mountains, West New Guinea)*. Baessler-Archiv, Neu Folge, Band XLV, 449–462.

Heller, J. (1962). *Catch 22*. New York: Simon & Schuster.

Herbart, J. F. von (1806). *Allgemeine Padagogik aus dem zweck der erziehung abgeleitet (Universal pedagogy)*. Gottingen: J. F. Rower.

Herbart, J. F. (1898). *The application of psychology to the science of education*. New York: Scribner.

Herrnstein, R., & Murray, C. (1994). *The bell curve: Intelligence and class structure in American life*. New York: The Free Press.

Hiebeler, R., Kelly, T., & Ketterman, C. (1998). *Best practices*. New York: Arthur Anderson/Simon & Schuster.

Hirsch, E. D., Jr. (1987). *Cultural literacy: What every American needs to know*. Boston: Houghton Mifflin.

Hirsch, E.D., Jr. (1997). *The schools we need: And why we don't have them*. New York: Doubleday.

Hirschman, A. O. (1970). *Exit, voice, and loyalty: Responses to decline in firms, organizations, and states*. Cambridge, MA: Harvard University Press.

Hirschman, A. O. (2001). *Crossing boundaries: Selected writings*. New York: Zone Books.

Hobbes, T. (1958). *Leviathan*. Indianapolis: Bobbs-Merrill. Original work published in 1651.

Hoffrage, U., & Gigerenzer, G. (1998). Using natural frequencies to improve diagnostic inferences. *Academic Medicine, 73*, 538–540.

Hofmeister, A., Prass, R., & Winnige, N. (1998). Elementary education, schools, literacy, and the demands of everyday life: Northwest Germany ca. 1800. *Central European History, 31,* 329–384.

Hofstadter, R. (1945). *Social Darwinism in American thought.* Philadelphia: University of Pennsylvania Press.

Holt, J. (1964). *How children fail.* New York: Pitman.

Holt, J. (1967). *How children learn.* New York: Pitman.

Holton, G. (1973). *Thematic origins of scientific thought.* Cambridge, MA: Harvard University Press.

Homer, B., & Olson, D. R. (1999). Literacy and children's conception of words. *Written Language and Literacy, 2,* 113–137.

Horowitz, R., & Olson, D. R. (in press). Texts that talk: The special and peculiar nature of classroom discourse and the crediting of sources. In R. Horowitz (Ed.), *Talking texts: Knowing the world through instructional discourse.* Newark, DE: International Reading Association and Mahwah, NJ: Erlbaum.

Hughes, R. (1928). *A high wind in Jamaica.* New York: Harper.

Hume, D. (1740). *A treatise on human nature* (L. Selby-Bigge, Ed.). Oxford: Clarendon Press, 1888.

Hume, D. (1987). Of civil liberty. In E. Miller (Ed.), *Essays moral, political and literary* (pp. 87–96). Indianapolis: Liberty Classics.

Huttenlocher, J. (1964). Children's language: Word-phrase relationship. *Science, 143,* 264–265.

Illich, I. (1994). *In the vineyard of the text.* Chicago: University of Chicago Press.

Ingersoll, R. M. (2001). Teacher turnover and teacher shortages: An organizational analysis. *American Educational Research Journal, 38,* 499–534.

International Herald Tribune (1980, February 14). p. 88.

Ipfling, H.-J., & Chambliss, J. J. (1989a). Herbart. *Encyclopaedia Britannica* (Vol. 5, p. 865). Chicago: Encyclopaedia Britannica.

Ipfling, H.-J., & Chambliss, J. J. (1989b). The history of education. *Encyclopaedia Britannica* (Vol. 18, pp. 1–90). Chicago: Encyclopaedia Britannica.

Jackendoff, R. (1999). The natural logic of rights and obligations. In R. Jackendoff, P. Bloom, and K. Wynn (Eds.), *Language, logic, and concepts* (pp. 67–117). Cambridge, MA: MIT Press.

Jackson, P. W. (1990). The functions of educational research. *Educational Research, 19,* 3–9.

Jakobeit, C. (1999). The World Bank and human development: Washington's new strategic approach. *Cooperation and Development.*

Jencks, C., Smith, M., Acland, H., Bane, M. J., Cohen, D., Ginits, H., Heyns, B., & Michelson, S. (1972). *Inequality: A reassessment of the effect of family and schooling in America.* New York: Basic Books.

Johns, A. (1998). *The nature of the book: Print and knowledge in the making.* Chicago: University of Chicago Press.

Johnson, D. M., & Erneling, C. E. (1997). *The future of the cognitive revolution.* Oxford: Oxford University Press.

Johnson, D. M., & Erneling, C. (2002). *Mind as a scientific object.* New York: Oxford University Press.

Johnson-Laird, P. (1998). *Mental models*. Cambridge: Cambridge University Press.

Kafka, F. (1999/1910). *The diaries of Franz Kafka, 1910–1923*. (M. Brood, Ed.). London: Vintage.

Kahneman, D. (1982). Bureaucracies, minds and the human engineering of decisions. In G. R. Ungson & D. N. Braunstein (Eds.), *Decision making: An interdisciplinary inquiry*. Boston: Kent.

Kahneman, D., & Tversky, A. (1982). On the study of statistical intuitions. In D. Kahneman, P. Slovic, & A. Tversky (Eds.), *Judgement under uncertainty: Heuristics and biases* (pp. 493–507). Cambridge: Cambridge University Press.

Kant, I. (1960). *Education* (A. Churton, Trans.). Ann Arbor: Ann Arbor Paperbacks, University of Michigan Press. Originally published in 1805.

Kant, I. (1966). *Critique of pure reason* (F. Max Muller, Trans.). Garden City, NJ: Anchor Books. Originally published 1881.

Karmiloff-Smith, A. (1992). *Beyond modularity: A developmental prespective on cognitive science*. Cambridge, MA: Bradford Books/MIT Press.

Katz, M. B. (2001). *The irony of early school reform* (2nd ed.). Boston: Beacon Press. Originally published in 1968.

Katz, S. (2001). *The knower and the known in folk pedagogies: A paradox exposed*. Unpublished doctoral dissertation, The Ontario Institute for Studies in Education of the University of Toronto.

Keating, D. (1996). Habits of mind for a learning society: Educating for human development. In D. Olson & N. Torrance (Eds.), *Handbook of education and human development* (pp. 461–482). Oxford: Blackwell.

Keil, F., & Silberstein, C. (1996). Schooling and the acquisition of theoretical knowledge. In D. R. Olson & N. G. Torrance (Eds.), *The handbook of education and human development* (pp. 621–645). Oxford: Blackwell.

Keil, F. C., & Wilson, R. A. (2000). Explaining explanation. In F. C. Keil & R. A. Wilson (Eds.), *Explanation and cognition* (pp. 1–18). Cambridge, MA: MIT Press.

Keller, C. M., & Keller, J. D. (1996). *Cognition and tool use: The blacksmith at work*. New York: Cambridge University Press.

Kenny, A. (1989). *The metaphysics of mind*. New York: Oxford University Press.

Kitcher, P. (1993). *The advancement of science: Sciences without legend, objectivity without illusion*. New York: Oxford University Press.

Kocka, J. (1999). Family and bureaucracy in German Industrial Management, 1850–1914, and From manufactory to factory: Technology and workplace relations at Siemens, 1874–1873. In *Industrial culture and bourgeois society: Business, labor, and bureaucracy in modern Germany* (pp. 1–50). New York: Berghahn Books.

Kohlberg, L., & Meyer, R. (1972). Development as the aim of education. *Harvard Educational Review, 42*, 449–496.

Korzybski, A. (1933). *Science and society*. Lakefield, CT: The International Non-Aristotelian Publishing Company.

Kripke, S. (1982). *Wittgenstein on rules and private language: An elementary exposition*. Oxford: Blackwell.

Kruger, A., & Tomasello, M. (1996). Cultural learning and learning culture. In D. Olson & N. Torrance (Eds.), *Handbook of education and human development.* Oxford: Blackwell.

Kuhn, D. (1991). *The skills of argument.* New York: Cambridge University Press.

Kuhn, D. (2000). Theory of mind, metacognition, and reasoning: A life-span perspective. In P. Mitchell & K.J. Riggs (Eds.), *Children's reasoning and the mind* (pp. 301–326). New York: Psychology Press.

Kuhn, D., & Pearsall, S. (2000). Developmental origins of scientific thinking. *Journal of Cognitive Development, 1,* 113–127.

Kuhn, T. S. (1962). *The structure of scientific revolutions.* Chicago: University of Chicago Press.

Kuhn, T. S. (1977). *The essential tension.* Chicago: University of Chicago Press.

Lagemann, E. C. (1997). Contested terrain: A history of education research in the United States, 1890–1990. *Educational Researcher, 26,* 5–17.

Lagemann, E. C. (2000). *An elusive science: The troubling history of education research.* Chicago: University of Chicago Press.

Lagemann, E. C., & Shulman, L. S. (Eds.) (1999a). *Issues in education research: Problems and possibilities.* San Francisco: Jossey-Bass.

Lagemann, E. C., & Shulman, L. S. (1999b) *Next steps: Reflections on education research and ways the National Academy of Education might help to further strengthen it.* NAE mimeo.

Lancey, D. (1996). *Playing on the mother ground.* New York: Guilford Press.

Larkin, P. (2001). *Further requirements.* London: Faber & Faber.

Latour, B. (1993). *We have never been modern.* New York: Harvester Wheatsheaf.

Latour, B., & Woolgar, S. (1986). *Laboratory life: The construction of scientific facts.* Princeton, NJ: Princeton University Press.

Lave, J., & Wenger, E. (1991). *Situated learning: Legitimate peripheral participation.* Cambridge: Cambridge University Press.

Lazarus, R. (1984). On the primacy of cognition. *American Psychologist, 39,* 124–129.

Lejewski, C. (1989). 20th century logic. *Encyclopedia Britannica, 23,* 239–242.

Lemann, N. (1999). *The big test: The secret history of the American Meritocracy.* New York: Farrar, Straus & Giroux.

Lemann, N. (2001, March 12). Education: Viewpoint. *Time,* pp. 74–75.

LeTendre, G., Baker, D., Akiba, M., Goesling, B., & Wiseman, A. (2001). Teacher's work: Institutional isomorphism and cultural variation in the U.S., Germany, and Japan. *Educational Researcher, 30,* 3–15.

Levin, H. (1998). Educational Performance Standards and the Economy. *Educational Researcher, 27,* 4–10.

Levine, D. (1994). Illiteracy and family life during the first industrial revolution. *Journal of Social History, 14,* 25–44.

Lewontin, R. (1976). The analysis of variance and the analysis of causes. In N. Block & G. Dworkin (Eds.), *The IQ controversy: Critical readings* (pp. 179–193). New York: Pantheon Books.

Lightfoot, S. L. (1983). *The good high school: Portraits of character and culture.* New York: Basic Books.

Linn, R. L. (2000). Assessments and accountability. *Educational Researcher, 29,* 4–16.

Literacy scores 'an alert.' (2002, March 13). *Toronto Globe and Mail,* p. A6.

Locke, J. (1961). *An essay concerning human understanding.* London: Dent. Original work published in 1690.

Lukes, S. (1973). *Emile Durkheim: His life and work.* Markham, Canada: Penguin.

Luria, A. R. (1976). *Cognitive development: Its cultural and social foundations.* Cambridge: Cambridge University Press.

Ly, A. (2001). *Young Children's epistemological understanding and their developing theory of mind.* Unpublished master's thesis, Ontario Institute for Studies in Education/University of Toronto, Toronto, Canada.

Macnamara, J. (1986). *A border dispute: The place of logic in psychology.* Cambridge, MA: Bradford/MIT Press.

Macnamara, J. (1999). *Through the rearview mirror: Historical reflections of psychology.* Cambridge, MA: MIT Press.

Makkreel, R. A. (1975). *Dilthey: Philosopher of the human sciences.* Princeton, NJ: Princeton University Press.

March, J., & Olsen, J. (1989). *Rediscovering institutions: The organizational basis of politics.* Toronto: The Free Press.

March, J., & Simon, H. A. (1958). *Organizations.* New York: Wiley.

Markman, E. (1979). Realizing that you don't understand: Elementary school children's awareness of inconsistencies. *Child Development, 50,* 643–655.

Mayer, M. (1961). *The schools.* New York: Harper.

McClelland, D. (1973). Testing for competence rather than for "intelligence." *American Psychologist, 29,* 107–132.

McCourt, F. (1996). *Angela's ashes: A memoir.* New York: Scribner.

McDermott, R. P. (1997). Achieving school failure 1972–1996. In G. D. Spindler (Ed.), *Education and cultural process* (pp. 82–118). Prospect Heights, IL: Waveland Press.

Mehan, H. (1998). The study of social interaction in education settings: Accomplishments and unresolved issues. *Human Development, 4,* 245–269.

Meier, D. W. (1999). Needed: Thoughtful research for thoughtful schools. In E. Lagemann & L. Shulman (Eds.), *Issues in educational research* (pp. 63–82). San Francisco: Jossey-Bass.

Meltzoff, A. N., Gopnik, A., & Repacholi, B. M. (1999). Toddlers' understanding of intentions, desires and emotions: Explorations of the dark ages. In P. D. Zelazo, J. W. Astington, & D. R. Olson (Eds.), *Developing theories of intention: Social understanding and self-control* (pp. 17–41). Mahwah, NJ: LEA.

Menand, L. (2001). *The metaphysical club: A story of ideas in America.* New York: Farrar, Straus & Giroux.

Messick, B. (1993). *The calligraphic state: Textual domination and history in a Muslim society.* Berkeley: University of California Press.

Meyer, M. (1961). *The schools.* New York: Harper & Brothers.

Meyer, J. W., Boli, J., & Thomas, G. M. (1994). Ontology and rationalization in the Western Cultural Account. In W. R. Scott & J. W. Meyer and

Associates (Eds.), *Structural complexity and individualism* (pp. 9–27). London: Sage.

Mill, J. S. (1865). *On liberty*. London: Longmans, Green.

Mills, C. W. (1959). *The sociological imagination*. New York: Oxford University Press.

Mischel, W. (1968). *Personality and Assessment*. New York: Wiley.

Montaigne, M. de (1580/1958). *Essays* (J. Cohen, Trans.). London: Penguin.

Montefiore, A. (1994). Review of M. Nussbaum, "Love's knowledge." *Journal of Philosophy, 9/02,* 105–109.

Moore, C., & Dunham, P. (Eds.) (1995). *Joint attention: Its origin and role in development*. Hillsdale, NJ: Erlbaum.

Moore, H. (1996). Why has competency-based training become the solution? *Prospect, 11,* 28–46.

Moore, J., & Newell, A. (1973). How can MERLIN understand? In L. W. Gregg (Ed.), *Knowledge and cognition* (pp. 201–252). Baltimore: Lawrence Erlbaum.

Morrison, E. (1974). *From know-how to nowhere: The development of American technology*. Oxford: Blackwell.

Mortimore, P., Sammons, P., Stoll, L., Lewis, D., and Ecob, R. (1988). *School matters*. Berkeley: University of California Press.

Moscovici, S. (1993). *The invention of society*. Cambridge: Polity Press.

Moscovici, S. (1998). Social consciousness and its history. *Culture & Psychology, 4,* 411–129.

Moustafa, M., & Maldonado-Coln, E. (1999). Whole-to-parts phonics instruction: Building on what children know to help them know more. *The Reading Teacher, 52,* 448–455.

MTA Cooperative Group (1999). A 14-month randomized clinical trial of treatment strategies for attention-deficit/hyperactivity disorder. *Archives of General Psychiatry, 36,* 1073–1086.

Murray, A. (1978). *Reason and society in the Middle Ages*. Oxford: Oxford University Press.

Nagel, T. (1974). What is it like to be a bat? *Philosophical Review, 83,* 435–451.

Nagel, T. (1986). *The view from nowhere*. Oxford: Oxford University Press.

National Commission on Excellence in Education. (1983). *A nation at risk: the imperative for education reform: A report to the nation and the Secretary of Education, United States Department of Education*. Washington, DC: U.S. GPO.

Neatby, H. (1953). *So little for the mind*. Toronto: Clarke, Irwin.

Neisser, U. (1976). *Cognition and reality*. San Francisco: W. H. Freeman.

Nelson, K. (1996). *Language in cognitive development: The emergence of the mediated mind*. New York: Cambridge University Press.

Nicholson, G. (1984). *Seeing and reading*. Atlantic Highlands, NJ: Humanities Press.

Nickerson, R. (1985). Understanding understanding. *American Journal of Education, 93,* 201–239.

Nickerson, R. (1993). On the distribution of cognition: Some reflections. In G. Salomon (Ed.), *Distributed cognitions: Psychological and educational considerations* (pp. 229–261). Cambridge: Cambridge University Press.

Nicolopoulou, A., & Weintraub, J. (1998). Individual and collective representations in social context. *Human Development, 41,* 215–235.

Nietzsche, F. (1979). On truth and lies a nonmoral sense. In *Philosophy and Truth: Selections from Nietzsche's Notebooks of the Early 1870s* (pp. 79–97) (D. Breazeale, Trans. and Ed.). Atlantic Highlands, NJ: Brill Academic Publishers.

Nissen, H. J. (1988). *The early history of ancient Near East, 9000–2000 B.C.* Chicago: University of Chicago Press.

Norris, S. P., & Phillips, L. M. (1987). Explanations of reading comprehension: Schema theory and critical thinking theory. *Teachers College Record, 89,* 281–306.

North, D. (1990). *Institutions, Institutional Change and Economic Performance.* Cambridge: Cambridge University Press.

Nussbaum, M. (1992). *Love's knowledge: Essays on philosophy and literature.* Oxford: Oxford University Press.

Oatley, K. (2000). The sentiments and beliefs of distributed cognition. In N. Frijda, A. Manstead, & S. Bem (Eds.), *Emotions and beliefs: How feelings influence thoughts* (pp. 78–107). Cambridge: Cambridge University Press.

Oatley, K., & Jenkins, J. M. (1996). *Understanding emotions.* Cambridge, MA, and Oxford: Blackwell.

Oatley, K., & Johnson-Laird, P. (1996). The communicative theory of emotions. In L. Martin & A. Tesser (Eds.), *Striving and feeling: Interactions among goals, affect and self-regulation* (pp. 363–393). Mahwah, NJ: Erlbaum.

Oatley, K., & Larocque, L. (1995). Everyday concepts of emotions following every-other-day errors in joint plans. In J. A. Russell, J-M. Fernandez-Dols, A. S. R. Manstead, & J. C. Wellenkamp (Eds.), *Everyday conceptions of emotion* (pp. 146–165). Amsterdam: Kluwer.

Oatley, K., & Nundy, S. (1996). Rethinking the role of emotions in education. In D. Olson & N. Torrance (Eds.), *Handbook of education and human development: New models of learning, teaching and schooling* (pp. 257–274). Cambridge, MA: Blackwell.

Oe, K. (1969). *A personal matter.* New York: Grove Press.

Olson, D. R. (1970). *Cognitive development: The child's conception of diagonality.* New York: Academic Press.

Olson, D. R. (1975). Review of J. B. Carroll & J. Chall (Eds.), *Toward a literate society. Proceedings of the National Academy of Education* (Vol. 2., pp. 109–178). Stanford, CA: National Academy of Education.

Olson, D. R. (1977). From utterance to text: The bias of language in speech and writing. *Harvard Educational Review, 47,* 257–281.

Olson, D. R. (1984). "See! Jumping!" Some oral language antecedents of literacy. In H. Goelman, A. Oberg, & F. Smith (Eds.), *Awakening to literacy* (pp. 185–192). London: Heinemann.

Olson, D. R. (1994). *The world on paper: The conceptual and cognitive implications of writing and reading.* Cambridge: Cambridge University Press.

Olson, D. R. (1996). Towards a psychology of literacy: On the relations between speech and writing. *Cognition, 60,* 83–104.

Olson, D. R. (1999). There are *x* kinds of learners in a single class: Diversity without individual differences. In J. S. Gaffney & B. J. Askew (Eds.),

Stirring the waters: The influence of Marie Clay (pp. 17–26). Portsmouth, NH: Heinemann.

Olson, D. R. (2001). Education: The bridge from culture to mind. In D. Bakhurst & S. Shanker (Eds.), *Jerome Bruner: Language, culture, self* (pp. 104–115). London: Sage.

Olson, D. R., & Astington, J. W. (1990). Talking about text: How literacy contributes to thought. *Journal of Pragmatics, 14*, 705–721.

Olson, D. R., & Bruner, J. S. (1974). Learning through experience and learning through the media. In D. R. Olson (Ed.), *Media and symbols: The forms of expression, communication and education* (pp. 125–150). The 73rd Yearbook of the National Society for the Study of Education. Chicago: University of Chicago Press.

Olson, D. R., & Bruner, J. S. (1996). Folk psychology and folk pedagogy. In D. R. Olson & N. Torrance (Eds.), *Handbook of education and human development* (pp. 9–27). Oxford: Blackwell.

Olson, D. R., & Kamawar, D. (1999). The theory of ascriptions. In P. Zelazo, J. Astington, & D. Olson (eds.), *Developing theories of intention* (pp. 153–166). Mahwah, NJ: Erlbaum.

Olson, D. R., & Katz, S. (2001). The fourth folk pedagogy. In B. Torff & R. Sternberg (Eds.), *Understanding and teaching the intuitive mind* (pp. 243–263). Mahwah, NJ: Erlbaum.

Olson, D. R., & Torrance, N. (Eds.) (2001). *The making of literate societies.* Oxford: Blackwell.

OME (Ontario Ministry of Education) (1995). *The common curriculum.* Toronto: Government of Ontario.

Ong, W. (1982). *Orality and literacy: The technologizing of the word.* London: Methuen.

Orfield, G. (2000). Policy and equity: Lessons of a third of a century of educational reforms in the United States. In F. Reimers (Ed.), *Unequal schools, unequal chances: The challenges to equal opportunity in the Americas* (pp. 401–426). Cambridge, MA: Harvard University Press.

Orwell, G. (1951). *1984.* New York: Oxford University Press.

Pacey, A. (1974). *The maze of ingenuity: Ideas and idealism in the development of technology.* Cambridge, MA: MIT Press.

Paley, V. G. (1992). *You can't say you can't play.* Cambridge, MA: Harvard University Press.

Parker, D. (1942). *Big blonde: The collected stories of Dorothy Parker.* New York: Modern Library.

Parsons, T. (1947). Introduction. In M. Weber, *The theory of social and economic organization* (A. Henderson & T. Parsons, Trans.). New York: The Free Press.

Parsons, T. (1951). *The social system.* Glencoe, IL: The Free Press.

Parsons, T. (1959). The school class as a social system: Some of its functions in American society. *Harvard Educational Review, 29*, 297–318.

Parsons, T. (1968). Emile Durkheim, *International Encyclopedia of the Social Sciences.* New York: Macmillan.

Parsons, T. (1970). On building social systems theory: A personal history. *Daedalus, 99*, 826–881.

Perkins, D. (1992). *Smart schools: Better thinking and learning for every child.* Cambridge, MA: MIT Press.

Perner, J. (1991). *Understanding the representational mind.* Cambridge, MA: MIT Press.

Peskin, J. (1992). Ruse and representation: On children's ability to conceal information. *Developmental Psychology, 28,* 84–89.

Peters, T. J., & Waterman, R. H. (1982). *In search of excellence: Lessons from America's best-run companies.* New York: Harper & Row.

Phenix, P. (1964). *Realms of meaning.* New York: McGraw-Hill.

Phillips, D. C. (1995). The good, the bad, and the ugly: The many faces of constructivism. *Educational Researcher, 24,* 5–12.

Piaget, J. (1932). *The moral judgment of the child.* London: Routledge & Kegan Paul.

Piaget, J. (1962). *Play, dreams and imitation in childhood.* New York: Norton.

Piaget, J. (1974). *Understanding Causality.* New York: Norton.

Piaget, J. (1983). Piaget's theory. In P. Mussen (Ed.), *Handbook of child psychology: Formerly Carmichael's manual of child psychology* (4th ed., Vol. 1, pp. 103–128). New York: Wiley.

Pinker, S., & Prince, A. (1999). The nature of human concepts: Evidence from an unusual source. In R. Jackendoff, P. Bloom, & K. Wynn (Eds.), *Language, logic and concepts: Essays in honor of John Macnamara* (pp. 221–262). Cambridge, MA: MIT Press.

Polanyi, M. (1958). *Personal knowledge.* London: Routledge & Kegan Paul.

Polanyi, M. (1967). *The tacit dimension.* Garden City, NY: Anchor/ Doubleday.

Polanyi, M. (1996). *Science, faith and society.* Chicago: University of Chicago Press.

Pope, W., Cohen, J., & Hazelrigg, L. (1975). On the divergence of Weber and Durkheim: A critique of Parsons' convergence thesis. *American Sociological Review, 40,* 417–427.

Popper, K. (1972). *Objective knowledge: An evolutionary approach.* Oxford: Clarendon.

Porter, A. C., & Smithson, J. L. (2001). Assessing reform implementation and effects. In S. Fuhrman (Ed.), *From the Capitol to the classroom: Standards-based reform in the States.* 100th Yearbook of the NSSE. Chicago: University of Chicago Press.

Porter, T. M. (1995). *Trust in numbers: The pursuit of objectivity in science and public life.* Princeton, NJ: Princeton University Press.

Postman, N., & Weingartner, C. (1969). *Teaching as a subversive activity.* New York: Delacorte Press.

Poussin, N. (1911). *Correspondence de Nicholas Poussin* (C. Jouanny, Ed.). Paris: Ecrits.

Pramling, I. (1996). Understanding and empowering the child as a learner. In D. R. Olson & N. Torrance (Eds.), *The handbook of education and human development* (pp. 265–292). Malden, MA: Blackwell.

Premack, D., & Premack, A. J. (1996). Why animals lack pedagogy and some cultures have more of it than others. In D. R. Olson & N. Torrance (Eds.), *The handbook of education and human development* (pp. 302–323). Cambridge, MA: Blackwell.

Provincial Committee on the aims and objectives of education in the schools in Ontario (1968). *Living and learning: The Hall-Dennis Report.* Toronto: Ontario Department of Education.

Ravitch, D. (1978). *The Revisionists revisited: A critique of the radical attack on the schools.* New York: Basic Books.

Ravitch, D. (1985). *The schools we deserve: Reflections on the educational crises of our times.* New York: Basic Books.

Ravitch, D. (1995). The search for order and the rejection of conformity: Standards in American Education. In D. Ravitch & M. Vinovskis, (Eds.), *Learning from the past: What history teaches us about school reform* (pp. 167–190). Baltimore: Johns Hopkins University Press.

Ravitch, D. (2000). *Left back: A century of failed school reforms.* New York: Simon & Schuster.

Ravitch, D., & Vinovskis, M. (1995). *Learning from the past: What history teaches us about school reform.* Baltimore: Johns Hopkins University Press.

Reisman, D., Denney, R., & Glazer, N. (1950). *The lonely crowd: A study of the changing American character* (abridged ed.). New Haven, CT: Yale University Press.

Resnick, L. B., & Hall, M. W. (1998). Learning organizations for sustainable education reform. *Daedalus, 127,* 89–118.

Ridgway, J., Crust, R., Burkhardt, H., Wilcox, S., Fisher, L., & Foster, D. (2000). *MARS report on the 2000 tests.* San Jose, CA: Mathematics Assessment Collaborative.

Ridley, M. (1999). *Genome: The autobiography of a species in 23 characters.* New York: Harper Collins.

Robinson, F. G. (1992). *Love's story told: A life of Henry A. Murray.* Cambridge, MA: Harvard University Press.

Rogoff, B. (1990). *Apprenticeship in thinking: Cognitive Development in Social Context.* New York: Oxford University Press.

Rorty, R. (1979). *Philosophy and the mirror of nature.* Princeton, NJ: Princeton University Press.

Rorty, R. (1989). *Contingency, irony and solidarity.* Cambridge: Cambridge University Press.

Rosenthal, R. (1968). *Pygmalion in the classroom: Teacher expectation and pupils' intellectual development.* New York: Holt, Rinehart & Winston.

Roth, K., & Anderson, C. (1988). Promoting conceptual change learning from science textbooks. In P. Ramsden (Ed.), *Improving learning: New perspectives* (pp. 109–141). London: Kogan Page.

Rothstein, R. (2002). *Out of balance: Our understanding of how schools affect society and how society affects schools.* Chicago: The Spencer Foundation.

Rozeboom, W. (1972). Problems in the psycho-philosophy of knowledge. In J. Royce & W. Rozeboom (eds.), *The psychology of knowing* (pp. 25–110). New York: Gordon & Breach.

Rummel, E. (Ed.) (1990). *The Erasmus Reader.* Toronto: University of Toronto Press.

Rutter, M., Maughan, B., Mortimore P., & Ouston, J. (1979). *Fifteen thousand hours: Secondary schools and their effects on children*. Cambridge, MA: Harvard University Press.

Ryan, A. (1987). Mill and Weber on history, freedom and reason. In W. Mommsen, & J. Osterhammel (Eds.), *Max Weber and his Contemporaries* (pp. 170–181). London: Unwin Hyman.

Ryan, A. (1995). *John Dewey and the high tide of American liberalism*. New York: W. W. Norton.

Ryan, A. (2001). Schools: The price of "progress": Essay review of D. Ravitch *Left back: A century of failed school reforms. New York Review of Books, 48*, 18–21.

Sacks, O. (1986) *The man who mistook his wife for his hat*. South Yarmouth, MA: J. Curley.

Salomon, G. (1983). The differential investment of mental effort in learning from different sources. *Educational Psychologist, 18*, 42–50.

Sarason, S, (1990). *The predictable failure of educational reform*. San Francisco: Jossey-Bass.

Sarason, S. (1998). Some features of a flawed educational system. *Daedalus, 127*, 1–12.

Satz, D., & Ferejohn, J. (1994). Rational choice and social theory. *Journal of Philosophy, 9102*, 71–87.

Sawyer, R. K. (2002a). Durkheim's dilemma: Toward a sociology of emergence. *Sociological Theory, 20*, 227–247.

Sawyer, R. K. (2002b). Unresolved tensions in sociocultural theory. *Culture and Psychology, 8*, 283–305.

Schachter, H., Pham, B., King, J., Langford, S., & Moher, D. (2001). How efficacious and safe is short-acting methylphenidate for the treatment of attention-deficit disorder in children and adolescents? A meta-analysis. *Canadian Medical Association Journal, 165*, 1475–1488.

Schauble, L., Klopfer, L. E., & Raghavan, K. (1991). Students' transition from an engineering model to a science model of experimentation. *Journal of Research in Science Teaching, 28*, 859–882.

Scheffler, I. (1974). *Four pragmatists: A critical introduction to Peirce, James, Mead, and Dewey*. London: Routledge & Kegan Paul.

Scheffler, I. (1997). *Symbolic worlds: Art, science, language, ritual*. New York: Cambridge University Press.

Schleiermacher, E. (1976). The Schleiermacher biography: Introduction. In H. P. Rickman (Ed.), *Dilthey: Selected writings* (pp. 37–77). London: Cambridge University Press.

Schlicht, E. (1998). *On custom in the economy*. Oxford: Clarendon.

Schoenfeld, A. H. (2002). Making mathematics work for all children: Issues of standards, testing, and equity. *Educational Researcher, 31*(1), 13–25.

Scribner, S., & Cole, M. (1981). *The psychology of literacy*. Cambridge, MA: Harvard University Press.

Searle, J. R. (1983). *Intentionality: An essay in the philosophy of mind*. Cambridge: Cambridge University Press.

Searle, J. (1997). *The mystery of consciousness*. New York: New York Review of Books.

Seigler, R. S. (1992). The other Alfred Binet. *Developmental Psychology, 28*, 179–190.

Shapiro, B. L. (1994) *What children bring to light: A constructivist perspective on children's learning in science*. New York: Teachers College Press.

Shields, C. (1993). *The stone diaries*. Toronto: Vintage/Random House.

Shore, B. (1996). *Culture in mind: Cognition, culture and the problem of meaning*. New York: Oxford University Press.

Shweder, R. (1991). *Thinking through cultures*. Cambridge, MA: Harvard University Press.

Silverstein, M., & Urban, G. (Eds.) (1996). *Natural histories of discourse*. Chicago: University of Chicago Press.

Simon, H. A. (2000). Discovering explanations. In F. Keil & R. Wilson (Eds.), *Explanation and prediction* (pp. 21–59). Cambridge, MA: MIT Press.

Singleton, J. (1989). Japanese folkcraft pottery apprenticeship: Cultural patterns of an educational institution. In M. W. Coy (Ed.), *Apprenticeship: From theory to method and back again* (pp. 13–30). Albany: State University of New York.

Smith, B. H. (1997). *Belief and resistance*. Cambridge, MA: Harvard University Press.

Smith, D. (1990a). *Texts, facts, and femininity: Exploring the relations of ruling*. London: Routledge.

Smith, D. (1990b). *The conceptual practices of power: A feminist sociology of knowledge*. Toronto: University of Toronto Press.

Smith, F. (1998). *The book of learning and forgetting*. New York: Teachers College Press.

Spence, J. D. (1996). *God's Chinese son: The Paiping heavenly Kingdom of Hong Xiuquan*. New York: Norton.

Spittler, G. (1998). *Hirtenarbeit: Die Welt der Kamelhirten und Ziegenhirtinnen von Timia* (pp. 241ff.). Koln: Rudiger Koppe Verlag.

Sprat, T. (1667/1966). *History of the Royal Society of London for the improving of natural knowledge* (J. I. Cope & H. W. Jones, Eds.). St. Louis: Washington University Press.

Spufford, F. (2002). *The child that books built*. London: Faber & Faber.

Stanovich, K. (1999). *Who is rational? Studies of individual differences in reasoning*. Mahwah, NJ: Erlbaum.

Staten, H. (1985). *Wittgenstein and Derrida*. Oxford: Blackwell.

Statistics Canada (1996). *Reading the future: A portrait of literacy in Canada*. Ottawa: Statistics Canada.

Stein, J. G. (2001). *The cult of efficiency*. Toronto: Anansi.

Sternberg, R. J. (Ed.) (1997). Intelligence and life long learning. *American Psychologist, 52*, 1029–1134.

Stich, S. (1983). *From folk psychology to cognitive science*. Cambridge, MA: Bradford/MIT Press.

Stock, B. (1983). *The implications of literacy*. Princeton, NJ: Princeton University Press.

Strauss, G. 1981, Techniques of indoctrination: The German reformation. In H. Graff (Ed.), *Literacy and social development in the West: A Reader* (pp. 96–104). Cambridge: Cambridge University Press.

Strauss, S. (2001). Folk psychology, folk pedagogy and their relations to subject matter knowledge. In B. Torff & R. Sternberg (Eds.), *Understanding and teaching the intuitive mind* (pp. 217–242). Mahwah, NJ: Erlbaum.

Taylor, C. (1989). *Sources of the self: The making of modern identity.* Cambridge: Cambridge University Press.

Taylor, I., & Taylor, M. M. (1995). *Writing and literacy in Chinese, Korean and Japanese* (Vol. 3). Philadelphia: John Benjamins.

Thagard, P. (2000). *Coherence in thought and action.* Cambridge, MA: MIT Press.

Thomas, R. (2001). Literacy in ancient Greece: Functional literacy, oral education, and the development of a literate environment. In D. R. Olson & N. Torrance (Eds.), *The making of literate societies* (pp. 68–81). Malden, MA: Blackwell.

Tishman, S., & Perkins, D. (1997). The language of thinking. *Phi Delta Kappan, 78,* 368–374.

Tishman, S., Perkins, D., & Jay, E. (1995). *The thinking classroom: Teaching and learning in a culture of thinking.* Boston: Allyn & Bacon.

Tomasello, M. (1999). *The cultural origins of human cognition.* Cambridge, MA: Harvard University Press.

Tomasello, M., & Call, J. (1997). *Primate cognition.* Oxford: Oxford University Press.

Tomasello, M., Kruger, A. C., & Ratner, H. H. (1993). Cultural learning. *Behavioural and Brain Sciences, 16,* 495–552.

Tönnies, F. (1887/1957). Community and society (*Gemeinschaft und Gesellschaft*) (C. P. Loomis, trans. and ed.). East Lansing: Michigan State University Press.

Toulmin, S. (1992) *Cosmopolis: The hidden agenda of modernity.* Chicago: University of Chicago Press.

Toulmin, S., & Goodfield, J. (1965). *The discovery of time.* New York: Harper Torchbooks.

Traub, R., Wolfe, R., & Russell, H. (1976–1977). Interface Project II and Ontario's Review of Educational Policy. *Interchange, 7,* 24–31.

Triebel, A. (2001). The roles of literacy practices in the activities and institutions of developed and developing countries. In D. R. Olson & N. Torrance (Eds.), *The making of literate societies* (pp. 19–53). Oxford: Blackwell.

Tyack, D. (1974). *The one best system: A history of American urban education.* Cambridge, MA: Harvard University Press.

Tyack, D. (1995). Reinventing schooling. In D. Ravitch & M. Vinovskis (Eds.), *Learning from the past: What history teaches us about school reform* (pp. 191–216). Baltimore: Johns Hopkins University Press.

Tyack, D., & Cuban, L. (1995). *Tinkering toward Utopia: A century of public school reform.* Cambridge, MA: Harvard University Press.

UNESCO (1995). *World symposium on family literacy, final report.* Paris: UNESCO.

Vendler, Z. (1970). Say what you think. In J. L. Cowan (Ed.), *Studies in thought and language* (pp. 79–97). Tucson: University of Arizona Press.

Visalberghi, E., & Limongelli, L. (1996). Acting and understanding: Tool use revisited through the minds of capuchin monkeys. In A. E. Russon, K. A. Bard, & S. T. Parker (Eds.), *Reaching into thought* (pp. 57–79). Cambridge: Cambridge University Press.

von Wright, G. H. (1971). *Explanation and understanding.* Ithaca, NY: Cornell University Press.

Vygotsky, L. (1986). *Thought and language* (A. Kozulin, Trans.). Cambridge, MA: MIT Press.

Walker, S. (1998). *The hyperactivity hoax.* New York: St. Martin's Press.

Weaver, W. (2002). The mystery of Ignazio Silone. *New York Review of Books, 69,* 32–37.

Weber, E. (1976). *Peasants into Frenchmen: The modernization of rural France.* Stanford, CA: Stanford University Press.

Weber, M. (1930). *The Protestant ethic and the spirit of capitalism* (T. Parsons, Trans.). London: Allen & Unwin. Original work published 1905.

Weber, M. (1948). *From Max Weber: Essays in sociology* (H. H. Gerth & C. W. Mills, Eds.). London: Routledge & Kegan Paul.

Weber, M. (1968). *The theory of social and economic organization* (A. Henderson & T. Parsons, Trans.). New York: The Free Press.

Wells, G. (1999). *Dialogic inquiry: Towards a sociocultural practice and theory of education.* New York: Cambridge University Press.

Wertsch, J. V. (1985). *Vygotsky and the social formation of mind.* Cambridge, MA: Harvard University Press.

Wertsch, J. V. (1991). *Voices of the mind: A socio-cultural approach to mediated action.* Cambridge, MA: Harvard University Press.

Westbrook, R. B. (1991). *John Dewey and American democracy.* Ithaca, NY: Cornell University Press.

Whiten, A. (1999). Parental encouragement in *Gorilla* in comparative perspective: Implications for social cognition and the evolution of teaching. In S. Parker, R. Mitchell & H. Miles (Eds.), *The mentalities of gorillas and orangutans in comparative perspective* (pp. 342–366). Cambridge: Cambridge University Press.

Whyte, W. (1956). *The Organization Man.* New York: Doubleday Anchor.

Wilder, T. (1938). *Our town: A play in three acts.* New York: Coward McCann.

Wilson, E. K. (1961). Introduction. In E. Durkheim, *Moral education: A study in the theory and application of the sociology of education* (E. K Wilson & H. Shnurer, Trans.). New York: The Free Press.

Wilson, R., & Keil, F. (2000). The shadows and shallows of explanation. In F. Keil & R. Wilson (Eds.), *Explanation and cognition* (pp. 87–114). Cambridge MA: MIT Press.

Wimmer, H., & Weichbold, V. (1994). Children's theory of mind: Fodor's heuristics examined. *Cognition, 53,* 45–57.

Wineburg, S. S. (1991). On the reading of historical texts: Notes on the breach between school and academy. *American Educational Research Journal, 28,* 495–519.

Winner, E. (1996). *Gifted children.* New York: Basic Books.

Winner, E., & Cooper, M. (2000). Mute those claims: No evidence (yet) for a causal link between arts study and academic achievement. *Journal of Aesthetic Education, 34,* 11–75.

Wirth, A. G. (1966). *John Dewey as educator.* New York: Wiley.

Wittgenstein, L. (1958). *Philosophical investigations* (G. E. M. Anscombe, Trans.). Oxford: Blackwell.

Wittgenstein, L. (1980). *Remarks on the philosophy of psychology and philosophy.* 2 vols. Oxford: Blackwell.

Wolfensohn, J. D. (1999). *A proposal for a comprehensive development framework.* Washington, DC: World Bank.

Wundt, W. (1916). *Elements of folk psychology* (E. L. Schaub, Trans.). New York: Macmillan.

Zajonc, R. B. (1984). On the primacy of affect. *American Psychologist, 39,* 117–123.

Zelazo, P. D. (1999). Language, levels of consciousness, and the development of intentional action. In P. Zelazo, J. Astington, & D. Olson (Eds.), *Developing theories of intention.* Mahwah, NJ: Erlbaum.

Author Index

Subject Index